Key Issues in Development

Key Issues in Development

**Damien Kingsbury, Joe Remenyi,
John McKay and Janet Hunt**

First published 2004 by
PALGRAVE MACMILLAN
Houndmills, Basingstoke, Hampshire RG21 6XS and
175 Fifth Avenue, New York, N.Y. 10010
Companies and representatives throughout the world

PALGRAVE MACMILLAN is the global academic imprint of the Palgrave
Macmillan division of St. Martin's Press, LLC and of Palgrave Macmillan Ltd.
Macmillan® is a registered trademark in the United States, United Kingdom
and other countries. Palgrave is a registered trademark in the European
Union and other countries.

ISBN – 13 : 978–1–4039–0044–9 hardback
ISBN – 10 : 1–4039–0044–2 hardback
ISBN – 13 : 978–1–4039–0045–6 paperback
ISBN – 10 : 1–4039–0045–0 paperback

This book is printed on paper suitable for recycling and
made from fully managed and sustained forest sources.

A catalogue record for this book is available from the British Library.

Library of Congress Cataloging-in-Publication Data
Key issues in development / Damien Kingsbury ... [et al.].
     p. cm.
  Includes bibliographical references and index.
  ISBN 1–4039–0044–2 (cloth)—ISBN 1–4039–0045–0 (paper)
  1. Developing countries—Economic conditions. 2. Poverty—Developing countries.
  3. Economic assistance—Developing countries. 4. Economic development—
  Economic aspects—Developing countries. 5. Economic development—Social
  aspects—Developing countries 6. Economic development—Political aspects—
  Developing countries. 7. Economic development—Environmental aspects—
  Developing countries. 8. Globalization—Economic aspects—Developing
  countries. I. Kingsbury, Damien.
HC59.7.K42 2004
338.9′009172′4—dc22   2003067560

10   9   8   7   6   5   4   3
13 12 11 10 09 08 07 06 05

Printed in China

Contents

List of Figures and Tables

Figures

Tables

Introduction

DAMIEN KINGSBURY

The idea of 'development' of the world's poorer countries is both highly contentious and central to international relations. Put simply, the study of development is concerned with how 'developing countries' can improve their living standards and eliminate absolute poverty. In the period since the end of the Second World War, and the subsequent decolonization process by which European colonial powers withdrew from their colonies in Africa, Asia and other parts of the world, the peoples and governments of most developed or industrialized countries have acknowledged that they have some responsibility to assist poorer countries to improve the lives of their poor. At one level, this is a simple matter of self interest – if people in poorer countries have more income they have more purchasing power and can generate more international trade, and hence, greater wealth all around. At another level, a basic humanitarian sensibility leaves many people in wealthier countries feeling that to allow poorer people to continue to stay poor is unjust. And for much of the late 20th century development assistance was seen as a way to persuade poorer countries to come into one of the two major ideological camps that dominated the Cold War era – the West or the Communist Bloc. The main powers of each bloc unashamedly used development assistance to maintain the support of poorer countries, to keep them in their 'sphere of influence'.

In the early 21st century, this bipolar ideological orientation has changed, but the fear that poverty can encourage conflict, perhaps on a global scale, was given a new lease of life by the preoccupation of the United States, its allies and like-minded countries, with global terrorism since the events of 11 September 2001. This has led to a refocusing on development designed to respond to a new perceived global 'enemy' – an anti-state, anti-materialist confederation operating under a banner of Islam.

From the viewpoint of many of its adherents, global Islam is seen as a foil to the perceived evils of global capitalism (or Westernism – defined as either Christian or materialist or both). And while some supporters of this form of Islam espouse a purely religious understanding of the conflict, many more are driven by desperation, poverty, inequity, and dispossession. All of this adds up to a deep – and in many cases well-grounded – sense of injustice, raising the question of whether enhanced development leading to greater global equity might dampen the zeal of at least the foot-soldiers of the movement. Might 'enlightened self-interest', which was the principal ideological motivation of Western donors fearful of the spread of communism in the 1950s and 1960s, provide a similar impetus for a renewal of development assistance today, so that increased 'development' might be seen as one thread in the 'war on terror'?

In most discussions about development, the term itself is bandied about as though its meaning is commonly understood and shared. This, of course, is not so. In the early post-war period development was primarily, and often exclusively, identified with economic growth, usually measured in terms of the average income per head of population of a given country (per capita GDP, or gross domestic product). However, as discussed further throughout this volume, development has a range of meanings, which while in most cases complementary or at least overlapping, may be quite distinct in the priority they give, for example, to equity, to political development and democratization, to gender, or to environmental issues and thus in their implications for action.

Even the terminology of development has changed and is continuing to change. For example, the term 'third world', which many less-developed countries preferred to use to describe themselves in the early Cold War period, was coined to contrast them to the 'first world' of the West (largely corresponding to the Organisation of Economic Development (OECD) countries) and the 'second world' – the socialist bloc states. Although still used, the term 'third world' has been effectively undermined by the collapse of the second world.

The whole approach to development, assumed for years to occur through a process of industrialization, is also now in question. The OECD world which 'industrialized' or 'modernized' decades ago, is now increasingly reliant upon service industries and higher technology rather than the heavy industrialized industries of the mid-20th century. Some analysts suggest that the idea of 'modernism', which they see as corresponding to heavy industrialization, production lines and bureaucratic organization, has, for many countries, more or less passed with the advent of the increasingly diversified, globalized, high technology types of work that now characterize the leading edge of developed economies. This suggests that the path to development may differ for countries endeavouring to lift themselves out of poverty today. Some may be able to 'skip' directly to a service industry, high technology approach. Others, however, see this development as simply a high expression of modernism, and a logical conclusion of technological development. They suggest that developing countries will have to proceed through the same industrialization process to reach that technological edge.

All of this is, of course, a very long way from the commodity producing and subsistence economies of most of the world's states, in which wages are low, employment conditions usually bad and unregulated, and in which many facets of modern (or post-modern) life taken for granted in OECD countries exist only as a dream. There has been a trickle down of technology, but for many people clean running water is not available, health conditions remain poor, medical support is limited or unaffordable, literacy is at marginal levels, and opportunities for personal growth are virtually non-existent.

The notion of 'third worldism' as a formula to express the common interests and joint organization of developing countries has also been challenged and largely undermined by the increasing variety of development experiences between and within these countries themselves. What really is the common feature of countries as diverse as Indonesia, Ethiopia, El Salvador and Bangladesh? Such countries are usually classified as less developed (LD) or least developed (LLD), with the latter status being used by the United Nations as a benchmark for entitlement to preferential assistance. The Least Developed, the poorest countries in the world, are those whose poverty is most profound, for whom special help is supposed to be available. Per capita GDP in such countries is generally less than US$2 a day and in some cases US$1 a day. What is more, for many of their inhabitants even these amounts would be regarded as a mark of wealth, as median incomes are invariably less than this. Examples of LLD countries include Laos, Cambodia, Burma and many of the states of sub-Saharan Africa. LD countries include South Africa, Egypt, the Central American states, India and Indonesia.

Some countries previously regarded as 'third world' and generally classified as 'developing', have managed to rise above such levels, on account of beneficial location, natural resources (especially oil), colonial (or post-colonial) good fortune, or, in exceptional circumstances, the right mix of policies combined with a competent and honest government. The average income of their populations is considerably more than in the bottom two categories, yet they are still some way from the income levels of the OECD countries. Industrialization may be taking place, but it is not consistent, and their economies tend to continue to be dominated either by commodity exports or light or simple manufacturing, often combined with a high level of foreign investment and ownership. Thailand, Malaysia, Chile and Argentina all fall into such a category of 'developing' countries, as perhaps does China.

All of this, however, privileges the economic above other aspects of life. The argument that it is difficult to consider other facets of life when one is hungry is persuasive, yet people in LD and LLD countries may still enjoy rich cultures and social structures, profound religious beliefs, as well as strong and complex social and kinship ties. And, at least as importantly, their hopes and aspirations are equal to, and often greater than, those of more economically privileged people. For example, a person consciously deprived of democracy is likely to appreciate its political advantages more than a person who can take it for granted. So too with human rights and their suppression, including those most basic desires of ordinary people everywhere, to speak freely and to be heard, to assemble and to organize around issues that affect them, and to be free of punishment – including torture, arbitrary arrest and detention, inhumane and inappropriate prison sentences and death – if they choose to do so.

Following this logic, rather than look rather to economic indicators as a measure of development, one might consider the nature of the state: whether its agencies function adequately, whether they are corrupt or untainted, the extent to which the government is autonomous of vested interests, and whether the rule of law applies consistently and equally, and across the whole of the territory claimed by the state.

In all of this, there is an assumption that, all other things being equal, such conditions do or should apply to all people more or less equally. Yet fully half of the world's population suffers various forms of discrimination, ranging from the 'glass ceiling' experienced by women and minorities in the developed countries, to forced abstinence from education or work in some others, and the otherwise culturally imposed roles that women are often forced to undertake, their lack of rights to redress, and their inferior status in almost all aspects of social, political and economic life. The role of women, their position in many societies, and the tension over the evolution of such positions has been one of the most troubled aspects of the development debate, and while there has been encouraging movement in some areas there has been depressingly little in others.

The issue of development, as especially material development, also implies the greater use of natural resources, often in ways that wilfully ignore the side-effects, such as water pollution from industrial sources, but also in ways in which people are genuinely unaware of the consequences, such as deforestation. One might ask, leaving aside for the moment the question of resource distribution, if a mother and father in a heavily over-populated country where large families are favoured would understand that continuing with such a tradition, especially in an era of broadly increasing life expectancy, could directly contribute to the potential ecological collapse of their own local environment? Or, indeed, one might also ask whether a local logger is thinking about the longer term when short-term survival continues to press. And then there are those whose faith in technology and the potential 'fixes' that it might provide, offers an easy rationale for not altering their otherwise ecologically unsustainable behaviour. The world is our home, yet we seem to insist on crowding and despoiling it, with little thought for how, and if, we can continue to live in our current manner, much less what sort of 'home' we are leaving to our children, our grandchildren, and subsequent generations.

How we live is generally ascribed to culture, which in its anthropological sense means a 'shared world view', or a social system of thinking and making sense of the world and what occurs within it. Yet the passive acceptance of such culturally embedded characteristics is at best fatalistic, and at worst implies an acceptance of a demonstrably inequitable and unsustainable status quo. Like languages, cultures are not static or immutable. Also like language, the only truly static culture is a dead one, and in this era of increasing and seemingly unstoppable globalization, in all its guises, all living cultures are transforming at historically unprecedented rates. Will development necessarily destroy ancient cultures or can development be achieved which respects and is consistent with different cultures in an evolving way? Can cultures whose practices are inconsistent with widely accepted human rights adapt to these universal principles? The question is how do we wish to direct such cultural change, and to what purpose?

This last question is profoundly normative, in that it asks not that we be aware of change in the world we live in, but that we identify certain types of change or outcomes as qualitatively better than others, and therefore preferable. The idea of 'development', as a normative judgement based on issues of moral duty, enlightened self-interest, and ideological preference, is probably more contested now than it has been at any time in the post-Second World War era. Yet the process of understanding development, what it means, and how it should apply is, undoubtedly, continuing to undergo substantial change and revision.

Within the OECD countries, the idea of per capita GDP as the primary measure of development, as noted above, began to give way to a more widely inclusive Physical Quality of Life Index (PQLI), developed in the 1970s. The PQLI emphasized development results rather than capacity for consumption, and measured infant mortality, life expectancy and adult literacy. This was, in turn, supplanted by the Human Development Index (HDI) in 1990, which combined life expectancy (as a proxy measure for good health), per capita income and a mix of educational measures, in an effort to measure capacity to make life choices as an alternative to GDP as a way of assessing development. These measurements, in turn, are now being challenged by the additional development criteria of human dignity, religious freedom, cultural maintenance, political expression, participation and empowerment, which give meaning to the often abused term 'democratization', and other so-called civil and politics 'rights'. In this, issues of 'governance' have become paramount.

In this respect, notions of 'development' continue to evolve in ways that increasingly address the range of concerns that are expressed by ordinary people in their daily lives, most notably in those countries or regions where such daily lives are often a struggle for existence, or at least an adequate existence. In particular, the expression of concerns and values that contribute to an expanding idea of 'development' are the product of an increased level of community participation in the development process. The emphasis on development has increasingly moved away from what the 'experts' say 'development' is, to what people seeking 'development' want it to be. In saying this, however, it should be understood that this process of change is only partial and not especially quick, in particular amongst the larger multilateral agencies like the World Bank or Asian Development Bank, and more traditionalist development planners.

The shift in the categorization of what constitutes development began to not only diversify 'ownership' of the meaning of development, but also reflected the diversity of responses to the development process. Some more successful post-colonial states, for instance, have moved up the Human Development Index scale while others, for various reasons, have tended to languish or indeed slide further down the scale, and yet others have had responses that have been inconsistent, in turn reflecting a different mix of policy prescriptions and circumstances. However, it has become increasingly clear that while, for the purposes of broad study, there is some advantage to such general categorizations, as a methodological tool such a scale is only partially helpful. All countries respond to and are influenced by a range of criteria that include history, material resources, economic infrastructure, trading links, political systems, conflict and the environment. Against this, while there are similarities between some countries, no two places are exactly the same. Hence, the study of development as it applies to people in real circumstances must, if it is to be meaningful, grapple with the specific outcomes in particular contexts, and not just broad theories.

Development is, perhaps the world's most critical problem, incorporating most of the world's pressing issues. At the same time, the subject of development has retreated to increasingly simple formulae in the minds of many of the people and governments able to address it meaningfully. Much has been achieved in the development field, in improving the lives of many of the world's people, but for many others little has advanced. Based on the overall fall in official development assistance from developed countries as a proportion of their GDP, it is clear that 'fatigue' has set in, and the global contest driving much work has ended. Certainly, the gap between developed countries and many, perhaps most, developing countries continues to widen, meaning that the world is and increasingly a less equal, rather than more equal, place.

In part, the problems of developing countries in 'catching up' with the developed world, or, in some cases, even maintaining their existing position, are self-inflicted. Poor and often corrupt leadership with totalitarian tendencies have all too often been experienced by developing countries over the past half century. And a refusal to informally accept as equal citizens members of non-governing ethnic groups has riven many multi-ethnic developing societies, undoing the basis for state development. However, in many cases, the problems faced by many developing countries are also a legacy of colonialism, in which disparate ethnic groups – proto-nations – were lumped together by colonial powers based on geo-political and military reach and with little or no regard for social cohesion, existing patterns of social organization, or the need for social and capital infrastructure. Similarly, the style and method of colonial rule very often imparted to aspiring independence movements little respect for, or understanding of, economic equity, legal principle, or political participation. Further, the often brutal methods of maintaining political control by many colonial powers and their often violent intransigence towards decolonization also informed and deeply influenced many post-colonial states.

Yet, it would be a mistake to see developing countries simply as a product of these historical circumstances alone. Post- (or neo-) colonial economic relationships have dominated most developing countries since, constructing them as suppliers of primary commodities to an often oversupplied world market that, as a consequence, has driven down prices and hence income available to such countries. Foreign political intervention has also been used to maintain in power governments that served elite interests, rather than the mass of the people. This process was especially notable during the period of ideological contest between the West and the Soviet Bloc. Very often regimes were installed or supported not because they addressed development issues, but simply because they were regarded as loyal 'clients' of one side or the other. The economic and political fall-out from this policy continues to reverberate to this day.

Most notably, for much of the past half century, developing countries have been encouraged to follow the industrializing lead of developed countries, borrowing heavily for (often questionable) major infrastructure projects and attempting to track along the path to economic 'take-off' expected by early development theorists. Indeed, this fixation with an often externally imposed model of economic development has often not suited the particular conditions of developing countries, and has exacerbated existing political and economic problems, or created new ones, such as deepening levels of indebtedness. There have, it is true, been some notable successes, particularly in East Asia. But a closer reading of these successes reveals a complex set of conditions that make them the exception rather than the rule. At present, only one broad model of development, based on neo-liberalism, is being promoted worldwide, but the question still remains whether or not there are potentially several development models rather than the one which currently dominates.

The 'aid', too, that has been offered to developing countries to help alleviate their problems can often be seen as means of buying off the sense of guilt of those in developed countries whose conscience is not shackled by parochial identity. Aid policies frequently target spending of aid money in the donor country on goods or services that usually have a short lifespan in the developing country and are unable to be sustained once the donor has left. In only a few cases are skills and knowledge successfully imparted to local partners in aid projects, creating a legacy of unfulfilled hopes, failed expectations, and political frustration (see de Waal 1999). The best, though rarest, aid projects are those that impart knowledge and skills and leave in place technology that is sustainable in local conditions. This represents the slow and incomplete transition from patronage to participation.

If most of the post-colonial era has been marked by wide-ranging policy failure on the part of many developing countries, then the developed countries also continue to bear responsibility. The policies of infrastructure development and industrialization encouraged by developed countries that required massive overseas borrowings by developing countries left a vast number of countries with crippling and often unsustainable debts. The answer to this has been further, renegotiated debt, mortgaging not just the present but the long-term future of many developing countries. And the policies that have been imposed by Western governments as a condition of debt 'relief' have, in most cases, been onerous and narrowly defined, leading to cuts in basic social services such as education and health care. The tighter economic embrace of global capital, particularly since the end of the Cold War, has left most developing countries with few, if any, options about the course that is supposed to lead to development. The largely 'off the shelf' economic model that is now being handed down by organizations such as the International Monetary Fund (IMF) and the World Bank is, in a real sense, simply not negotiable. Yet it has been precisely this patronizing and unilateral view of the options for development that have themselves failed in the past. The 'experts' continue to believe their own propaganda and to ignore the mounting evidence. The one or two that announce that the emperor (or the empire) has no clothes are invariably cast out (see Stiglitz 2003).

Yet what has been learned about development over the past half century is that much of the development process to date has, based on a wider set of criteria, been inadequate. Development fads have changed while the lives of many poor people remain much the same. It is now clear that investment in new industries to modernize the economy (1950s) has been inappropriate or inadequate; that investment in education alone (1960s) has in most cases not been sustained to reveal the benefits it could have delivered; that investment in basic needs (health, agriculture, etc) (1970s) has not been enough or sufficiently applied; that investment in 'getting policies right' to facilitate technology transfer (1980s) has been misguided, mishandled or was simply unsustainable; and that investment in alliances that were intended to achieve sectoral reforms, especially in finance and export-led development (1990s), has not achieved the sort of gains in development that have led to a sustainable reduction in poverty on a global scale.

In all of this, remarkably, and perhaps dangerously, little attention has been paid to the physical impact that various attempts at development have had on the planet on which we all live. As noted at the Johannesburg Summit on Sustainable Development in August 2002, over the next half century the population of the world's 49 poorest countries will triple and the global population is expected to be in excess of nine billion people. In terms of economic distribution, around half of the world's population lives on less than US$2 a day, which as noted above is understood by some planners to constitute absolute poverty, while more than 150 million children remain undernourished. Eighty per cent of the world's wealth is held by 15 per cent of its people, who also use a disproportionate share of world resources (UNPD 2001). Natural resources, including arable land, forests and sea life, are diminishing at an unsustainable rate, while more than 11,000 species risk extinction, including a quarter of all mammal species and 30 per cent of fish species (WWF 2002). Remaining forests, which produce oxygen and absorb carbon dioxide, are estimated to reduce by almost half over the next 20 years. Global warming from the production of greenhouse gasses continues. Scarcity of clean water affects more than a billion people, and water loss is becoming a major problem in Africa and Asia.

Facing a less forgiving international economic and ideological order, with little scope for error, traditional 'modernist' development is being challenged by models that are more reflective, more critical and more participatory. This development challenge is reflected in efforts by some practitioners to utilize more participatory approaches to development planning, and to challenge orthodox approaches to development project design, implementation and monitoring. Greater focus on the account-ability of decision makers in developing countries also reflects these new trends. As a result, much of the focus has shifted to giving attention to governance issues which, it has been repeatedly shown, when ignored can be manipulated by narrow sectional interests for narrowly defined personal gain. Accountability, transparency and mandate are key themes in this new approach to development, with advocates for pro-poor policies, fairer international economic relations, and sustainable poverty reduction challenging globalization and free-market capitalism for control of the development agenda. This shift in focus and emphasis poses fundamental challenges to earlier conventional approaches to development, and redefines the roles that key stakeholders play in priority setting. Moral hazard and poor governance are two of the issues that are now attracting greater attention. Equally important are shifts in process that challenge development professionals to genuinely 'democratize' the development process and set out key performance indicators that do more than give lip service to the interests of the poor. Thus, the success or failure of development will be assessed through their eyes.

It is important to note that these trends were unlikely to have come forward while the Cold War continued. While developing countries remained pawns in a larger game, it was commonly regarded as too costly to the big powers to allow issues of governance, fairness or justice to play a real role in determining stakeholder influence. While there remain significant vested constraints, with the passing of the Cold War the pressures are different. Disenfranchised stakeholders are asserting their voices and poverty reduction can (and no doubt should) be a real goal of the global system.

About the book

This book acknowledges that development is a contested and, in some senses, unstable idea, having progressed from the early post-war years, when it meant little more than increasing average income, to, more than 50 years later, including a range of conditions and circumstances that impact on life in countries that continue to variously define themselves in the modern, or post-modern, world. A common understanding of a post-modern world that has evolved since the end of the Cold War is that which has transcended industrialization and largely relies on information flows and processes as the basis for its economy. Critics have argued, however, that post-modernism is in fact a variety of modernism, which continues to rely on a (sometimes off-shore) manufacturing sub-strata and continued access to primary commodities, while also using the higher level of information technology now available . That is to say, the world is increasingly locating economic sectors along state lines, with different states playing different roles, i.e. high technology information providers, industrial manufacturers, and basic commodity providers. The primary categories continue to exist, if in an increasingly global, rather than local, economy.

Assuming, then, that the major global economic changes involve a reorganization of states as primarily differentiated contributors to commodity, manufacturing and information components of the global economy, the questions that arise revolve around the relative weightings of these sectors and the political judgements that consent to such a reorganization. In this there is a very real tension between the structural exigencies of the 'neo-liberal' (free-market-led) global economic agenda and the potential agency of politics in which allocation of resources reflects ideological (interest-based), rather than mechanistic, economic considerations. There is a suggestion in this that, following the neo-liberal paradigm, economic development is increasingly market rather than state led. However, this assumes that what markets achieve is development broadly defined. The neo-liberal philosophy that structurally links free markets (which are almost never actually free) and democracy (generically regarded as political development) fundamentally fails to note a long history of state intervention in markets alongside democracy. It is also based on the unfounded assumption that markets unrestrained will deliver broadly distributed wealth, and that neo-liberal economic theory and practice is somehow politically value-neutral which, demonstrably, it is not.

From this tension arises the question, yet again, of what is the purpose of development? As discussed in this book, development continues to mean the material advancement of people, especially the world's poor. But material advancement, especially if understood as simple economic growth, is not enough by itself, and, indeed, may not even be realized without other component aspects of development, which include the capacity to ensure adequate distribution of the benefits of such growth, ecological sustainability in the way the growth is achieved, and the governance to ensure that the processes to achieve such growth are agreed in a politically inclusive manner and operate under the rule of law.

Development here is, therefore, understood as a process not just of growth or, at its most benign, poverty alleviation, but also of empowerment. The universalist claims to rights, for example, as a part of an overarching (although inconsistent) globalization of standards, also includes accountability and transparency. On the other hand, the growing tendency towards localism is increasing the pressure to put decision making into the hands of ordinary people. In this, it has been argued by some development commentators there is a further tension between universal prescriptions and local conditions. As discussed in the chapter on community development (Chapter 9), the contributors to this volume would agree that any application of development practice must be attuned to local conditions. However, none of the contributors to this book would also resile from the universality of certain normative development outcomes, including the full and disinterested application of law, and active political participation and representation of people whatever their race, sex, creed, or social status. These mutually reliant outcomes, which might be termed 'inclusive governance', both implicitly and sometimes explicitly underpin the contributions to this book. It is this underpinning, or philosophical orientation, that makes this book a somewhat more original contribution to the development debate than many others, which have been far more equivocal about or disinterested in such matters.

For the purpose of the book, and as already indicated, development means the process by which the people and states outside the industrialized world attempt to improve their conditions of life, through material and social means. In this development implies change, affecting most, if not all, areas of life. The idea of development is a multi-dimensional and, by definition, interdisciplinary field in which economic, political, technological, social and cultural factors interact. Development has also been portrayed as synonymous with 'modernization', in this sense including the ideas of industrialization, economic and organizational efficiency, delineated formal political institutions and functions, the pursuit of rational decision making and the fundamental alteration of social and cultural patterns. However, as these criteria have not proven to be universally successful there are increasingly alternative or more inclusive paradigms for defining development.

In this respect, the book considers a wide range of what its authors believe to be the key issues in the development debate. These include definitions of levels of development, global influences on development, measurements of development, economic issues, the contribution of international aid, political and civil development (often referred to under the over-used rubric of 'democratization'), the issue of gender, the idea of development as 'modernization', theories of underdevelopment, regional variation, the environment, and community development. The focus of the book is widely international and employs a geographically broad range of examples, other than where it addresses geographically specific issues (that themselves have wider implications for the field of study, such as the Asian economic crisis, sub-Sahara Africa's development failure, or the United Nations-led state-building exercise in East Timor).

Joe Remenyi's opening chapter asks the question 'What is Development?' At one level this is a basic question, but, as intimated above, it can quickly descend into a complex and contested range of responses. To this end, Reminyi offers a more detailed discussion of what constitutes development, locating at development's core the idea of poverty alleviation, and tracing its origins from the beginning of the post-Second-World-War era. Remenyi's focus on poverty alleviation as the core of what constitutes development addresses perhaps the most basic issue in the development debate; that if people remain hungry or without adequate shelter, education or other basic services, then all else becomes redundant. This establishes the basic premise for the rest of the book.

Any study of development must trace the key debates on the political economy of development since the beginning of the post-war era. John McKay outlines these major trends and conditions within the emerging global system, and the dominant ideas on the nature and genesis of development. At one level, the second half of the 20th century was an era of unparalleled growth and prosperity. But this has only occurred within certain countries or regions. A key question then, which McKay seeks to answer, is why some countries have been able to prosper while others have stagnated or gone backwards. Within mainstream economic thought there has been a strong assumption that growth in some regions will eventually 'trickle down' to the more peripheral areas, given certain conditions and policies. Thus, according to this theory, poor countries can catch up and benefit from the earlier growth experience of others, and pass through a similar process of development, albeit at a later date. This is the essence of the theories of modernization that were popular in the 1950s and 1960s, and which made a return under the guise of 'neo-liberalism' from the 1980s. These ideas still inform the dominant international institutions in the development field, notably the IMF and the World Bank.

As McKay discusses, the underlying assumptions of the various permutations of free-market capitalism came under sustained attack during the 1960s, from what has become known as the 'dependency school', originating especially in Latin America. One view, put by theorists such as Baran, Frank and others, argued that developing countries could not develop in this 'trickle down' manner, because the processes of global change that gave rise to prosperity in developed countries resulted in the simultaneous impoverishment of the poorer regions. These dependency ideas themselves were also criticised, partly because of their over-reliance on global rather than local factors, but especially for their inability to account for the rapid growth that was clearly going on in parts of East Asia at the time. In turn, the economic crisis in Asia in 1997–8, the continued crisis in Africa, and the seemingly remorseless progress of globalization, partly through the expansion of the multinational corporations, has seen a revival of interest in 'neo-dependency' approaches. The chapter, then, explores the history of ideas about development, asking what has been learned from the last 50 years in terms of theory and the design of more appropriate policies.

Within development, a major consistent focus has been on development assistance, usually referred to as aid. Considering this, Janet Hunt's chapter on aid looks critically at multilateral and bilateral aid, and the distinctions between official development assistance (ODA) and private aid programs. The chapter assesses the contributions, styles and shifting orientations of the major multilateral aid organizations and aid donor countries, the international commitment to aid, how aid is employed in bilateral relations, and the role of non-government organizations (NGOs) in the aid agenda/s and as contributors to the effective application of aid. It also considers what aid has achieved since the beginning of the 1960s, and where it is heading in the 21st century. Hunt sets aid within the context of other more significant factors in development, such as globalization, trade and financial policies, indebtedness (some of it aid-driven), and intrastate conflict. Her chapter also addresses public perceptions of aid, and the issues of public and political support for the aid regime.

The international focus on aid has changed in the period during and after the Cold War, with aid levels declining and distribution patterns changing. Since poverty reduction is a key goal of aid (and a focus of this book), Hunt also considers the extent to which aid can contribute to poverty reduction. The question of aid and power relations raises the further question of who primarily benefits from aid, noting that aid is often far less benign than it initially appears.

The issue of globalization is one that looms increasingly large over many areas, not least that of development, and was therefore considered critical to include in this overall study. While Kingsbury notes that development is sometimes defined in global terms, he questions the specificity of particular development issues, reflecting what some observers have called a 'global–local' dichotomy. Beyond countries, there are also wider challenges and changes to communities at all levels brought about by various aspects of globalization. As Kingsbury notes, globalization has been broadly taken to mean economic globalization, especially of a free-market capitalist type. This implies that critiques of globalization have focused on this dominant type of globalization rather than globalization as such. Global capitalism, freed of the restraints that can be applied by states, is no longer easily restrained by a politically and often economically fragmented international community. As a result of this, Kingsbury notes, in order to prosper communities must attract global capital – those that do can, indeed, prosper, while those that do not tend to wither. Yet in order to appear attractive to global capital, communities in developing countries often have to undercut their competitors, in what amounts to a downward cycle, if not spiral, of poverty. Kingsbury suggests that what is said to be a reduction of state sovereignty is just another domain for elite domination, or state variation, which opens the way for exploitation.

As with development, defining globalization solely as an economic phenomenon artificially constrains its meaning. Other, non-economic types of globalization, are equally important. These may include the spread of normative ('universalist') humanist political and social values, such as civil and political rights, political participation and representation, equality before an impartial law and so on (which is often contained within the term 'democratization'). Communication and aspects of culture are also increasingly globalized, in terms of technology, ownership and spread of media, and shared popular preferences. In these senses, development can be understood as comprising economic, political and cultural elements, all of which engage in a wider world and all of which are in some ways ultimately transformed by it. In all of this, there remains a capacity for a normative type of globalization, which implies a process intended to achieve the greatest amount of happiness among the greatest number of people.

Following from this increasing tendency towards globalization, Reminyi examines the economic model that has in large part come to define, if not the global standard, then at least the dominant economic paradigm in development, that of neo-classical (or neo-liberal) development economics. In this he notes the critical importance of money, structural adjustment within the context of greater demands for transparency and accountability. Goal setting and the role of competing and complementary financing strategies are then used to illustrate the different roles that can be taken by the public and the private sectors.

Reminyi also looks at trends in the meaning of development and the role of economics. In terms of capacity for economic efficiency and hence competitiveness, Reminyi asks whether notions of comparative advantage remain applicable, and how this is related to globalization and the contribution that gains from trade make to economic development. Despite the extra-state demands of globalization, Reminyi continues to see a role for government in economic planning, in particular relating to the public sector in planning, infrastructure development and policy making.

Reminyi's identification of the importance of governance then raises the issue of political development, as further explored by Kingsbury, who notes that traditional approaches to development focused heavily on economic criteria, often at the expense of political development. However, in many countries where the process of economic development has been poor or uneven, a view has developed that this may have been a consequence of poor governance and a lack of political accountability. Indeed, it has been argued that better governance and accountability enhances economic development.

Nowhere has the failure of economic development, and governance, been more pronounced than in sub-Saharan Africa, where deterioration of social and economic conditions over the past two decades has confounded development efforts. Following Asia's financial crisis of 1997–8, which raised major governance issues relating to economic development in South East Asia, the issues gained further prominence. These failures in Africa and Asia have presented major challenges to development theory and practice, and each in their different ways can said to be at the heart of the development process. Most notably as McKay observes, rapid economic growth and then collapse in Asia has posed questions for both dependency theorists and the proponents of free-market policies, while the continued crisis in Africa is an indictment of the entire development 'profession'. This chapter examines these two very different crises, and considers in particular the nature of the crises in the two regions, and the various explanations that have been put forward to account for these serious events. McKay considers whether the crises in Africa and Asia are separate, unrelated events, or two symptoms of some basic problems in the global system.

Within this, McKay notes the variations between countries in terms of the severity and causes of the crisis, the policies that had been adopted, or had failed to be adopted, in the period leading up to the respective crises, and the relationship between them with the onset of crisis conditions. This then leads to considering the impact of trade, investment and other liberalization policies, and the relationship between the crises and the nature of the global systems of trade, investment and finance.

Given expressions of broadly anti-Western sentiment in a number of developing countries, McKay then looks at the level and nature of resentment in Asia and Africa against the West, and its economic, political and strategic implications. And continuing with a theme developed in earlier chapters, McKay also considers the relationships in various countries and regions between democracy, transparency, good governance, economic development and the crisis. He explores the extent and nature of recovery from the crisis in various countries, especially in Asia, and the policies for restructuring and reform, including the role of international and regional agencies in facilitating recovery, and the extent to which these actions were effective.

In discussion of the success or otherwise of the application of economic models, issues of governance and, hence. accountability have become critical. As Kingsbury notes in the following chapter, good governance and accountability are generally accepted as being more prevalent in societies that have a participatory and representative (democratic) political process. As Kingsbury also argues, while there may be practical difficulties in lifting material living standards, there are few impediments, other than those that are politically imposed, to political development. And in countries where there has been economic development, people's greater access to education and information has also enhanced the political development agenda.

Yet, as Kingsbury discusses, the idea of political development immediately calls up debate about political theories and ideologies, in particular about where political power does or should lie, and about the role of 'tradition' and 'culture' in political processes. There are debates about universal versus local values, the form and structure of the state, the principle model of political organization, about who should be included and who not and how and why, about the legitimacy of the state and the relationship between the government and the state. Key questions revolve around the responsibilities of the state to its people, usually defined as citizens, and what responsibilities citizens in turn have to the state. Further issues explored here include universal criteria and obligations that can be said to apply to political relationships and how they are enforced, as well as the limits of state sovereignty.

Kingsbury argues that political development includes broad notions of citizenship, an open representative electoral process and certain basic rights concerning freedom of speech and assembly, and freedom from arbitrary arrest and inhumane punishment. Without these safeguards, people's participation in a political process leaves them vulnerable to the exercise of arbitrary power in repressive states. A key component contributing to, and reflecting, political development, Kingsbury suggests, is the growth and activity of civil society. The criteria for political development outlined in this chapter all imply good governance, in which the institutions of state operate transparently, efficiently and according to a legal code that meets the above mentioned criteria. Such institutions must also require that civil, political or economic (business) bodies that come under their administrative jurisdiction comply fully and fairly with the legal code.

Proceeding from political development and addressing the intersection of global institutions, local participation and poverty alleviation, Reminyi discusses notions of local participation in the development process, in particular in poverty reduction. Within state agencies and the now ageing Bretton Woods institutions (see pp. 131ff), Reminyi identifies a gradual recognition that the existing development strategies are in need of reassessment and revision if absolute poverty, which continues to afflict a billion people worldwide, is to be ended. Reminyi says that participatory poverty reduction is linked to rural democratization that parallels international trends towards smaller government. Within this context Remenyi considers the issues of what poverty is, who the poor are, and how persistent poverty can be overcome within the context of the institutional changes. In this he addresses poverty as a practical issue requiring more effective targeting of poverty reduction resources, in particularly through local participation in sustainable poverty reduction.

To assess the efficacy of this core function of development Remenyi addresses the development 'balance sheet', in particular taking the view that measuring development cannot be divorced from the need to measure the impact of development on reducing poverty. The ability to measure the impact of development upon poverty is important, as claimed outcomes of past development projects have in many cases not translated into identifiable gains in poverty reduction.

To this end, Remenyi presents a range of means of assessing development, considering the several dimensions of poverty. Novel notions dealing with functional poverty, the poverty pyramid and a participatory weighted poverty index are presented in contrast to the UNDP's Human Development Index and the 'dollar a day' (or two dollars a day) standard promulgated by the World Bank. Within this critical understanding of measuring development, Reminyi considers income-based indicators of development, and the validity of absolute and relative measures of poverty, as well as indicators identified by the poor themselves. He discusses the importance of household income and gender differences, how the gap in income across countries is or can be breached, and the role that income differences between countries play in relation to sources of investment opportunities and gains from trade. Reminyi then moves to consider relevant 'civil society' indicators dealing with crime, democratic processes, demographic trends, and human rights. The chapter concludes by considering how development stands after half a decade, and what the prospects are for the future of development, again noting that poverty alleviation is the critical criterion for understanding and assessing development.

The next chapter picks up on themes of the focus, purpose and methods of development raised by Remenyi and Kingsbury, to consider ideas of community development. Community development is intended to enhance the social and local decision making process – the 'empowerment' – of people who are the target of development projects, and to give them more practical political power over the goals and outcomes of the development process. Kingsbury posits that the movement towards community development reflects a fundamental re-orientation of development towards a grass-roots or local-level process of democratization. Such an approach has been shown, in a number of cases, to produce real, tangible and appropriate benefits to people at the local level, as well as providing a greater sense of self worth and the capacity to make many of their own decisions. It also has the benefit of working within and preserving aspects of local culture that give meaning to community life, and which assist in maintaining and enhancing the social cohesion that is necessary when successfully engaging in a process of change.

The move towards this focus on social and cultural development derived from critiques of top-down aid projects and decision-making. Many such projects failed to meet the needs and desires of ordinary people at the local level, were often not based on local experience and were frequently unsustainable once the aid provider had left. In all, such aid benefited the aid provider, in that they were given a job and a social purpose, but had little, and sometimes negative, impact on the aid recipients. In other cases, decisions about aid projects have been taken by traditional representatives or chiefs, sometimes with the outcome that the decisions have reflected their own somewhat more limited interests, to the exclusion of those of the more marginal people in their areas.

In the formative stages of this more 'grass roots' form of development, local decision makers might require assistance and education, which has been shown to be most successfully undertaken through what has been referred to as 'participatory development'. In this, the external agency works with local people in assisting them to make decisions for themselves, to reflect on their decisions and to secure such decisions against external incursions. The balancing act for the 'participatory development worker' is to assist and, where necessary, guide but to do so in a way that continues to reinforce local decision making, needs and aspirations.

Related to community development or local empowerment is the development or empowerment of women within the development context. In Chapter 10, Janet Hunt focuses on the gender aspects of development, in particular how women have largely been 'made invisible' and left out of the development process. While policies have more recently sought to include women in development the results are mixed at best, and women have always carried the largest share of the domestic material burden in societies in developing countries, beyond child rearing and home maintenance, including domestic husbandry and agriculture, and, more recently, in paid employment. Hunt also notes that men have been more readily accommodated into the cash economy, although the benefits of their access to cash has not always contributed to the welfare of family members.

As Hunt explains, gender is understood as the socially ascribed roles of men and women in any society based on their sex. Hunt examines how gender-defined roles have been differentiated traditionally and how the development process has influenced or changed this, and how this influence or change has impacted on gender relations and the distribution of the benefits of development, often to the detriment of women.

In many traditional societies, the roles of the sexes are clearly and separately defined, in some cases with sanctions being placed on the transgression of gender roles. Gender roles in traditional societies can reflect a balance (or imbalance) of responsibilities around modes of production. However, the process of development destabilizes and reorients aspects of traditional modes of production, especially in relation to cash cropping, employed labour and the social impact of industrialization, often leaving women with heavier work burdens. Understanding the gender impacts of proposed development is a key issue.

Hunt's chapter links many of the issues raised in earlier chapters and views them through a gender lens. If development is to reduce poverty, then it must transform women's lives, since women are disproportionately represented among the world's poor. Hunt explores the relationship of gender considerations to macro-economic trends of the past 20 years, to globalization and trade liberalization, to the environment and attempts to make development sustainable, and to the focus on community development.

While all of the preceding issues are critical to an understanding of development, it is the degradation of the earth's capacity to sustain life that presents short-term problems and critical long-term threats. That is to say, no development can take place outside the context of the physical environment, yet, until recently, this has been the most neglected area in development debate. Kingsbury, therefore, considers aspects of the environment that increasingly demand to be thought of as fundamental parts of the development agenda. This demand has been partly as a consequence of the rise in the profile of environmental issues in developed countries and, hence, among many bilateral and multilateral aid agencies and aid organizations, and partly in response to environmental issues that have arisen in developing countries due to increases in population and particularly as a direct result of a range of development processes. Kingsbury notes that the environmental record in development has, to date, been poor, and environmental degradation has continued at a pace that is unsustainable in absolute terms. There is debate about how long current development processes can continue before the global ecology collapses, but Kingsbury says there is no longer serious debate about such an eventual collapse should there not be a fundamental shift in development thinking, planning and implementation.

The environmental impact of development has manifested in a number of ways. In particular, the sheer increase in the global population, the consumption of natural resources implied in such growth and the human and industrial pollution that has been produced is perhaps the single most important issue. Assuming no significant change in human behaviour, there would need to be a considerable, perhaps drastic, reduction in the world's population in order to accommodate finite natural productive capacity and to find alternative and more sustainable natural resources. However, as Kingsbury notes, the only significant signs of population reduction, apart from natural or human calamities, have been in the most developed societies. This implies that global society will have to develop significantly further before there is any in-built tendency towards population reduction. The indicators suggest that there may be serious environmental breakdown before this 'natural' process can take place.

In terms of the quality, rather than sheer quantity, of human behaviour, Kingsbury discusses some outstanding examples of unsustainable environmental degradation that are directly linked to the development process. These include the loss of the world's forests, and associated desertification, as probably the world's foremost specific environmental problem. Beyond the issues of deforestation, the diversion, use and pollution of the world's waterways for human and industrial purposes has both reduced the amount of potable water and negatively impacted on plant and animal life. Fisheries, in streams as well as in oceans in areas near sources of pollution, have been significantly affected, with a severe impact on marginal populations who still rely on this supply of protein and potable water for everyday needs. And, as Kingsbury notes in this chapter, governments of developing countries are more inclined to go softly on such industry, as they cite their economic inability to provide alternative means of waste disposal while pointing out their contribution to employment and economic development. The same is often said about issues such as air pollution, which have been shown to impact on wider aspects of the global environment, such as the ozone layer and global warming. To this end, there has increasingly been discussion about 'appropriate development' and 'sustainable development', two ideas that often overlap, and these issues are discussed in this chapter.

As noted at the outset, much of the world continues to focus on issues of development, and when attention is properly turned it is widely recognised that the problems of development are global in both their reach and their potential impact. Yet at the same time the urgency felt by some about such global development issues is far from shared by all, and has resulted in this retreat from tackling the complex issues. The reduction to increasingly simplistic formulae for addressing the continuing problems of development reflects the various types of 'fatigue' that has beset many wealthier countries in relation to poorer countries. Much of this, in turn, can be attributed to the lack of ideological imperative that characterized the period from around 1950 to 1990. A new ideological imperative – that of neo-liberalism – prevails, but it is less generous, less sympathetic (and much less empathetic), and fairly inflexible in the choices that are on offer.

This book, then, attempts to discuss these key issues and explore some of the ways forward for development in this evolving period of global reorganization. If it provides material to work with and to consider critically it will have gone a long way towards achieving its primary goal.

Chapter 1

What is Development?

JOE REMENYI

> Development is a process directed at outcomes encapsulating improved
> standards of living and greater capacity for self-reliance in economies
> that are technically more complex and more dependent on global
> integration than before.

The concept of development has undergone significant change since the
end of the Second World War. This chapter considers the paths by which
development has come to be widely understood today as a people-centered
historical process. It will be argued that the present understanding of
development as a people-centered process intimately linked to governance
issues. It will be argued that this process has been a response to lessons
from experience rather than the consequence of a victory of one line of
thinking among the competing range of ideas about development.

The evolution of thought on development has not been uniform or even.
Rather, progress in thinking has been disjointed, awaiting the accumulation of anomalies until it was no longer possible to adhere to convenient
but unsustainable assumptions. Among the critical but false assumptions,
four are fundamental:

(i)   blind faith in the belief that Western 'scientific' methods are superior
       to traditional practices
(ii)   the belief that there is no gender dimension to development
(iii) the proposition that the elimination of poverty can be achieved by
       realizing sustained economic growth, poverty targeting notwithstanding
(iv)   the priority of economic development over all else, so that governance
       issues are incidental to economic development.

The disciplinary perspective from which one examines thinking on
development does make a difference to the issues. This chapter is
unequivocally focused on 'people in poverty' and pays particular attention
to the evolution of views of development that place at their centre the
notion of people seeking a better life. In this perspective economic
development has a 'service' role to play to ensure that the centrality of
good governance and human rights issues are not only not ignored, but
also used to ensure that poverty alleviation is firmly placed on the centre
stage of development policy and development in practice.

The definition of development presented at the outset of this chapter¹ submits a challenge to revise thinking on development. In particular, little attention is given to the idea that contemporary development is a response to decolonization. There is a strong argument that can be made that the colonial heritage of many developing countries complicated the process of development. It is undoubtedly true that the need to regularize national borders, deal with internal civil unrest from groups reluctant to accept incorporation into emerging new states, and the competition engendered by the opposed interests of the Cold War combatants has complicated the task of state-building and development planning. However, it is also true that much of the literature on decolonization and the colonial heritage of developing countries is little more than apologetics for why corruption and the triumph of elite groups over the poor majority have dominated the development experience of so many developing countries.

The road from Bretton Woods

It is important to note that what we refer to as the modern era of development began with the end of the Second World War, which marked the beginning of an unprecedented period of science and technology transfer. It was also the beginning of an era of government intervention, inspired by Keynesian and Socialist philosophies, that was meant to be enlightened though paternalistic approaches to economic management and national progress. At the international level, the end of the Second World War also saw the creation of international governance structures, the so called Bretton Woods institutions (the World Bank, the International Monetary Fund and associated United Nations agencies), that were to dominate the environment within which international development and official development assistance were to be administered.

The spectre of stagnation

The industrialized economies of Europe and North America welcomed the end of the Second World War. But, the political leaders of these warring economies also feared the transition to peace. There was a real concern that the end of war may result in such a collapse of demand from the military sector that the Western alliance economies, all of which had become adjusted to wartime conditions for almost a decade, might plunge into a period of widespread unemployment, possibly on the scale of the 1930s depression. Among economists and international public policy activists, the spectre of post-war demobilization was associated with the threat of economic stagnation, not the start of what hindsight reveals as a generation of full employment growth (see, in particular, Hansen 1941). In this environment of uncertainty, the revitalization and modernization of poor and technologically backward economies presented an opportunity to avoid international economic stagnation. Development of economically backward areas was to create investment opportunities and demand for the output of industries desperate to find peacetime customers.

Thus, fear and opportunity mixed to give birth to the new industry of 'foreign aid and development planning'. The age of the development professional dawned. Armed with the tools of Keynesian demand management economics, the political and economic thinkers and leaders of the Western alliance welded the interests of *donor* economies to those of aid recipients. Among the Eastern-bloc economies, led by the example of the early successes of Soviet economic progress, similar processes were evident, though the driving force was political and ideological rather than economic.

Whether assisted by donors from one side of the Cold War or the other, the development outcomes sought were documented in grandiose five-year national development plans. For much of the last 50 years, no self-respecting developing country could be without a five-year plan. Yet, the history of modern development has shown that, all too often, these plans were built on false assumptions and poor quality data.

Modernization first

The modern era of development began brash and confident that the world, and developing countries in particular, could be remade within a generation or two. Poverty would be vanquished, but only if backward economies were modernized; modernization was the first order of business.

More than a generation had to pass before the concept of development could evolve beyond its intrinsic association with modernization. It is difficult to avoid the conclusion that for at least the first 30 years after 1945, development professionals and national leaders in donor and recipient economies alike, actively sought to avoid having to acknowledge that improving the welfare of poor people in developing countries is the *raison d'etre* of development of poor economies.

Development is both a process and an outcome

Development is a process intended to achieve a well-defined outcome. But, the definition to which we subscribe must be just as relevant in reverse (i.e., in describing the opposite to development, de-development), as it is in the identification of successful development. The definition towards which we will work describes a process that is more than economic progress, more than technological re-organization of society, more than the embrace of modernity, more than the pursuit of freedom, and more than the triumph of democracy or people power.

Development is a process of growth towards self-reliance and contentment. It is a process by which individuals, groups and communities obtain the means to be responsible for their own livelihoods, welfare and future. The opposite, de-development, is when the capacity for self-reliance and contentment deteriorates, typically because the means to be responsible for one's own livelihood, welfare or future has been lost to war, civil unrest, natural calamity, or the need to flee and adopt the life of a refugee. The modern era of development consists of a patchwork of experiences that include examples of success (Japan, Singapore, Malaysia, China, South Korea, Taiwan, and Botswana), failures (Zimbabwe, Nigeria, Sierra Leone, Kenya, Angola, Mozambique, Argentina, Venezuela, Philippines, North Korea, Lebanon, Sudan and Iraq), and some in-between (notably Thailand, Egypt, Israel, Morocco, Turkey, Tanzania, South Africa, Ghana, Chile, Peru, Mexico and Brazil).

Economics first

It is not an exaggeration to say that through at least the 1950s and 1960s, and probably well into the 1970s, development of poor countries was seen by a vast majority of development professionals, policy makers and academics as synonymous with economic development. Almost no attention was given in the modernization- and investment-driven development strategies of those years to development as being about the improvement of people and their circumstances at household level.

The theories of economic development and economic growth that dominated thinking about development in the 1950s and 1960s regarded the improvement of people's livelihoods and standards of living as little more than by-products of the building blocks of modernization, i.e., (i) economic returns to successful accumulation of capital, and (ii) economic growth fuelled by productivity improvements arising from the transfer of technology from technologically and economically advanced areas to technologically and economically backward areas. The late comers to development were believed to be at an advantage because they could pick and choose from a vast range of ready-made and tested technological developments and new industries 'off the shelf' (see Agarwala and Singh 1958, also Little 1982, Meier and Seers 1984, Meier 1995, Seligson and Passe-Smith 1998, and Dutt 2002, Volume 1).

Complicit in the push for modernizing 'economic development at all costs', were professionals from disciplines with whom macroeconomic managers and development planners needed to cooperate. In addition to economists, especially those from various branches of macroeconomics, the key actors in the planning and implementation of development were technical professionals from all aspects of engineering, agriculture, administration and planning, demography and the law. Quite rapidly, a new breed of development professionals emerged. In the main these professionals shared a commitment to modernization. They also believed that the combination of Keynesian macro-economics plus centralized planning and resource management skills honed during the war years, undergirded by modern science, provided everything that would be needed to initiate and manage a process of economic growth (i.e. development), that would ensure gradual abolition of structural unemployment and poverty from poor countries and the world at large. These widely and firmly held beliefs reflected a time when development professionals served a concept of development that was, at best, naïve and, at worst, biased because it was founded on spurious assumptions and informed by data of questionable quality.

The foregoing comment does not apply to all contributors to the development literature or development practice during the period 1950–2000. Some notable exceptions are found it the pioneering work of agriculture and rural development specialists, such as University-of-Chicago-based economist Ted Schultz who spearheaded belated attention to human capital development (see Schultz 1962, 1964), David Norman and colleagues in the international agricultural research centre system who mainstreamed the systems approach to our understanding of traditional agriculture (see Norman 1974, 1980, Zandstra *et al.* 1981), and Robert Chambers, Gordon Conway and others who pioneered qualitative data collection and poverty analysis using rapid rural appraisal (RRA) and participatory methods in all phases of the project cycle (see Chambers 1983, Uphoff 1982, Cernea 1985, 1991, and McCracken, Pretty and Conway 1988). Similarly, from a completely different perspective and quite independently, Ester Boserup's path-breaking work on gender (Boserup 1970), and Sen's analysis of poverty and entitlements (Sen 1981), are also critical exceptions. However, it is only in the 20 or so years since 1980 that the link between poverty and development has been given explicit attention in the mainstream professional journals and other development literature. Core to this shift is the realization that participatory development is a powerful means of data collection, planning, problem solving and inclusive program implementation.

Schism in the ranks

Post-Second-World-War reconstruction in Europe under the Marshall Plan was an important lesson for the nascent development industry. In the years immediately after the end of the War in 1945, more than $US17 billion in reconstruction aid (equivalent to about $US420 billion at 2000 prices) was directed at the rebuilding and modernization of war-ravaged European economies. Technology transfer and massive investment in infrastructure quickly brought moribund European economies on line, seamlessly integrating them into a global economy such as the world had never seen. The lessons for the development of poor and technologically backward economies appeared clear. They too would have to be integrated into the world economy. The keys to integration were identified as investment, technology transfer and free trade.

In 1949, US President Harry Truman encapsulated the lessons of the Marshall Plan for Europe into his Point Four programme for the development of technologically backward and poor economies. He heralded Point Four as a phase in the development of states that would bring economic progress to poor countries, underwrite world peace and keep developing countries from falling under the influence of communism. In all, the Point Four programme represented a marriage of what was perceived to be mutual interests. The fear of global stagnation, the challenge of the Cold War, and the prospect of profitable investment opportunities in the untapped markets of poor economies were combined into a message that declared the development of poor economies to be in the self-interest of all concerned. The advocates of peaceful decolonization, the architects of prosperity in established industrial economies, and the anti-communist hawks found common ground in this grand liberal–democratic vision of development. Development was to be a win–win game, with the foreign aid offered under the Point Four programme providing an auspicious beginning to the modern era of development and official development assistance.

President Truman's initiative in launching Point Four in 1949 reflected not only American opinion, but also a vision shared by America's allies in Western Europe and the Pacific. This vision was of a brave new world, saved from communism and poverty by the power of science and investments in modernization.

However, the existence of a widely shared global vision did not mean an absence of disagreement on the outcomes that development of poor countries was meant to deliver. The developed economies, those which were to form the *donor* country group, located primarily in the temperate zones of the northern hemisphere, wanted development to deliver a world economy that obeyed the rules that had been articulated in the post-war meetings at Bretton Woods, NH, USA, in July 1944. These rules were to be policed by the newly created Bretton Woods institutions, the International Bank for Reconstruction and Development (IBRD), later to be known simply as the World Bank, the International Monetary Fund (IMF), the

General Agreement on Tariffs and Trade (GATT), and several UN development agencies. These institutional innovations represented a new set of mechanisms to serve mutual interests by bringing capital from lending governments in developed economies to borrowing governments in developing economies.

The first of the rules that was supposed to be observed was that countries that have a surplus of labour should develop by fostering the growth of economic activities that are labour-using, while the capital-intensive high-tech economic activities would be the preserve of economies with more capital than labour. If all economies followed this simple rule, then the global economy would be free to grow in ways that are consistent with international comparative advantage. The second rule was that participating governments are committed to promoting freer trade, so as to ensure that growth is fostered by trade and development is not hindered by obstacles to access to markets. Both of these rules genuflect before the altar of free trade, the mantra of which is the Smithian doctrine that 'the wealth of nations is limited only by the extent of the market'.

History shows that the proliferation of tariff and non-tariff trade barriers, including producer subsidies, and legal obstacles to untrammeled competition and access to domestic markets in developed and developing countries alike, has meant that the commitment to freer trade has been observed more in rhetoric than in reality by developed and developing countries. The strictures of competition and the discipline of market forces have, in the main, been accepted only when it has been in the unequivocal self-interest of the political elites in the countries concerned. Recourse by governments to tariffs and other interventionist strategies to promote local development through new industries or import replacement has been a politically safe way to appear to shift the cost of development onto foreigners, while at the same time underwriting the interests of elite groups (see, e.g., Prebish 1950, Chenery 1955, Hirschman 1958, Ellis 1961, Cairncross 1962, Furtado 1970, Bhagwati and Desai 1970, Balassa 1971, Bauer 1971, Amin 1978, Griffin and Kahn 1978, Amacher, Haberler and Willett 1979).

For donor countries, it made all kinds of sense for economically backward and highly populated developing countries to specialize in labour-intensive economic activities. Moreover, donor countries rightly saw development as offering them the opportunity to tap new markets. Neither of these ideas, however, squared at all well with the aspirations of people from many of the world's poorest and most highly populated economies. Specialization in labour-intensive industries, it seemed to them, would merely trap them into a low-tech set of options for the future. In the minds of the national leaders of developing countries across Asia, Africa and South America, development meant modernization, which meant domestic capacity building in high-tech, capital-intensive industries as well as up-grading of the scientific base of production in traditional rural industries.

It is not surprising, therefore, that a study of the development plans of most developing countries during the period 1950–70 reveals a commitment to industrialism and a rush to develop economies that are as near as possible to the high-tech end of the modernization spectrum. Hidden behind tariff walls to protect their infant industries, some developing countries even sought to establish steel plants and chemical industries that would be wholly dependent on imports for raw materials and other essential inputs. In effect, freer trade was traded not for fair trade, but for a belief in economic development through investment in import replacement, comparative advantage notwithstanding (see, e.g., Prebisch 1950, Nurske 1953, Lewis 1955, Rostow 1960, Kuznets 1966, Furtado 1970, Chenery and Syrquin 1975, and Amin 1978).

In hindsight, one can understand and even share the desire on the part of most developing countries to join the club of scientific leading countries with their own high-tech industries and sectors. It is natural for political leaders to see value and strength in breaking free from dependence on foreigners for all things scientific and modern. Besides, Europe's Common Agricultural Policy and (later) the USA's commitment to massive subsidies to its farm sector represented an example that was politically more palatable than freer trade and the limits to development planning that the economics of comparative advantage appeared to require. The line of least resistance and political self-interest clearly led to development strategies that gave priority to modernization over all else, behind protective tariff walls if necessary. It will come as no surprise, therefore, to find that in the development plans devised for developing countries in the three decades after the Second World War, the interests and needs of poor people come after the resource needs of modernization, concern for demographic trends excepted. India's development plans through the 1960s are a case in point, the initial commitment to self-reliance and home-spun technologies in the Ghandi-inspired first Indian Development Plan of the later 1950s notwithstanding (see Mahalanobis 1963).

Waiting for the demographic transition

Population growth has always been a contentious issue in development. Concern that rapid population growth in populous poor economies would undermine gains made in economic development formed a solid foundation for population control programmes, that went as far as forced sterilizations during the reign of Indira Ghandi as Prime Minister of India in the 1960s and 1970s. Demographers, however, pointed to the demographic transition that had happened in economically advanced economies.

The growth of populations in developed economies could be mapped to show that beyond certain key levels of economic achievement, fertility rates declined, causing the gap between plummeting death rates and very high, even rising, birth rates to shrink (see Figure 1.1). The theory of demographic transition offered the world hope that economic development would, in time, achieve the same result in developing countries. Development professionals were resigned to the view that it may take a generation or two before the fall in fertility rates would begin to overwhelm the impetus given to population growth as a consequence of falling death rates.

It is not simple to determine whether population trends in developing countries hinder or assist the process of development. Those who believe firmly in the essential role of birth control and other measures targeted at lowering the number of births tend to belong to the camp that holds firmly that population growth can be too rapid and needs to be contained for development to take hold and pass onto a phase of sustainability. Others argue that population control programmes divert attention from the development initiatives that will bring on the demographic transition all the more quickly.

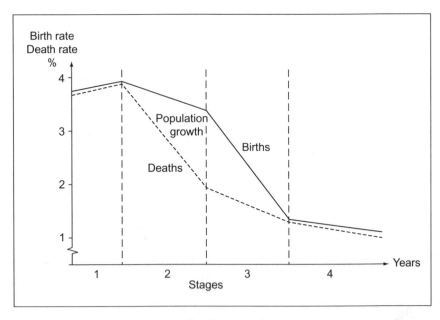

Figure 1.1   *The demographic transition*

This battle of opinions and ideas still rages, though the progress of developing countries in the latter decade of the 20th century is clearly revealing falls in fertility rates (the average number of life-time births per adult female), that is slowly closing the gap between crude death rates and crude birth rates. At the start of the 21st century, developing countries are challenged by ageing populations and declining birth rates; exactly the opposite of the situation in 1950.

Researchers are still undecided about whether the effectiveness of birth control programmes, or the impact of sustained improvements in key indicators of development (e.g., improved income per person, declining infant mortality, rising basic education achievement rates among fertile women, etc.) are the cause of recent demographic transition trends in developing countries. Whichever way it turns out, the trend toward significantly lower fertility rates in the world's populous poor countries, significant parts of Africa excepted, is one of the most welcome trends in contemporary development. This is because declining fertility rates make it easier for poor people to take charge of their own poverty reduction strategies and to sustain whatever gains they make. Declining fertility rates do tend to lead to smaller families and lower dependency ratios (the number of economically active household members as a proportion of family size). Lower fertility rates and lower dependency rations tend to be important indicators of improving trends in the incidence of poverty.

Demographic transition in modern development has been anxiously awaited for at least the last two generations. Now that it is upon us, the world of development professionals and political leaders is ambivalent about its effects. In donor countries the concern is that populations will decline as population growth rates fall to well below replacement levels. In developing countries there is a rising tide of concern over aging populations and the need to plan for the day when local economies will be under pressure to support a rapidly rising cohort of aged people (see UNFPA 1978–2002).

The rediscovery and loss of a poverty focus

A hallmark of the 13 years during which Robert McNamara was president of the World Bank, 1968–1981, was the rediscovery of the importance of placing poverty reduction at centre stage in development (McNamara 1981). However, the good beginning that McNamara oversaw at the Bank was gradually diverted by two important developments in thinking on poverty and the environment in which poverty alleviation has to take place. The first watershed was the link forged between the idea that poverty created disabling traps that keep poor people poor. Escape from

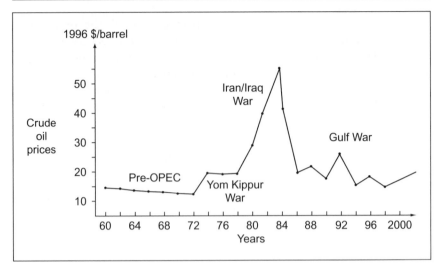

Figure 1.2   *Crude oil price trends 1960–2000*

these poverty traps demands, it was believed, government intervention and policy prescriptions that will ensure that poor people have secure access to basic needs. The intellectual link between basic needs and development had its equivalent among some religious leaders in the literature on liberation theology. Liberation theology strengthened the alliance between religion-based development agencies, religious communities working in community development, and secular development professionals committed to promoting basic needs-based development (see Hillar 1993, Boff and Clodovis 1984).

The second *gestalt* in thinking flowed from the oil crisis of 1973, which launched a decade long hiatus in the world's energy markets, marked by the escalation of global oil prices, under the leadership of the Organisation of Petroleum Exporting Countries (OPEC), from $US3 per barrel in 1973 to $US30 in 1979 (see Figure 1.2).

Basic needs

On the surface, the movement to give greater prominence to basic needs in development planning was a positive evolution in thinking on development. It resulted in a decade or more of renewed vigor given to programmes that sought to ensure availability of basic needs to the poor and the upgrading of literacy, numeracy and health maintenance skills in rural communities. However, the argument for increased priority to basic needs in development planning gradually deteriorated into the rhetoric of welfare. The welfare needs of the poor diverted attention from the need to lift the productivity of the poor and the environments in which they lived. Policies targeted at the poor took on a paternalistic tone. The attitude that poor people needed help to escape their poverty remained. But the side-effects of paternalism nurtured the elitist belief that technical-assistance professionals already knew the sort of help that poor people needed to overcome their poverty. In reality, the development profession of the earliest development decades revealed an intellectual arrogance in the common approach to development in practice. Paternalism obscured the truth, confusing charity with development assistance, education with knowledge, and poverty with ignorance, genuine concern for basic needs notwithstanding.

The essential switch in mindset, by which understanding and attitudes to development as a poverty-reduction-focused process is clarified for at least two decades if not more. This conclusion will raise the hackles of the champions of basic needs approaches to development with a human face. Nonetheless, a dispassionate assessment of the literature leaves one with the uncomfortable conclusion that at the beginning of the development decade of the 1970s, the meaning of development remained essentially technocratic, paternalistic and elitist. Little or no value was given in development planning to the knowledge that poor people have of how poverty effects them, why they cannot escape their poverty unaided, or what realistic and attainable poverty alleviation targets are.

The notion that development has to be about *pro-poor* growth was not considered in development thinking pre-1980. The well-intentioned views of the advocates of development with a human face notwithstanding, it was unimaginable that pro-poor growth could be as high if not higher than 'trickle-down' growth. The 30 years from 1969 to 1999 were dominated by the struggle of leading thinkers on development to overcome the myopia of entrenched attitudes and prejudices. Critical among these assumptions was the belief that the poor have little if anything to contribute, that they are a burden on society, and that the poor themselves are, in part at least, responsible for their own plight because of their ignorance, laziness or blind commitment to outmoded customs and traditions.

The stern determination with which these assumptions were held meant that it was difficult for Western-trained development professionals to automatically see that the poor are victims of the systems in which they struggle to survive. Instead the poor were perceived and portrayed as people to be re-educated, pitied and not trusted because they are constrained by irrational commitments to restrictive social and cultural customs, misguided beliefs born of ignorance, and irrational aversion to risk and innovation because of ignorance and the fear of change. These dominant negative views of the poor prevented the development profession from seeing what was always there to see: that it is not possible to have *real* poverty-reduction-based development without a deep appreciation of the problems and constraints facing poor households.

The conviction among development professionals that poverty reduction is a victory that can be won by recourse to the exemplars of modernity remained common until well into the 1980s. Even NGOs embraced these prejudices, reflected in the predominance in their client base of programme participants drawn from levels of the poverty pyramid well above those where the poorest of the poor are to be found. If one examines the development literature throughout the 30-plus years to 1985, very little of it examines governance issues, social capital development, institution building, or capacity building for self-reliance. The development profession had passed well into the 1990s before there was widespread acceptance of the proposition that poverty-reducing development is a victory that demands a partnership with the poor and radical change to the circumstances and opportunities available to households at the bottom of the poverty economy. It is in the exceptions to this observation, especially as it came to be practised in farmer-inclusive farming systems research, pioneering work on gender in community development, and the radical resurrection of the people-orientated role of NGOs in development, that the truth of this observation can be found.

The importance of the pioneers in thinking on the role of agriculture, gender and participatory approaches to community development cannot be over-estimated. In a very real sense the literature on farming systems, induced innovation, women as farmers, the structure of household budgets, and community problem analysis brought thinking on development back on track. This literature put people first without defining the needs of the poor in welfare terms. In contrast to the literature on basic needs, the agricultural economists and social scientists who wrote about the role of the poor in development elevated the role of the poor by identifying them as critical parts of the solution to poverty. In so doing the poor became not only beneficiaries, but also a resource for development that is poverty reducing.

Energy crisis

The OPEC-led revolution in energy pricing, and the attention subsequently given to how development can or should take a more sustainable approach to the use of non-renewable resources was pivotal to the evolution of thinking on what constitutes development. The urgency of the energy crisis, the perceived need to build development investments around the recycling of petro-dollars, and the apparent threat that OPEC presented to the extant balance of power in the world order, sidelined concern for poverty as a core issue in development. Poverty and the poor of the Third World almost fell off the development agenda through the later 1970s and the 1980s, even though the success of OPEC was matched by the emergence of super-poor oil-importing countries.

The energy crisis of 1972–1980 precipitated a reassessment of development issues dealing with sustainability and resource management. The Club of Rome, an independent NGO committed to raising awareness of resource constraints to development and economic growth, led world debate by publishing *Limits to Growth* in 1972, followed by *Mankind at the Turning Point* in 1974. Economists responded to the fear that at current rates of consumption known supplies of certain key raw materials would soon be used up. Rejecting the notion that the world is running out of non-renewable resources, *The Economist* magazine proclaimed, 'that there is no shortage of oil, only a shortage of cheap oil'. Individual economists similarly challenged the doomsayers, confidently predicting that high prices would bring forth a flurry of new exploration and the discovery of substitutes or more efficient uses for expensive minerals, including oil, that would solve the problem of current shortages. The outcome of this debate, however, has not yet been reached.

For poor developing countries, however, the OPEC-led energy crisis spelt the beginning of what was to mature into a chronic debt burden in the 1990s. Fearing the political consequences of immediate adjustments to high energy prices, many of the poorest developing countries, especially in

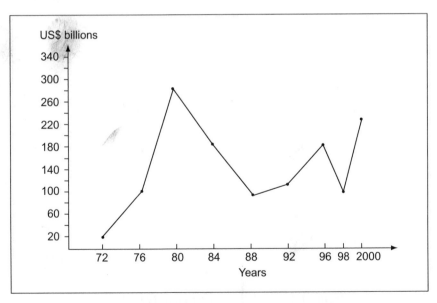

Figure 1.3 *OPEC crude oil export revenues 1972–2000*

Africa, borrowed heavily to sustain previous levels of consumption of oil and petroleum-based products, especially fertilizer and plastics.

The energy crisis has not yet 'gone away'. Rather, the world, and developing countries in particular, have learnt to give greater respect to the role of comparative advantage in the identification of sustainable development strategies. At the same time, the energy crisis initiated a global adjustment to permanently higher energy prices. Structural adjustment took on a new meaning in development planning, for developed and developing countries alike.

The development experience since 1972 has shown that the economies that recovered best from the realignment of energy prices were those that took the hard decisions to adjust to the new regime of radically altered price relativities. The shock wave that followed in the wake of OPEC's triumph in the 1970s flowed through the international economy unabated into the 1980s and beyond. For the first time since the end of the Second World War, the total value of international trade declined in the opening years of the 1980s, heralding a development decade of disappointment and frustration that culminated in the Asian economic crisis of the late 1990s.

In the main, donor countries responded to the challenge to world order from OPEC by cutting commitments to official development aid. Some of the more important donors, the USA and the Europeans in particular, also shored up the subsidies they paid to strategic voter groups, such as farmers, domestic producers dependent on exports, and finance sector companies. In an alliance between the US Federal Reserve, the World Bank

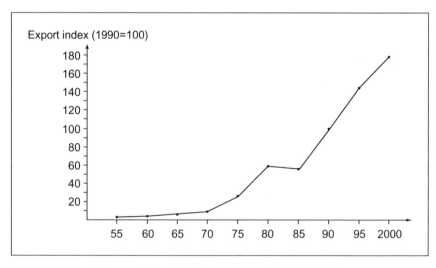

Figure 1.4   *Global export trends 1995–2000.*
Data Sources: WTO, World Bank

and the IMF, the cause of development was yet again derailed in the early 1990s because of concern that some of the major commercial banks of the Western world would go bankrupt if default by highly indebted poor countries was allowed to happen. Quite suddenly, the cause of *development* shifted from concern for the needs of the poor or poverty reduction to concern for the rule of law and guarantees that loan contracts between developing country governments and commercial lenders would be honoured. The tragedy of the Asian economic crisis of 1996–1999 can be traced to this shift in priorities, the problems of corruption, poor government and ill-directed development spending notwithstanding (Stiglitz 2000).

The significance of the Green Revolution

It was during the tenure of Robert McNamara at the World Bank that the Green Revolution in agriculture unfolded. This 'quiet revolution' was built on a unique partnership between science and farmers in developing countries, matched by three complementary shifts in thinking about development and poverty alleviation:

(i)   the discovery of the importance of successful farming systems to technology transfer
(ii) the discovery of the critical contribution that women make to rural production, especially in the poorest households, and
(iii) the discovery of the constraints to self-employment and income generation by poor households that can be lifted by the application of microfinance.

The Green Revolution did not begin in the 1960s, but with the realization in the late 1950s by the then Provost at Cornell University and Vice President for International Programs at the Ford Foundation, FF (Frosty) Hill, and his colleagues at the Rockefeller Foundation, that modern agricultural technology was not giving farmers in developing countries better results than traditional methods. Hill and the Foundation despatched several young scientists to India, Pakistan, the Philippines, Mexico, Colombia and Nigeria to study the performance of modern farming methods in farmers' fields, not on the research station. Among them was David Hopper, a graduate student of Professor Ted Schultz at Chicago University, an economist who was to win the Nobel Prize for his writings on education and development. Hopper's results clearly showed that poor farmers in India were behaving quite rationally in rejecting modern farming methods in favour of traditional farming practices and seeds. The outcome confirmed the need for situation-specific research to develop better technologies for tropical and semi-arid agricultural environments. Ford and Rockefeller combined to provide the means and the momentum needed to establish the first two international agricultural research centres, IRRI for rice and CIMMYT for wheat and maize, in the Philippines and Mexico respectively. The research programme set for these institutions was to adapt modern scientific methods to the circumstances of poor farmers. The package of high yielding varieties (HYVs), and instructions on how these were to be used (including applications of water, fertilizer and chemicals to control weeds and pests), formed the basis of what has come to be called the Green Revolution technologies. Farmers adopting HYVs found that yield gains were substantial, especially where irrigation was available.

With minimal commitments to extension services, farmers adopted HYVs, so that, by the end of the 1980s, HYVs had displaced traditional varieties and farming practices throughout irrigated agriculture, but less so in rain-fed agriculture. Nonetheless, the impact of IRRI, CIMMYT and the other crop- and livestock-based international agricultural research centres (IARCs) was pervasive and profound. The Green Revolution taught an ever-expanding circle of development professionals that understanding farming systems or the constraints that face poor households in rural circumstances cannot be done unless these households are consulted and involved. It is not enough to simply do the research on the research station; field trials in partnership with farmers are essential.

The realization that poor farmers have an essential role to play in the generation of appropriate agricultural technologies is at the root of contemporary participatory approaches to almost every aspect of the project cycle in development. It is this impact of the Green Revolution that is by far the most important, falling consumer prices for rice, wheat and corn notwithstanding. HYVs and the package of new farming methods that have arisen out of the scientific research programme of the IARCs are a passing fad, quickly replaced by the next generation of new seeds and scientific progress. Participatory methods, however, have engaged the poor in the solution of their own problems, opening opportunities for real and sustainable progress in the personal efforts of farmers and their families to escape from poverty and remain out of poverty.

Gender sensitive development

No matter how hard one might search, it is almost impossible to find development literature before 1970 that accorded any special importance to the role of women or gender issues in development. Parallel with the integration of farming systems research into our understanding of the

challenges in rural development, stands the discovery of the important role that women play in rural production in developing countries. Ester Boserup's seminal book, *Women's Role in Economic Development*, published in 1970, presented evidence to show that in some African countries women are responsible for not less than 70 per cent of agricultural production. Boserup demonstrated the folly of ignoring women and proceeding as though men are the key to progress. Gradually the shift to integrate women and women's issues into the mainstream of development thinking took hold. By the end of the 1980s, it was simply illegitimate to approach any topic in development without serious attention to gender as a critical cross-cutting issue. The integration of gender into development thinking must be judged a major leap forward in the understanding of the concept of development and our appreciation of what it means to say that development has taken place. Yet, the struggle to bring gender issues into the mainstream of development practice is on-going (see, e.g., World Bank 2002, and http://www.worldbank.org/gender/prr/).

The radical feminist literature aside, professional understanding of gender issues in development has evolved through three main stages. In the first stage it was necessary to clearly define and statistically describe the role of women in development (WID). In the second stage, the effort shifted to a more inclusive approach to development thinking and planning, encapsulated in the phrase 'women and development' (WAD). WAD engaged women and sought to increase the number of women involved in all aspects of development, at least in proportion to their importance in specific areas, such as agriculture, health, education, or community development. The third phase progressed to a focus on gender as opposed to women versus men. Gender and development (GAD), is the current thrust, opening the gate to more holistic approaches that recognize the need to change the way men behave and the manner in which children are accounted for if poor women and poor women's issues are to be incorporated into development planning.

Microfinance-led development

Since the earliest efforts to accelerate agricultural development in poor countries, the need for subsidized rural credit to enable poor farmers to adopt new technologies and move into cash-based production systems was taken as a given. Poor farmers and rural communities in developing countries were depicted as stuck in a poverty trap, characterized by an absence of capacity to save, an absence of investment opportunities, and constrained by obstacles to progress born of ignorance and prejudice.

In the late 1970s, Yale graduate Professor Mohamad Yunus, an academic at Chittagong University, Bangladesh, began an experiment that questioned each of these characterizations. His creation, the Grameen Bank, is built on participatory partnerships with poor people. The business of the bank has thrived because it has listened to the poor and learned that the poor do need to invest, the poor do have investment opportunities, the poor can and do save, the poor need money management services, the poor are trustworthy, and the poor are driven by self-interest and the desire to have a better livelihood, as are most people.

Through the tools that microfinance affords development professionals, millions of poor people, and especially poor women, have been given the opportunity to take responsibility for their own welfare, their own livelihoods, and their own future. This outcome is not a miracle. Rather, it is an outcome of development strategies that succeed because they are built on the right priorities, and respond to the revealed needs of the clients targeted. Successful microfinance providers know their market intimately and harness the unique knowledge that poor people have of poverty and their vigorous desire to climb the economic ladder to a better quality of life for themselves and their families.

Women tend to dominate the client list of microfinance providers not because of a gender bias in how the providers operate, but because women have demonstrated that they are among the best customers of microfinance programmes. However, the beneficiary list of microfinance reveals no similar statistical trend favouring women. Indeed, by serving female clients, microfinance providers have found that the profile of their pool of beneficiaries is spread across gender and age boundaries (see, e.g., Reminyi 1991, Todd 1996, Ledgerwood 1999, Reminyi and Quinones 2000, Rutherford 2000, and Rhyne 2001).

Microfinance has been the favoured 'fad' in development since at least 1990. However, there is every reason to believe that it is a fad that will not pass quickly. Microfinance has an intuitive appeal because it serves the desire of poor people to participate in and benefit from development directly and almost immediately. Microfinance relieves the liquidity constraint that is chronic in poor households. It does so by facilitating and promulgating institutional innovations designed to enable individuals, groups and communities to mobilize local resources, engage in wealth creation, and obtain the means to have greater control of their personal fortunes and prospects. Microfinance is, therefore, very people-centered, but is dependent upon growth in individual and household capacity for self-reliance for sustainable success. This characteristic elevates successful microfinance to a unique position as a quintessential example of the meaning of 'development' at the grass roots and in practice.

A matter of focus and perspective

At global, regional and national levels the development experience since 1945 has resulted in a restructured post-colonial world economy. The defining characteristic of this new world is the globalization of production, finance, exchange and access to new knowledge. Modern nation states must contend with qualitatively different forms of competition for markets and resources. National economic robustness in the face of globalized markets for the essentials of modern living is an outcome of development that is more important than ever before. The achievement of robustness as a consequence of development is as important to governments as it is to enterprises, households and individuals. Economists have long understood the importance of choosing economic policies and strategies that bequeath the economy, the business, the household or the individual the ability to withstand and quickly recover from unexpected external shocks or internally generated disruptions to economic planning, business activity, or individual budgeting. Economics has long argued that investment and wealth creation strategies that are designed to withstand the cold winds of competition will also serve the goals of robustness, whereas development strategies that fly in the face of comparative advantage and competitive production systems does the opposite.

The development experience from 1945 to 2000 cannot, therefore, be divorced from political choices that favour competitive over protectionist policies, or vice versa. The history of contemporary development, especially during the Cold War years to 1990, has been complicated by the impact of the ideological struggle fostered between competing economic and political systems. Despite the end of the Cold War with the collapse of the Eastern Bloc in the late 1980s, this struggle continues, albeit on a different scale. Entrenched elite groups who had been kept in power because of the success with which they courted one side or the other are now jockeying to retain their positions of privilege and authority. In the process governance systems are coming under pressure to give greater attention to grass-roots issues in development. Ironically, while the pressures for globalization is increasing with freer trade, lower levels of official development assistance, and increased flows of direct foreign investment in developing countries, there is a parallel shift in political accountability to domestic stakeholders as access to resources from the Cold War combatants has dried up. This has meant that, at local levels, the struggle to achieve governance systems that are inclusive of the poor, responsive to the needs of the poor, and able to protect the vulnerable from the greed of the great and powerful is gaining ground. Regional competition (e.g., between China and ASEAN) and national stakeholder concerns are gradually filling the political vacuum left by the departure of Cold War alliances. The dismemberment of the USSR has not, however, equated to the death of the socialist ideal in goal-setting and the realignment of national priorities. Instead, so-called transition economies, including China, Poland and Vietnam, are demonstrating to the world that a variety of political recipes, consistent with real gains in poverty-reduction-grounded achievements in development, can be realized under a variety of evolving political models.

The development record has forced a reconsideration of the role of government in development. Faith in the ability of paternalistic governments to plan development and ensure that the rights of the individual are protected has waned. In its place governments have come under pressure to favour market-driven solutions to public policy, and to devote increasing attention to the creation of environments in which non-government agents (i.e., individuals, households, firms, communities) are expected to be responsible for their own welfare, their own wealth accumulation, and the level of their participation in the use and growth of the community's stock of social capital.

Nothing has altered how we think about the role of government in development more than the end of the Cold War. The loss of the capacity to play the East off against the West has forced a significant number of developing country governments to give greater attention to placating the calls of domestic stakeholders for a voice in government and national development. Regional trade relations and socio-cultural issues (especially the tensions generated by the on-going conflict in the Middle East, competition for secure sources of affordable oil, diplomatic tensions between Muslim and Christian societies, and the Pandora's Box of the war on terrorism) are also looming larger in national political agendas than previously. But it is the question of governance, associated issues of the rule of law, and donor country aid fatigue (arising from an unwillingness to continue to tolerate past levels of corruption and incompetent government in developing countries), that have combined to put people, people's aspirations, and poverty reduction back onto the centre stage of development.

The scientific approach taken to the challenge of development in President Truman's Point Four programme of 1949 stands in stark contrast to the key issues engaging the world development community (i.e., smaller government, more democratic and accountable government, and more transparent national development priority setting processes) at the start of the 21st century. This contrast is a measure of the progress that has been made in our understanding of what constitutes cutting-edge development, as reflected in the Millennium Development Goals adopted by the United Nations in 2001. These goals embrace political strategies, sectoral visions, and funding priorities that are far more focused on poverty reduction than ever before. Gone are the universal welfare blankets associated with crude Keynesianism and basic needs. In their place are targeted safety nets for the vulnerable and a growing recognition of the need for enhanced investments in people. The spread of user-pays pricing policies and cost recovery mechanisms in public finance are adding to the pressures that are shifting the balance of accountability towards tax payers and consumers. Nonetheless, it continues to be the case that most developing countries still support public sectors that are far larger than is typical in donor economies. Given that this fact is an artifact of history, and that there is little or no reason to believe that governments in developing countries need to be more pervasive than in developed economies, it is not difficult to understand why contemporary development priorities accord a much higher place to public sector downsizing and privatization than was the case in 1949, or in any year since 1990.

Concluding observations on the concept of development

The concept of development has been presented here as a participatory, people-centered process intended to reduce the incidence of poverty and achieve better livelihoods for all. This interpretation is based on a study of the lessons of history and familiarity with the intellectual struggle waged among development professionals in their effort to refine their under-standing of development. A key lesson highlighted in the chapter is that the separation of development as a *process* from development as an *outcome* is illegitimate if we are to do the concept of development justice. Development as a process and development as an outcome are two sides of the same coin.

At a practical level, however, the separation of process and outcome is important. As a process, development practitioners are reminded that development involves the identification of roles for government, private sector, and individuals that bear directly on the welfare outcomes that people experience. Hence, inclusiveness, consultation and accountability are critical elements of development as a process.

As development practitioners it is important for us to accept the responsibility that we have to ensure that the outcomes of development are those intended. One of these outcomes is about governance and the important role that development has played in nation building. Develop-ment should add to the legitimacy of governing structures and endorsed leadership roles given to people, the law, and public institutions. But, the idea that poverty alleviation and social justice are only relevant if it serves the interests of those seeking legitimacy in government must be unreservedly rejected. Democracy and participatory structures in society are perverted if the only circumstances in which they are recognized and accepted are where they align with the self-interests of governing elites.

Development must always be about poverty reduction and the creation of the means by which poverty can be kept at bay. It is from the success with which these twin goals are achieved that legitimacy in government at local or national level flows. The study of development has much to do with understanding the manner in which governments have sought to reconcile goals that are in competition with the needs of the poor or pro-poor economic growth. Hindsight reveals, however, that development in practice is a process by which individuals, groups and communities obtain the means to be self reliant; responsible for their own livelihoods, welfare and future.

Chapter 2

Reassessing Development Theory: Modernization and Beyond

JOHN McKAY

In this chapter we explore the key ideas put forward, especially in the last half century or so, on the political economy of development and underdevelopment, and place these concepts within the context of the major trends, conditions and prevailing ideologies within the emerging global system. The dominant ideas on the nature and genesis of the very process of development have themselves gone through a series of transformations during this period, but some strong counter arguments have also been put forward in opposition to the generally accepted tenets in the field. At one level, the last 50 years have been characterized by unprecedented growth and prosperity, but only within certain countries and regions. A basic question within development, then, must be why some countries have been able to achieve spectacular progress while others have stagnated or even gone backwards.

Within mainstream economic thought there has been a strong assumption throughout this period that growth in successful regions will eventually 'trickle down' to the more peripheral areas, given certain conditions and policies. Thus, poor countries can catch up and benefit from the earlier growth experiences of others, and pass through a similar process of development, albeit at a later date. This is the essence of the theories of modernization that were popular in the 1950s and 1960s, and which, in a modified form, made a return to the mainstream of policy making in the 1980s. These ideas still inform the dominant international institutions in the development field, notably the World Bank and the International Monetary Fund (IMF). However, these prescriptions have come under sustained attack from a number of different directions since the 1960s. These theories and the assumptions behind them were first criticized from what became known as the 'dependency school', originating especially in Latin America. Several authors argued that the underdeveloped world could not develop in this 'trickle down' manner, because the very processes of global change that gave rise to prosperity in the North resulted in the simultaneous impoverishment of the countries of the South.

In turn, these ideas were also criticized, partly because of their over-reliance on global rather than national factors, but more particularly for their alleged inability to account for the very rapid growth that was going on in parts of East Asia at the time. If growth at an unprecedented rate was possible in South Korea, Taiwan and the other 'Tiger' economies, there could be nothing wrong with the global system as such, it was argued. The problem must rest with the internal policies of the poor countries: to be successful they needed to do more to emulate the East Asian 'miracle' economies. However, the onset of the Asian financial crisis in 1997 has caused a dramatic rethink of that position.

Mainstream ideas of modernization have also been criticized from a quite different direction. Several authors have questioned the often unspoken assumption that development is to deliver to every global citizen a lifestyle that is similar to that now prevailing in the rich countries. They have dismissed the idea that development must always be the same as 'modernization', which is, in fact, nothing less than 'Westernization'. This perspective has also been taken up by the growing environmental movement, which has argued that it would be physically impossible for everyone in poor countries to live the sort of lifestyle now prevailing in North America or Western Europe. The costs in terms of resource depletion, pollution and general environmental degradation would simply be too great.

In spite of these criticisms, and especially since the end of the Cold War and the onset of the Asian crisis, the mainstream paradigm seems to be as entrenched as ever. However, the impacts of the turmoil in Asia, the continued crisis in Africa, and the seemingly remorseless progress of 'globalization', centred around the expansion of the multinational corporations, is now seeing a revival of interest in 'neo-dependency' approaches.

This chapter will explore these major currents of thought, and will evaluate some of the major theories that have been advanced. However, the main perspective will be from that of the new millennium, asking what we have learned from the last 50 years in terms of development theory and the design of more effective policy approaches.

The global context for development ideas and policies

Ideas in development theory and practice cannot be divorced from the broader assumptions, aspirations and beliefs of any age. These more general modes of thought set the scene for more specific discussions of what development is, or should be, and the most appropriate policies and methods that can be harnessed in the search for this elusive promised land of happiness and prosperity. It could be argued that debate about development, its nature and how to achieve it, is *the* central issue in the whole of Western social science. The early towering figures in the field, writers such as John Stuart Mill and Karl Marx, were essentially theorizing about development. The Enlightenment was fundamentally concerned with progress towards an ideal society, and how the harnessing of rational thoughts, policies and actions might allow the realizations of this goal. But similar ideas of progress can be found in other non-Western modes of thought. In Japan, for example, it has been argued that a unique approach to the philosophy of economics was developed, one that was rather different from studies emerging in the West. However, the focus here was on economics as 'administering the nation and relieving the suffering of the people' (Morris-Suzuki 1989), a notion which is not so far from the concerns of development. In traditional China, Confucius (who died around 479 BC) was convinced that he lived in an age of acute crisis, perhaps similar in some ways to our own times. He was, he believed, witnessing the collapse of civilization (Leys 1997), and his entire project was concerned with the ways in which a better society might be built, and how it might be governed. Thus, it could be said that development and progress.are absolutely central ideas in Western thought, but such concepts can also be found in other traditions.

The genesis of modern development thought in the West is usually dated to the end of the Second World War. The European colonial empires had earlier expressed some concern for the improvement of their subject peoples, but it was really only after 1945 that development was seen as a worldwide priority. New technologies and logistical systems developed during the war were seen as being modified to fight a new battle against global poverty. The initiation of the Marshall Plan for the reconstruction of Europe, a similar plan for Japan, and the establishment of the major Bretton Woods institutions, notably the World Bank and the IMF, signalled a new determination to avoid the economic and social problems of the 1930s that heralded a global conflict. However, there have been numerous changes of fashion in development thought since 1945, reflecting the ebb and flow of a series of wider debates.

The first of these concerns the position and role of the nation state as the fundamental unit of analysis and policy making. The system of international relations that emerged in the post-war world and was centred on the United Nations and related institutions enshrined the special position of the sovereign state as the recognized authority over the space defined by its national boundaries, as the legal body able to pass laws and initiate policy, and as the only legitimate user of armed force to ensure its stability and will. This position has been broadly retained into the new millennium. The field of development studies generally uses the nation as its primary unit of analysis, and most of the statistics we used are collected on this basis. However, the growth of broader economic and political units, such as the European Union, has taken a number of powers from individual countries, and the growth of international treaties of various kinds has had a similar effect in some specific matters. At the same time a large number of regions within individual countries have been campaigning for, and in some case achieving, much greater autonomy. Thus, the power of the nation state is being whittled away from above and below, a process which some have called the 'hollowing out of the state'.

A related question concerns the extent to which the government of a nation can act as the most important catalyst for change and the key controller and co-ordinator of all kinds of development programmes. In the 1950s and 1960s there was a general assumption that governments must play these key roles, and be the organizers of a wide range of services. However, we are now in an era in which many commentators and politicians see the private sector as being much more important, urging that the size of government and the range of its powers must be minimized. The conviction that markets can deliver the benefits of development more effectively than governments is a central tenet in the neo-liberal paradigm that has held sway for the last two decades, and which has resulted in what Toye (1987) has called the 'counter-revolution' in development thought. There are important differences between opinions in various countries here. Support for the minimalist state come most enthusiastically from the United States, the United Kingdom and Australia, while much of Western Europe has retained its traditional range of government responsibilities. The transformation of the Asia into an economically powerful region raised the possibility of new creative possibilities for government activities. Most analysts have now accepted that Asian governments were absolutely central to the progress of Korea, Taiwan and Singapore, and in the more recent dramatic development of China. Some writers have even suggested that the Asian model of development brought together the most useful aspects of the capitalist and socialist systems into a new 'third way', which was the most efficient way yet devised of generating growth (Johnson 1987, Wade 1990).

Notions of power are central to development thought – some would even argue that power is the pivotal concept in the whole corpus. Certainly, debates about the use of power, and the ways in which the tools of development can be manipulated to enhance the influence of one group against all possible opposition, have been crucial. During the Cold War, both the United States and the Soviet Union saw aid and development programmes as a major weapon in the battle to gain support for their ideologies and systems. Genuine independence of policy was not favoured by either side, hence the rise of the non-aligned movement. However, some leaders were able to play-off one side against the other, gaining benefits from both. The end of the Cold War saw an end to both these constraints and opportunities. Whole regions of the globe, especially most of Africa, suddenly became peripheral to the global system and were simply ignored by Western politicians, businessmen and investors. This situation may have changed again after the terrorist attacks on the United States on 11 September 2001. In the 'war on terror' we have returned to the Cold War slogan that 'either you are with us or against us'.

In the period since the end of the Cold War it has become common to regard liberal democracy as the only viable economic and political system in the modern world – 'the only game in town'. Francis Fukuyama (1992) called this the 'end of history', in the sense that the long period of conflict between rival ideological systems was clearly over. This has again raised the question of whether there is only one way of achieving development, and one manifestation of having arrived as a modern nation. However, this assumption has come under sustained attack. The whole debate about 'Asian values' at a time when growth rates in that region were clearly superior to those prevailing in the West, was one form of questioning. The environmentalists' view that not all nations can possibly have the lifestyle prevailing in the West has already been mentioned, but other authors are now raising some rather different, but just as difficult, questions. Hernando de Soto (2000) has asked why capitalism has triumphed in the West but has been so spectacularly unsuccessful in a number of other regions. Oswaldo de Rivero (2001) has raised the prospect that not all economies can ever aspire to sustained growth and development. Many are simply non-viable. Thus, the old assumption that development can be achieved by all if the 'correct' policies are implemented is being increasingly questioned.

These debates raise further questions about democracy, freedom and the involvement of local communities in the process of development. Democracy is, of course, a noble aim in itself, but it is also open to a wide range of alternative interpretations. Not surprisingly, a number of Asian commentators, confident in the economic success of their region, have proposed that Asia can develop its own form of democracy and its own definition of human rights. These concepts would not be the same as the Western ideals, but would be just as valid (Mahbubani 1998, de Bary 1998, Bauer and Bell 1999, Bell 2000). Nobel prize winner Amartya Sen (2000) has proposed that we should regard development as freedom.

Development, he suggests, involves the removal of the major sources of unfreedom – tyranny, poor economic prospects, social deprivation, inefficient public facilities, and so on.

Finally, the question of democracy and freedom raises the question of how far we see development as being a process initiated and implemented by outside forces and actors, or as an essentially internal transformation fuelled by local initiative and self help. The emphasis in the field on the role of outside 'experts', the inculcation of new and foreign values and methods, and the central role of aid have all conspired to downgrade the role of local mobilization. This is especially true in an era of globalization, when many commentators predict that cultural and economic convergence on some kind of international best practice is bound to take place. In the present era, the whole question of the relationships between globalization and development theory is opening up as a new battleground in the conflict of ideas and ideologies (see, for example, Jomo and Nagaraj 2001; Schuurman, F. 2001; Petras and Veltmeyer 2001).

Theories of modernization

None of the complexities, counter arguments or self-doubts introduced in the previous section was allowed to cloud the simple but powerful message espoused by the proponents of modernization theory. During the 1960s and part of the 1970s, there appeared, within all of the social sciences, studies of aspects of modernization, each couched in the particular language and concepts of the particular discipline, but all carrying the same beguiling promise: all nations, however poor, were able, with the implementation of 'correct' policies to achieve a modern standard of living by following exactly the same growth path as that pioneered by the Western nations.

Examples of such studies can be found in sociology, geography and political science, but it was in economics that the seminal work was published, with the appearance of Rostow's *The Stages of Growth* (1960). But this is more than just a study in economics, which is part of the reason for its influence over the years. Rostow, as he has made clear in some of his later reminiscences (Rostow 1984) has always had a strong interest in economic history, and has also written in detail on the importance of politics in the development process (Rostow 1971). Yet, somewhat paradoxically, Rotow's many critics have derided his attempts to produce a universal theory of development, one largely divorced from the historical and institutional realities of particular societies, and have been particularly scathing about his political positions.

Rostow proposed that the path to development and modernity involved the movement by any nation through a series of stages:

- The traditional society
- The pre-take-off society
- Take-off
- The road to maturity
- The mass-consumption society.

The framework is full of hope – every nation has the capacity had the potential to pass through these stages and achieve mass consumption. The image of take-off is particularly evocative, full of power and hope as the nation is able to launch itself into a bright new future. The book was also written as a deliberate counter to the numerous Marxist theories that were appearing at this time. The subtitle of the book – 'a non-communist manifesto' – written at a time when Communist expansion was feared in all parts of the underdeveloped world, emphasized that successful development could be achieved without a revolution. The most important mechanism in the whole process, the fuel needed to achieve take-off, was investment derived principally from domestic savings. If the savings rate could be moved from the normal 5 per cent of GDP to 10 per cent or more for a sustained period, then take-off could proceed. A major role of the political system, especially in the early stages, was to create the organizational mechanisms and the political will to achieve these sustained increases in savings and productive investment. Rostow was at pains to point out that there was nothing automatic or inevitable about these processes. Unless economic policies and political systems were managed effectively, then a nation's move from one stage to another could stall.

While roundly criticized, as we will see later in this chapter, this theory has been widely quoted and used by both theorists and policy makers. In a number of more recent interviews and books, Rostow has claimed that history has entirely vindicated his theory. The fall of the Soviet Union has demonstrated the unviability of the Communist alternative, while the success of East Asia has underlined the importance of high rates of savings and investment (Rostow 1990).

Rostow's theories, and their symbolism, matched the mood of their time. There was much discussion in policy circles of the need to escape the 'vicious cycle of poverty'. There were several versions of this concept, but in general terms it described the ways in which the processes of poverty and underdevelopment were self-reinforcing. Low or non-existent rates of growth meant that savings and investment rates were low. Insufficient investment was made in productive facilities of various kinds, ensuring that low levels of growth persisted. Funds were not available for better schools, universities or hospitals ensuring that nations could not find a way out of poverty through investment in human resources. Lack of investment in roads, ports and other infrastructure kept economies working at low levels of efficiency. A way out of this persistent cycle of poverty was needed, and the modernization theorists provided a hope that this might be possible.

The Harrod–Domar growth model, which also became popular at this time, provided some economic sophistication to the emerging propositions (see, for example, Hettne 1995). Growth could be self-sustaining, leading to a 'virtuous cycle of growth'. Increases in output and income would be accompanied by a higher marginal propensity to save, leading to more investment and a new round of expansion and income growth. This model, based on Keynesian theory, also proposed that initial impetus for growth could come from foreign aid, providing the first round of investment in the absence of domestic savings.

The emphasis on modernization within economics was mirrored by a range of other (and some would say complementary) studies in other social sciences. In politics, for example, there was much research on political modernization and the generation of more effective political institutions, inevitably made in the image of the West. In geography, a number of studies concentrated on 'spatial modernization', involving the spread of infrastructure and other symbols of modern life, and the gradual expansion of the *core* into the more backward *periphery*. In psychology, too, there was an attempt to explore the ways in which more 'modern' personality traits could be engendered and fostered. These studies enhanced the work going on in economics, and gave it added breadth, but in all these studies the basic assumptions were essentially the same as those put forward by Rostow. There were, however, some genuine attempts to make modernization theory more sophisticated through what has become known as *dialectical modernization theory* (Martinussen 1997). This attempted to unravel the complex relationships between the 'traditional' and 'modern' sectors. Gusfield (1967), for example, argued the traditional institutions could be revitalized through contact with modernizing influences in other parts of the society. This represented a significant advance over the numerous studies of the 'dual economy', which saw a much clearer distinction between the modern and more traditional parts of the society.

Some assumptions in the rather optimistic modernization framework were questioned in various works by Gunnar Myrdal and Albert Hirschman, both of whom demonstrated that both 'virtuous' and 'vicious' cycles could operate simultaneously to produce growth in some areas and stagnation in others. Earlier, economic theory had been used to suggest that inequalities will not last for long because labour will migrate from low wage areas to regions where rewards are higher. Similarly, capital will move to regions where the returns are higher, usually in areas which are currently backward but with high investment potential. Thus, growth will take place in the more backward areas, removing the initial inequalities. Both Myrdal and Hirschman attacked this kind of equilibrium analysis. Myrdal suggested that two kinds of forces would be at work. *Spread* effects would serve to distribute growth from richer to poorer regions or countries, while *backwash* effects tended to intensify existing inequalities. The relative strength of these two forces would depend on a range of circumstances and policy frameworks, thus it was impossible to predict some kind of universal process of the kind postulated by Rostow. Myrdal suggested that trade within or between countries could give rise to strong backwash effects. Thus he proposed a theory of *circular and cumulative causation*, with spread and backwash effects often leading to permanent, and ever deepening, levels of inequality.

Many of Hirschman's idea were quite similar, but he developed a particular analysis of the role of government in the management of these processes. He argued that development is by necessity an unbalanced process, and it would also be unrealistic to expect government planners to invest in various sectors of the economy in a finely balanced way. In particular he considered the balance between investment in *directly productive activities*, such as factories or plantations, and the infra-structure needed to support these facilities, which he termed *social overhead capital*. Growth may occur by concentrating on the development of infrastructure, thereby reducing production costs and encouraging further investment in production, or the reverse may be preferred. If production is privileged, inefficiencies in infrastructure will appear, forcing catch-up investment. Either strategy may work, and the choice of the more appropriate will depend on local circumstances. The work of Hirschman and Myrdal grew out of the tradition of modernization studies, and used some of the same theoretical assumptions, but their attention to inequalities and the persistence or even intensification of these differences provides a direct link to some of the more radical critiques that began to appear in the 1960s.

The challenge of dependency theory

Several basic assumptions of modernization approaches in general, and of Rostow's influential thesis, began to be identified in the 1960s. A basic objection was that the optimistic tone of much modernization theory flew in the face of the actual situation in the underdeveloped world. Inequalities were not being narrowed as conventional economic theory predicted.

Rather, the world was becoming increasingly divided between the powerful *core* regions and the impoverished *periphery*. In Myrdal's terms, the *spread* effects were being overwhelmed by the much more powerful forces of *backwash*. One of the regions where this reality appeared to many observers to be most pronounced was in Latin America, and it was from here that an influential set of new theories began to emerge, a movement which still has some influence. This became known as the *dependencia* or dependency school.

Much of the initial impetus for this mode of thought came from the work of the United Nations Economic Commission for Latin America, and in particular from the work of Raul Prebisch. The central argument, in what became known as the 'Prebisch thesis' was that the basic assumptions of neo-classical economics, propositions that were essential for the achievement of trickle-down effects, did not exist in the real world. The economic landscape did not primarily consist of small producers and buyers, each operating in a perfect marketplace with none able to exert power over these market processes. Rather, global commerce took place between the rich and powerful developed economies and the much weaker peripheral countries. Not surprisingly, the rules of the trading system were systematically manipulated in favour of the powerful Western-based corporations to the benefit of the already rich countries (DiMarco 1972). In particular, Prebisch rejected the orthodox Ricardian arguments in favour of each nation specializing in the output of goods for which it had a special comparative advantage, and trading these goods through the international system. He argued that none of the 'late industrialisers', such as the United States, Germany and Japan had been able to use such a strategy for their development. Rather, they had gone through the early stages of industrialization behind protective tariff walls until they felt competitive enough to confront the global market on equal terms. Specialization would not encourage industrial development of the kind needed in Latin America; instead the region would be condemned to a peripheral position as a supplier of primary products.

These arguments were taken a stage further, and given much greater exposure in the English-speaking world, by Andre Gunder Frank, who, in 1967, produced his classic *Capitalism and Underdevelopment in Latin America*. He argued that development and underdevelopment are in fact simply two sides of the same coin. The rich countries achieved growth by systematically exploiting their colonies and the rest of the underdeveloped world, and this process had been going on for several centuries, at least since the Spanish penetration of the New World. By the 20th century, no part of the globe was too remote to remain untouched by the impacts of the international economic system of imperialism and domination. Thus, it was nonsense to regard, as Rostow had done, the underdeveloped world as in some kind of pristine initial state. The poor countries had in fact been underdeveloped in the process of incorporation into the global system. They were impoverished, and the structural changes that had been imposed upon them made future development of a real and autonomous kind much less likely. Once the goods in which they specialized were no longer needed by the world market, or if a cheaper source was found, they would simply be discarded without the possibility of returning to their old internally orientated system of production. The poorest regions of Latin America were not those that had been ignored by the world market. Rather they were those that had in the past had a very close relationship, but had outlived their usefulness. Latin America as a whole, he suggested, had progressed most during the two world wars, when the countries at the core of international capitalism had been otherwise engaged and the periphery was left to develop in its own way.

Many similar ideas were developed at roughly the same time by Celso Furtado (1964), who also became a very influential figure in the dependency movement. He also argued that capitalism had expanded throughout the globe, particularly after the industrial revolution in Europe. No region was left untouched, and in all cases new hybrid structures were left behind, with profound implications for future development prospects. The penetrated economies were generally char-acterized by the existence and interaction of three distinct sectors:

- A 'remnant' economy consisting mainly of subsistence farmers, but with a small amount of cash crop production
- A domestic sector producing goods and services for local consumption
- The internationally orientated sector producing goods for the world market.

This classification was used as the basis of a later analysis of the Brazilian situation (Furtado 1965), written at the time of a political and economic crisis in that country. Here he dealt in more detail with the class implications of the structures of underdevelopment. Many earlier theorists had dismissed the role of the elites in Latin America as simple collaborators with international capitalism in the exploitation of their lands. But here Furtado presented a much more nuanced analysis, pointing out that there is a real diversity of class interests in Brazil. Crucially, he suggested, the Brazilian economy lacked an elite that was committed to the generation of genuine and autonomous industrialization. Institutional arrangements would need to be flexible enough to allow such a group to assume power. This is a crucial advance in thinking about development and one that we will take up again with reference to the successful industrialization of East Asia. Furtado's thinking was taken a stage further again in a return to a general analysis of Latin America (Furtado 1969), which represents one of the fullest statement of the dependency thesis. The export of primary products, he urges, cannot advance development at all, but, more importantly, the structures of the economy and the society strongly inhibit any movement towards a more productive and sustainable future. He called for a complete reform of institutional arrangements and in the exercise of political power. Relationships with the outside world, and with the United States in particular, needed a complete overhaul, as did relations with the multinational corporations. New technologies needed to be developed and harnessed internally, and, in the early stages at least, the state sector would have to play a leading role as a catalyst for development. The countries of Latin America could achieve many of these difficult tasks more easily by developing productive arrangements for regional co-operation. While these basic assumptions and propositions were generally accepted by many later theorists, a number of writers developed particular components of the analysis in more detail. Three of them, all of whom have particular relevance for current debates, are considered briefly here: Arghiri Emmanuel, Samir Amin and Immanuel Wallerstein.

Emmanuel (1972) produced what, at the time, was a very influential analysis of the ways in which international trade re-enforces income inequalities at a global level. Goods exported from high-wage countries have a consistently higher price on the world market compared with exports from underdeveloped countries with much lower wages, not because these first world exports are inherently more valuable but because rich countries have the political power to manipulate the markets and set prices favourable to their own products. This argument, although widely criticized in several quarters, is still repeated by some authors in the current debate about globalization and the supposed benefits of large-scale expansions of world trade.

Amin's particular contribution, on the other hand, was to elaborate Furtado's analysis of the internal structures of underdeveloped countries (see, for example, Amin 1976, 1977). He looked at the development of both the export-orientated and domestic sectors, and at the linkage (or lack of it) between the two. Areas involved in export activities, usually of primary products, would have higher wages than found in the rest of the economy, but the multiplier effects of these investments would be far less than in developed economies. Most of the supplies of specialized machinery would come from core countries, as would even some of the food and more luxury items consumed by the labour force. This lack of productive linkage meant that the two parts of the economy were quite isolated from each other. The export sector would, in fact, have its closest relationships with the areas to which its output was exported, again in the core countries.

Amin termed this separation between sectors *disarticulation*, a character-istic feature of almost all underdeveloped countries. The maintenance of the export sector required the compliance of members of the local elite, who would be bought off through higher wages, corrupt payments or the supply of luxury goods. The obvious gaps between rich and poor would inevitably cause deep resentments that could lead to political instability, and, to ensure the maintenance of order, large sums would have to be spent on the import of military hardware and in rewards to the military forces to maintain their loyalty. This would exacerbate a balance of payments situation already made dire by the progressive decline in the relative value of the primary products being exported. The shortfall in hard currency could only be met by opening up yet further mines, plantations or other export activities, but this would lead to yet another spiral of deepening disarticulation and internal inequality.

Wallerstein's contributions have been voluminous, and have partly involved some very detailed historical analysis of the emergence and development of the global economy, founding a whole school of analysis that has become known as *world systems theory* (see, for example, Wallerstein 1974, 1979, 1984, Hopkins and Wallerstein 1982). But he is also important for his introduction of an entire new category into the debate about the structure of the core and the periphery. He pointed to the need for a category of countries that could act as go-betweens or mediators between the rich and the poor nations, and could help to diffuse any tensions that might arise from global inequalities by providing examples of what could be achieved within the system. This group, which included countries like Australia, Canada, Spain and South Korea, he termed the *semi-periphery*, and their role was to demonstrate that revolution or even drastic reform was not at all necessary.

As we have seen, in much of dependency theory there was the assumption that external forces were all-powerful and simply swept away any lingering remnants of the old structures. As a number of critics pointed out, this is clearly too extreme, and, even in the newer versions of modernization theory, important interactions between the modern and traditional sectors were postulated. A number of the later dependency writers attempted to remedy this shortcoming, notably Fernando Cardoso (Cardoso and Faletto 1979, Cardoso 1982). These writings point to the complex configuration in various Latin American countries of competing or co-operating groups and classes, each influenced by external forces and each attempting to use these external elements to their own advantage, although no class or group is strong enough to control this environment. This represents a considerable advance, and many of these ideas are now being used to analyse the new situation of globalization and the local responses to it, as we will see later in this chapter.

Dependency theory has also been criticized from a variety of other perspectives. A number of Marxist scholars have taken issue with the methods and assumptions used, suggesting that they are a misrepresentation of the true Marxist position. Several writers have argued that the dependency theorists have missed the true essence of capitalism and instead have portrayed it as a simple zero-sum game. Bill Warren is one of the prime examples here. His basic position is that, while capitalism may have a number of abhorrent features, it is necessary to strip away the original feudal situation found in most underdeveloped regions, and this can only be accomplished by outside imperialist forces that are essential for the establishment of capitalism, which is in turn a pre-requisite for the transition to socialism. From the other side of the ideological spectrum, a number of critics have pointed to some gains that have been made in the development of a number of countries, especially in Asia. This has been contrasted with the performance of those countries that have attempted a more self-reliant approach, and it is to this miracle of growth in Asia that we now turn.

The Asian miracle: challenges for modernization and dependency approaches

It has been claimed, with justification, that the spectacular growth that has taken place in East Asia since the 1960s represents the most profound and rapid economic, social and political transformation that has ever taken place. It is little surprise, then, that the Asian experience should have attracted so much attention and presented such a challenge to all existing theories of development (see, for example, Rowen 1998, Leipziger 2000, Berger and Borer 1997). The recent history of the region has generated an enormous literature, and spawned a number of comparative studies seeking to explain why Asia has been so much more successful than either Latin America or Africa (Gereffi and Wyman 1990). However, there is still no agreement about the Asian experience and what its implications are: each side in the debate has attempted to enlist the Asian success story to support its own entrenched position

The modern-day descendants of the modernization theorists have stressed the importance of adherence to neo-classical postulates in countries such as South Korea and Taiwan. The key to success, they argue, was the avoidance of any protectionist tendencies. Rather, the entire emphasis was on exports as the key engine of growth. Competitiveness in export markets required close attention to labour and other production costs, and to the careful management of macro-economic policy and exchange rate settings. Increased interaction with companies in other countries allowed productive familiarity with advances in management systems and technology. Continued competitiveness also demanded an ongoing program of reform, resulting in progressive privatization of government enterprises, trade liberalization, structural adjustment, reforms in corporate governance and the fundamental democratization of the political system.

The responses of the adherents of dependency theory have also been predictable. In the early stages of the developments in South Korea, for example, a number of critics questioned how 'real' this development was, arguing that this was a classic example of dependent development, relying on politically motivated support from the United States and essentially exploiting low-cost labour resources. Unflattering comparisons were made with North Korea's emphasis on self-reliance. Yet as the evidence of continued progress mounted, and as the North Korean competition faltered, the emphasis switched to the lauding of the South Korean model of autonomous development. It was emphasized that the early stages of industrialization took place behind high tariff walls, and the government played a very important role as initiator and co-ordinator of new initiatives (Amsden 1989, Wade 1990). The nature and role of the South Korean state has received particular attention. Peter Evans (1995), for example, has argued that East Asia has been far more successful than Latin America because the state has been both *autonomous* and *embedded*. Unlike its counterparts in Latin America, the state in Asia has not been hostage to particular vested class interests, but has been autonomous and able to act independently in the interests of the whole nation. Yet, the state has been closely integrated into society, positioned to receive messages for all parts of the community and able to interact with all of these levels, and, in particular, the business community, to ensure that plans and targets were effectively met.

Yet, the Asian experience has also presented some different challenges to development theory by highlighting some factors that are outside all of the major existing theories. One set of writers has highlighted the role of culture in development, and pointed to the wide variety of experience in different parts of the world, thus questioning the generality of any development theories. Much has been made of the common Confucian heritage in Korea, Taiwan and China. This philosophy emphasises the ethical responsibilities of both rulers and the ruled and, it has been argued, was useful in instilling a high level of work ethic and response to authority in these countries. Confucianism also places great reliance on education and self-cultivation in the development of society, and, as a result, the level of investment in education has been extremely high. Thus, there has been a renewed interest in culture as an important variable in the development process. Comparisons have been made between what has been called the

'Confucian rate of growth' and the lesser performers, labelled, for example, the 'Hindu' and the 'Buddhist' level of performance. More broadly, the Asian experience has drawn attention to the capacity of the state to initiate and control growth (Weiss and Hobson 1995), and to the capacity of the population to contribute skills and initiative.

Some commentators have also pointed out that both Korea and Taiwan had a special strategic position during the Cold War, being American allies on the front line against Communism. This allowed them to gain special advantages from the United States, including access to military and development aid, and preferential access to American markets for their products, especially in the early stages of growth. The Western world generally turned a blind eye to the blatant copying of products and technology, something that would not be tolerated now.

Rather than supporting one of the existing models of development, a number of researchers have suggested that the Asian model of growth is in fact a case unto itself. Chalmers Johnson (1987) has gone so far as to suggest that the success has been based on the combination of some of best features of both the capitalist and socialist systems, yet avoiding the major weaknesses of each. The Asian companies have been energetic and entrepreneurial, have concentrated on improving their productivity levels, and have been able to develop new product lines and penetrate new markets, as older lines become less profitable. Yet, the prevailing ethos of the societies has been generally much more egalitarian than in countries such as the United States. There has been great attention to the avoidance of the grosser forms of income inequality, giving a much greater sense of social cohesion and stability. At the same time, some of the strengths of more centrally planned economies were utilized, especially in the early stages of development. The state was both active and efficient, avoiding the lethargy and waste that characterized the Soviet system. Importantly, the population felt that it was involved in a great and vital national enterprise, and was willing to work enormously hard and make sacrifices in the interest of future generations. This is not to argue that everything in Asia was perfect, as the onset of the Asian crisis demonstrated, however the enormous success of the model cannot be denied.

But this successful experience and the later onset of the Asian crisis leads us to two further questions, both of which are concerned with the question of the applicability of this model to other parts of the underdeveloped world. First, several commentators, as well as policy makers from around the world, have urged various governments to adopt the Korean or Taiwanese models of development, but it is far from clear whether such a transfer can work. As we have seen, many aspects of the Asian transformation can be interpreted as being very culturally and historically specific. Cultural values in regions such as Africa are far different from those in Korea, and countries could not now expect to derive the economic advantages that Korea and Taiwan were able to derive during the Cold War. Even if it were possible to transfer development models in this way, do nations that adopt such a high growth path to development risk the sort of damaging crisis that befell Asia in 1997? Is it possible to adopt these methods in the early stages of growth and then undertake a careful and appropriately sequenced series of reforms that can avoid later instability? This latter question is of great relevance to China at the moment. Many features of the Korean model, including the creation of some large conglomerates based on the example of the Korean *chaebol*, have been adopted, but there are fears of how the economy will be adapted and reformed in the longer term. We will return to these issues in Chapter 6, which deals, in part, with the lessons of the Asian crisis.

The neo-liberal ascendancy

Since the 1980s, development thought and policy has been dominated by what has become known as neo-liberal thought, or what Toye (1991) has called the New Political Economy. In part, this has resulted from a particular reading of the important Asian experience described above, as well as the decline of the dependency movement as a result of criticisms from both within and outside the 'progressive' strands of development thought. The movement also gained much momentum from the fall of the Soviet Union, and the consequent discrediting of socialist alternatives to capitalism, which gave rise to a more self-confident West willing to reassert many of the elements of the old modernization model (Colclough and Manor 1991).

Certainly, there are many elements that are a simple return to modernization, notably the often unstated belief that there is one path to development that all nations can follow in a series of stages. The goals of development are also portrayed as unproblematic, involving a simple movement toward the modernity that is portrayed as so successful in the West. All good comes from external sources, with outside norms and methods being essential to the breaking down of traditional barriers to growth. Many of the core mechanisms for growth are also similar to those cited in the earlier period. Savings rates are still a central element, supported by foreign investment. But there are also some important new elements and emphases. In particular, the role of government is much more clearly stated than in the earlier paradigm, or rather the involvement of government is simply dismissed. Elites and politicians, in particular, are uniformly portrayed as rent-seeking villains, willing only to look after their own narrow interests rather than the good of the entire society (Toye 1991).

Thus, while markets may not be perfect, they are portrayed as infinitely preferable to governments controlled by a 'kleptocracy'. Indeed, market failures are seen as more often resulting from an excess of government interference in the economy rather than from a dearth of regulation. Government services, even including health and education, must be pared back in the interests of balancing the budget and creating an environment conducive to foreign investment. Similarly, foreign exchange rates must be managed (i.e., devalued) to encourage export competitiveness.

Many of these policy measures have been promulgated by international institutions, notably the IMF, to deal with the periodic crises that have plagued much of the underdeveloped world; hence, many of these themes will be taken up in more detail in Chapter 6. But it is also true that much of the neo-liberal doctrine is embedded in the large body of literature supporting the move towards globalization, and it is to this important topic, and to some of the counter-voices that we now turn.

Globalization and development theory

In the early years of the new millennium, the central talking point, both among policy makers and the general public, is globalization. There even seems a general agreement that this new wave of change is inevitable, and that all nations must either seek ways of accommodating this new reality or risk irrelevance as the rest of the world marches into this glittering future. Yet, there is surprisingly little consensus on exactly what the term means. At one level it can simply involve the expansion of economic activities such as trade and investment across national boundaries. But it is frequently used to highlight closer economic integration, greater policy reform and openness, and greater interdependence between countries. More controversially, the term has sometimes been used to describe (or predict) tendencies towards convergence by all countries towards similar political systems, lifestyles and even tastes in entertainment or fast foods.

Given the looseness of the concept, it is not surprising that a number of voices have been raised to criticize several of the claims that have been made in the name of globalization. John Gray (1998) has challenged one of the basic tenets of the supporters of globalization, that this is a new era involving a profound set of changes to many aspects of global economy and society. Rather, Gray suggests, there have been several similar periods before in world history – in the mid-19th century and again in the years leading up to the First World War in particular – when there were high levels of international trade and investment. In these earlier cases the experiment with *laissez-faire* economics proved to be short-lived, principally because of the extreme levels of income inequality that were generated in the process. This polarization led to political instability that quickly forced new systems to be adopted. In both earlier examples, the longevity of the experiment was no more than 10–15 years. This, Gray argues, means that we have not entered a new and stable period in which an unprecedented set of conditions and processes will result in a permanent transformation of all aspects of life. Rather we are seeing a return to an old and failed experiment, and this current incarnation is bound to disappear in the same way quite quickly, and for basically the same reasons.

Not surprisingly, the remnants of the old dependency school have also criticized globalization as yet another manifestation of the Western desire to dominate and exploit the underdeveloped countries. Petras and Veltmeyer (2001) have denounced the concept of globalization, and the wide range of hype and jargon that has grown up around it, as an attempt to throw an ideological veil over a continuation of an old process to promote the economic and political interests of international capitalism. The existing world order is being re-made to serve the greed, class interest and desire to increase the profits of this small group. An important part of this process is the restructuring of the capitalist state to serve this new kind of imperialism. Many groups have felt marginalized and even exploited by this powerful set of global forces, and we have recently witnessed a number of mass demonstrations against globalization and some of what are regarded as its key institutions, the World Trade Organization, the IMF and the World Economic Forum, for example. Most dramatically, in the aftermath of the 11 September 2001 terrorist attacks on the United States, the President of the World Bank observed that issues of development and income inequality had now been highlighted in the most tragic way. The world, he argues, cannot afford to allow these inequalities to remain, much less grow, or the despair in the Third World and the anger that this engenders, will seriously destabilize the international system. This theme, which has been called 'the politics of resentment', will be taken up in more detail in Chapter 6 in our analysis of the economic crises in Africa, Asia and Latin America.

The supporters of globalization argue that the best chance for growth in the poorer countries remains with the liberalization of world trade and the reform of internal policies. As noted in the previous section, many of the arguments used here are not very different from those used to advance the claim of modernization theory over the last 50 years, although some important new elements are also apparent. 'Trickle-down' theory is alive and well, and is firmly incorporated in the structural adjustment packages forced on a series of crisis-ridden countries by the IMF. Currently there is lively debate raging about the empirical evidence on whether the gap between rich and poor countries is in fact growing or declining as the result of these policies. One group led by members of the United Nations

Development Programme argues that the gulf is getting wider, while others suggest the opposite. Dollar and Kraay (2002) have argued that inequality has, in fact, decreased since 1975, mainly because of rapid growth in China and India, and 'globalizing' countries have done much better than others. However, several other commentators have questioned these figures and the assumptions behind them.

Moving beyond these arguments, a number of elements of a new agenda for development have been proposed by some writers who are responding to what they see as innovative elements in the global debate. The whole modernization approach has been seriously questioned by those seeking to go beyond what they regard as an outmoded modernist paradigm. Any attempt to impose any unidirectional or single path to development has received some harsh criticism from those researchers using a post-modern approach. Traditional concerns for the things described so far in this chapter have been replaced for some by a whole new agenda concerned with knowledge, identity, meaning and the like (Parfitt 2002, Schuurman 2001). Some have gone so far as to suggest that the whole development project is now moribund, and we have entered an era of 'post-development' (Sachs 1992b, Rahnema 1997).

In part, this involves a whole new set of concerns into the debate, but many of the older issues are also rejected or turned on their head. The assumption that the underdeveloped world can be treated as a homogeneous and undifferentiated whole is completely dismissed. The development path of a society, and, indeed, its choices about the goals of development itself, are historically conditioned, and heavily influenced by the pattern of institutions that has emerged over the years. We should not regard any set of institutions, not even the market, as indispensable or the best choice – everything depends upon the context and the historical legacy. Similarly, the overarching belief in progress that characterized the modernist approach has been replaced for some by a greater sense of pessimism or a desire to simply avoid the most dangerous risks. The state, regarded by many for so long as the guardian or even the catalyst of development is now seen by this group as part of the problem. Rather, they argue, our real hope is with civil society and its struggle for emancipation. It is civil society that must define goals, objectives and methods. This, of course, raises some serious issues about the old methods of development assistance and the role of aid and the 'expert'. The process of development is here conceived as a form of discourse, one shaped by disparities of power. Escobar (1995) has argued that development is not a set of aims or knowledge that is gradually uncovered and acted upon, but an imposed set of constructs and values. The Western concern has been to win markets, gain access to raw materials and avoid being swamped by massive increases in the populations of impoverished countries. The West with its blind faith in technology and the effectiveness of planning has treated the Third World as a child in great need of guidance. Thus, the discourse of development can be envisaged as a web of power relations in which some are empowered and others disempowered. The poor are seen as the problem to be solved by the experts who are able to bring programmes for health care, education, social development or whatever. Accordingly, this school argues that all earlier categories of development thinking have fallen into the trap of paternalism, or what is now often called 'trusteeship' (Cowen and Shenton 1996, Parfitt 2002). The aim of development must be to escape from this trap and to reflect the real needs and goals of the people involved, although it is far from clear how this is to be achieved.

Another important element in the current debate concerns the role of different kinds of political and economic regimes in encouraging or inhibiting growth. These questions relating to institutions and economic development are important and timely, although far from resolved. Not surprisingly, the neo-liberal mainstream argues that Western-style democracy is essential to progress, although some interesting counter arguments are now appearing (see, for example, Clague 1997). Not surprisingly, given our earlier discussion, much of the counter argument is coming from Asian countries, which see themselves as being successful but not necessarily following conventional or Western models. In an interesting new study, Sylvia Chan (2002) argues that the common label of 'liberal democracy' contains two different elements that may in fact be contradictory, i.e., many of those who are strongest in their support of economic liberalization are, in fact, quite opposed to many democratic ideals. Thus, she argues, we need to decompose the whole notion that is at the centre of the neo-liberal agenda. Similarly, when we turn to the question of whether it is conducive to growth, she suggests we need to recognize on one side three key elements of 'liberty' – *economic, civil* and *political* liberty – and three key conditions that need to be achieved to promote growth – *security, stability,* and *openness and information*. After surveying the Asian growth experience she concludes that such liberties and outcomes have in fact been achieved under national systems that are not democratic in the Western sense. Development may well be possible using alternative regimes and models that are more congruent with local conditions, histories and institutional frameworks.

Conclusion

We have seen that the history of thinking about development is rich and varied, and with a strong tradition of vigorous debate. We have followed the main lines of this debate from 1945 to the present day and seen how certain ideas have waxed and waned in popularity, and then sometimes returned in a slightly modified form in a later period. But what is really striking is how little has really changed in both the theoretical debates and in the construction of policies. There are strong similarities between the modernization theories of the 1950s and the current structural adjustment prescriptions of the IMF. In the same way, many of the concepts put forward by the dependency school in the 1960s are still with us. Some features have been refined and reworked, but the basic points about unequal power and the exploitation of the poor countries remain. The phenomenon of globalization is seen by some as adding some new dimensions, but for most people in Africa or Asia the realities and hardships of everyday life remain pretty much the same as ever. Development is certainly about power, and the poor have, as always, little or no power either to set their own goals or to mobilize the resources needed to achieve them.

Chapter 3

Aid and Development

JANET HUNT

As development thinking has changed, so have fashions in aid. This chapter considers the various ideas and approaches that have shaped international development assistance over its 50 years, looks at the various motives for co-operation, and assesses the current state and role of development co-operation in light of globalization. It also considers the role development co-operation can play towards achievement of the Millennium Development Goals and what future there is for aid.

The purpose of aid

The purpose of aid, or why countries give aid, rests on a range of inter-related values about what might be called an international social contract. That is, there is a broad understanding amongst developed countries that, in order for the world to be, or to be seen to be, a moderately equitable place, or at least to alleviate some of the worst suffering, there needs to be some form of international assistance. For some developed countries this follows a perceived sense of responsibility following the process of decolonization. For others, it is intended to assist less developed states, to reduce the probability of their further decline and potential for instability. Many donors provide aid not only for humanitarian reasons, but to enhance their own economic and political interests, through encouraging their own exports, or shaping the economic policies or political persuasion of recipient countries.

Historical background

It is generally believed that the idea that wealthier countries could assist poorer ones to develop originated at the end of the Second World War. However, Rist (1997: 65) points out that its origins are really earlier than that, since in the period between 1929 and 1941, the League of Nations had responded to Chinese requests for assistance with the provision of some 30 technical experts in areas such as health, education, transport and rural co-operatives. Following the war, assistance started on a much larger scale with the formation of the United Nations and its specialized agencies and the establishment of the international financial institutions. In 1944, the Bretton Woods Conference agreed to form the International Bank for Reconstruction and Development (IBRD) and the International Monetary Fund (IMF). The initial role of the IBRD, better known as the World Bank, was to raise capital for the reconstruction of Europe and Japan, while the IMF was to promote international monetary stability. The first loans for assistance in developing countries were to Latin American countries in 1948 and 1949 (Hellinger, Hellinger and O'Regan 1988: 14, Ryrie 1995: 4–5).

US bilateral assistance began with the establishment, in 1948, of the Economic Cooperation Administration (Marshall Plan) to assist with Western European reconstruction in the face of advancing communism in Eastern Europe. In 1952 its functions were transferred to the Mutual Security Administration in a clear move to integrate foreign economic aid with military aid to meet Cold War objectives (Zimmerman 1993: 8).

The idea that there could be a concerted international effort to address poverty and underdevelopment is attributed to President Truman's inaugural speech in January 1949, in which he announced continuing support for the UN, the Marshall Plan, the establishment of NATO and, in Point Four, said:

> We must embark on a bold new program for making the benefits of our scientific advances and industrial progress available for the improvement and growth of underdeveloped areas (Rist 1997: 71).

The underlying theory was that growth in developing countries would create development, and that it would be achieved through large investments of capital, coupled with technical expertise. The emphasis was on modernization and industrialization, using surplus labour from rural areas, to achieve import substitution (Tarp 2000: 19–23). Keynesian economic theory was the order of the day, with its emphasis on government investment adding further intellectual support for the value of providing foreign aid.

European aid programmes developed strongly in the 1960s, as European nations recovered from war and were in a position to join the effort to assist the developing countries. In particular, as decolonization of Asia and Africa proceeded, former colonial powers, such as France and Britain, launched major development assistance programmes in their former colonies.

As the USA and Western European countries used aid as a tool in the Cold War, so did the USSR and China. The USSR was active in supporting Eastern European reconstruction, but later turned its attention to other 'fronts' in the Cold War, notably in Asia and parts of Africa.

Although aid from Organization for Economic Co-operation and Development (OECD, i.e., 'developed') countries accounts for the largest proportion of aid by far, it is important to recognize that non-OECD countries, particularly the Eastern Bloc during the Cold War and the Arab countries in the period in the lead up to and during the oil boom of the early 1970s, have provided assistance to developing countries. The richer socialist countries not only assisted poorer socialist nations, such as Cuba, Vietnam, Mongolia, and North Korea, but to persuade them to a more sympathetic position, they also assisted capitalist developing countries, among them Egypt, India, Iran, Iraq, Algeria, Indonesia, Brazil and Pakistan (Nayyar 1977: 4). While the USSR was the major donor, other Eastern European countries, such as East Germany and Czechoslovakia, and later China, were all involved, the latter particularly assisting African countries such as Tanzania and Somalia from the 1960s onwards (Nayyar 1977). By 1988, aid from the socialist bloc had begun to fall, to US$4.7 billion, with 90 per cent of that coming from the Soviet Union (OECD 1989: 175). Soviet aid to sub-Saharan Africa alone, for example, dropped from US$2.1 billion between 1980 and 1984 (Adade 1991), to effectively nothing after 1989. However, even when Soviet aid was at its peak, it was primarily in military supplies to client states in Africa, South-East Asia, and Latin America (see Klare and Anderson 1996: 3–8). Today, following the end of the Cold War, and as a result of the economic 'opening' in the former communist world, the Soviet Union and other Eastern bloc countries, notably the Baltic states and the states of former Soviet Central Asia, are themselves recipients of OECD aid.

As a consequence of the first oil price boom, Arab assistance began in the early 1970s and rose rapidly, with average spending of US$6 billion a year in the mid–late 1970s, mainly through bilateral channels to African Arab and Muslim states. Saudi Arabia has been particularly active, and in 1976–77 it was the second largest donor of official development assistance, after the USA. However, since the late 1970s, aid from the Arab world has declined. By 1988 it was down to US$2.3 billion, of which most was Saudi Arabian aid, going to agricultural development and structural adjustment in African countries.

Interestingly, the idea of providing aid through non-government organizations preceded these government initiatives. The origins of non-government aid can be traced to between the First and Second World Wars, often in response to the victims of war and conflict, although it should be recognized that the Red Cross had already been established as early as 1863 (Stubbings 1992:5), while 'proto-aid' charitable organizations, notably Christian missions, existed prior to that. As Smillie notes (1995: 37–39), Save the Children was founded in 1919 to help the child victims of the First World War. Foster Parents Plan (now Plan

International), which began in 1937, was a response to the Spanish Civil War, again to help the child victims. Oxfam began in 1942, during the Second World War, to provide famine relief to victims of the Greek civil war; CARE started by sending food parcels from the USA to Europe in 1946 and World Vision began slightly later, in response to the victims of the Korean War. These are among the major international non-governmental organizations (NGOs) today.

The late 1940s and the 1950s was a period of optimism, in which people believed that it was indeed possible to eradicate the hunger and misery resulting from under-development. They recognized that the task was a large one, required a significant commitment of resources and should be thought of as taking at least a decade (Hoffman 1997).

How much aid, to whom?

In the early years of aid, it was felt that 6 per cent growth was needed in developing countries to address the poverty and misery people were experiencing. To have the capital necessary to invest to gain this level of growth, it was suggested, would require 0.7 per cent of the gross national product (GNP) of the developed nations (Jolly 1999: 36–37). This is the origin of the target for aid set in 1970, but still current today, more honoured in the breach than in its realization.

Only five countries – Denmark, Netherlands, Sweden, Norway and Luxembourg – meet the 0.7 per cent target, and, since the early 1980s, aid levels have been falling steadily from around 0.36 per cent GNP to an average of 0.22 per cent GNP (German and Randel 2002: 149).

German and Randel note that though wealth per person in donor countries has more than doubled since 1961 (from US$13,298 to US$29,769), aid per capita from countries on the OECD's Development Assistance Committee (DAC) has fallen from US$71 in 1961 to US$66 per year in 2000 (German and Randel 2002: 145).

By the first half of the 1950s, aid already amounted to some US$8 billion a year (at 1987 values). Over the decades it grew in volume, if not as a percentage of GNP, until the total *volume* of OECD aid peaked at US$62.7 billion in 1992. It has declined since to US$53.7 billion in 2000 (Tarp 2000: 85, German and Randel 2002: 145). While US aid was significant in the early decades, by 1980 the European countries were providing more than twice as much as the US (Ryrie 1995: 10). In dollar terms, Japan and the US now contribute the largest amounts of aid, but as a percentage of their GNPs their contributions are small, especially that of the USA (0.28 per cent and 0.10 per cent of GNP respectively).

In efforts to bring greater focus on to the quality and direction of aid, over the years, two other significant indicators have been added to the basic measure. One relates to the proportion of aid going to Least Developed Countries (LLDC) and Less Developed Countries (LDC), the other to the proportion of aid being spent on Basic Social Services (BSS), such as health services, education, potable water, and sanitation (Jolly 1999). The emphasis on the Least Developed Countries reflected concern in the UN and among NGOs at the distortions of aid that led to relatively high proportions flowing to middle-income developing countries. It was championed by the United Nations Conference on Trade and Development (UNCTAD) and NGOs at a 1981 UN meeting on Least Developed Countries, where donors agreed to contribute 0.15 per cent of GNP to these nations. Almost a decade later, donors had reached 0.09 per cent, somewhat over half way towards the goal. The LLDCs, which comprise the world's poorest nations, now receive 29 per cent of global aid from the DAC countries (German and Randel 2002: 151–2), a slight increase on the proportion spent in LLDCs in the mid-1990s (approx 25 per cent) (Reality of Aid 1997–1998: 246). The measure of Basic Social Services was proposed by United Nations Children's Fund (UNICEF) and United Nations Development program (UNDP) at the World Summit on Social Development in 1995, as part of a proposed compact in which 20 per cent of development assistance and 20 per cent of developing country government expenditure should be devoted to basic services in areas such as health, family planning, education, nutrition, water and sanitation. However, infighting over the definitional issues and difficulty of measurement means that although the DAC started measuring spending on BSS, the proposal has not been taken up very effectively. Nevertheless, the exercise revealed a very low level of expenditure on sectors such as basic health and basic education, which, in 1995 and 1996, were a mere 1.8 per cent and 1.2 per cent of total Official Development Assistance (ODA) respectively for the 12 donors who managed to report against these measures (Reality of Aid 1997–1998: 249). Mehotra (2002:532) reports that average funding to basic education actually fell in the late 1990s, and funding to health averaged only 2 per cent of ODA in that decade. Mehotra believes that around 10 per cent of ODA currently goes to basic social services (Mehotra 2002: 533).

The geographical distribution of aid has changed significantly over the decades. In 1961, almost a quarter of all aid went to the Middle East and North Africa, 20 per cent to South Asia, and less than 10 per cent to sub-Saharan Africa (Ryrie 1995: 12). By 2000, DAC donors provided 30 per cent of their assistance to sub-Saharan Africa, 12 per cent to South and Central Asia and only 12 per cent to the Middle East and North Africa.

Over 70 per cent of aid is provided through bilateral channels, that is, directly from one country to another. The remainder is provided through multilateral organizations, which include the various specialized UN agencies, such as the World Food Program, World Health Organization,

UNICEF, UN High Commission for Refugees, and United Nations Development Program, and the international financial institutions, especially the concessional arms of the World Bank and the various regional development banks (e.g. Asian Development Bank, Inter-American Development Bank).

What has shaped levels and distribution of aid?

There can be no doubt that the Cold War and foreign policy objectives have had a major influence on both the levels and distribution of aid. This has been particularly the case for the US and a number of larger aid donors (by volume) such as France. As Ryrie says,

> ... in 1991, one country, Egypt, received no less than 32 per cent of American aid and Israel, a relatively rich country, 8 per cent. These figures exclude military aid. Nicaragua and Honduras between them received another 4 per cent, while the whole of sub-Saharan Africa got 3.6 and India, 0.8 per cent. (Ryrie 1995: 13)

Zimmerman traces the US–Egypt aid relationship as a central part of the USA's Middle East policy to influence the Arab world, but notes that:

> diplomacy that used economic aid to advance US strategic interests has impeded use of those resources to stimulate self-sustaining development. (Zimmerman 1993: 106)

If aid has not been wholly effective in relation to its publicly promoted humanitarian objectives, it may have been far more successful in achieving its other, less trumpeted, yet often more calculated goals.

Some of the better known abuses of aid include the way Japan has used aid to leverage votes from small states to support its pro-whaling stance in the International Whaling Commission, and the use of aid by numerous donors to promote trade through a host of mixed-credit schemes. The use of Australian aid to promote Australian technology and support Australian exports to China is a classic example of the use of aid to promote the commercial objectives of the donor (Bain 1996). The dramatic skewing of US aid in favour of Israel and Egypt for foreign policy purposes is another example of the political use of aid. A recent example of this was the pledge in December 2001 from the US to Pakistan of over US$1 billion in debt forgiveness, investment trade and refugee relief (Jefferys 2002: 3). This is clearly associated with the US Government's 'war on terror' (Human Rights Watch 2002) and its need to maintain a close alliance with Pakistan because of its engagement in neighbouring Afghanistan. Finally, aid can be used as an international response when tough political decisions are not made. The cases of Rwanda and East Timor stand out as examples of the way in which the international community responds with aid when it has failed to deal with the political source of the crisis. However, Tarp (2000) shows that the aid of smaller countries, such as Sweden, has been better shaped by the needs of recipient countries than that of other, larger donors.

The decline in aid since 1992 illustrates that the end of the Cold War did affect levels of aid, although other factors were also at work, notably the rise in private-sector investment in selected developing countries. Since the end of the Cold War aid has been shaped by new agendas, influenced by the view that aid is only effective where 'good policies' are in place. 'Good policies' is code for policies that are consistent with the Washington consensus, or neo-liberalism. The major effect on the geographical distribution of aid immediately after the Cold War was the rapid rise of aid to Eastern Europe and Central Asia, including the emergency in former Yugoslavia. At the same time, a commitment to the 1996 DAC goals of halving the proportion of people living in poverty with its associated social goals, has influenced donor governments to re-assess where aid is going, what effect it is having, and whether the goals can be reached. The focus has turned to assisting those countries where poverty is significant but where 'good governance' policies are in place. Many donor countries are reducing the number of countries to which they provide aid, and are assessing the mechanisms through which aid is provided, to try to make it more effective.

Shifts have also occurred in the sectoral distribution of aid. In the early period there was a very strong emphasis on economic infrastructure development; recent figures show that the largest allocation now is to social infrastructure (31 per cent), with economic infrastructure spending at 17 per cent of total aid. Eight per cent of global aid is now spent on emergency assistance, with a similar proportion of aid expenditure on debt relief. Despite their high public profile, support to NGOs is only three per cent of official development assistance (German and Randel 2002: 151).

What has aid been like?

Though the goals of aid have remained much the same, the ways donors aim to achieve them have changed considerably over the years. Mosley and Eeckhout have found that:

> The project aid component of aid budgets has declined severely from the early 1970s (sometimes to the point of collapse) and other aid instruments have expanded to fill the vacuum, notably technical co-operation, policy-conditioned programme aid, support for the private

sector and for NGOs and emergency assistance. (Mosley and Eeckhout, in Tarp 2000: 131)

As mentioned above, in the early years, much aid was in the form of infrastructure projects, such as roads, bridges, power stations and the like, using Western technology and capital, but Robert McNamara's emphasis on Basic Needs in 1972 extended the 'development project' into new areas, such as agricultural development, health and education. The processes of development immediately became more complex and less predictable than the physical infrastructure projects. In particular, a trend towards large 'integrated rural development projects' greatly increased the complexity of development tasks. The weaknesses and problems that such projects faced led to greater focus on government policy environments as a key factor in successful development.

Following the oil price shocks and the US dropping of the gold standard (see Chapter 9), and the consequent economic upheavals, at the end of the 1970s Keynsian economic policies gave way to neo-classicism. In line with this, the World Bank's promotion of Basic Needs approaches ended, and attention turned to macro-economic policies. The economic recession at the beginning of the 1980s, and the associated debt defaults first triggered by Mexico, led to a major re-think in development circles. An aid mechanism was needed now which could quickly help stabilize the economies of deeply indebted poor countries, where private sector investment had dried up. Thus began lending and balance of payments support that was predicated on IMF directed 'structural adjustment' programmes, requiring recipient countries to liberalise and deregulate their economies. By the mid-1990s, the World Bank had also moved towards emphasizing structural adjustment packages, becoming 'about a third of World Bank lending and just under 20 per cent of the bilateral aid budgets of the OECD countries' (Mosley and Eekhout 2000: 136–137). As Mosley and Eekhout note there were at least three major problems with this type of assistance:

- weak implementation – 'about half of the first wave of adjustment reforms were not implemented', largely for reasons of political corruption and mismanagement
- ineffectiveness – many countries found that the reforms did not stimulate supply in their economies
- negative side-effects – there were costs in terms of increased poverty and reduction in services caused by the public expenditure cuts.

Though countries undergoing structural adjustment found that their export trade improved, investment deteriorated and the impacts on poverty and growth were unconvincing (Mosley and Eekhout 2000:

138–139). Morrissey (2000) cites evidence from Latin America that shows that even with increased trade, many developing countries are more vulnerable to negative influences on the trading environment, such as hyper-competitive pricing for imports against a local manufacturing market, and that in a bid to compete primarily on the basis of low wage rates, developing countries tend to bargain each other downwards, which has a negative impact on levels and distribution of income.

Thus, the next phase was to shift to other mechanisms, notably through the private sector and, on a much smaller scale, through NGOs. For example, there were significant increases in World Bank funds to the International Finance Corporation, which supports private sector development in the developing world through a catalytic and advisory role in raising project finance and investment in developing country companies (Ryrie 1995: 121–161). The OECD emphasizes that, in general, 'countries which have used market opportunities and developed dynamic private sectors have fared better than those that have not' (OECD 1989: 78–79). It thus urges donor governments to assist poor developing countries to meet the preconditions for developing a vibrant private sector, among them, 'strengthening developing countries' policies, institutions and infrastructure in the widest sense, including training' (OECD 1989: 80). Among the requirements that aid is now addressing are the abolition of monopolies, strengthening competition, an appropriate regulatory environment, efficient banking, transport and communication facilities.

It should be noted that the private sector of donor countries has long been involved in development co-operation, as the managing agents of the development projects supported by the donors. Such involvement of the private sector of donor countries has been roundly criticized as costly to developing countries. Tying may include requiring firms who manage projects to be registered in the donor country, procuring commodities, such as food aid, from donor sources, and placing donor country expatriates in developing countries as technical advisers. A study by British Official Development Assistance found that the costs of certain types of purchases, namely heavy vehicles and agricultural tools, were up to 47 per cent higher than the cheapest international alternative, and on average prices of tied goods were 20 per cent higher (cited in Simons 1997). From April 2001, the UK untied all its aid other than that through NGOs and universities (Reality of Aid 2002: 15). However, it remains true that tying aid still adds between 10–30 per cent to the cost of aid, thus reducing its value to the developing countries (Simons 1997: 187, Reality of Aid 2002: 14–15). After considerable NGO criticism, donors finally agreed to partially untie aid to the Least Developed Countries from the start of 2001, though technical assistance – still a large component of total aid – was exempted. The Dutch have untied their technical assistance, but most other donors still fully or partially tie it to their nationals. In 1999, UNDP estimated that a quarter of all aid – US$14 billion – was spent on technical assistance, with the World Bank suggesting that 100,000 foreign technical experts were employed in Africa alone at that time – an incredible number.

The linkage of tertiary education places to universities in donor countries is a further aspect of aid tying, which has also distorted educational aid strongly in favour of tertiary education, rather than basic and primary education. For example, examining Australia's educational assistance in the first half of the 1990s, around 70–75 per cent went to tertiary level while only 6–10 per cent went to primary and secondary combined. This despite the fact that research has consistently shown high social rates of return for spending on primary education (Simons 1997: 130–133). As Australia has a higher than average expenditure on basic education compared to other DAC countries, the significance of the issue is evident.

A more recent mechanism for aid is the development of sector programmes (e.g. specific programmes within a sector with specific objectives in areas such as health, agriculture, education, etc) which fall somewhere between the project level and the macro-economic support of structural adjustment lending. These enable donor funds to be integrated into sectoral budgets to expand programmes in agreed ways and, in theory, facilitate donor co-ordination to support developing country government planning and priorities. However, in reality, the weakness of donor coordination, and the extent of donor intervention and oversight, means that such strategies are far from the ideal of giving recipient governments a greater chance to drive development (Reality of Aid 2002:17).

One of the rapidly growing areas of aid in the early 1990s was emergency assistance. Total OECD aid for emergencies, around US$1 billion in 1990, rose dramatically to over $3.4 billion in 1993 (Simons 1997: 280). It continued to grow through the 1990s, so that some 8 per cent of all aid (over US $4.2 billion) in 2000 was spent on emergency assistance. This growth reflects the growing number of international emergencies, both natural disasters and complex humanitarian emergencies brought on by conflict (German and Randel 2002:151). The role of aid in conflict and post-conflict environments has become a new area for practice and study.

Other major changes in aid in more recent decades have reflected greater attention on the social and environmental rather than just economic aspects of development. The struggle to gain recognition that aid could contribute to gender inequality when it should be enhancing gender equity has been a long hard one (see Chapter 10) and, whilst all donors now have gender policies, the translation of policy to practice is more difficult. It has been almost as difficult to ensure that environmental sustainability was an integral consideration in aid efforts, despite the attention brought to these issues by the Rio Earth Summit in 1990 and advocacy by environmental NGOs. Most recently, efforts to bring human rights thinking into development co-operation, with a rights-based approach to development, have struggled to gain legitimacy and to be translated into practical application. In addition, changing global circumstances have brought a range of new aid agendas to attention, among them preventing the devastating spread of HIV/AIDS, combating the trafficking of people, and promoting drug control through aid support to farmers to convert from opium growing to other crops.

How effective has aid been?

Clearly the stated purposes of aid are related to economic growth, the reduction of poverty and the alleviation of suffering. Aid is, thus, correctly, assessed against such criteria. Clearly, over the years there have been some successes, but they are not as great as many think they should have been. One reason for this is that aid has, in fact, been badly distorted by other agendas, whether diplomatic, commercial or related to the economic self-interest of OECD countries. At the March 2002 Financing for Development Conference the USA was disparaging about the effectiveness of past aid, but as one NGO representative present reported, 'unfortunately, they did not explore the reasons for that ineffectiveness, such as its political capture, funnelling to middle-income rather than low-income countries, distribution to client states and tying to donor country goods, in all of which the US is a leading culprit' (Zwart 2002).

Because of the above mentioned distortions, the efficacy of aid has been ambiguous. However, while recognizing the ambiguity of aspects of aid and its efficacy, Cassen notes that aid has helped make possible a number of significant achievements, from raising food production to building infrastructure (1994: 224). According to Cassen: '[T]he majority of aid is successful in terms of its own objects. Over a wide range of countries and sectors, aid has made positive and valuable contributions' (1994: 225). However, as Cassen also notes, this does not mean that all is well with aid – it has not always been used in the places where it is most effective, and the degrees of its misuse have ranged from the less to the more reprehensible (1994: 225). More reprehensible failures from the donor side, according to Cassen, include using aid for commercial or political ends without regard for its supposed development objects, or from failing to learn from past mistakes in its application. However, Cassen does not discuss the 'reprehensibility' of aid misuse by recipient countries, which could be said to include corruption, redirection of aid, predatory official behaviour towards nominal aid recipients and so on.

One approach to assessing the effectiveness of aid is to examine evaluations of aid programmes. The World Bank published a review of evaluations of development assistance in 1995 that drew five conclusions about the conditions that were necessary to make aid effective. These were:

- ownership by the government and participation of affected people – linked to the government's own commitment to poverty reduction
- strong administrative and institutional capacity – an environment of 'good governance'
- sound policies and good public sector management – meaning governments facilitating open markets and investing in infrastructure and people
- close coordination by donors – to simplify aid management for recipient governments
- improvements in donors' own business practices – to focus less on inputs and more on the effects of development at the country level (World Bank 1995).

By 2001, the World Bank had shifted its emphasis more to what might be termed fine tuning, which was based on the assumption that there was a qualitative improvement in individual operations. In particular, it noted the need for:

- strengthening country and sector assistance by linking instruments (specific forms of bank development assistance) more logically with objectives, taking note of past performance
- emphasis on non-lending activities, especially in 'poor performing' countries
- strengthening guidance in instrument selection, to fully exploit synergies between instruments (Battaile 2001).

Much of the debate about the effectiveness of aid has been at a macro level, and has focused on the extent to which aid has contributed to growth in developing countries. Hansen and Tarp (2000) review these studies of aid effectiveness. The Burnside and Dollar study has been particularly influential recently in donor, especially World Bank, circles. Their 1997 study concluded that 'aid has a positive impact on growth in a good policy environment' (Hansen and Tarp 2000:116). This fed into the World Bank's own study authored by Dollar, *Assessing Aid*, in 1998. Their work has indeed shaped a great deal of aid thinking in the late 1990s and subsequently, in that a strong emphasis has been placed on countries having in place sound policies. At a time when donors were reducing the number of countries to which they provided aid, in an attempt to gain more focus and effectiveness in their aid programs, consideration of developing country policy environments appears to have played a significant part in their selections (Battaile 2001: 2–3).

Hansen and Tarp suggest that Dollar and Burnside's conclusions are, at best, questionable. They revisit the same data, but conclude instead that aid has a positive impact on growth even where policies are poor. When other studies are also considered (e.g., Hadjimichael *et al*. 1996), the conclusion they draw is that aid has a significant impact on growth, 'as long as the aid to GDP ratio is not excessively high' (Hansen and Tarp 2000: 118, Tarp 2000: 45). As they point out, in any case, the countries whose policy environments are most conducive to good aid results may be those who need aid least. On the other hand, there is also the view that countries that most need aid can quickly become aid-dependent and are not able or encouraged to develop their own economic foundations, or that inappropriate aid simple establishes a higher level of external debt with no quantifiable improvement (see Kanbur 2000: 410–416).

The debate remains a lively one, with arguments about whether aid should be provided only after governments have instituted particular policies, or whether aid can be used to help them move to those positions. For example, efforts by the World Bank in Indonesia to reduce corruption, sell off state enterprises, reform the banking system, and strengthen the legal system would be a case of the latter approach. This has had mixed success, due, in part, to incomplete application of requirements, continuing corruption across all levels of government, judicial ambiguity and, not least, because of the country's potential and actual political instability.

Aid has always had its critics, both from the left and the right of the political spectrum. Even early on, the Basic Human Needs approach to aid was criticized for being an attempt to thwart developing country efforts to push for a new international economic order (Galtung 1997). In another relatively early critique of aid, Weissman *et al*. (1975) take the view that development assistance is simply a new form of post-colonial control and imperialism:

> Whatever the form of aid, or even trade, we see no realistic way in which rich nations can transfer resources to the poor without pursuing their own profits and expanding their own power. (Weissman 1975: 13)

Over a quarter of a century later, the NGOs that together wrote and published *The Reality of Aid* assert that the conditionalities increasingly associated with aid enable the donors to exert power over developing countries. The trends of the 1980s and 1990s, as they say, brought about a new global order:

dramatically at odds with the New International Economic Order. Dramatic rises in world interest rates, the dominance of the neo-liberal market ideology in governments in the United States and the UK, and faltering state-led industrialization in the South were accompanied by the explosion of debt for Brazil and Mexico, and later among more than 50 of the poorest countries. (Reality of Aid 2002: 6)

As they point out, despite the rhetoric of the Development Assistance Committee about a new emphasis on partnership and ownership of development programmes and projects, the donor countries' imposition of countless conditionalities served to push the Washington Consensus policies onto aid receiving countries, particularly through economic adjustment programs to deal with the debt crisis. The contrasts between the policies developing country governments are forced to pursue and those enjoyed by developed countries is the ultimate hypocrisy that NGOs decry:

> southern governments are forced to privatize and liberalize, while OECD restrictive practices, tariff and non-tariff barriers cost developing countries US $160 billion a year. (Reality of Aid 2002: 5)

Hancock (1989) also criticizes official development assistance as a concept, though his grounds are different, and, unlike NGOs, he has no faith that it can be reformed. He argues that the bureaucratic institutions that manage aid are secretive, bloated, and self-serving. He is particularly critical of a host of failed and unsustainable projects which have often left governments indebted, while donor-country private corporations responsible for the project implementation walk away with handsome profits. Furthermore, relative to other economic flows, he says, aid is insignificant (see Chapter 9), and, indeed, the so-called 'donor' countries have, in fact, been net recipients of funds from the developing countries since the early 1980s. At the same time, Hancock says there is enough aid to do harm:

> ... it is often profoundly dangerous to the poor and inimical to their interests; it has financed the creation of monstrous projects that, at vast expense, have devastated the environment and ruined lives; it has supported and legitimised brutal tyrannies; it has facilitated the emergence of fantastical and Byzantine bureaucracies staffed by legions of self-serving hypocrites; it has sapped the initiative, creativity and enterprise of ordinary people and substituted the superficial and irrelevant glitz of imported advice (Hancock 1989: 189).

The list of damage goes on. NGOs have also made concerted criticisms of a number of major aid projects, specifically those supported by the

World Bank and/or the Asian Development Bank, such as those at Kedung Ombo, Narmada, and Arun (Nepal). These campaigns have led in turn to a range of demands for changes in World Bank *policies* in areas such as information disclosure, resettlement, the Inspection panel to monitor Bank compliance with its own policies, indigenous peoples' policy and various improvements in environmental and social policies (Fox and Brown 1998, Rumansara 1998, Siwakoti 2002).

Others, such as de Waal (1989, 1997) and Maren (1997), have been critical of humanitarian relief aid in particular. Alex de Waal's criticisms of the relief response in Dafur, Sudan during the 1984–1985 famine, were well-founded and have had an impact. He argued that food aid was not the key response – since most of the deaths were health related and in some cases the health risks were actually increased by the congregations of huge numbers of people at relief centres. Furthermore, he says, 'the food was committed late, delivered late, and to the wrong people'. De Waal made constructive suggestions as to how to avoid such problems in the future, and his work has been influential.

The level and strength of public support for aid seems to reflect the ambivalence about aid that these criticisms indicate. While in most donor countries there is a very high level in principle of support for giving foreign aid, that support is, as Ian Smillie says 'a mile wide and an inch deep' (Smillie 1999: 72). In fact, as Smillie points out, aid needs to be far more effectively focused on poverty, more money has to spent on explaining to the public why aid is important, and a broad definition of enlightened self-interest, combined with humanitarianism, needs to be used to convince the public that an investment of good aid now may avert far greater costs later.

The International Development Targets/Millennium Development Goals

The idea of setting some International Development Targets derived from a series of United Nations World Conferences held in the 1990s, particularly the World Summit for Children, held in New York in 1990 and the World Summit for Social Development held in Copenhagen in 1995. These conferences themselves set a series of goals for governments to achieve in their Action Plans.

In 1996, at an important meeting of the OECD Development Assistance Committee, which also placed great emphasis on effective partnerships and 'locally owned' development strategies, donors agreed to a series of goals to be reached by the Year 2015. These goals are:

- halve the proportion of people living in extreme poverty
- universal primary education (with elimination of gender disparities in primary and secondary education by 2005)
- reduction in under-five mortality by two-thirds of the 1990 level
- reduction of maternal mortality by three-quarters of the 1990 level
- universal access to reproductive health care services
- reversal of the trends in loss of environmental resources through national strategies.

Achieving such goals will depend on both national budgetary support and donor financing. Mehotra suggests that an additional US$70–80 billion are needed (Mehotra 2002: 5330). This focus on poverty reduction was taken up by donors, among them Australia, the UK and New Zealand, in the latter cases following major reviews of their ODA (Simons 1997, DFID 1997, 2000, Ministerial Review Team 2001), often combined with reductions in the number of countries receiving support and some emphasis on 'good governance' or 'good policy' in the selection of recipients. Thus, the UK's Department for International Development's (DFID) White Papers place significant emphasis on eradicating poverty, although as Slater and Bell (2002) note, they do not challenge the virtues of neo-liberal globalization or acknowledge that there may be contradictions between the poverty eradication goals and the widening inequality that current forms of globalization are creating. This is particularly salient in light of Hanmer and Naschold's findings that, 'according to the projections, the target of halving extreme poverty by 2015 will be met if, and only if, low levels of income inequality accompany growth' (Booth 1999). The World Bank's publication on the more widely and more recently agreed Millennium Development Goals concludes that 'too many countries are falling short of the goals or lack the data to monitor progress'. In particular, the nations of Africa look least likely to achieve the targets on present trends.

The targets have caused donors to focus more closely on the quality and effectiveness of aid, and particularly its impact on poverty reduction, rather than on more general measures of growth and development. However, reconciling the demands for performance against these targets with the notions of partnership accepted by the DAC's 1996 document, *Shaping the Twenty First Century*, may be more difficult. Wood (1999) recognized this, asking what donors would do when developing countries ask for support which differs from donor views and experience of 'proven strategies for success' (Wood 1999:19). Further, he asks whether the key issue where donors lack capacity is not the level of aid provided, but the type of aid. This appears to be the motivation for Foster and Leary's study of differing modes of aid financing for different circumstances.

The Monterrey Financing for Development Conference, held in March 2002, was essentially concerned with ways to finance the Millennium Development Goals using a mix of methods, among them domestic and international resources from private and public sources, trade, debt relief and other measures. Interestingly, the conference made explicit reference to the linkage between debt relief and these goals, as well as providing an opportunity for a significant number of countries to announce commitments to substantially increase official development assistance. The US, for example, announced a 50 per cent increase by 2005, but with strong conditionality related to good governance, sound economic policies, and investments in health and education, while EU countries committed to boost their aid to an average 0.39 per cent of GNP by 2006.

There is a growing interest in 'innovative sources of finance' to supplement the meagre contributions of ODA. Whilst debt reduction through the World Bank's Debt Relief for Heavily Indebted Poor Countries programme is seen as one way in which additional funds can be released for social investment (particularly since the introduction of Poverty Strategy Reduction Papers as a precondition for debt relief), another idea slowly gaining support, particularly in Europe, is the currency transaction tax. This would be a very small tax on all foreign exchange transactions, which currently amount to around $350 trillion per year (Forex 2002). At a 0.1 per cent tax rate, even with a 50 per cent reduction in foreign exchange dealing, this would provide US$175 billion annual revenue. A German study commissioned by its Foreign Ministry, however, suggests a much lower normal taxation rate of 0.01 per cent which would raise some US$17–20 billion per year, with a surcharge which would cut in if a currency was under speculative attack (Zwart 2002: 10). Whilst much debate remains about how such a mechanism would operate and how funds so gained would be directed for development, political opposition to the idea and challenges to its technical feasibility are slowly wearing down. Others point out that more funds are lost to developing countries through capital flight than they receive in ODA, so measures to prevent such losses would be extremely valuable. Boyce, for example, says that capital flight from the severely indebted low-income countries of sub-Saharan Africa was greater than their combined public external debts over the period 1970–1996 (Boyce 2002: 244). Capital flight from Indonesia in 1997 was said to amount to $70 billion, at that time approximately equivalent to the country's total foreign debt, which underpinned the radical devaluation of its currency. Indonesia's economy was not expected to significantly recover from the effects of the 1997 crash until at least 2010, assuming no other major disasters. Malaysia, on the other hand, imposed restrictions on the flow of capital and by 2002 had effectively recovered from the 1997 economic crash.

Aid in an era of globalization

One major purpose of official development assistance had been to supply capital to the developing world, but by 1977 private capital flows to developing countries had already exceeded official development assistance by a ratio of two to one (Williams 1997: 43). As globalization proceeded, the question emerging was what specific role would development assistance play in a world in which private financial flows were increasing so rapidly? Between 1990 and 1996, private international finance to developing countries increased from US$44.4 billion to US$256 billion – more than six times the aid flows. However, the bulk of the investment was directed to around a dozen countries in East Asia and Latin America, notably China. Very little is flowing to the Least Developed Countries, nor are the social sectors such as health and education the targets of this investment. In 1997, the financial collapse in East Asia, which reverberated through Thailand, South Korea and Indonesia in particular, illustrated the dangers of rapid withdrawal of speculative capital and the collapse of a country's currency.

As noted, every day more than one trillion dollars is traded globally in currency exchanges (Oxfam 2002: 36). One week of currency exchange is worth more than a whole year's worth of trade in goods and services globally. More than 40 per cent of these transactions involve round trips of less than three days. This rapid movement of speculative capital leads to great volatility and instability in financial markets, and can quite suddenly plunge millions of people into poverty. So, while flows of private finance may be contributing to the development of a limited number of nations, the problem with the global capital flows from a human development perspective is their size and volatility, and their capacity to undo development gains virtually overnight.

Much of the theory of globalization rests on the promotion of trade as a driver of economic growth. As Oxfam (2002) notes:

> if developing countries increased their share of world exports by just five per cent, this would generate US$350 billion, seven times as much as they receive in aid. The US$70 billion that Africa would generate through a one per cent increase in its share of world exports is approximately five times the amount provided to the region through aid and debt relief. (Oxfam 2002: 6)

According to Oxfam, 'the potential of even a one per cent increase in world export share for each developing region could reduce world poverty by 12 per cent' (Oxfam 2002:7). Yet, as they go on to show, trade theory is not being borne out in practice for much of the developing world, as poor people, far from benefiting from global trade expansion are, as noted earlier, losing out. Trade restrictive practices by the developed world are frustrating developing countries' aspirations, Oxfam estimates that the total cost to developing countries of all export restrictive practices is over US$100 billion annually. Thus, trade liberalization has proceeded in a highly asymmetric manner. Many developing countries have been forced to liberalize by conditionalities attached to structural adjustment loans, but developed countries have resisted any equivalent policy shifts, blocking equitable access to their markets for developing country produce. As Australia's former Governor-General, Bill Hayden, was fond of saying, the subsidy given to a European cow is greater than the annual income of three poor people in the developing world. Or put another way, 'total OECD agricultural subsidization exceeds the total income of the 1.2 billion people living below the poverty line' (Oxfam 2002: 113). When average per-capita income in low income countries is just over $400 per year, and US farmers receive average subsidies of $21,000 per annum, something seems seriously awry (Oxfam 2002: 112–113). Unless trade liberalization proceeds in a more equitable manner, current trends, which are seeing a widening of the gap between developing and developed countries in their share of world income, are likely to persist and even worsen (Oxfam 2002: 66–70).

Thus, both trade and the growth of private sector investment in developing countries may have the potential to supersede official development assistance, but at present, the geographically limited benefits and the negative trends associated with both these phenomena lead one to conclude that official development assistance will still be required by many of the poorer countries for some time.

One consequence of globalization has been the use of aid to boost the private sector, support the financial sector, and support trade liberalization policy generally. Kragh *et al.* (2000) review the various aid instruments that donors use to stimulate the private sector, among them investment support funds, 'enabling environment' support programmes, privatization and commercialization programmes and business partnerships (Kragh *et al.* 2000: 319–330), noting that, while this type of support remains only a small part of official development assistance, it is growing, and can contribute to poverty reduction as well as overall growth. Morrissey (2000: 375–391) notes that aid can be used both for short-term compensatory assistance as countries liberalize trade, or to support the development and necessary infrastructure for regional trade agreements. Kovsted (2000) recognizes that, following a series of international financial crises since the 1980s that impacted negatively on developing countries, aid is also now being used to help strengthen the financial sectors of developing countries, reducing the risks of 'systemic failure'. Such assistance can also aim to safeguard the economy 'against excessive volatility and contagion from both domestic and international financial markets' (Kovsted 2000: 333), for example, through improved financial information and analysis and better regulation. One of the more popular forms of support has been to micro-finance institutions that appear to meet donor interests in both stimulating markets and assisting the poor simultaneously.

It is arguable that widening inequality and the stresses and strains of globalization have also contributed to the number of intra-state conflicts in the 1990s. Addison (2000) says:

> How to prevent and end violent conflict, deal with its humanitarian debris, and help countries recover, is now *the* most important set of issues facing the donor countries and their development, foreign policy, and military institutions. (Addison 2000: 392).

Emergency aid

There has been a significant growth in emergency humanitarian assistance in the face of the demands during the 1990s in former Yugoslavia, Bosnia, Rwanda, Ethiopia, Somalia, Sudan, Honduras, Guatemala, Mozambique, Afghanistan, North Korea, Angola, Sri Lanka, East Timor and many more. As Jeffreys (2002:2) shows, emergency humanitarian aid is rarely dispersed according to need, rather it depends on the geo-political interests of donors. While there has also been considerable debate about the extent to which aid may prolong conflict, many aid organizations have made a considerable effort to ensure that the victims of conflict are assisted in ways that avoid fuelling violence through a deeper appreciation of the dynamics of conflict. Apart from the obvious role of aid in assisting refugees and displaced people affected by conflict, aid is being used in the transition to peace and democracy, for example, in supporting peace talks and monitoring peace agreements, the establishment or re-establishment of institutions, macro-economic assistance, the conduct of elections, supporting justice systems – including international criminal tribunals for the former Yugoslavia and Rwanda, (now declining) landmine awareness and clearance, and the restoration of livelihoods in the longer term. The complexities of providing aid in these contexts should not be underestimated, particularly where political instability persists and power shifts constantly at many levels. While this is not a new use of aid, the scale and frequency of such uses is what has changed, and it is likely that, based on the increasing role of the UN in these types of operations, this trend will persist in the future.

The contribution of aid to peace building is but one use of aid as a 'public good'. A global 'public good' may be considered any issue which has trans-boundary benefits, or addresses trans-boundary problems. Among the most obvious are global environmental challenges such as climate change, deforestation, trans-boundary pollution, the spread of disease (especially HIV/AIDS), the drugs trade and people trafficking, and reducing population growth (Kaul 1999). A new motivation for aid involves its use for these purposes which may distract from the poverty-reduction focus.

Already, a significant proportion of development assistance is being spent on these types of activity. For example, the Simons Review of Australian aid in 1997 noted that AusAID had made contributions to support five major international environment conventions; for example, AUD$43 million had been committed to the Global Environment Facility (GEF) alone between 1994–1997. The Review commented that 'around 80 per cent of the projects approved for GEF funding have been in the areas of climate change and biodiversity'. It went on to say that although these were issues of enormous international significance, there was a risk 'that the aid program can end up being diverted from its core purpose by supporting too broad a range of environmental programs and objectives' (Simons 1997: 234). Interestingly, as Hopkins (2000: 436) points out, many of these global public goods initiatives provide some global regulation in the face of market failure and, thus, present an alternative to the neo-liberal paradigm. They also, however, reflect the use of aid for purposes of self-interest to developed countries, such as the sums being spent on slowing or halting the flow of people to developed countries and combating the trade in illicit drugs. Interestingly, the broadened agenda for development assistance may be one of the factors that is leading to political support for some of the increases in aid announced in 2002. There are difficult tensions between maintaining the focus of aid on poverty reduction and building constituencies in the developed countries for reviving flagging aid budgets. The 'global public goods' use of aid is a vehicle for rebuilding constituencies, but it clearly creates the risk of pursuing multiple objectives that cannot all be met.

What future for aid?

After 50 years, what might the future of aid look like? There are several scenarios that might be considered. One thing we need to realize is that the paradigm of development, as first envisaged in the 1950s has changed, and that today the key concept is not 'development' but 'globalization'. And for those who hold the reins of power this means economic globalization according to the neo-liberal agenda. Thus, aid will be seen increasingly within this context.

Bearing this in mind, there are three main possibilities for aid in the future. The first indicates that, since trade and private sector finance is seen as the driver of growth, and growth is still seen erroneously as leading somewhat automatically to development, aid will be of less and less relevance and will decline. The second, sees aid as actively helping to promote the trade liberalization and broader neo-liberal agenda. The third, sees aid being used to address global market failure, which might include the emphasis on global public goods, to address challenges the market cannot accommodate, and the idea of aid as some sort of global welfare for the countries and people who remain excluded by globalization. This would include the increased use of aid as emergency assistance to populations affected by environmental disasters and conflict.

Until the announcements from the USA and EU at the Financing for Development Conference in 2002, the long-term decline of official development assistance seemed the most likely scenario. Development assistance has been on a long-term decline since the 1960s, and despite high levels of public support across the OECD, political commitment to aid has been weak at best. A 1995 UNDP survey of polls found, on average, 79 per cent of those polled in 19 countries supported aid. However, a 1998 AusAID/ACFOA poll also found that, while public support was high, at 84 per cent in favour of foreign aid, the level of confidence in its effectiveness is considerably lower, with only 46 per cent thinking government aid was effective. People believed that aid was only having a small impact on global poverty. These doubts are consistent with polls in other countries that show a high level of scepticism about whether aid actually reaches those in need. The weakness of political will seems related to this scepticism as well as domestic pressures on budgets. Unless development assistance can demonstrate tangible outcomes, the case for its demise is one that politicians under pressure at home will all too easily embrace. Hence, the pressure for aid effectiveness and quality is closely linked to the idea of maintaining an aid program at all.

A second scenario is that aid will continue to be used *to advance the neo-liberal agenda, and increasingly the Western security agenda* further. In particular, the indebtedness of many countries resulting from aid-related loans will continue to provide donors with a means to enforce neo-liberal policies more or less directly. The most recent mechanism is through the Poverty Reduction Strategy Papers which have to meet the approval of the IMF and World Bank before debt relief can be granted. The partnership principles will be sorely challenged if civil society and governments views in the indebted countries conflict with the requirements of the international financial institutions. In Australia a growing part of the aid budget in the Pacific is now dedicated to the Pacific Policy and Management Reform Program, which 'rewards' Pacific nations that adopt governance approaches consistent with liberal democracy and economic liberalism. That programme is now larger than the aid budget to any single nation in the Pacific (AusAID 2001).

Clearly, the use of US aid in the future is designed to meet its security objectives and promote liberal democracies globally. The massive aid already granted to Pakistan post-11 September 2001 sends one signal – that the issue is less about democracy and more about alliances in the war on terror – but the President's statement on US International Strategy in September 2002 indicates that US aid will be intimately connected to its security policy for years to come. In his seven-point plan, designed largely to outline the new security agenda of the US, there is a lengthy exposition of how US aid will be used to 'expand the circle of development by opening societies and building the infrastructure of democracy' (Bush 2002). Noting that 'a world where some live in comfort and plenty, while half of the human race live on less than two dollars a day, is neither just nor stable', Bush's statement goes on to assert that aid is a moral imperative. However, recognizing the failures of ODA in the past, without acknowledging the political reasons contributing to their failure, the US statement goes on to set the agenda for the kind of aid it will provide in future. A Millennium Challenge Account, which provides five billion dollars above existing aid disbursements for specific projects including health and education, will be used to support countries that, among other things, 'encourage economic freedom'. US aid will also be used to 'open societies to commerce and investment' in the belief that trade and investment will drive growth. This is the neo-liberal agenda writ large. At the same time there will be funding for health, education and agricultural development, though the latter emphasizes 'new technologies', which no doubt includes genetically modified crops, a controversial issue in many developing countries. No doubt the incentive of aid and the threat of its withdrawal will be used to help maintain the US 'war on terror' alliance. The importance of economic and democratic liberalism in this will depend on the significance of the recipient nation to the military objectives, as the case of Pakistan has already shown. This approach to aid will only reinforce public scepticism but it will maintain political support for aid.

The third scenario sees aid address aspects of global market failure. This will see the expansion of *aid to address a range of global public goods, so that it better serves the immediate interests of developed countries, while also acting as a sort of global welfare fund.* Thus, the component of aid used to fund programmes dealing with global environment, health, people smuggling and other trans-boundary issues will increase, and the poverty-reduction objective will be further muddied, although still there. One development of this will be the use of aid to secure access to, or control of, scarce natural resources as pressures on soil, land, water and marine life, and forestry resources increase over the next decades. It is likely that the future will see a significant increase in conflict over the control and management of such natural resources. There will remain some focus on poverty-reduction objectives, but increasingly countries with policies less acceptable to donors will lose any long-term development assistance, and will only find themselves in receipt of assistance for emergencies and for humanitarian goals, mostly through local NGOs. This approach is likely to maintain public support for aid more than any other.

In reality, aid policies and programmes are likely to combine some elements of current trends and all three strategies, with different emphases in different countries according to their position in the global context. Donors will vary in emphasis and the strategies applied to different aid-receiving countries will also vary according to geo-political factors, their engagement with or marginalization from global trade, and their adherence to neo-liberal economic frameworks. As the world heads towards 2015 the NGO community will no doubt keep the pressure on to see the International Development Targets met, and while this can provide an opportunity to press for quality and accountability for outcomes for the poor, it is also likely to lead to a more vigorous debate about the other conditions necessary beyond aid if these targets are to be achieved. The challenge to the dominant model of globalization has yet to gain strength.

Chapter 4

Globalization and Development

DAMIEN KINGSBURY

There is much to separate and distinguish developing countries, and each needs to be understood in its own context. However, there is also much that developing countries share in common, in terms of their internal structures and conditions, and their relations with and links to the rest of the world. In a significant part, where developing countries do experience internal conditions in common, this is a consequence of their external relations, and the increasing standardization or homegenization of those relations. In particular, how development has been defined, the methods of achieving development and the conditionalities that have been applied to developing countries have all reflected an increasingly standardized global agenda. Even the material and cultural aspirations of many in developing countries have increasingly come to reflect a more global set of influences, as have the means by which culture is dispersed. While particularities remain local, the shared and imposed circumstances of development reflect an increasing tendency towards the global.

Amongst the commonalities between developing countries is that most people are living in poverty, with many living in absolute poverty. Most developing countries are also overwhelmingly net exporters of one or two, usually unprocessed, primary goods, and net importers of manufactured goods, especially technical and electronic goods. Where developing countries do export manufactured goods, they are often textiles, clothing and footwear, or of simple construction, older technology, or already partially processed manufactures.

Where people in such country have a job, or some means of income, there is a good chance they will have a small, portable transistor radio, which plays music based on a popular US format. If these people live in or visit a big city, they might pass by an American-style fast food outlet, where the cost of a meal is as much as most people would be lucky to earn in a day, or, in some cases, in a week. However, the customers of this fast food outlet, who probably arrived by a fairly new Japanese or Korean car, may be wearing brand-name sports shoes and jeans, and drinking an American-brand soft drink with their fashionable treat.

The government of this country would probably hold elections and thus claims to reflect the common aspirational political standard of 'democracy', although irregularities could be common and patron–client relations remain an important source of political power, in large part due to the relatively recent adoption of a representative voting system. The government would also most likely be a recipient of an IMF structural adjustment package as a consequence of earlier, poorly invested or squandered loans for infrastructure projects. However, to qualify for this further loan, the government will have had to significantly cut its public service, including funding for schools and teachers, and public clinics and hospitals and their staff.

It will also have reduced tariffs on imported goods, but will have found that prices for its export commodities have fallen by around half, in real terms, over the past two decades, placing further pressure on government revenues. Competing against subsidized commodities, especially food and other agricultural products, in developed country markets has disadvantaged exports. If the gap in income between rich and poor in this country was not getting any greater (and it would have already been significant), there is a fair chance that it was not reducing much either. These are just some of the possible, and probable, circumstances for a person in a developing country in the era of globalization.

The issue of development, almost by definition, is a global one and has, as a consequence, been defined in global terms. From the formulation of development models to the provision of aid, loans and other funds to multilateral, bilateral and NGO aid projects, the response to issues raised by the development question has been one defined in global terms. This has been, in some cases, quite appropriate, and in others not. Similarly, the impositions and advantages of global economic integration and linkages, including through banks and other financial institutions, foreign multi-nationals and foreign investment, and other aspects of global integration, such as communication and culture, have impacted on almost all developing countries in one form or another. This has left many developing countries facing what has become a 'cookie-cutter' or 'off-the-shelf' format for future development. One size, or policy programme, is suggested to fit all, especially by the international agencies that are so often the arbiters of 'correct' policies.

While many of the issues facing developing countries are similar, the particular circumstances for each country vary, often even within a single country. Similarly, with a process of global integration occurring at a state level, local communities have increasingly looked to themselves, their context, their past and their cultural markers as a means of defining or preserving local identity in the face of a potentially homogenizing world. So too have some governments asserted a local particularism, although in the field of politics this has most often been by way of denying local political aspirations. Unfortunately, the use, and abuse, of power has a universal quality that transcends local particularity. In terms of local context, the pressures that arise, for example, in a tropical country with high rainfall and relatively high soil fertility will be quite different to those of a semi-arid or arid country, mountainous territory will have different requirements to flat ground, industrialization raises different issues to agriculture, a literate work force will have different capabilities and expectations to an illiterate one, and so on. Beyond countries, there are in some cases also issues that correspond to groups of countries within a particular region, for example in trade policy (e.g., ASEAN). And there are, of course, wider challenges and changes to communities at all levels brought about by various aspects of the process of global integration.

The meaning of globalization

Of the thousands of texts that have been written on 'globalization' in recent years, most have their own definition, not all of which agree. However, the broadly prevailing (but also most generalized) view of globalization is that it is a proposed or actual situation where there is a process or series of linked processes that lead towards greater interaction or integration. The primary context for both the process and the outcome is economic, being manifested as an increasingly integrated or inter-dependent global market. Stiglitz (2003) posits globalization as the closer integration of the countries and peoples of the world which, in turn, has derived from the reduction in costs of transportation and communication and the breaking down of barriers to the flow of goods, services and capital across borders.

Kearny's survey of globalization (2001) opted for economic criteria accounting for 90 per cent of the globalization phenomenon, allocating the difference to political, cultural and environmental criteria. Such an integrated market is understood to operate on the principle of *laissez-faire* capitalism, in which barriers between states, such as tariffs, no longer exist and in which local economic unities (such as local regions or states) compete on the basis of comparative advantage. Comparative advantage might be, for instance, a specialization in a particular form of production, or it could be what a country does best or, in some cases, at all. For many developing countries, their 'comparative advantage' is low wage rates, which is simply selling down the cost of labour as the lowest common economic denominator. In principle, economic globalization could also be met through the standardization of central economic planning (the model employed under 'communism'), although this was never achieved in practice. That is because the contemporary global economic condition in which there is a tendency towards integration was made possible, in practical terms, by the collapse of such centrally planned economies ('international communism'), and the claimed failure of state interventionist or Keynesian economic policies in otherwise capitalist societies (despite the success of state interventionist capitalist societies such as Singapore).

However, many proponents and critics of economic globalization also argue that the world remains a long way from an idealized free-trade model. Some even suggest that pro-free traders are less interested in free trade, as such, but rather the untrammelled pursuit of profit, which can be achieved by free trade where that suits, but by government intervention or protection where that suits. Critics of globalization argue that the notion of free trade based on comparative advantage works primarily to the benefit of industrialised countries that can take advantage of cheap labour and goods produced in developing countries. Where free trade does not deliver such advantages to developed countries, they employ protectionist policies to support globally non-viable but domestically politically important industries (legislated United States farm subsidies of US$270 billion between 2002 and 2012 being a prime case in point). That is to say, what has been happening has been less economic globalization, which implies a degree of equal access, than it has been an internationalization of capitalism, which does not imply such an equality of access (Beck 2000: 199–200). Even the IMF has recognized that economic globalization has not been an unmitigated success, stating that: 'a large part of the world's population – especially in sub-Saharan Africa – has been left behind by economic progress. As a result, the disparities between the world's richest and poorest countries are now wider than ever, with increasing incidences of poverty within countries' (IMF 2002: 1).

While the economic definition of globalization is probably the most important, because it impacts directly on how people live, other interpretations of globalism include a more generalized interdependence, the collapse of time/space, communications, culture, political institutions, global institutions, and levels of global intervention. Many also identify the collapse of effective distance, at least for the some, via improvements in transportation and communication, as critical aspects of globalization (see, for example, Robins 2000, Thompson 2000, Herman and McChesney 2000, Tehranian 1999, Giddens 1991, 1995, Lubbers and Koorevaar 1999, 1998, Lubbers 1996). Tehranian, in particular, notes that communication is the defining quality of the post-industrial age and that it is as a consequence of enhanced communications that globalization has been able to both occur and to occur in particular ways. Conversely, it has also been the globalization of communication that has allowed for a global response to globalization – a social globalization aimed at limiting the free reign of unfettered economic globalization (Florini 2000: 1923). Gurtov

(1994: 6–11) suggests that interdependence generally is the defining characteristic of globalization, and sees that occurring in both positive and negative ways, citing previously local types of issues arising across international boundaries, including responses to investment and ownership, voluntarist aid programmes, legal disputation, terrorism, and so on. Globalism, therefore, can, in many respects, also imply a cross-pollination of influences, or a tendency towards a common point. This can apply to economics, but equally as to politics and socio-cultural matters.

One controversial and much discussed, but poorly documented, aspect of globalization has been its impact on cultures, and the capacity for the preservation of tradition and custom. The symbols of globalization, such as television and generic clothing (image and self-image) and the elite culture of consumerism, have become commonplace if not universal, while the impact of material aspiration has entered almost every corner of the globe. For many, the 'protection' of cultures is critical, and, in cases where there is an unthinking onslaught, the gradual acclimatization to external influences is often preferable to complete social dislocation. However, the preservation of culture assumes that it is, or can be static, and preserving the particular in the face of the encroaching universal is a fraught process and one not guaranteed to succeed. There is in this, though, an assumption that what amounts to culture is inviolable or somehow static. There are numerous examples of traditional patterns of behaviour being not only at odds with increasingly globalized norms of behaviour, but with members of their own community. Cultures that have customs that oppress women are far from universally freely endorsed by those women, while cultures that imply economic or political repression or subjugation may have a long history but are not always universally subscribed to. And then there is the notion that even in an increasingly homogenized world there is or can be a uniformity of culture or of cultural responses, and that material conditions, environment, and history will all continue to contribute to shaping a range of world views.

In all of this, there is the equation submitted by Amartya Sen that the purpose of development should define its application, and (in a slightly less utilitarian but more complex way) he defines development as being a process intended to achieve the greatest amount of happiness among the greatest number of people. This happiness, he says, comes from freedoms to do and achieve things, and freedom from negatives, such as hunger, illiteracy and oppression. Sen's version of development too represents a type of globalization, but a positive type with which most anti-globalization critics would feel fairly comfortable.

The IMF goes so far as to say that globalization is not about economics so much is it is a 'political choice in favour of international economic integration, which for the most part goes hand in hand with the consolidation of democracy' (IMF 2002: 1). The assumption here is that countries exercise 'choice' in liberalizing their economies, and that as they do so they will also liberalize their political institutions. The causal logic implied here is that economic liberalization will lead to economic growth, which will, in turn, lead to the development of an educated middle class which will, in turn, press for greater democratization. While there have been some instances of economic 'choice' and of political liberalization that agree with this proposition, there have also been many more examples of states that have liberalized their economies through coercion, and often while maintaining authoritarian political structures. Capitalism has been shown to be a prerequisite for democracy, but democracy has not been a prerequisite for capitalism.

One way in which development and globalization fit neatly together has been in the development paradigm that 'development' equals economic growth, which, in turn, implied industrialization. The standard development model implied a standardized development outcome. This has been shown to be far from the case, consequently raising questions about the evenness and depth of the globalization process, and the influence of local conditions. In these senses, development can be understood as comprising economic, political and cultural elements, all of which engage in a wider world and all of which are in some ways ultimately transformed by it.

Related to the idea of the globalization of ideas, but with less of a structural linkage than between economic and political development, is what Beck calls a 'cosmopolitan democracy', or the establishment of 'cosmopolitan rights for all' (Beck 2000: 93). Beck notes that rights, as such, are best protected for those who enjoy them when they are enjoyed by all. However, as Beck also notes, assuming a 'realist' international relations theory position (in which states achieve beneficial outcomes primarily through the capacity to impose their will), the paradox in such 'cosmopolitanism' is that rights are only guaranteed by states in what is still largely an anarchic world order, and that guaranteeing rights beyond states implies global governance which, to date, does not exist. There is, however, a view of what constitutes 'universal' human rights that is normatively applicable regardless of circumstances. The UN Declaration of Human Rights is one such vehicle for the expression of such values, while global organizations such as Amnesty International and a number of transnational NGOs also promote a universalist agenda. As Pettman notes, human rights are a general moral claim to matters of fundamental interest (Pettman 1979: 76) and, as such, apply to the condition of being human, rather than to being the citizen of a particular state. Similarly, the idea of 'democracy' has become increasingly universalized, if only in rhetoric (see Chapter 7). However, while normative terms are prone to being over-used and reduced in meaning, their acceptance as representing a set of ideas around which codes of behaviour are supposed to cohere in turn, at least to some extent, represents a global agreement. So too is there global acceptance, it could be argued, of the idea that within each polity there is, or should be, a type of social contract to ensure that states and their elites function more or less in the interests of all citizens and in which citizens agree to work more or less co-operatively to the larger benefit (and where states and elites fail to function as such they are recognized as being dysfunctional or malignant). The problem, of course, is that the normative quality and practical application of such 'agreement' is largely defined by each country's elites, often to their own benefit, and the capacity of the global community to formally enforce such norms, through a conventional monopoly of violence, does not functionally exist. Where the 'global community' does enforce sets of 'norms', they are more often interpreted and enforced by a small number of key states (e.g. the US), and too often appear to reflect at least some of the fundamental interests of those states rather than a larger global norm (e.g. the Persian Gulf War of 1991). Such states can and do argue that the interests they represent are global, and they might actually believe this. However, the unilateral character of such representation of global interest necessarily implies a particular perspective, and that perspective may not be, and often is not, universally shared.

In response to what is perceived as unilateralism, another phenomenon that can be and sometimes is global in its reach and aspirations is 'terrorism' (that is, acts of attempted political persuasion by the use of terror), which has been highlighted in the period since 11 September 2001. It is overstating the situation to suggest that terrorism literally reaches into homes across the globe, and in significant part the impact of terrorism, as it has manifested in North American, South-East Asia and Africa, has come from the global reach of the news media. However, in the post-Cold War era, via the news media, terrorism has reached into homes across the globe in a symbolic sense, and its targets have been manifestations of developed global identity (embassies of the primary global power, the World Trade Centre, foreigners' night club, foreigners' hotel). Because of the somewhat diffuse and seemingly unconnected nature of its targets, the geographic breadth of its reach, and its global aspirations, terrorism in the early 21st century has increasingly become portrayed as the primary transglobal threat (USDS 2002).

Key globalization organizations

Globalization is represented by two broad tendencies, one of which is increasingly pervasive, sometimes recognized by its symbols, but which is otherwise not easy to pin down. Of this tendency, the global reach of

American-styled popular music and English-language films, associated Western styles of clothing, and the generic use of English (particularly its popular terminology) stand out, although shifting across to a more specifically identified arena are global brand names, such as Coca-Cola, McDonald's, and Nike (or Pepsi, KFC, and Adidas). Such branding, however, starts to imply not just familiar signification, but also global corporate reach, such readily identifiable names of which include Exxon-Mobil, Microsoft, and General Motors (or Royal Dutch/Shell, IBM and Ford). Less readily, to most people, are 'faceless' organizations such as Citigroup, Itochu, and Axa, or mining companies such as Rio Tinto or AngloAmerican. These are typical of the world's largest trans-national corporations. But it is global 'public' institutions that perhaps most fully carry the standard of globalization. Such institutions in some ways fulfil the types of functions found under the governments of sovereign states, yet there is no global government for them to answer to. In this way, these organizations are sometimes perceived as being a law unto themselves, running a global agenda, but on behalf of unstated interests.

These are organizations that represent what could be called 'global interest', or which are explicitly in favour of globalization. These organizations have come to be publicly identified with globalization, and to some extent with the juggernaut quality that globalization represents to many people. Most influential among these organizations are the World Trade Organization (WTO), the International Monetary Fund (IMF), the World Bank (WB) and the United Nations (UN). The first three are targeted at various aspects of economic development within the context of a global economy. The UN and its numerous agencies tend to focus more on the political, humanitarian and social aspects of global development.

The WTO is the world's main international organization to promote order and co-operation in world trade, and, as such, is the world's dominant pro-globalization multilateral organization (see Supachai 2002). The WTO was created out of the 125 member state Uruguay Round of the General Agreement on Tariffs and Trade (GATT) negotiations in 1995. The primary difference between the WTO and the GATT is that the WTO is a permanent organization with judicial power to rule on international trade disputes, whereas GATT was based on a series of meetings, or 'rounds', without permanent status and with no judicial power. The WTO also covers services, while the GATT included only trade. However, like the GATT, the focus of the WTO includes tariffs, and non-tariff barriers to trade, natural resource products, textiles and clothing, agricultural and tropical produce, other articles covered under the GATT system, anti-dumping regulations, subsidies, intellectual property, dispute settlement, and services. According to the WTO, its purpose is to achieve by consensus 'legal ground rules for international commerce' that are then ratified by member state legislatures to increase the flow of trade (WTO 2002a). The WTO has a rule-making and dispute settlement function that is, in effect, legally binding on member states and which has been strengthening since the WTO's inception (see Gagne 2000).

Of particular relevance within the context of development, the WTO represents a large proportion of developing countries, with three-quarters of its membership self-defined as developing, less developed (LDC), or least developed (LLDC). In principle, special provisions for developing, less-developed and least-developed countries are put into all WTO agreements, including 'longer time periods to implement agreements and commitments, measures to increase their trading opportunities and support to help them build the infrastructure for WTO work, handle disputes, and implement technical standards' (WTO 2002b). According to UNCTAD, the 49 least developed countries are identified by the UN as such in terms of low GDP per capita, weak human assets, and a high degree of economic vulnerability. (UNCTAD 2002) At the time of writing, the key definition for least-developed country was based on a daily per capita income level (even though this said nothing about median per capita GDP, which is a more accurate assessment of how most people in a given country actually live). However UNCTAD had not yet determined whether the level for determining LLDC status would be at per capita US$1 or US$2 a day (the latter criterion potentially including a very much larger number of developing countries than the former), and did not base it calculation on purchasing parity power (PPP) (the relative capacity for a denominated unit of currency to purchase a set good in a particular environment). The definition for what constituted LLDC was also determined by restrictions on trade capacity or opportunity, and other related criteria. But even if a WTO member announces that it is a developing country, this does not automatically mean that it will benefit from the unilateral developing country preference schemes, such as the Generalized System of Preferences (GSP): 'in practice, it is the preference giving country which decides the list of developing countries that will benefit from the preferences' (WTO 2002b). More importantly, since the formation of the WTO, none of the countries that were members of GATT that have negotiated accession have been allowed to use the transitional periods set out in the WTO Agreement. It is also worth noting that under GATT, tariffs were primarily reduced between developed countries, which also benefited from a subsequent increase in trade. In this, many developing countries were left further outside the global trading environment (Martin and Schuman 1997: 108–114). As a minor concession under the WTO, however, developing countries were eligible to benefit from technical assistance provided by the WTO Secretariat and WTO Members.

Perhaps less identified as a globalizing institution than the WTO, the IMF has been at least as pervasive in reshaping the global macroeconomic climate, and, in particular, in bringing to heel many states that have otherwise been reluctant to accept the full and far-reaching effects of access to globalization via economic deregulation. The main impact of such deregulation has been in the the flow of global finance, which leapt from $17.5 trillion in 1979 to over $3000 trillion by the end of the 20th century (Held *et al.* 1999: 208–9, see other references in this collection) and which dominates all other forms of global capitalism, including stock markets and the like. The IMF was established in 1946 as a part of the Bretton Woods Agreement of post-war reconstruction, to promote international co-operation on finance, encourage stability in exchange rates and orderly systems for exchanging money between countries, and to provide temporary assistance for countries suffering balance of payments problems. Especially since the late 1970s, the IMF has played an active role in lending money to redress balance of payments problems caused by previous bad loans. In doing so, through what it calls 'structural adjustment programs' (SAPs) the IMF has commonly imposed free-market 'reforms' on countries that have requested loans. SAPs commonly consist of raising interest rates to reduce domestic consumption and to attract foreign capital, reducing tariffs and non-tariff barriers to trade, reducing commercial taxation rates, establishing 'free-trade' (non-taxable) zones for foreign investment, and cutting government spending, most commonly in administration, education and health. Like the WTO, the IMF believes that world prosperity is enhanced by greater exchange between nations, and these policies are intended to facilitate the integration of developing economies into the global market.

Also established under the Bretton Woods Agreement is the IMF's sibling organization, the World Bank (WB), which is, in effect, a global development bank, or a multilateral bank that provides long-term (and lower interest) loans primarily for major infrastructure projects, such as water and sanitation, natural resource management, energy supply and so on. Increasingly, in practice, the WB also helps to restructure broad economies, through what it calls 'adjustment projects', which support governments undertaking policy reforms, such as improved public sector management. Because of its policy of providing 'soft loans' primarily for development projects, the WB does not attract the criticism that is sometimes directed at the harder-focused IMF. However, being derived from the Bretton Woods Agreement of 1944 for post-war reconstruction and to stabilise global currencies, the ideological orientation of the WB and the IMF is closer than even their sometimes overlapping functions, and the WB also uses its economic leverage, notably through the 'Integrated

Framework' for 'trade capacity building', to encourage borrowing countries to adopt free trade or pro-economic globalization policies.

While the WTO, IMF and WB are 'inclusive' economic global organizations, not all 'global' institutions are as nominally inviting. The Organization for Economic Cooperation and Development (OECD) is comprised of 29 members that are exclusively developed or industrialised countries, including in North America, Western Europe (including Czech Republic, Hungary and Poland) and Japan, South Korea, Australia and New Zealand. While it claims to support a broad and socially equitable agenda, including governance, development and sustainability (such terms having widely interpretable meaning), the OECD's main function is to provide economic arguments for globalization, such as data demonstrating the positive contribution made by multinational corporations to economic development. In that it includes countries from around the world, but does not include non-industrialised states in its membership, the OECD's perspective tends to be driven by the rather narrowly defined economic interests of global capitalism that, as noted, have been claimed to lead to structural global imbalances.

While the WTO, IMF, WB and OECD are primarily orientated towards achieving global economic outcomes, the other major global institution is the United Nations. The purpose of the UN is to promote and maintain international peace and security through friendly relations and dispute resolution, and to support human rights (UN 1945). In a large part, this role came out of a global desire to promote peace and international harmony following the catastrophe of the Second World War. The globalizing aspect of the UN derives from its requirement that its 191 member countries commit to being good global citizens, abide by UN agreements and conventions, and support its various agencies. UN agencies include the Security Council, the Economic and Social Council, the Trusteeship Council, the International Court of Justice, and offices including the High Commissioner for Refugees (UNHCR), Conference on Trade and Development (UNCTAD), the UN Children's Fund (UNICEF) and the UN Development Program (UNDP). The UN is also linked to the IMF, WB, World Health Organization and similar inter-governmental organizations through co-operative agreements. The United Nations recognizes that broader global responsibility requires international institutions, as well as supporting the case for reform of international institutions, including its own Security Council, to make them more representative. Related to the above, the UN has sponsored a Global Compact to establish and promote a shared set of core values regarding labour standards, human rights and the environment. In this sense, the UN is as close to a global government as exists, although the fact that its agreements and conventions largely rely on the co-operation of member countries means that it has very little scope for enforcing its decisions and they are, consequently, frequently observed in the breech.

New or old?

The public idea of globalization has gained currency since the 1980s and in particular from the 1990s, following the end of the Cold War and the subsequent opening up of global markets. However, the term itself was first coined in the 1960s, following the rise of trans-national corporations. A number of theorists even argue that it began with the first circumnavigation of the globe in 1519–1522 (despite that set of linked voyages being a rather tenuous venture), or that the 'world system' (i.e. globalization) goes back some 5000 years (see Frank and Gills 1992). Global exploration proceeded quickly and by the end of the 19th century global trade and investment, as a proportion of global capital, was at a record high. At the same time, those few parts of the world not already colonized were becoming so. This event, or series of events, not only integrated virtually all parts of the world into common administrative groupings, it also reorganized much of the economic activity in the colonies towards providing unprocessed or semi-processed goods for European and North American markets. In this respect, the colonies were linked to what were to become the developed countries in ways that implied their structural economic subservience, and which set many of the opportunities or lack thereof that came to define the newly independent states in the post-colonial era.

The First World War brought global economic expansion to a halt, and, although it continued again in the 1920s, it was severely buffeted by the Great Depression of the 1930s. However, during this time there were also increasing global standards applied to measurements of weights, distance, time, and space. The post-Second-World-War period saw the emancipation of virtually all of the world's colonies and marked an era of both greater global interaction and greater global competition, not least between two great rival ideologies; capitalism and economic central planning (generally, although inaccurately, described as 'communism' or 'Marxism'). The 'long boom' from the early 1950s until the mid-1970s, saw consumer-driven global capitalism develop at a functionally unprecedented rate. This paralleled the struggle of most post-colonial states to become economically functional within the increasingly globalized system (as discussed in other chapters).

Other aspects of globalization from this time included major improvements in global communications, especially through telephone and satellite technology and an increasing level of international air travel, which speeded up communications and enhanced both international business and the global spread of ideas. The aforementioned collapse of economic central planning (signified most clearly by the tearing down of the Berlin Wall and the end of the Soviet Union), the advent of computerization and the related introduction of the internet, shifted global communication, and hence global business, to another plane, seemingly to 'shrink' the world, at least for the lucky billion or so who live in developed countries, or who comprise the elite in developing countries. Notably, the flows of trade and finance that have ensued are now at unprecedented levels (see further discussion of this in Chapter 6), and this alone is argued to be a, and perhaps the, defining characteristic of globalization. And along with unprecedented production, trade and integration, so too have the by-products of such development become global (see Chapter 11). For most, however, globalization has not meant greater access to global resources, but being buffeted by material circumstances that are often the consequence of decisions taken by otherwise unconnected people on the other side of the globe. And for many who do have access to that most pervasive medium of global communication – television – the global messages are overwhelmingly trite and often culturally and spiritually corrosive.

While there is no doubt that globalization exists as an idea, there are varying perspectives on what globalization actually means, or to the extent of its pervasiveness. These views could be broadly categorized as according to hyperglobalists, sceptics, and transformationalists.

Hyperglobalists

Hyperglobalists are broadly that group that could be called the 'boosters' of globalization; those whose theoretical arguments give legitimacy to others who act often in their own interests. The hyperglobalists, exemplified by Kenichi Ohmae, regard the world as dominated by transnational corporations that in an unregulated environment are the source of efficiency and unstoppable progress and vehicles for the creation and dispersal of wealth on a global scale (at least to those countries that embrace such globalization). Within this, the capacity for states to erect barriers to global trade has reduced their legitimacy in such a global environment (Ohmae 1996, 1995, 1991) This view of globalization posits it as the ultimate expression of modernism (which one development paradigm held as synonymous with development) and as the logical endpoint for human development.

The hyperglobalist position argues that globalization is a fact, and that it is and should be unstoppable. The primary statistic to support the hyperglobalist case that the world is indeed economically integrating, and at a vastly increased rate, is the turnover of foreign exchange, which increased by 10 times between 1979 and 1997 relative to global GDP (Guellen 2001: 6). Hyperglobalists argue that economic globalization is in everyone's benefit, often in the near to middle term. Proponents of this position cite evidence to support the assertion that inequalities in global income and poverty are decreasing, claiming that this is a consequence of states complying with the largely free-market requirements of economic globalization (Ben-David *et al.* 2000). The World Bank, for examples, argues that where poorer countries have lowered their tariff barriers they have increased employment through shifting industry towards export-orientated markets, which generally earn more that industries that compete for local markets. The World Bank cites the example of China's engagement with global trade, and its growth in income from $1460 per capita in 1980 to $4120 in 1999. Or to look at it another way, in 1980 American citizens earned 12.5 times as much as Chinese, but by 1999 the difference was only 7.4 times (though this still represents a strong advantage). The World Bank also claims that income disparity is decreasing in Asia and Latin America (although this was before various financial crises beset some Asian and Latin American states). In such circumstances, if incomes are lower that tends to reflect lower education and productivity standards, although as capital accumulates there is a capital shift towards more capital- and knowledge-intensive industry that generates high income. Where poverty has increased, this has reflected a failure to integrate into the global economy (World Bank 2002a, 2002b).

Indeed, in many countries, notably in East Asia but also in some cases in Latin America, per capita GDP has increased relative to the United States (WB-GNI 2002) However, in many cases this is a consequence of a complex array of factors, including history, proximity or access to natural resources and markets, industrial predisposition, and prior industrialization or infrastructure development. Further, such statistical information is not based on the exchange rate between currencies, i.e., it is not denominated in single currency (such as US dollar) terms. Rather, such analysis is based on the parity purchasing power (PPP) of particular currencies within their own countries, and there are numerous arguments to suggest that, while PPP gives a better indication of real income value, it does not provide an overall, especially macro-economic, picture (nor does it distinguish between lower cost local products and higher cost, often higher technology, imports).

While the hyperglobalization group argues that globalization does not make the world more economically unequal (see Lindert and Williamson 2002), there is not absolute agreement on this point. Duncan suggests that globalization may indeed increase economic inequality in some countries, notably through the economic 'shocks' this can induce. But he suggests that this can still be overcome through 'risk management' and other internal structural adjustments. And he still says that poverty is rising in countries that do not open themselves to globalization (Duncan 2000). Similarly, the UNDP generally favours the advantages of globalization, but note that it also has 'negative, disruptive, marginalizing aspects' (UNHDR 1999: 1).

Sceptics

The sceptics' position on globalization is generally that if it does exist, it has been overstated, that it is not especially new, and the effects on world trade are primarily amongst the developed economies of North America, Western Europe and Japan. This, sceptics say, represents and increase in economic internationalization, but not in economic globalization; that domestic investment remains greater than foreign investment, that the volume of trade is small relative to the size of trading economies, that most companies locate most of their staff in their home countries and that large areas of the world are little touched by such internationalization or globalization (Hirst and Thompson 1996, Wade 1996: 66–84). Such sceptics also note that, far from becoming an anachronism in a 'borderless' world, the state is stronger that in any previous period (a view that found renewed impetus from the unilateral 'realism' of the US post-11 September 2001). Not only is the state stronger or more unilateral, at least in some cases, sceptics claim, but there has also been a significant rise in the number of independent states over the primary period of contemporary globalization, from 159 UN members in 1990 to 191 by 2002 (UN 2002), with numerous more attempting to assert independent state status.

However, while the state is still understood as the primary manifestation of collective political will, the increase in the number of states in a significant part reflects the failure of pre-existing states, and the consequent assertion of a more local political identity. Moreover, most of the states that have come into being in that period were beholden to multilateral organizations for their political or economic survival, and were in that sense more a product of globalization than a reaction to it. Finally, the increase in the quantity of states did not imply a qualitative assertion, and while there were more states the capacity of states to exercise independent authority in the realm of macro-economic policy had diminished significantly over this period. There were, however, exceptions to these macro-economic 'rules'.

The Prime Minister of Malaysia, Mahathir Mohamad, has been one of the more successful critics of globalization, rejecting IMF intervention and policies in Malaysia following the 1997 South-East Asian economic crisis and instituting monetary and financial controls which saw Malaysia recover from the crisis more quickly and thoroughly than its neighbours. Since then, Mahathir has continued to accept capitalism and foreign investment, while lambasting the *laissez-faire* aspects of globalization, arguing that the 'one size fits all' policies pursued by the WTO, IMF and WB 'tend to favor the agenda of richer countries that dominate them' and 'hinder the ability of the individual country to choose the set of policies that suits its own development needs'. In particular, Mahathir has espoused the 'selective' acceptance of globalisaton, in particular the timing, manner and extent to which a country participates in globalization. He also argued for the selective protection of strategic industries 'for the good of the country'. To that end, a country must retain a decisive and independent political leadership (Mahathir 2002).

Positioned at the further end of the sceptics scale are those oppositionist groups that not only doubt the claims for globalization, but which regard it as being actively negative. The broad view represented by such groups claims that rather than globalization leading to a reduction in income inequality, it actually increases such inequality, through the failure of the global 'trickle down' effect (in which the spending of the rich contributes to the wealth of the poor) to adequately 'trickle down'. In particular, they often cite the UNDP 1999 Human Development Report, which notes that over the decade to 1999 the number of people earning $1 or less a day had remained static at 1.2 billion, while the number of people earning less than $2 a day had increased from just over 2.5 billion to 2.8 billion. Further, the report noted that the gap in global income between the world's richest 20 per cent and the world's poorest 20 per cent have increased from 30:1 in 1960 to 82:1 by 1995. While there were net global improvements in some areas, such as the reduction of infant mortality, this could not be attributed to globalization as such. A range of other indicators did, however, show that the world's poorest countries largely remained exceptionally poor, and in many cases were slipping by comparison with developed countries (UNHDR 1999: Ch 1).

Further, the poorest 20 per cent of the world's population enjoyed just 1 per cent of global GDP, global export markets, foreign direct investment (FDI) and the world's telephone lines. The world's richest 20 per cent, by comparison, enjoyed 86 per cent of global GDP, 82 per cent of the world's export markets, 68 per cent of FDI and 74 per cent of the world's telephone lines. According to Oxfam:

> The world's 48 poorest countries have seen their share of world trade decline by more than 40 per cent since 1980 to a mere 0.4 per cent. ...
> The agriculture and textiles sectors, in which poor countries are most

competitive, remain subject to a prohibitive array of high and escalating tariffs, quotas, and seasonal restrictions. (Oxfam 2002, see also Kamal-Chaoui 2000)

Another way of looking at it was that the world's richest 1 per cent earned as much as the world poorest 57 per cent (Elliott and Denny 2002).

Like Oxfam, organizations such as The South Centre and the Group of 77 (developing country groups) are critical of the IMF and the WB for failing to live up to their rhetoric on poverty alleviation and, though structural adjustment policies, in many cases exacerbating poverty. Such organizations also call for developing country debt to be cancelled, particularly where such debt is low in absolute terms but also unsustainable. They are also critical of the WTO for promoting policies that encourage trade at the expense of developing countries (South Centre 1998, G77 2002).

Depending on the method of analysis, most of the critiques of capitalist globalization could be understood as variations on a left-liberal political agenda. That is, such critiques tend to posit equity before capital accumulation and the supremacy of the social and political over the economic. In particular, there is a wholesale rejection of the idea that markets should function without accountability beyond 'market forces'. As a consequence, this coalescing of groups around such core ideas has resulted in a competing form of globalization, in which networks of groups, organizations and even countries combine to pressure or protest against economic globalization's otherwise seemingly unstoppable march. A key network in the anti-economic globalization debate is the World Social Forum (WSF), the explicit leftist orientation of which looks towards rebuilding leftist politics through a loose alignment of like-minded organizations within a globalized context. While the WSF is a global organization, it was founded in Brazil and its orientation has remained with the world's poorer countries. In this, it 'stand[s] in opposition to a process of globalization commanded by the large multinational corporations and by the governments and international institutions at the service of those corporations' interests, with the complicity of national governments' (WSF 2002: pt 4). Various (mostly quite small) left-wing political parties around the world have constructed generally similar Marxian critiques of economic globalization, seeing it as essentially the global spread of capitalism in which the global poor are exploited by the global rich, while a number of organizations have arisen specifically in response to economic globalization, notably around specific meetings of the WTO (e.g., Seattle 1999, Genoa 1998).

Following from, and in some aspects related to, the 'sceptics' position, within the critique of globalization there is also a significant environmental debate, which is critical of globalization's pursuit of profit at the expense of the natural environment, and the exploitation of developing countries' often lax environmental regulations. This follows on from globalization's lack of commitment to or exploitation of the local, in which neither foreigners nor elites are directly subject to the consequences of local environmental degradation. Organizations such as Friends of the Earth, Greenpeace, the World Wildlife Fund and others are all critical of the environmental record of global capitalism, notably over global warming, deforestation and the depletion of other non-renewable natural resources, and the production and inappropriate disposal of harmful bi-products.

Friends of the Earth, for instance, have constructed a 'WTO environmental scorecard', which identifies WTO decisions that have had a direct negative environmental outcome, notably on 'dirty' petroleum products in Venezuala, overturning European preferences for Caribbean (low pesticide) bananas, overturning a European ban on hormone-treated beef, and against a US ban on shrimp fishing that harmed turtles and other sealife (FOE 2002). Greenpeace similarly notes that trade liberalization has been undertaken without an environmental impact assessment, that it has not introduced environmental precautionary measures, and has side-stepped responsibility on international environmental law such as the Kyoto Protocol on Climate Change (Greenpeace 2001). Many such organizations argue that there needs to be trade sanctions to enforce environmental goals. Interestingly, these organizations are themselves global, although representing very much an alternative vision to the conventional global free-trade developmentalist model.

Transformationalists

Within the globalization debate, there is a group that has been identified as 'transformationalists', which in some areas intersect with the sceptics' position, and which sees globalization as a part of a historical process of multiple transformations. These transformations vary from place to place and time to time, in terms of extent and intensity of change, and the speed and impact of such change (Held *et al.* 1999). In some senses, the transformationalist understanding of globalization corresponds to the debate between modernism and post-modernism, the former equating with hyperglobalization, and the latter with a transformationalist under-standing. In particular, the plural quality of the transformationalists' understanding, emphasizing difference, inconsistency and diffuse centres of power, contrasting with the actual or claimed singularity of hyperglobalization. Giddens has argued, for instance, that the process of globalization has been uneven, and while it co-ordinates it also aids the process of inter-state fragmentation, with states proceeding in less a uniform direction than displaying opposed or competing tendencies (Giddens 1990: 64, 175). In a not unrelated manner, many observers note that globalization is less 'global' than it is regional, being reflected not only in increased trade and investment between OECD countries but also through the development of trading blocs or groupa, such as the North America Free Trade Agreement, the European Union, the Association of South-East Asian Nations, the Southern Common Market (Latin America), West African Economic and Monetary Union, the Asia-Pacific Economic Cooperation forum, and others.

Others, meanwhile, have argued that the process of globalization has produced a complex series of inconsistently related outcomes that serve to create uniformity in some spheres at some times but competing tendencies in others. The distribution of income within developing countries could be a case in point, with many developing countries manifesting an increasing gap in income distribution. Kohl and O'Rourke noted that in East Asia, income inequality fell while economic growth was led by export demand, which was, in turn, supported by higher education levels. However, where export growth exceeded educational capacity, income inequality grew. They also note that while factors other than globalization appeared to be more important in determining income inequality, the 'shocks' introduced by globalization could and often did exacerbate such inequality (Kohl and O'Rourke 2000: 44–46). And even in a relatively successful economy such as Malaysia, income inequality shifted only slightly over the 20 years from 1970 to 1989 (Yusoff *et al.* 2000), while in Argentina globalization was recognized as being a significant contributor to income inequality (Bebczuk and Gasparini 2000). However, in other cases, the impact of globalization has been at best ambiguous and in some cases clearly positive (e.g., Sinagpore, Taiwan, Hong Kong).

In this, the political value-judgements applied to the policy implications of globalization, especially economic globalization, are paramount, at least in those states able or willing to assert a degree of autonomy from the globalization paradigm. Perhaps in this the distinction needs to be made between developed and developing countries, and the economic capacity for diversification between developed countries (types of complex manufactures and information-based systems), and between developed and developing countries, and the relative homogenization of economic capacity (simple primary exports and labour intensive production) on the part on many developing countries. Within this, it should be noted, a small number of countries have made the leap from developing to developed status, in particular the 'four tigers' of East Asia. But the conducive circumstances of these countries has been identified as specific, and their feat has not been widely replicated.

In all of this, the alleged modification of state sovereignty is in one sense just another domain for elite domination. It is less that state sovereignty is being reduced, but that there is a variation in the role and function of the state, in particular variation that has implications for dividing elite and common interest along international lines, which can in turn manifest as corruption, oppression and so on. The 'state', as an idea, is only sacrosanct for those who have, or who believe they have, a vested interest in its maintenance. To this end, the state, as an institution, has had to variously accommodate differing sources of pressure; from international institutions in the realms of economics and politics, on one hand and demands from 'localisms' (community groups, separatists, etc) on the other, which have tended to weaken the institutional independence of many states, and to some observers have led to a 'hollowing out' of 'globalized' states. The biggest impact on the functioning of the state has, therefore, been in how states rearrange themselves in light of such external influences. The hyperglobalists' singularity implies a Fukyama-ist 'end of history', which instead of achieving hegemony has remained challenged, and it is probable that the 'democratic fatalism' – the necessary advent of democracy as the political expression of liberal capitalism – implied in this totalising idea is mistaken. But in the global contest of ideas and information, the normative and historical claim to such a singularity is perhaps the greatest intellectual challenge to the idea of the state.

'Realism'

In some areas of debate, globalization is taken to mean economic globalization, especially of a *laissez-faire* capitalist type. There are two points worth noting here. The first is that there is nothing new about global trade or what might be called global 'economic imperialism'. The second is that there is implied to be something wrong with economic globalization as such, whereas it more probably refers to global *laissez-faire* capitalism. Critics of economic globalization would, on the face of it, be happier with a more equitable global distribution of wealth that would, by definition, also constitute 'globalization'.

Global capitalism, of the free-market type, has developed a life of its own, though, in ways that could not be easily constrained by what remains a politically and often economically fragmented international community. In simple terms, if global capital is unhappy with one site of investment it can, relatively simply, pick up and move to another. The logic of this process is that, in order to prosper, communities must attract global capital, and those that do (and do so within proper investment guidelines) tend to prosper, while those that don't sink. Yet in order to appear attractive to global capital, communities often have to undercut their competitors, which in turn calls forth their competitors also cutting in what amounts to a downward cycle, if not spiral, of poverty. The wage structures of Indonesia and the Philippines well illustrate this cause and effect model, with both competing against each other for foreign investment on the 'comparative advantage' basis of low wages and each driving the other lower and lower in international dollar terms.

There is, however, some debate about whether the term 'realism', in its international relations sense, accurately describes globalization. Assuming realism to mean the capacity of states to protect their own interests or impose such interests on others, a critical assessment of globalization would argue that it does reflect the 'realist' policies of the world's economically developed states, not least of which is the US. However, another analysis could argue that the interdependence implied in globalization is at odds with the independence implied in realism, that realism tends more towards protectionist economic policies, and that alliances are displaced by collective security. (Gurtov 1994: ch 2) However, a critical analysis of both realism and globalization would suggest they are variations on the same theme, that they both enhance the capacity of selected states, that WTO/IMF/WB prescriptions do function as a type of protectionism, and that collective security is only limited to those states that are part of the globalization alliance or which are strategically important to the globalization agenda.

This then posits a type of 'neo-realism' in international relations, in which dominant states define domestic policy in spite of globalizing tendencies, in which the give and take of international relations is increasingly negotiated (although with the obvious capacity for pressure), and in which states themselves are seen to be acting less on behalf of the direct interests of their citizens as much as on behalf of ideological assumptions about what is best for the state, which includes what might be termed its other 'stakeholders', such as the corporate sector and, in some cases, government institutions. That is, the role of the state is becoming redefined or reorganized rather than disappearing.

Conclusion

There is a case to suggest that globalization slowed in the last years of the 20th century, not least in response to the Asian economic crisis of 1997. But this was probably a temporary slowdown, and did not mean that the process of globalization is in decline, at least not for the foreseeable future. That is, the various elements of globalization do appear to be progressing more or less inexorably. For those who abhor globalization and see little or nothing positive in it, this may well be cause for dismay. For those who champion or look forward to it, it is cause for some satisfaction. But for most, it simply is, in much the same way that the formation of nations in the 19th and 20th centuries was in part a constructed process and in part an imposed consolidation of political and economic territorial imperatives. There were then many who felt (and may still feel) uncomfortable about such territorial incorporation, but on the whole the idea of ordering of the global community into states was a necessary precondition for political survival.

In one sense, the linkages and interdependencies that have come to characterize intra-state relations are coming to be replicated on a global scale. In the way that the train, mail and telegraph increased regional integration, so too global shipping, airlines, telecommunications and the internet are increasing global integration. The oil for the machinery of national integration was industrialization, most successfully brought about through capitalism and the trade it implies. The oil for the machinery of global integration similarly remains capitalism and the trade it implies.

The difference between national integration and global integration, however, is that national integration and the terms upon which it was founded largely followed a long integration of regional peoples, whereas global integration has been relatively sudden, at least in its post-communist phase, and unaccountable in its application. Further, the construction of states has implied both rights and obligations on the part of both the state and its citizens, and within that a type of social contract. The notion of global rights and obligations exists in public rhetoric, but is a very long way from being supported in the objective conditions of the lives of a very large proportion of the world's population. In economic terms, states increasingly have global obligations, which are functionally paid for by their citizens. However, in so far as 'rights' exist, they exist at the state level, with global intervention occurring only where a case can be made that such intervention is in the clear global interest (or in the interest of a global power with the capacity to persuade others). Similarly, in so far as there is potential for a 'social contract', there is little doubt that if the world was one political community much of it would decry its conditions and question its position in such an agreement.

This, then, reflects the reality of globalization, which is that regardless of the rhetoric of its usefulness, its capacity to produce growth or other forms of development, it is essentially a unilateral arrangement that reflects particular ideological views (see Cox 1996: 23). This unilateral arrangement, or the ideology it represents, does not necessarily reflect the views of the people of developed countries (although it may if they understood what sorts of compromises they might have to make in a more equitable, sustainable world), but of the major corporations and the governments that are symbiotically linked to them. In this sense, capitalism is more able to proceed in a *laissez-faire* manner globally than it is within states. And, equally, the moderating factor on state-based capitalism, which is government that in theory represents the will of its citizens, does not exist in the 'anarchic' international environment. It is from this point that globalization and development can proceed in one of two general directions.

The first direction is that, corresponding to economic relations and the agreements that allow them to exist, global institutions will come to form the machinery of a functional global government, operating as an effective federation joined in common interest. As global capitalism develops, it may be that it will need to ensure that developing countries do in fact grow richer (if in a more sustainable manner) in order to continue to provide the markets that capitalism cannot survive without. This will then require that the obvious imbalance in global wealth in part be addressed through sheer economic necessity. The other direction that globalization can proceed in is, after having fantasized about genuine *laissez-faire* economics, which have historically never existed, capitalism's free market theorists will achieve their goal of unregulated (or 'self-regulating') economic activity with no role for 'government'. Unfettered capitalism's internal logic will, according to this theory, ensure the greatest potential for global growth and the most pragmatic distribution of economic good. An alternative view is that such unfettered capitalism will simply see the accumulation of wealth in some places, but not in others. The problem with this scenario, however, is that, even assuming that such theory can translate in practice before short-term greed produces environmental unsustainability, the social and economic cost that is already being borne by much of the world's population will increase and will, almost inevitably, result in some form of political response.

It has been argued, for example, that global Islam's critique of the West is in large part fuelled by such structural inequality, expressed as repression (see, for example, Chirzin 2002), and that this has in turn created the grounds for radical and terroristic responses. In this, it has employed the communications tools of globalization, although these have been used to profoundly reject globalization's *laissez-faire* policies. Less religiously motivated, it was a similar (though perhaps not as profound) economic imbalance that motivated the rise of theoretical and then practical state-based 'communism' in the late 19th and early 20th centuries, initially expressed as terror, and then as revolution. As noted by Plekhanov, in the Russian context over 100 years ago, the underprivileged 'suffer not only from the development of capitalism, but also from the scarcity of that development' (in Kochan 1963: 204). It was the failure to address the shortcomings of both capitalism and the distribution of capitalism's benefits that led directly to the Russian Revolution of 1917, in which three decades of high-level foreign investment was appropriated by the Bolsheviks (Kochan 1963: 174, 199–200). It would take little imagination to conceive of a similar global response to global capitalism's capacity for rapaciousness. However, in this there may be a glimmer of hope. Recognizing the radical option as a response to an unrestrained global capitalism, it may be that, as occurred in states a century or so earlier, there will become a compromise, in which the demands for equity are tempered by moderation and reform, and in which the desire for unrestrained profit is similarly tempered. It may be that there will be conflict before such a balance is struck. But without a balance between developed and developing countries, and between global capitalism and global equity, the future looks exceptionally bleak.

Chapter 5

The Economics of Development

JOE REMENYI

The most influential contribution that Western economics has made to the understanding of the human condition is the proposition that a world in which individuals act freely in their own self-interest, will not degenerate into chaos, but evolve into an orderly society in which scarce resources are optimally allocated. From this one contested idea economics has built a family of theories that underlie the mainstreams of thinking on economics since before the appearance of Adam Smith's influential book, *The Wealth of Nations,* in 1776.

From this proposition derives the theory of comparative advantage, which posits that a country will always do best if it specializes in activities in which it can maintain competitiveness against all comers. Further, core to economics is the notion that markets matter, which is why economists spend so much energy arguing that the role of government is to ensure that markets operate efficiently to equate the wants of consumers/savers on one side of the market with those of producers/investors on the other.

This chapter explores these ideas, concentrating on explaining mainstream thinking on economic development. The chapter does not seek to justify or explain away the criticism that liberal market economics has been the source of great suffering in developing countries, arising especially from policies directed at structural adjustment and enforced odious debt repayment. This is because experience has served to confirm the importance of competition, the ability of even the poorest person to choose what is in their personal best interests, and the important role that good government can play to protect the interests of the vulnerable and create environments for individuals to get on with the job of sustainable wealth creation. Hence, the goal of this chapter is to elucidate:

(i)   why economics places such great stress on efficient markets as critical to economic development

(ii) what economists mean when they describe economic development is a process of capital accumulation

(iii) why asset creation is as important as income generation for robust and sustainable development, and

(iv) why the processes associated with economic growth demand effective
      and non-corrupt governance systems to ensure that domestic welfare
      gains arise from the integration of developing economies into global
      markets for goods, services, resources, financial flows and informa-
      tion exchange.

Economic development in perspective: setting the scene

The developing world consists of more than five times as many sovereign
states as there are donor members of the Development Assistance
Committee (DAC). However, the 20 DAC countries enjoy access to
economies that are four-times as productive as the sum of those in
developing countries, delivering eight times the spending power of the
rural industry dominated developing world.

The gross differences between developed and developing countries
reflected in Table 5.1 are much smaller than was the case at the start of
1950. Yet when we examine structural economic differences between
developed and developing economies, and compare recent growth rates in
key economic aggregates, the contrasts that remain are significant (see
Table 5.2).

Developing economies are far more dependent on agriculture than is the
case in developed countries. Even though the overall contribution of
agriculture to developing country GDP has declined from more than 70 per
cent to less than 12 per cent during 1969–1999, this is still six times the
level for DAC economies. In some more populous developing countries,
such as China, Bangladesh, India and Indonesia, agriculture still accounts
for between one-fifth and one-quarter of national production, while across
Africa south of the Sahara the proportion is typically twice that level.

In step with the falling importance of agriculture, developing economies
are expanding their services sectors and their involvement in global
competition for export markets. South Asia excepted, the economies of
South-East and North Asia, especially China, South Korea, Taiwan,
Singapore and Malaysia have out-performed the rest of the developing
world in taking advantage of growth based on export expansion. A high
proportion of foreign direct investment (FDI) to GDP for all of Asia, other
than South Asia, arises because of the high number of these export
initiatives brought to fruition through FDI joint ventures, along with
government directed support. In agriculture the impact of the Green
Revolution on food production is evident in the doubling of the index of
food production by developing countries. This has delivered cheaper food

Table 5.1 Global relatives: population and income estimates in developed and developing economies, 2000

	Developed[1] Countries	Developing[2] Countries	Africa-Middle East: SoS[3]	Other	Asia: South	Other	Latin America[4]	Non EU Europe[5]
Number of countries	20	111	35	13	6	13	21	23
Population								
millions	955	5,178	674	295	1,380	1,830	524	475
% annual, 1990–99	0.6	1.6	2.6	2.2	1.9	1.3	1.7	0.2
% 15–64 years	64	62	53	59	60	66	63	67
% distribution	15	85	20	5	22	36	9	8
persons/sq. km	29	51	27	26	278	115	25	20
% urban	77	41	34	58	28	34	75	67
GNP								
$US billions	25	6	0.3	0.6	0.6	1.5	1.8	0.9
PPP[6] $US/capita	27	7	1.5	5	2	4	7	7

1 Countries that are members of the OECD-based Development Assistance Committee
2 Counties receiving Official Development Assistance
3 South of the Sahara
4 Includes all Caribbean countries
5 Includes all former Soviet bloc countries
6 Purchasing power parity measure of income per person

Source: Data from World Bank, WDR, 2000–01

Table 5.2 Structural differences, developed and developing economies, 2000

	Developed[1] Countries	Developing[2] Countries	Africa-Middle East: SoS[3]	Africa-Middle East: Other	Asia: South	Asia: Other	Latin America	Non EU Europe[4]
% of GDP								
Agriculture	2	12	18	15	28	13	8	10
Services	64	54	50	47	47	41	63	58
Exports	17	20	21	19	9	28	13	23
Military spending	2.4	2.9	2.3	7.0	3.1	2.5	1.8	4.0
ODA[5]	n.a	0.7	4.1	1.0	0.9	0.5	0.2	0.6
FDI[6]	2.0	2.7	1.2	0.9	0.7	3.4	3.4	2.2
Food Production Index[7]								
1979–81	93	72	79	70	70	67	80	n.a
1996–98	108	135	124	138	122	152	124	n.a
Annual growth rate (%)								
consumption/person[8]	2.2	1.9	-1.2	–	2.6	5.6	0.6	–
exports[9]	6.5	8.2	4.4	–	9.6	12.6	8.7	4.4
GDP[10]	2.4	3.3	2.4	3.0	5.7	7.4	3.4	-2.7

1 Countries that are members of the OECD based Development Assistance Committee
2 Countries receiving Official Development Assistance
3 South of the Sahara
4 Includes all former Soviet bloc countries
5 Official Development Assistance
6 Foreign Direct Investment
7 1989–91 = 100
8 Average, 1980–98
9 Goods and services, 1990–99
10 Average, 1990–99

Source: Data from World Bank 2002a.

Table 5.3 *Income poverty by region, selected years, 1990—98*

	People living on less than US$1 a day (millions)		% of population living on less than US$1 a day (per cent)	
	1990	1998	1990	1998
East Asia and Pacific	452	278	28	15
Excluding China	92	65	19	11
Europe and Central Asia	7	24	2	5
Latin America and the Caribbean	74	78	17	16
Middle East and North Africa	6	5	2	2
South Asia	495	522	44	40
Sub-Saharan Africa	242	291	48	46
Total	1,276	1,199	29	24
Excluding China	916	986	28	26

Source: Data from World Bank 2002a.

to consumers, especially in urban areas, enabling general consumption spending to grow more rapidly than income per person, especially in the non-food sector.

The situation of economies in Africa south of the Sahara remains parlous, however. Despite gains in food production in excess of population increase, private sector consumption per person has declined in recent years. Given the low level of income and even lower levels of absolute consumption by the average African, this trend is not welcome. ODA dependence in Africa remains significantly above that for almost all other developing areas, the small South Pacific economies excepted, and the level of direct private investment lower than elsewhere.

Table 5.3 provides data on key trends in the incidence of global poverty, two of which need to be highlighted.

First, the locus of global absolute poverty is shifting from Asia to Africa, despite the setback to poverty reduction in ASEAN economies following the Asian economic crisis of 1996–2000. Second, the evidence indicates that the global incidence of absolute poverty may now be in decline, with World Bank data suggesting that from 1980–1998 the absolute number of poor (i.e., those living on less than US$1 per day) declined by at least 200 million. Over this period, average per capita income in developing countries grew from a little less than US$1,000 in 1980, to almost US$1,400 in 2000. This is a significant achievement, the sources of which are:

(i)   positive trends in international trade
(ii) more effective financial resource flows into developing countries
(iii) improved poverty targeting in current and development spending
(iv) lower levels of corruption.

Income indicators of trends in the incidence of poverty are consistent with trends in most non-income measures of the quality of life. Infant mortality has been almost halved from 107 deaths per 1000 live births in 1980 to 58 in 2000. Similarly adult illiteracy has been halved to 25 per cent, and life expectancy has increase by more than a decade. School enrolment at primary level now typically averages well in excess of 80 per cent of the eligible age group, though secondary school participation continues to elude 40–50 per cent of children in developing countries. A rise in the age of first marriage of girls by between 5 and 10 years has contributed very significantly to the halving of fertility rates.

Seven common characteristics of economic development

There was a time when economic development was regarded as synonymous with development. The central place given to economics and economists in the design of the post-Second-World-War global institutions and rules of the 'global' game of development, commonly known as the Bretton Woods system, goes some way to explaining why this was so. The World Bank (WB) (known until the 1960s by its full title, the *International Bank for Reconstruction and Development (IBDR)*, plus its soft-loan window, the *International Development Association (IDA)*), the International Monetary Fund (IMF), the General Agreement on Tariffs and Trade (GATT), and the United Nations Development Program (UNDP), were the means by which the world community would harness its new-found confidence in Keynesian macroeconomic management to reconstruct the known world. It seemed an irrefutable truth that successful development would flow almost automatically if only the economics was right.

The benefit of hindsight shows that the rules of the game and the inexorable forces of globalization notwithstanding, there are seven characteristics of economic development that are common to the development experience of all countries. These seven characteristics are features of a historical process that we have come to identify as economic development:

(i)   Economic development involves greater specialization and division of labour, which reduces self-sufficiency, but increases trade. An important source of greater division of labour is the reorganization of production, including the use of economies of scale. However, to the leaders of many developing countries, this free-trade-comparative-advantage scenario seemed to trap the late-comers in specializing in industries that are the least modern and the least dynamic, essentially labour intensive, rural, low-technology industries. Developing countries have therefore generally sought to reject this free-trade, comparative-advantage, liberal-market model of development.

All of the alternative economic development strategies replaced free trade and open competition on world markets with development plans for modernization and industrial development behind steep walls of protective tariffs and trade restrictions. These powerful alternatives to the neo-classical comparative advantage model dominated the economic development record from 1950. It is only since the cessation of the Cold War that the free-trade-comparative-advantage-based model for the development of a competitive and robust economy has gained ascendancy. It is worth noting here that the pressure for structural adjustment in developing economies arises in large part because of the economic distortions that emerged in response to the adoption of non-market responsive, non-competition orientated economic development strategies.

It would appear that the non-market-based alternative strategies of economic development have not stood the test of time. The lesson here is not that neo-liberal market economics is always right, but that in choosing development priorities it is the efficiency with which that capital is deployed that is critical. The contrast between the economic development experience in Latin America/Africa and that in North Asia is instructive. In the former (e.g., Mexico, Venezuela, Argentina, Kenya, Nigeria and Tanzania), blind commitments to industry development through import-substitution resulted in investment that supported inefficient import dependent industries, incapable of supplying local consumers at internationally competitive prices. In the latter (e.g., South Korea, Taiwan, and China), public sector support for investment in automobile production, electronics and other high-tech industries have tended to be conditional on industry strategies targeted at serving global markets.

(ii)   Greater specialization also means more trade. In order to oil the wheels of exchange, economic development encourages the replacement of barter with cash transactions. Gradually, the demand for money takes on a momentum of its own, pushing the reach of monetised markets into the remotest villages and the poorest households. Money makes for more efficient trade by reducing the transactions costs of buying, selling and saving. Money is also a medium of exchange that is more flexible, durable, divisible, transportable and accountable than barter goods. As the opportunities for wage employment expand in rural areas, so too does the demand for money as the only practical link between one's wage and one's need for consumer durables, investment goods and commodities imported from remote markets. The spread of the money economy has gradually but inexorably displaced barter and subsistence systems of livelihood in all developing countries.

In the modern economy money is a commodity in its own right, for which a market exists to set prices (interest rates) and bring suppliers (lenders) and users (borrowers) into contact. The importance of these money markets increases as economic development proceeds. The supply of money is a function of the rate at which liquidity in the economy is generated or taken away. Traditionally, economics has presented the relationship between money supply, liquidity and the quantity of money needed to finance all the transactions that occur in a given period of time with a disarmingly simple equation describing the 'quantity theory of money'. The equation takes the following form:

$$M.V = P.T$$

Where   M = quantity of money in circulation
        V = the velocity at which the money circulates in the economy
        P = the average price level
        T = the number of transactions
    M.V = the quantity of 'liquidity' in the economy
    P.T = total expenditure in the economy
             (consumption expenditure plus investment expenditure)

In the poorest sections of the economy, savings mobilization programmes that simply transfer money from poor households into bank deposits or into government coffers, reduces both M and V in the markets in which the poor buy and sell goods, services and their labour. Unless these savings are recycled back into these same markets, (which development strategies that rely on financing modernization by drawing resources from the traditional sectors of the economy do not do), a liquidity crisis will ensue. Contractions in P.T, the number and value of transactions in the markets where the poor find their employment and their basic needs, must follow to the disadvantage of the poor.

(iii) Economic development is associated with an increase in the range of effective choices. New and cheaper commodities add to the real income of poor people, even if they decide not to spend their saved income. 'Social goods', such as education, health, transport, power and sanitation infrastructure add to the quality of life, but they can also expand the range of economic activities that institutional innovations (such as increased specialization, new credit institutions, expanded marketing opportunities) and technical progress open to increasing numbers of individuals, groups, households and firms.

Earlier economic theory posited that income inequality would get worse before it got better. However, more recent studies have shown that the development experience of the developing economies that have performed the best, in terms of sustained growth rates in income per head, are those that have chosen economic development strategies that are equity promoting. The developing economies that have had the most disappointing record in terms of growth of income per head are also those economies in which governments have been most tolerant of deteriorating levels of equity (see Meier 1995).

Development policy advisers also linked the conventional belief that economic development demands sustained high rates of investment with the observation that rich people save more than poor people. Hence, if a maximal level of development investment is to be funded from domestic savings, income equity has to slide. The error in this thinking lay in the fact that it does not follow that the savings of the rich will flow into uses that advance national productivity or reduce the incidence of poverty. In many instances these savings merely fuel speculative investments in land or other potential sources of capital gains, instead of increased output or increases in the nation's stock of physical and human capital. In contrast, strategies of economic development that promote greater equity in the distribution of income, by feeding on the high demand for greater and more diverse forms of consumption from people on low incomes, stimulate demand, bringing forth added investment and faster growth in income per head as the market place seeks to meet the demands of consumers and investors.

A common method by which social scientists have measured income equity levels is by the construction of a 'Lorenz Curve' and the calculation of what is known as the Gini coefficient. The Lorenz curve is a straight line when x per cent of income goes to x per cent of households, no matter what level of income or proportion of households one considers. When equity is not uniform, the Lorenz Curve traces the actual relationship between these two statistics. The more the Lorenz Curve bends away from the diagonal, the greater the inequality in distribution of income. If the Lorenz Curve is the same as the diagonal, the Gini coefficient equals zero, indicating zero inequality in income distribution. The closer the Gini Coefficient gets to unity, the greater is the inequality in distribution of income across households.

Gini coefficients for selected economies are shown in Table 5.4. These indicate that income inequality if often greatest in the poorest countries, despite anomalies such as Brazil and some of former member states of the Soviet Union. Wealthy donor countries tend to have levels of income

Table 5.4 Gini coefficients for selected developing countries

Least equity								Most equity
Country	Year	Gini	Country	Year	Gini	Country	Year	Gini
Sierra Leone	1989	62.9	Nigeria	1997	50.6	Tanzania	1993	38.2
C African R.	1993	61.3	Zambia	1996	49.8	India	1997	37.8
Brazil	1996	60.1	Russia	1998	48.7	Indonesia	1996	36.5
Guatemala	1989	59.6	Malaysia	1995	48.5	Australia	1994	35.2
RS Africa	1994	59.3	Philippines	1997	46.2	France	1996	32.7
Paraguay	1995	59.1	Kenya	1994	44.5	Germany	1994	30.0
Colombia	1996	57.1	Turkey	1994	41.5	Japan	1993	24.9
Zimbabwe	1991	56.8	USA	1997	40.8	Denmark	1992	24.7
Chile	1994	56.5	Cambodia	1997	40.4	Belarus	1998	21.7
Mexico	1995	53.7	PR China	1998	40.3	Slovakia	1992	19.5

Source: Data from World Bank 2002a.

inequality that are far lower than the poorest developing countries in Africa, Latin America and Asia.

(iv) It is not necessarily the case that the role of government must increase with economic development. It is conventional wisdom that the industrial revolution in Britain meant a decline in the role of government and the ascendency of *laissez-faire*. In Germany and France the opposite was true. In the USA, the experience was similar to that of Britain. Throughout most of the period 1950–1990, there was very little evidence that smaller government would result from successful economic development in developing countries.

The pervasiveness of economic planning in contemporary development is unique to the economic history of recent generations. Development planning has its roots in several places, two of which are critical. First, the leaders of most newly independent post-colonial developing countries were greatly impressed by the apparent success of centralized planning in the Soviet Union during the period 1920–1950. At that time the Soviet bloc was seen as threatening the West for global economic ascendency. Second, Keynesian macroeconomic management gave its imprimatur to widespread government intervention in even the most advanced of the market-orientated economies. Economic planning was accepted as an important new approach to economic management which, when properly done, ought to be an effective means of accelerating economic growth beyond the rates of advance that free market forces could be expected to produce.

The great depression of the 1930s and the unemployment plagued 1920s, seemed to suggest that market failures, not full-employment equilibrium, are the norm. Traditional economics had taught that whenever the economy is in disequilibrium, equilibrating forces will come into play and bring the economy back towards full-employment equilibrium. The tragedy of the 1930s depression severely challenged the faith of economists in this core tennet of conventional economics. Keynes attracted many converts to his views, the foundations of which can be summarised in three critical propositions:

(a) Full employment growth requires demand management because the inability of unemployed people to register their demand in the market is not a sign of inadequate demand, but a sign of massive market failure. The Keynesian solution was to support income transfers that would allow the poor to buy the things they need, thus creating the market signals that will reverse the downward spiral of sales, employment and income.

(b) The paradox of thrift, which overturned the convention in traditional economics to generalise from the situation of the individual or the household to that of the national economy. Economists had a tendency to attribute recessions/depressions to the normal consequences of 'living beyond one's means'. Keynes demonstrated that while an increase in savings as a result of greater caution and more conservative spending habits can augment the wealth and well-being of the individual, if everyone does the same the demand for commodities will decline and induce a depression generating downward spiral away from full-employment equilibrium. Keynes shifted the ground from the supply side, [in which the demand for labour (employment) is a function of the productivity of labour (output per hour) relative to the cost of labour (the wage rate)], to the demand side, [in which the demand for labour is derived from the demand for commodities and services, including export demand].

(c)   The economics of poverty and less-than full employment is not the economics of stability and efficient market forces. By this proposition Keynes suggested that the economy could get trapped in a less-than-full employment situation in which low-level stagnation is the norm rather than the natural tendency to return to full employment equilibrium. Only if governments intervened to manage further growth, keep interest rates low enough to keep investment profitable, and so encourage further technical progress, could the stationary state and global stagnation be avoided.

In Keynes' view, the problem of markets is not that markets do not work, but that market failures are more widespread than conventional economic theories accepted. He attributed this anomaly to the commitment that conventional economics had made to the belief in the full-employment stability of the economy. Keynes' *General Theory* accepted the centrality of the self-interested-'maximizing' individual as a description of the typical economic actor, but he questioned the assumption of a stable full-employment equilibrium. Keynes believed that the normal condition of the economy is not at or above full-employment but in less-than-full-employment disequilibrium. Keynes further observed that in less-than-full-employment situations employers are not forced by competition to pay workers what the theory of productivity indicates that they are 'worth', but they will pay 'whatever they can get away with'.

When recovery from the 1930s depression came, it was not attributed to the operation of market forces but to the intervention of governments guided by the principles of demand management and Keynesian macroeconomic policies. For developing economies this experience seemed to point the way ahead. The Second World War further confirmed the effectiveness with which governments are able to intervene to achieve widespread economic changes and shifts in sectoral priorities in production. The strategies of economic development proposed for poor countries was a mixture of demand management, direct government intervention in investment, and vigorous government-controlled supply-side management. Domestic conditions in the developing world encouraged the view that leadership from the top – i.e., the political resolve to modernize and catch-up to the rich countries – was critical to successful economic growth and social development. It is little wonder, therefore, that at the start of the modern era of development, the consensus view was that government had to be the leading exemplar of modernity and the mechanism that would enable developing economies to avoid the traps of market failures.

(v) The external sector is that part of the economy involved in international trade, foreign resource flows (essentially finance and labour), and technology transfer from abroad. In most developing countries the external sector remains relatively small so long as subsistence production is the dominant source of livelihood. Consequently, the external sectors of developing economies have typically been associated more with the 'modern' than the 'traditional' sector of the economy. However, as the significance of programmes directed at food security, rural development, new industries and export-led growth increases, the importance of the external sector as a source of employment and income will rise.

All developing economies encounter balance of payments constraints that become more pressing with advances in economic development. Foreign exchange is needed to pay for machinery, materials and technologies that cannot be domestically produced. Foreign aid can relieve this constraint by providing the necessary foreign exchange at concessional rates, but no economy can rely on foreign aid alone. As the process of increasing specialization accelerates and export industries (including tourism) are developed to generate the foreign exchange earnings needed for modernization and technology transfer, the economy is inexorably drawn into the complex web that makes up the global economy.

From greater earlier trade, in the half century to 1950, the volume of world trade increased at a meagre 0.5 per cent per annum, while the competition for markets sent traditional food and primary product export prices on a long-term downward spiral. Immediately after the Second World War, therefore, there was great scepticism among many economists and policy makers, especially those from developing countries, about the extent to which the newly emerging independent states of Asia, Latin America and Africa could rely on foreign trade as the engine of their development.

In this sceptical environment, developing economies turned inward, looking to protected domestic markets as the base for import-substituting industrial development. However, despite this decision, the import dependence of most new industries for continuing technology transfer and key raw material inputs saw trade as a proportion of developing economy GDP rise from less than 10 per cent at the end of the Second World War to between 20 and 30 per cent by the close of the 1980s.

Economists resisted any diminution in the importance of 'comparative advantage' as the basis on which poor countries ought to nurture structural change in their economies. However, they were also conscious of the resistance among the leaders of developing country to adopt conventional economic principles of industrial development that seemed to lock them into specialization in labour-intensive, low-technology export industries. These leaders believed that if poor countries were ever to catch-up to the rich countries, they would have to not only grow rapidly, but in ways that diversified their exports beyond low-technology labour-intensive products. This anomaly remained with development economists until well into the 1980s; it is only since that the anomaly has been recognized as a falsehood of the 'catch-up' view of development.

The power of trade liberalization as an engine of poor country development has had to be rediscovered, based, in part, on the important role that export-led economic growth has played in the most successful economies of East and North Asia, especially China, South Korea, Taiwan and Singapore. A complementary lesson has been taken from the disappointing development experience of those developing countries that based their development strategies on policies that eschewed export-capable industrial development and embraced the isolation of protectionism.

Other sources of closer ties to the international economy in the development experience of poor countries are based on global flows of private foreign investment, the activities of transnational corporations, the

Table 5.5   *Financial and resource flows to developing countries, 1960–2000 (US$, billions)*

	1960	1970	1980	1990	2000
Exports	26.7	59.6	580.2	734.2	1290.2
Imports	30.1	64.3	490.7	793.5	1327.0
ODA	2.5*	7.0	27.3	55.6	49.5
Net FDI	n.a	2.2	4.4	24.6	166.7
Net Long Term Debt	3.1*	13.1	107.0	128.4	264.7
Workers' Remittances	n.a	1.2	14.0	25.4	52.4
Debt Service Ratio (%)	8.0	9.2	93.4	163.8	398.9

* 1965
Sources: Data from World Bank, IMF, UN and OECD.

Table 5.6   *Change needed to gain the equivalent of a 10 per cent increase in
export receipts*

10 per cent gain in developing country export receipts (2000, US$, billions)	+ 129.0
Percentage change needed for an equivalent increase in foreign exchange receipts:	
Bilateral ODA	+ 261 per cent
Workers' remittances	+ 246 per cent
Direct investment	+ 74 per cent
Net long term loans	+ 49 per cent

rise of developing-country-based multinationals, private and public technology transfer, flows of official development assistance (ODA), the remittances of guest workers, and economic links associated with labour migration, refugee resettlement and global debt management. Table 5.5 summarizes the relative importance of each as a source of resource flows.

The most important source of foreign exchange for developing countries is export earnings. All other sources of foreign exchange amount to not more than one-quarter of the total receipts earned from exports. In other words, more can be done to benefit access to foreign exchange resources by developing countries by getting trade relations right than by any other means. In order to achieve a gain equivalent to a 10 per cent increase in export earnings, whether by improved access to rich country markets or higher export prices, the equivalent change in each of the alternative sources of foreign exchange is many multiples of 10 per cent (see Table 5.6).

(vi)   Economic development is reflected in shifts in the distribution of employment from the rural to the urban and services sectors. It does not follow, however, that this process is also associated with the displacement of workers from their traditional economic engagements. The fear that productivity improvements in agriculture constitutes a spectre of a growing pool of displaced workers is not supported by the experience of developing countries. Shifts in the distribution of employment occur because the growth of job opportunities is not concentrated in traditional agriculture. Even though increases in agricultural output can result in increased levels of seasonal employment, especially at planting and harvesting times, the rate of growth of employment opportunities in traditional livelihood areas do not keep pace with the rate of growth of population during the course of economic development. Economic development has tended, therefore, to be associated with a continuous decline in the proportion of the workforce in agriculture and growth in urban living.

The drift to the cities in developing countries is associated with the rapid increase of livelihood- and income-earning opportunities in urban areas. Parallel with the decline in the importance of agriculture as a source of employment and household income, is an increase in demand for a more highly skilled workforce. The great mass of unskilled workers has encouraged the growth of 'informal sectors' in every developing country.

Economists view the economy as made up of sectors between which there are linkages, but each sector can be analysed as a separate and largely independent entity. The five basic sectors are agriculture, industry, trade, services and government. In recent years, economists have added a financial sector, a foreign trade sector and an informal sector. The addition of these new sub-divisions reflects the emphasis given to them as part of the structural transformation that all developing economies experience in the course of development.

An important issue in early theories of economic development was whether development ought to proceed on a 'balanced' growth path, with all sectors advancing on a broad front (see Nurske 1953 and Rosenstein-Rodan 1943) or an 'unbalanced' path with leading industries and sectors dragging the rest of the economy along into the new world of modernity (see Hirschman 1958). Balanced growth theories of economic development maintain a relatively constant relationship between the value of output coming from each sector in an effort to capture the economies of scale that were believed to come from broad-based economic development. The problem with balanced growth strategies was that they demanded a co-ordinated minimum critical effort, and the 'big-push' involved proved to be beyond the resources and administrative capacity of most developing country governments. Unbalanced growth focused attention on the linkages between the sectors, with development strategies designed to exploit the backward and forward linkages of new industries as the way to achieve the structural transformations associated with modernization.

The decline of the agriculture sector relative to the rest of the economy has long held the attention of economics as a key indicator of successful development. In classical economics the decline of agriculture was attributed to the belief that agriculture is subject to 'diminishing returns'. This is so because the supply of 'quality' land is limited. Hence, as more and more land is brought into production, the opportunity cost of continuing to invest in bringing inferior land into cultivation increases, encouraging a shift in the pattern of investment away from agriculture. The apparent widespread existence of unemployment or under-employment in agriculture seemed to confirm this observation. It encouraged the conclusion that the only way in which rural unemployment and under-employment can be effectively reduced is to move labour out of agriculture.

(vii) Industrialization is not a process that is confined to manufacturing, but is about technology transfer and adoption of more capital intensive and specialized production processes, both of which are engines of economic development. Hence, in the course of economic development not only is manufacturing industrialized as producers adopt more disaggregated, more specialized, and more capital intensive methods of production, but so too is agriculture industrialized, the services sector industrialized, and foreign trade industrialized. Even the civil service is industrialized as computers are harnessed to the task of information management, documentation and storage. Greater division of labour facilitates industrialization, but industrialization does not occur until traditional techniques of production, distribution or marketing are exchanged for more capital intensive technologies. It is in this sense that industrialization is a ubiquitous characteristic of development.

Institutional background

It is useful to be reminded of the devastation that ushered in the modern age of economic development. The Second World War had left a legacy of refugees and destruction that is almost unbelievable. At the end of 1945 there were some 60 million refugees in Europe, representing 55 ethnic groups from 27 devastated nations. If one adds the plight of refugees and displaced persons in Japan, China, South-East Asia and the Pacific to those in Europe, the scale of dislocation and economic destruction facing the world at that time dwarfs anything that the development experience of the world has seen since 1950. At the beginning of 1995 there were an estimated 20 million refugees worldwide! While this number is unacceptable, the scale of the global refugee problem is well within dimensions that the world has demonstrated an ability to handle, though the nature of the contemporary refugee problem, especially in Africa and Asia where the greater number are to be found, is unique and less tractable than it was in the immediate post-war period.

The first United Nations Monetary and Financial Conference was convened at Bretton Woods on 1–22 July 1944. Its task was to design the financial and institutional reforms that would be needed to deal with post-war reconstruction and global recovery. The experts who met in New Hampshire, representing 44 sovereign states, were very aware of the task before them. The great depression of the 1930s and the inflation-ravaged stagnation of the decade that followed the First World War were recent memories. The architects of the Bretton Woods institutions were fearful that the poverty of Europe and Asia would result in global stagnation for the lack of effective demand to sustain economic growth and full employment. Their proposals, therefore, targeted financial reconstruction as the key priority. But, they also saw in the emerging nations of the tropics a potential source of new investment opportunities and potential sources of new competition. Both needed to be 'managed' in order to ensure that adequate capital will be available for sustained long term growth.

The World Bank was designed to channel long-term capital for the development of member states. The IMF was designed to finance short-term imbalances in international payments in order to stabilize exchange rates and ensure that transition to sustained long-term growth would not be held back for want of short-term financial assistance. The institutional evolution of the Bretton Woods system of global governance reveals growth in awareness of the complexity of the development challenge.

The World Bank began operations in June 1946. The Soviet bloc states chose not to become members and with few exceptions (Hungary, Poland, Czechoslovakia) remained outside the system until after the break-up of the USSR. The Bank's first loans were made for post-war reconstruction, but by 1949 the emphasis in bank lending had moved to finance for economic development. Its first development loans were project-based, restricted to governments or to private enterprises with their government's guarantee, and intended to make available finance when private capital is not available on reasonable terms. World Bank lending was, therefore, not intended to displace private lending. It was intended to fill what was believed to be a failure in private-sector financial markets to reasonably meet the development investment needs of member states. Early lending by the Bank emphasized, therefore, funding of infrastructure and construction of public utilities. It was not until the 1970s that the Bank turned to agriculture and rural development as priority areas for funding.

In July 1956, the International Finance Corporation (IFC), was created as a specialized United Nations agency affiliated with the IBRD to provide funding to private enterprises in the developing countries where private-sector sources are found wanting. IFC loans recognized the importance of private investment in development and created a means by which the Bank could assist potential private-sector investors without the need for government guarantees to back loans made. Four years later, a parallel specialized agency, the International Development Association (IDA), was added to the Bank's armoury to meet the special financial needs of the poorest developing economies, colloquially known as the Least-Developed Countries (LLDCs). IDA offered the Bank a 'soft-loan' window, funded by special subscriptions from the 26 wealthiest member states. Through the IDA facility, the Bank was able to offer the neediest countries development finance on far more flexible and generous terms. At times, an IDA loan will include grant elements to cover project components, such as research, training or social welfare for vulnerable groups, that are judged to be socially important or subject to significant 'externalities' that make these components unattractive to private investors.

Throughout the period 1950–1980 the IMF and the GATT played complementary roles in international development. Both institutions were committed to promoting freer trade and assisting nations to avoid or overcome short-term balance-of-payments problems and debt repayment difficulties. The GATT has hosted a succession of 'rounds' aimed at achieving reform in particular areas of international trade. The Uruguay Round (1986–1994), addressed freer trade in agriculture and services. but it also resulted in further reforms to GATT, which ultimately cleared the way for the emergence of the World Trade Organization (WTO).

The Uruguay Round was preceded by the Tokyo Round (1972–1979) and the Kennedy Round (1964–1967), both of which sought lower tariffs generally, agreement on the treatment of export subsidies and new codes on non-tariff barriers to international trade. A full list of all the GATT Trade Rounds and the Doha Round initiated under the auspices of the WTO in 2002 are summarized in Table 5.7.

A complement to the Bretton Woods financial institutions is the set of United Nations specialized agencies that are dedicated to the promotion of development in the Third World. The first of these agencies to be affiliated to the UN was the International Labour Organization (ILO 1946), which had originally been created in 1919 as an office of the League of Nations under of the Treaty of Versailles. Its brief was to facilitate the improvement of the conditions of labour and living standards generally. The ILO has led the push to redraft development policies in ways that are employment creating and was the first agency to recognize the importance of the 'informal' sector in most developing countries. A parallel organization in agriculture is the Food and Agriculture Organization (FAO), which also has a history that can be traced through predecessor organizations back to the League of Nations. In the post-Second-World-War period, however, the FAO has acted as the premier technical agency in agriculture for the UN system. In particular, the FAO is the technical assistance arm of the UN Development Program (UNDP) and the World Food Program (WFP). Table 5.8 provides an overview of the range of agencies that operate within the UN system.

1994 marked the 50th anniversary of the Bretton Woods system. This event prompted some reassessment of performance of the Bretton Woods organizations in the development experience of developing countries. The results highlighted on-going problems and options for reform. Both the World Bank and the IMF continue to be under strong pressure from the non-government sector in particular, leading members of which have called for the abolition of both as institutions that have 'outlived their

Table 5.7 *The GATT/WTO Trade Rounds*

Year	Place/name	Subjects covered	Number of countries
1947	Geneva	Tariffs	12
1949	Annecy	Tariffs	13
1951	Torquay	Tariffs	38
1956	Geneva	Tariffs	26
1960–1961	Geneva	Tariffs	26
1964–1967	Geneva (Kennedy Round)	Tariffs and anti-dumping measures	62
1973–1979	Geneva (Tokyo Round)	Tariffs, non-tariff measures, 'framework' agreements	102
1986–1994	Geneva (Uruguay Round)	Tariffs, non-tariff measures, rules, services, intellectual property, dispute settlements, textiles, agriculture, creation of WTO	123
2002–2004	Doha	All goods and services, tariffs, non-tariff measures, anti-dumping and subsidies, regional trade agreements, intellectual property, environment, dispute settlement, Singapore issues	144

Source: Data from World Trade Organization, 2001, 'Trading Into the Future', http://www.wto.org.

use-by dates'. The basis of these critical evaluations can be traced to disquiet over the effectiveness of 'structural adjustment' loans, the apparent inability of the Bank and the Fund to deal with corruption and misuse of loan monies without penalizing the poor in client states, and the changing roles that the Bank and the Fund have cast for themselves since the start of the 1980s.

The role of the IMF remained focused on short-term balance of payments adjustments, trade facilitation and reform of the exchange rate system until the first structural adjustment loan to Turkey in 1980. This loan pioneered use by the IMF, in concert with the World Bank, of a strategy of 'conditionality' to govern continuing access to Bank and Fund financial assistance. In effect, the Bank combined its 'leverage' with that of the Fund to encourage adoption of policy advice that the two institutions

Table 5.8   *Bretton Woods and affiliated United Nations development agencies*

Name	Acronym	Year created	Purpose
International Labour Organization	ILO	1919	Improve conditions of labour and living standards
Food and Agriculture Organization	FAO	1945	Eliminate hunger and improve nutrition
International Monetary Fund	IMF	1945	Short-term balance of payments finance
World Bank	IBRD/WB	1946	Long-term development finance
UN Children's Fund	UNICEF	1946	Promote the welfare of children
UN Education Scientific Cultural Organization	UNESCO	1946	Promote world peace through collaborative projects
General Agreement on Tariffs and Trade	GATT	1947	Promote freer trade
World Health Organization	WHO	1948	Promote international cooperation for improved health
UN High Commissioner for Refugees	UNHCR	1951	Refugee assistance, protection and resettlement
International Finance Corporation	IFC	1956	Private-enterprise development finance
International Development Association	IDA	1960	Soft loan window for Fourth World
World Food Program	WFP	1961	Development through food aid and emergency relief
UN Conference on Trade and Development	UNCTAD	1964	Promote development through international trade
UN Development Program	UNDP	1965	Development assistance through technical aid
UN Capital Development Fund	UNCDF	1966	Grants/loans for the 30 least developed countries
UN Fund for Population Activities	UNFPA	1967	Family planning and population control
UN Industrial Development Organization	UNIDO	1967	Promote industrialization in developing countries
UN Environment Program	UNEP	1972	Guide and co-ordinate UN environmental activities
International Fund for Agricultural Development	IFAD	1974	Eliminate rural poverty and promote food production

believed would enable the client government to return the national economy onto a footing that would enable the country to meet its international loan repayment obligations and create a solid base for future economic growth. The priorities in the process were clearly taken from a strict neo-classical, rationalist, approach to macroeconomics, plus the protection of debt repayment obligations, even where repayments may involve greater deprivation and hardship for the poor and the vulnerable.

Since that first structural adjustment loan, the IMF has entered into a large number of similar loans, the consequences of which have been to cement the IMF into a role in economic development policy making and debt management that was not envisaged at the time of its creation. It has also blurred the distinction between the role of the Bank and the Fund, which has provided critics of these two organizations with a platform for their reform, if not their abolition.

Economic development in historical perspective

The economic development record since 1950 is spectacular in many respects. However, it is not uniformly so for all developing countries. The differences in the economic growth trends between regions of the globe and between countries within a region are very significant. Even so, we should not dismiss unfairly the sustained economic growth rates that have been achieved, which far exceeded those that the wealthy donor economies managed in their run to the top of the income and wealth stakes.

In a study of growth rates for the World Bank it was reported that European per capita income growth rates averaged between 0.74 and 1.35 per cent per annum between 1800 and 1950. It was further estimated that in the century to 1950, England achieved an average annual growth in

Table 5.9   *Decade average annual GDP per head growth rates (% p.a.)*

	1950–1959	1960–1969	1970–1979	1980–1989	1990–1999
DAC donor economies	2.8	3.7	2.1	2.3	1.8
Developing economies	2.3	3.1	2.9	2.0	2.0
High income	2.7	3.5	3.0	2.2	5.0
Middle income	2.4	3.1	3.0	0.6	2.3
Low income	<2.0	1.8	2.6	3.9	0.4

Source: Calculated from data in World Bank, World Tables, and *World Development Report*, various issues.

income per head of only 1.2 per cent, France 1.4 per cent, Germany 1.6 per cent and the USA 1.8 per cent. Only Japan (2.8 per cent) and the Soviet Union (4 per cent) achieved sustained per capita growth rates in excess of 2 per cent per annum, but these two countries also began from a far lower base in 1850 than the others. Developing economies, on the other hand, have recorded average income-per-head growth rates equal to or in excess of 2 per cent per annum in every decade since 1950. The data are summarized in Table 5.9.

Modelling key economic development variables

A common experience for village people in developing countries is the pressure they feel to leave the village and find work in town, in a nearby city, or maybe even a government-created 'export zone'. Whichever of these employment options a villager is drawn into, the decision to leave the village and become involved in urban-based employment introduces them to a radically different timbre of daily life and livelihood. One thing that is not unfamiliar, however, is the conviction that hard work brings its own reward. Every person who responds to the pull of employment in an urban setting does so because they have a need to find for themselves a livelihood that will allow them to save enough to finance investments in their own future and the future of fellow family members. Hidden in this simple scenario are the fundamental identities of economic accounting and growth in capacity to generate income.

It is not unusual for individual savings activity in developing countries to involve one or more forms of 'hoarding' (i.e., holding cash until needed). Hoarding is one of the most unproductive forms of saving. Hoarding may protect an asset, but it is a strategy of saving that does not use the asset to create an income stream. Furthermore, if inflation is a feature of the local economy, hoarding will result in a negative return as the purchasing power of the money saved is eroded by price rises. For the sake of this illustration, however, let us assume that the villager does not hoard his savings but sends whatever surplus there is home to the village for 'family' support. That part of these remittances used to support family livelihood standards forms another addition to consumer spending. However, that part of the remittance which is used by the family to pay for the education of fellow family members, improve the nutritional and health status of the family, or to pay for income-generating asset purchases is 'investment'. Investments in education and the availability of labour power within the household represent increases in the family's stock of human 'capital'. Investments in income generating assets represent accumulations in depreciable physical capital.

That is, income can be regarded in either of two ways: from the point of view of the worker's decisions about how they allocate their supply of 'income' between consumption spending and productive savings; or from the point of view of the food suppliers, shop-keepers and others who supply the urban worker with the goods and services purchased. These consumption purchases represent their sales, while the amount remitted back to the village as 'savings' represents their 'investment', held by them as 'stock not sold'. In order to explore the nature of these economic relationships further, let us consider the nature of the relationship between the income earned and the decisions taken about the level of consumption expenditures.

In urban employment, income earned can increase for either of only two reasons.

(a)   Longer hours are worked at the same wage rate,

or

(b)   A higher wage rate is paid for the same hours of work.

We can assume that the employer will only choose to lift the wage rate if it is profitable to do so (possibly because the worker has become more 'productive' with experience and is able to produce more in the time worked). The employer will prefer to increase the hours worked by employees if demand has driven prices up and made each item sold more profitable. In either case the employee is the beneficiary of higher income.

Consider now what the urban worker does with the increase in income, irrespective of whether it comes from an increase in hours worked or a rise in the hourly wage rate? It is possible that the worker will elect to spend all of the increase on higher personal consumption. More likely, however, some of the increase in income will be spent on higher consumption and some saved. In other words, at this point in our modelling, we do not allow spending beyond the limit of current income. There is no borrowing or lending in this system. Since that portion of the increase in income that is not consumed must add to the worker's savings, it must also be the case that the proportion spent on consumption, plus the proportion saved, must sum to 1 to account for the whole of the increase in income.

This, then, tells the story of the migrant worker in a particular way. The story is distorted because it is a snapshot and grossly simplified compared to reality. Nevertheless, if the propensity to consume were to increase, the worker's savings would fall. We can follow this through in terms of the possible impact of this change on the flow of resources back to her family. Similarly, if there is a bout of inflation that is higher than the rate at which income increases, real income will fall. These equations give us enough information to begin to explore at least some of the possible impacts of changes such as these on savings flows, demand for consumer goods, and investment. With respect to inflation, economists have long held that it is one of the most regressive forms of 'taxation' that bears most heavily on the poor.

It is folly to assume that we can describe the whole of the economic development process using simple economic identities. Even complex models using dozens of equations fail to do justice to the full range of nuances that are commonplace in everyday economic activities. Nonetheless, the simple 'circular flow' model that can be described are instructive. It demonstrates the close association that there is between the flow of savings, hours worked, the wage rate, income and investment expenditures.

We have deliberately simplified the picture we have drawn on the basis that if we cannot describe these relationships in the simplest circumstances, we will not be able to do so in far more complicated real world situations. We have not, therefore, allowed the pictures we draw to include a finance system, borrowing and lending facilities, foreign trade, or a government sector. Rather, our purpose has been to illustrate, in as simple a way as possible, the importance of the link between income earned, wage rates, consumer demand, savings flows and investment. From this simple model the absence of the ability to borrow because there is no finance and banking sector ought to be clear. If the level of planned or desired expenditure on investments exceeds available savings, then the only way that the shortfall can be met is if income is increased or consumption reduced. If we were to add a government sector, the national government could look to foreign aid or international borrowing as alternative or complementary ways in which to fill the gap in savings.

In a sense, the money that our hypothetical urban worker sends back to their family in the village is like 'foreign aid'; a transfer of resources from one party to another at a cost to the recipient that is below the true market value to the giver of the resources transferred. To the urban worker, the opportunity cost of the savings sent home are the things that the worker would have done with those funds if they had been retained for personal use.

A simple model of dynamic economic development

In order to get to the complicated world of economic growth, more than a sequence of snap-shots that we derive from the simple world of comparative statics is needed. As can be seen from the following, the dynamics of change, however, can be 'pictured' using situations that are not all that much more demanding than those we have already described.

Output is a function of investment

The technical relationship between investment and output can be assumed to be fairly stable in the short term, although the nation's capital stock can and does change. While the investment:income ratio does tend to be fixed in the short term, it will vary between competing technologies. This ratio defines a direct relationship between investment and the expected change in income arising from that investment.

For the managers of macroeconomic policy in developing countries, this implied that economic development could be achieved if adequate attention could be given to savings mobilization to fund higher rates of investment, and technology transfer to fuel modernization of the economy. Underlying the macroeconomic economic growth relationship is the belief that the main determinant of economic growth is continuing investment in modernization, financed from savings generated by sustained growth in income.

In essence, this is not unlike the story that is embedded in the modelling of the urban worker. The availability of work in urban settings is limited by the investments that create new jobs in established industries or in new fields of economic activity, such as electronics, pharmaceuticals, engineering and information technology. However, once the urban worker has found a job, future prospects for the worker and their family back in the village is dependent on the productive use of savings from income earned.

Competing strategies of economic development

It is a fallacy to say that developing countries have a clear choice between competing strategies of development. In fact, there is a spectrum of strategies based on chosen priorities that will combine several strategies simultaneously. The government might, for example, dominate investment activity in the new industry sector, leaving agriculture essentially to the private sector. At the same time, the nation's development priorities might reflect goals that aim at reducing national dependence on agriculture as a source of GDP but increase the gains made from participation in international trade. Consider the 'development diamond' shown in Figure 5.1.

The strong impression that one can draw from the long-term trends in structural characteristics of developing countries suggests that in 1950 the Third World was far less dependent on international trade than it was in the 1990s and will be in the future, but it was far more dependent on agriculture. The role of government in developing economies has expanded in every respect. As a source of investment the government sector has assumed the role of entrepreneur and leading risk taker in addition to its traditional role in infrastructure development. Figure 5.1 is an attempt to summarize the

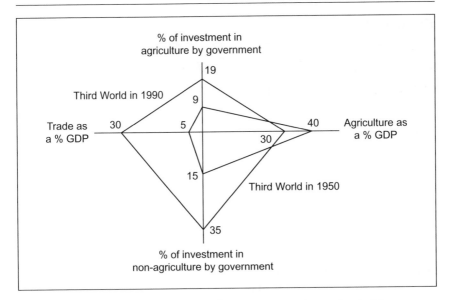

Figure 5.1 *Competing development strategies and priorities*

primary emphasis in the mix of development strategies that have been followed by low income economies since the Second World War.

The development experience of high-growth, high-income developing countries confirms the importance of judicious government leadership, choice of competitive industries to nurture, and equity-promoting development policies. A closer study of the 'success' stories of north and east Asian economies adds to these observations lessons that redefine our understanding of an appropriate role for government in economic development. These new perspectives give greater weight to policies that impose on new industries performance indicators consistent with competitive development, and confirmation of the importance of 'investing in people' and 'getting prices right'.

These lessons indicate that current received wisdom ought to place far less stress on the uncertainties associated with the existence of 'economies of scale' requiring government intervention to realize. Further, it appears that fears of market failures, which have been used to sanction increased government intervention, centralized planning and regulated development of new industries have been grossly overstated. This conclusion does not imply that there is a lesser need for governments to intervene where market failures exist. On the contrary, the contribution of government to sustainable economic development will be advanced if governments spend more time and resources ensuring that markets work, redressing the sorry absence of adequate and effective competition policies in developing countries.

Chapter 6

Crises in Africa, Asia and Latin America

JOHN McKAY

Why study crises?

Recent crises in Africa, Asia and Latin America have generated a huge amount of debate about both their causes and policy implications, and for very good reasons. Crises of the dimension, for example, of the Asian crisis of 1997–1998 are very traumatic events in their own right, resulting in losses of income and assets that affect very wide sections of the community, and with ramifications that can often be seen for decades afterwards. Job losses are usually dramatic, made much worse in most countries by the absence of any kind of social safety net. In the case of many African countries, which have been in seemingly permanent crisis for some three decades, the impacts are catastrophic. As Arrighi (2002) has noted, it is perhaps now more realistic to replace the term 'African crisis' with 'African tragedy'. High levels of poverty and hunger are compounded by the impact of the HIV/AIDS epidemic to produce a human and environmental disaster.

But crises are also of much interest because of what they can tell us about economic and political systems in various countries and regions, and at the wider global level. The stresses and tensions that lead to crisis can be very revealing about these systems and how they function, or malfunction. Similarly, we can also learn much about policy responses by national governments and international organizations in terms of their effectiveness and their impact on the lives of the people in the country concerned.

Even more fundamentally, crises are usually the periods in which national or international systems change or are transformed by outside pressures. During periods of relative prosperity, or at least stability, the pressures for change are much less urgent, and, as a result, there is a tendency for existing ways of operating to continue. It is only when some form of crisis creates a national or international emergency that change is forced on often-reluctant governments and the wider community.

However, there may also be a danger inherent in regarding crises as unusual or even aberrant phenomena. A number of writers have pointed out that periodic crises seem to be an integral part of the international capitalist system, or perhaps of all political and economic systems yet devised. For example, Joseph Stiglitz (2002) has argued that we should not really be surprised that Asia suffered a crisis in 1997 and 1998. Rather we should ask why, contrary to previous experience in all other regions, including Europe and North America, the region had been so remarkably stable and dynamic more or less continuously since the 1960s. This raises some interesting and fundamental questions about how the global system is organized. In particular, recent crises in Asia and Latin America have called into question the architecture of the international financial system. Similarly, the responses of international agencies such as the World Bank and the International Monetary Fund (IMF) have received much scrutiny, and there have been many calls for significant structural reforms as well as fundamental changes in approach.

These debates are also instructive in providing clear evidence of the complex linkages between economic, social, political and strategic factors. The consequences of crisis in any nation are not purely economic, of course. Stock market crashes, currency fluctuations, balance of payments problems and other economic manifestations of crisis are matched by other impacts, such as unemployment, famine, political instability, ethnic tensions, and so on. Similarly, the causes of crisis are never purely economic either. While the mismanagement of economic policy may be important, there are frequently problems of the more fundamental failure of the state. External factors or shocks, such as rapid increases in the price of oil, also interact in complex ways with internal forces.

In this chapter we consider the general nature and causes of crisis, as well as looking more specifically at recent problems in Africa, Asia and Latin America. In the next section we review the historical evidence on a number of crises, going back to the 19th century, and evaluate the theories that have been put forward to explain these serious events. Next, we ask whether recent changes in the global economy and its rules of operation (or its lack of rules) may have increased the likelihood of crises taking place. These themes are then taken up in separate sections on the recent crises in Africa, Asia and Latin America. Finally, in a short conclusion, we attempt to draw some general lessons from this experience.

Regional crises in historical context

One result of the recent crises in Africa, Asia and Latin America has been to create renewed interest in the longer-term historical evidence on crises in various countries and regions. Most attention has focused on the Great Depression of the 1930s and the contrasts or commonalities with the experiences of the 1980s and 1990s, but there has also been a return to the historical analysis of several periods of upheaval during the 19th century, and some important re-interpretations of earlier evidence (see, for example, Kindelberger 1978, Fishlow 1985, Ghosh 2001). It is no accident that most interest has been generated by those crises that have threatened to have serious impacts on the West: if a crisis is no longer just 'out there' in Africa or wherever, even if troubling images appear nightly on the world's television screens, it is much less disturbing than one that threatens to strike also at the rich nations.

During the 19th century, various kinds of crises occurred – in the 1820s, 1850s, 1870s and 1890s – but most of these were confined to small groups of countries. In this sense they were quite different from the Great Depression of the 1930s, which was global in its impacts. The crises of the late 1970s and 1980s were again more restrictive, affecting Latin America, Eastern Europe and Africa, but not Asia. The 1995 crisis in Mexico was even more limited in scope. The Asian crisis was of course confined in its primary stages to one region, but it threatened to spread to other regions, especially Latin America and Russia, and a number of commentators argued that the entire global system was being seriously destabilized. It was in this sense that Paul Krugman (1999) extended his analysis of the Asian crisis to herald the 'return of Depression economics'.

But this intense level of enquiry, resulting now in a very large literature, has failed to yield any consensus on the predominant causes of these crises. The conventional view, what in Chapter 2 has already been introduced as the *Washington consensus,* stresses that crises are essentially caused by internal weaknesses of policy, failures to implement the optimal mix of measures that include trade and financial liberalization, privatization of government-owned assets, tight monetary and fiscal settings, and the general strengthening of market-based systems throughout the economy. It follows then that the appropriate policies to deal with crisis situations emphasize steep increases in interest rates, cutbacks in government spending, increases in taxes, and a range of *structural reforms* designed to deal with the problem features of the national economy. This set of policy prescriptions has provided the foundation for the various IMF programmes to assist crisis-ridden countries in a range of continents and at various times.

This dominant paradigm has received a great deal of criticism from a number of directions. Several commentators have criticized the exclusive concentration on the internal causes of crisis. While not denying that weaknesses in national institutions and policies are important in many situations leading to economic disasters, they argue that external factors are often just as important, and in many instances paramount. External features that have been cited in various circumstances include the structure of the international financial system itself, the activities of hedge funds and other new financial instruments, the policies of the international agencies such as the IMF, the policies of stronger Western countries (especially the United States), and the activities of multinational corporations. Since the Asian crisis of 1997, much attention has been paid to the impacts on individual countries of the liberalization of flows of international finance. Stiglitz (2002), for example, has argued that the primary cause of the Asian crisis was the vulnerability to rapid changes in the inflows and outflows of foreign funds that resulted from the premature removal of restrictions on the movements of international capital to and from countries such as Korea. In such situations, the poor development of regulatory regimes coupled with rapid inflows of funds can quickly result in the formation of a 'bubble' economy, which can even more rapidly plunge into crisis once the bubble bursts.

More fundamentally, a number of writers have argued that crisis is the direct and inevitable result of the ways in which various regions have been incorporated into the global capitalist system. The precise details vary from region to region, and many forces are specific to particular historical periods, but, as we shall see in relation to Africa, Asia and Latin America, crises have been explained by some researchers as the result of long-term structural factors rather than specific and internal policy failings. Thus, for such writers, crisis becomes practically synonymous with underdevelopment, the result of long-term forces and structures rather than shorter-term, local departures from 'normal' conditions (see, for example, Arrighi 2002, Frank 1980).

These fundamental differences of opinion on the causes of economic crisis inevitably lead to sharp conflicts over the most appropriate policy responses to the onset of a crisis. The policy prescriptions that flow from the Washington consensus described above are, of course, restricted to internal policy reforms. By contrast, those writers who have emphasized the external or global causes of crisis have paid more attention to the reform of international financial institutions and of the basic structures of the global economy. The IMF has been criticized for being too concerned with the need to pay back loans owed to international lenders, often with dire consequences for the welfare of local residents. As we shall see, the IMF has also been criticized for its failure to learn the lessons of the Great Depression of the 1930s. Through the work of John Maynard Keynes, in particular, it became accepted by many monetary authorities that the policies put in place initially to deal with the Great Depression were entirely inappropriate, and, in fact, made matters even worse. By emphasising cuts in government expenditures, imposing tariffs to protect local industries, and increasing interest rates governments in the 1930s deepened the Depression and ensured a greater contagion effect from one country to another. Yet, it was just such contractionary policies that were imposed on Asian countries in 1997, when what was needed was a strong stimulus to encourage growth, and industrial expansion in particular (Stiglitz 2002).

A number of attempts have been made to bring together internal and external factors that might be responsible for the onset of a crisis, to produce a more complex and sophisticated analysis. One example here, and one I will use particularly in relation to the Asian crisis, is the theory of *regime dynamics*. Here the term regime is not used in the commonplace way, which simply refers to the nature of the incumbent government. Rather, the regime operating in a particular country constitutes its political and economic institutions, the various political and economic alliances that operate within the nation, and the policies of the government and the business sector that will be modified in the context of changing political and economic contexts. Interest in the concept of regimes has been stimulated by the simple question of why individual economies continue to differ from one another, and why these differences persist rather than converging on international 'best practice'. Certainly, national systems undergo change, even fundamental transformation as the result of some kind of crisis, but this also raises questions about the mechanisms of such change and about the relative strengths of local and international factors. Social pressures for restructuring accompany growth, exacerbated by changes in the global economy. Capital and the state adjust their strategies to these changing environments, but within previously established social contexts. These national systems have all evolved, often over long periods, to meet the needs of the local conditions and the heritage of unique institutional configurations. Boyer and Hollingsworth (1997) emphasize that there is no single optimum institutional configuration for any economy, rather a very large array of possible arrangements. The best choice depends upon the external environment and the precise nature of the societal problems that need to be solved. They argue that not even the market should be regarded as the ideal and universal institutional arrangement for co-ordinating economic activity, and numerous problems can arise if efforts are made to organize the world exclusively in terms of markets. All institutional arrangements have their own strengths and weaknesses, and the best choice at any time will depend on the precise context. Hence no new institution, not even the market, can simply be borrowed and implemented in any given social setting. It is not just the nature of the individual institutions that varies between nations, it is the unique configuration of these components in the entire economic system that is important (Gao 2001: 18).

Perhaps the most difficult task in this kind of analysis is to understand how and why regimes change. Pempel (1998) argues that any regime is faced with a variety of pressures for change, but not all changes will destabilize a regime: some will merely cause minor re-adjustments. He recognizes several levels of disturbance in any system. Some pressures can be accommodated by the system with only minimal adjustments. But fundamental pressures may be sufficient to bring about a true *regime shift*. Gao (2001) suggests that such a shift may take some time, as the forces for change gather strength and the fundamental contradictions in the existing regime are revealed, and as a new regime emerges, made up of some new elements and some remaining fragments from the old system, but combined in a unique new configuration. Thus, in this method of analysis, crisis is the result of often long-term contradictions that build up in an existing regime and which then force fundamental change. This process of change is often highly disruptive and contested, and will usually result in a period of low growth or even chaos before a new regime becomes established.

Thus, theories of crisis in various parts of the world have been developed from a wide variety of intellectual and ideological perspectives. The dominant paradigm, that of the Washington consensus, sees crises as the outcome of policy failures within individual countries. These problems need only be short-lived if the correct (and usually harsh) policy reforms are undertaken. If this is done successfully, the nation can then return to a path of normal growth within a benign international system. At the other end of the spectrum, some analysts see crises as almost permanent, and certainly inevitable, features of the global capitalist system. The precise nature of a crisis will vary according to the position of the nation concerned in the global division of labour, but all crises derive from the same basic source. Between these two extremes are a number of other explanations, some internally focused, others stressing the international dimension. Some authors have attempted to combine internal and external analyses to produce more complex explanations. Some theories are short-run in nature, while others emphasize more basic structural factors. A variety of these approaches will be outlined in more detail in the later sections of this chapter on the crises in Africa, Asia and Latin America.

Has the risk of crisis increased in recent years?

A number of analysts have suggested that the risk of crisis is now significantly greater than it was some decades ago. Attention has been focused particularly on the changing volume and nature of international financial flows, the progressive removal of state regulations controlling such flows, and the ways in which the introduction of these new financial systems have been supported by alliances between some governments in the developed world and the emerging financial industry.

There is no doubt that the volume of international financial flows has increased dramatically since the 1970s. In earlier periods, the amount of money flowing between two countries was made up of two components: first, payments for goods traded, and second, investments and loans from one country to another. Both of these flows continue to be important, and both have grown dramatically in recent years; however, in terms of sheer volumes of finance, these items have been overwhelmed by a new component, speculative capital. Gray (1998) estimates that as much as $1.2 trillion moves across national borders every day, which is around 50 times the value of international trade. He suggests that some 95 per cent of this capital is speculative in nature, often using a complex new array of derivative financial instruments based on options and futures. Around $900 billion is traded daily on the foreign exchange markets of the world, considerably more than the total foreign exchange reserves of the world's central banks, ensuring that the financial authorities, even in the largest and richest countries are very limited in their power to act in the national interest against currency speculators. Even John Gray (1998), who is generally sceptical of claims that the current era of globalization is as new and revolutionary as some commentators would have us believe, acknowledges that this is a completely new feature of the world economy. The most carefully researched critique of this new world of speculation has been developed by Susan Strange (1986, 1998). She has coined the term *casino capitalism* to describe this new phase in the global economy, but she has more recently argued that things have moved on so fast since her original book was published that it is now better to talk about *mad money*. This frenetic movement of capital has a clear logic, she argues, but it is simply the logic of short-term profit, with no thought of the consequences for nations or communities.

Several factors have given rise to this new situation. One of the most important of these has been the rapid growth in the amount of money available on world financial markets. This growth in liquidity began in the early 1970, when rapid rises in the world price of oil flooded the markets with *petrodollars* seeking profitable investments. This source of money was quickly supplemented in August 1971, when President Nixon, in an attempt to solve the problems that the United States government was having in financing the Vietnam War, unilaterally abrogated the Bretton Woods system, refusing to allow the continued exchange of US dollars for US gold reserves. In essence, this allowed the US government to simply print more money to pay for spiralling balance of payments deficits. As we shall see, a number of commentators have tried to make a direct link between this decision and the onset of the Asian financial crisis in 1997. Still more money became available on financial markets in the 1970s and 1980s as the result of rapid industrial development in East Asia. So much money became available for investment that only a small fraction of it could be absorbed into traditional channels. Thus, the second factor in the development of this new economy has been the rapid emergence of new financial instruments and products, and, equally importantly, the reform of existing government regulations to allow them to flourish. Existing banks were progressively freed from many of the limitations that had previously restricted their activities, and, even more important, was the emergence of a new range of non-bank financial institutions. At the same time, foreign exchange rates were progressively deregulated, allowing markets rather than governments to set these rates. But for these new financial products to work more effectively and speedily, new technologies were needed for the instantaneous transfer of funds across the globe, and these were soon available thanks to advances in computer and satellite systems. However, one vital piece was still missing: a push strong enough to overcome the reluctance of some governments to give up the national controls that still existed in many economies, and which were seen by many officials (correctly as it turned out) as necessary for continued stability in the financial sector. This final impetus was provided by the emerging alliance between the United States government and the dominant players on Wall Street. The US government used extremely tough measures to ensure that even the most reluctant governments were persuaded to deregulate their systems, and, in particular, remove any restrictions on inflows of capital.

We have noted that speculative capital is by far the largest component of international money transfers, and Susan Strange's metaphor of the casino highlights the risky and unstable character of much of this activity. In speculation, as in the casino, bets are being made, this time on the future value of currencies, commodities, or shares, and some punters will win and others will lose. Given the instability that often results in hardship for ordinary citizens in the countries affected, would it not be more desirable to remove much of this uncertainty in markets by returning, for example, to more regulated exchange rates? The answer is that it is the very uncertainty inherent in the new system that allows some people to make very large amounts of profit from speculation.

While all of these changes have been taking place in the financial system, there have also been important developments in the more traditional sectors, which are now frequently called the *real economy* – a telling comment on the nature of much financial activity! In spite of continuing protectionist policies in the European Union and the United States, restrictions on world trade through tariffs and other means have been progressively reduced through a series of agreements negotiated within the General Agreement of Tariffs and Trade (GATT), which, soon after the conclusion of the Uruguay Round in 1993, became known as the World Trade Organization (WTO). This is one factor in the rapid growth of world trade, which since 1945 has expanded some twelve-fold, compared with a five-fold increase in global output. But this increase in trade also reflects a growing internationalization of production through expanded foreign investment, especially by large, multinational corporations, a process which began on a large scale in the 1970s. At this time, profit levels for the large corporations of the developed world were being hit by the combination of three factors. First, the shocks to the international finance system provided by the Vietnam War and the dramatic increases in the world price of oil in 1972–1973 and 1979 pushed up cost structures for many companies and resulted in strong inflationary pressures in many countries. Secondly, the 1970s were also a period of rapid wage increases in much of the developed world, with serious consequences for inflation and production costs. Thirdly, the global recession triggered by the oil price increases resulted in a significant and extended drop in demand for many industrial products. The total impact of these pressures saw a serious crisis in profitability for established companies, resulting in strenuous attempts to cut costs. The strategy favoured by many corporations was to move production offshore to cheaper locations, saving particularly on labour costs. But for this to be successful, several new features had to be in place. Global production networks, in which components made in several locations are brought together for final assembly and export of world markets, can only work effectively if cheap and efficient transport is available. This was provided by the complex of innovations that has become known as the containerization revolution. A global network of production also requires an efficient and reliable means for monitoring, controlling and co-ordinating production and quality levels. This became available through rapid advances in computer and satellite technology. Perhaps most important of all, the institutional basis had to be available in the new host countries to ensure that investment could be made on favourable terms. An increasing number of national governments, especially in Asia, were willing to provide such a favourable environment for foreign investment as part of their emerging strategies of export-oriented industrialization. The spectacular success of the Newly Industrialising Countries of Asia was initiated by the *Four Dragons* (or *Four Tigers*) – South Korea, Taiwan, Hong Kong and Singapore – and their strategies for growth were quickly adopted by a number of other countries in South-East Asia. The *Little Dragons*, notably Thailand, Indonesia, Malaysia and Vietnam, hosted those labour-intensive industries that by the 1980s had become uneconomic in the original Dragons.

This movement towards international production has continued to the present, resulting in a rapid growth in the levels of direct foreign investment (FDI). Flows of such investment increased steadily, with a very rapid expansion in the 1990s, but since 2000 there has been a serious downturn, although this may turn out to be temporary. In 1982, the total value of all FDI inflows was $59 billion, but this increased to $203 billion in 1990, $386 billion in 1996, and a staggering $1492 billion in 2000. Following the terrorist attacks on the United States in September 2001 and the more general stagnation in the world economy, there was a marked slowing of the flows in 2001 to $735 billion. However, the vast majority of these capital movements have been to developed countries. In 2000, some 82 per cent of all FDI was in developed countries, and only 16 per cent to the developing world. However, it is worth noting that the recent downturn in flows has shown up much more in the developed countries, with the proportion going to developing countries rising to 28 per cent, much closer to the average figure since the 1980s (UNCTAD 2002). During the 1990s, the flows of investment to developing countries were dominated by investments to Asia, with some two-thirds of all developing country flows. By contrast, flows to Africa were generally only one-tenth of those to Asia.

A number of writers have argued that the recent rapid increases in FDI flows have heralded a new period in the nature of global financial flows. Eichengreen and Fishlow (1998) have contrasted this new era with earlier episodes on the basis of the dominant form or origin of financial flows, recognizing three distinct periods and modes of investment:

1. *The era of bond finance.* This was a long period of distinctive international financial flows originating in the 19th century, and consisting of loans guaranteed by government, municipal or private organizations. Strong bond markets emerged in London, Paris, Berlin and Amsterdam to service the emerging capital markets particularly in the United States, Canada, Australia, Latin America and Russia. This early period was somewhat volatile, with frequent defaults. Much of this investment was in infrastructure projects. A number of changes took place in this system in the early part of the 20th century. The United States emerged as an exporter of capital rather than an importer, and, by the 1920s, a number of financial intermediaries emerged, notably investment trusts. The nature of the projects being financed and the countries of destination also changed, widening to include some much more risky markets. The system received a fatal blow in the global Depression of the 1930s, with most countries defaulting on their debts.

2. *The era of bank finance.* As has already been described, the late 1960s and early 1970s saw a period of rapid increase in liquidity resulting from

increases in oil prices, and the emergence of new financial instruments, supported by a new consensus on the need for financial reform and liberalization. At the same time, new financial markets emerged, notably the Eurodollar market, and these actively pursued possible new investment destination in the developing world. Large investment flows took place initially to Latin America, but then to East Asia and Africa. When the burden of this debt became too much, and when it became clear than a substantial proportion of the money had been invested in unproductive projects – what Susan George (1988) has called 'castles in the sand' – the result was the crisis of Third World debt. This crisis began with the Mexican default of 1982, and in many ways is still with us.

3.   *The era of equity finance.* This period has been characterized by an emphasis on investment in shares in companies around the world, and Eichengreen and Fishlow date this phase from the end of the 1980s. By then there had been significant changes in the financial regulatory systems of many countries, but equally important was the emergence of pension funds and insurance companies as major investors. By 1990, lending to Latin America was greater than at the peak of the bank lending period, and flows to Asia were also very large. In 1994, Mexico was again in trouble, but this was passed off as a local effect attributable to particular national circumstances. The money kept flowing, encouraged by low interest rates in the United States and much of the developed world. Financial flows to Asia were enormous in the mid-1990s, but a rapid loss of investor confidence, beginning in Thailand in the middle of 1997, heralded the onset of the Asian financial crisis.

Thus, financial flows from the developed to the developing world have been closely tied to crises of various kinds and in different regions. These crises may have had some common origins, although many commentators have argued that local factors such as poor standards of regulation, corporate governance and general economic policies have also been very significant. However, it is clear that the impacts of these events have been quite different in particular regions. So it is to the specific manifestations of these recent crises in Africa, Asia and Latin America that we now turn.

African crisis, African tragedy

Sub-Saharan Africa is now clearly the most impoverished region of the world, and many statistics could be cited to illustrate different facets of this unfortunate condition. The total GNP of the 48 economies that make up the region is some US$300 billion, roughly the same as that of Belgium, which has a population of 10 million, compared with some 600 million in that part of Africa. This total GNP is also rather less than the rich countries devote annually to farm subsidies. South Africa contributes around 40 per cent of this total income, and Nigeria some 11 per cent, leaving the combined income of the other 46 countries at US$140 billion for a combined population of 450 million (Mills 2002). In 1975, the per capita GNP of the region stood at 17.6 per cent of the global average: by 1999 this had dropped to 10.5 per cent (Arrighi 2002). Around 40 per cent of the population lacks access to safe water, and 33 per cent have no access to health services. Two million children die annually before their first birthdays: infant mortality rates have risen to 107 per 1000 compared with 69 in South Asia. Some 70 per cent of the world's HIV/AIDS cases are in Africa: 9 per cent of all 15 to 49-year-olds live with the disease.

This is certainly a crisis, but unlike, for example, the Asian financial crisis, this is not a short event with a quick onset and a relatively rapid recovery. This has been a long, slow deterioration, especially since the 1970s. The causes are complex and multifaceted, embedded in pre-colonial, colonial and post-colonial history and in the cultural history of Africa's diverse population. Space only allows us here to consider just some of the most important factors involved.

Arrighi (2002) and others have argued that one of the most important causes of the African tragedy is the form in which Africa has been incorporated into the global economic and political system. By the time of European colonization in the late 19th century, Africa had already been devastated by several centuries of Arab and European slave trading from the region, and this was exacerbated by decades of further exploitation. Whatever the shortcomings of Japanese colonial rule in Korea and Taiwan, (and this period from 1905 to 1945 witnessed some extraordinary acts of cruelty), the colonial power left behind a level of human resource development and infrastructure that was far in advance of anything that was achieved by the Europeans in Africa, and this was a important factor in the early development of East Asia. Many of the African states that achieved independence in the 1960s had very arbitrary boundaries, cutting through many major ethnic groups, and many had difficult geographies because of their size, shape, harsh terrain, poor climates or very uneven population distributions (Herbst 2000). The fragmented nature of many African societies and political systems, and the very old tribal antagonisms that existed between a number of groups, worked against the consolidation of state power and authority in many of these new countries. The result, was a large number of weak, poorly organized or even dysfunctional states. Few, if any, states were able to mobilize the resources needed to compete in the new, globalizing economy that emerged from the late 1970s onwards. Many were, in fact, faced with civil wars, insurrections or armed conflicts over access to scarce resources. Recently,

Africa has suffered from a large number of internal conflicts, certainly more than any other region, and, by 2001, the number of internally displaced people had reached 13.5 million (Mills 2002). In many states, the major priority of the ruling elites has been the consolidation of their own power and wealth rather than programmes to enhance the wealth of the total society.

A lack of adequate human resources has been a particular problem for the continent. To make matters worse, Africa has suffered from a serious flight of skilled people in recent years. It is estimated that 60,000 doctors, engineers and university staff left Africa between 1985 and 1990, and this exodus has continued at a rate of 20,000 per year since then (Mills 2002). Add to this the impact of a range of debilitating diseases, and the extent of Africa's problem of skills and labour becomes very clear.

A further basic problem facing Africa has been its clear marginalization in the global system that has emerged since the late 1970s, and especially since the end of the Cold War. During the Cold War a number of debilitating 'wars by proxy' were fought in Africa by the superpowers, but few if any economic benefits were received. Since the early 1990s, Africa has been largely seen as irrelevant in global economic, strategic and political terms. The continent now accounts for less than 1 per cent of annual global financial flows. By 2001, sub-Saharan Africa accounted for a total FDI stock of only US$116 billion, compared with US$1243 billion in East and South-East Asia (UNCTAD 2002). China alone now attracts more than 10 times as much FDI per year than the whole of Africa. International investors see Africa as poor, politically unstable, lacking in human resources and with inadequate infrastructure. There are also few domestic sources of investment given the low level of average incomes, and as a proportion of wealth or exports, African countries remain among the most heavily indebted in the world. Savings rates in Africa are the lowest in the world, less than half of those found in Asia, and some 40 per cent of all the domestic wealth that does exist is held outside the continent. Arrighi (2002) has argued that as a result, Africa has always been very dependent on foreign capital, but this turned away from the continent in the drastic restructuring of the global economy that took place in the 1980s.

Partly as the result of the failure to create productive export industries capable of generating significant export earnings, Africa has been unable to make any headway in paying off the debt that has been accumulated over previous decades, but particularly since the 1970s. In 1999, Africa's debt was estimated to be some $201 billion. In many African countries external debt is now larger than total GDP, and in some cases debt servicing requirements in terms of interest repayments alone far exceed total export revenues (Gibb *et al.* 2002). A debate continues over the question of how the international community should respond to the continuing burden of debt in poor countries, many of them in Africa. One influential group has lobbied for the forgiveness of debt under the banner of the loose alliance called Jubilee 2000. In 1996, the World Bank created its Highly Indebted Poor Countries (HIPC) Debt Initiative to allow poor countries to break free from these past debts. By 1999, $3.4 billion had been set aside for debt relief, but Jubilee 2000 has consistently argued that much more needs to be done. In fact, little real assistance has been given to poor countries, notably those in Africa, although a number of promises for action have been made. Critics of debt relief, on the other hand, have argued that there is no point in cancelling debts until there is tangible evidence of real reform in Africa, otherwise yet more external assistance will be wasted (Easterly 2001).

Given this multitude of problems, what are the prospects for reform and reconstruction? There have been many grand plans for African reconstruction in the past, including a series of studies by the World Bank (1981, 1984b, 1986), the Lagos Plan of Action produced by the Organization of African Unity (1981), and the United Nations *Plan of Action for African Economic Recovery and Development, 1986–1990* (United Nations 1985). The actual impact of these ambitious programmes has been very disappointing, but there is now some renewed hope for progress based around the recent launch of the New Partnership for African Development (NEPAD). This is a joint initiative of the African leaders themselves, but it has been endorsed by a meeting of the World Economic Forum in Durban in June 2002 and by a meeting of the G8 in Canada later in the same month. In July, also in South Africa, the African Union was launched, replacing the old Organization of African Unity, and this was partly meant to symbolize a new and united beginning to co-operation in the region in support of NEPAD.

The aim of NEPAD is to put an end to poverty in Africa, reduce its marginalization in the world economy, and forge a more equal relationship with the developed countries. A primary target is a growth rate of at least 7 per cent, but in order to achieve this there must be peace, good governance and effective policy-making on the continent. To achieve this, four core initiatives have been proposed:

- *The Peace, Security, Democracy and Political Governance Initiative*, which aims to bring an end to conflict in the region and encourage good governance and a respect for human rights.
- *The Economic and Corporate Governance Initiative*, designed to strengthen economic management in governments and in the private sector.

- *The Capital Flows Initiative*, which aims to bring greater resources to Africa by encouraging investment, debt relief and higher levels of development assistance.
- *The Market Access Initiative*, under which there will be attempts to open foreign markets to more African exports. There will also be encouragement for greater diversification of African production and the movement into higher value products.

It is much too early to judge how effective this new initiative will be, and some community groups have already denounced NEPAD as a sell-out to foreign interests, but many commentators see this as one last chance to bring some hope to the people of Africa after decades of devastation and poverty.

Dragons in distress: the 1997 financial crisis in Asia

We have already seen in Chapter 2 that the dramatic rates of growth achieved in a number of East Asian countries from the 1960s onwards posed a major challenge to analysts of the processes of development, and opinions varied widely as to the basic causes of this economic success. Similarly, the catastrophic crisis that hit the region in 1997 has also given rise to widely varying theories about the causes and implications of these events. Some commentators have argued that the causes of the Asian crisis were basically *internal* and resulted from the growing contradictions and inefficiencies that had emerged within the economic and political systems of these countries. Their policy response has been to call for fundamental reforms of corporate governance, economic policy making, the political systems and the relationships between the government and the private sector. By contrast, other researchers have suggested that, while there were certainly some internal shortcomings, the basic causes of the crisis were essentially *external*, relating particularly to the shortcomings in the structure of the international financial system. Their policy responses have centred on the need for a new architecture of regulations governing these global flows of funds.

The onset of the crisis is usually dated to 2 July 1997. Following a period of ineffective and very expensive attempts to maintain the peg on its exchange rate with the US$ – it is estimated that the Thai government spent US$23 billion in a vain attempt to defend the currency – the Thai *baht* was floated. Within weeks the Indonesian *rupiah* was also floated, and both of these events were interpreted by the international financial markets as important warning signals about the economic vulnerability of the whole region. Very quickly the exchange rate in Thailand went from

25 *baht* to the dollar to 56. In Indonesia, the fall in the value of the *rupiah* was even more dramatic, from 2300 to the dollar to 17,000. Before the end of the year, the contagion of crisis had also spread to South Korea. By November 1997, South Korea had a serious shortage of foreign exchange reserves, partly as a result of a failed attempt to defend the *won,* and there were fears that the country would default on the payment of its international loans. In December, the government was forced to call on the International Monetary Fund for assistance, and the largest ever emergency loan of US$58.3 billion was put in place. Similar, but smaller, loans were also obtained by Thailand and Indonesia. A number of other countries in the region were also affected by the crisis, notably Malaysia, but the governments did not find it necessary to seek IMF assistance.

The impact on the most affected countries was catastrophic. The Indonesian economy declined by at least 14 per cent in 1998, and by some estimates inflation was running at 60 per cent. Both Thailand and Korea experienced declines of around 6 per cent, closely followed by Malaysia at 5.1 per cent. Unemployment became a serious problem throughout the region, although the precise levels are open to some dispute. World Bank estimates suggest that by June 1998 unemployment had risen to 16.8 per cent in Indonesia, 8.8 in Thailand, 6.9 in Korea, and 5.0 in Malaysia. However, some governments in the region have presented very different estimates. According to the government of Indonesia, for example, at the height of the crisis unemployment there was around 40 per cent, with a further 20 per cent underemployed. The social effects throughout the region were very serious, with marked increases in poverty levels. The poor were badly hit, of course, but many small and medium-sized businesses were also destroyed (Haggard 2000). In the midst of the crisis, Korea managed to hold a presidential election, with a relatively smooth transition to the new government of President Kim Dae-Jung, but in Indonesia there was widespread political unrest, culminating in the overthrow of President Suharto.

Given the magnitude and importance of these events, it is hardly surprising that the Asian crisis has generated an enormous literature from an wide variety of disciplinary, theoretical and ideological perspectives (see, for example, Stiglitz and Yusuf 2001, Jomo 1998, Agenor *et al.* 1999, Pempel 1999, Woo *et al.* 2000, Jackson 1999, Haggard 2000). However, there is a wide divergence of opinion on the basic causes of the catastrophe, its policy implications, and the appropriateness of the conventional management measures invoked by the IMF.

As was noted above, one major school of thought has paid particular attention to the internal causes of the crisis, stressing failures of macro-economic policy and corporate governance. However, these authors have focused on quite different aspects of internal policy failures and, hence, have invoked quite different policy responses. Not surprisingly, the emphasis has been different in each of the countries being analysed, properly reflecting contrasts in each national experience. Much of this literature has been unashamedly triumphalist, proclaiming that the Asian model, which had for many years been touted by some as more effective than the orthodox neo-classical paradigm, did not work after all. The aspects of policy failure that have been stressed by different authors and with relation to specific countries include:

- *Prudential regulation.* One important aspect of the crisis was the failure of a number of important financial institutions, especially some of the large banks, and the inability of regulatory bodies within governments to monitor and control levels of debt, exposure to bad debts, and dangers from over-exposure to currency fluctuations. These issues were apparent in all of the affected countries, but perhaps most seriously in Korea, where many of the large conglomerates had become over-extended and had very high gearing levels. To compound the problem, a number had taken out these large loans denominated in $US, because of the much lower interest rates in the international markets compared to the local system, and were, thus, highly vulnerable to any devaluation of the *won*. Many of these loans were also of a very short-term nature.

- *Corporate governance.* Companies, it has been argued, exhibited similar failures in their lack of monitoring, risk management, transparency and reporting mechanisms. Many companies not only had high debt/equity ratios, but also had in place systems of cross-guarantees from one component of a conglomerate to other members. Thus, failure in one area of business had the potential to destabilize the entire structure. Accounting systems were inadequate, if not deliberately secretive, making it impossible for investors to gain a true picture of company health. Companies have also been criticized for their obsession with growth and market share, without adequate regard for the profitability of their operations.

- *Exchange rates.* Many countries affected by the crisis, tried for far to long to defend their currency exchange levels, and in the process wasted large amounts of precious foreign reserves. Several commentators have argued that the crisis clearly demonstrates the superiority of floating exchange rates.

- *Cronyism.* Several critics have pointed to the bad effects of close relations between governments and individual companies, emphasizing the dangers of corruption, preferential deals, and poor investment decisions (Kang 2002, Lindsey and Dick 2002). Governments were often unwilling to take appropriately tough decisions because they had close relations with many of the companies involved.

- *Technology and productivity.* In an article that evoked an enormous amount of debate, Paul Krugman (1994) argued that Asia's rapid growth was fragile in the longer term because it was not based on gains in productivity, which he suggested were the mainspring of modern progress, but on the application of larger and larger amounts of capital and labour to the production progress. Such a system could not go on for ever, and growth was bound to slow. Some other commentators have pointed to this factor, the inability to generate high levels of productivity growth through technological advances, as crucial to the onset of the crisis.
- *Moral hazard.* It has been suggested that many firms in Asia had no incentive to change their behaviour and become more efficient because they knew that governments would always look after them and give them rewards. This not only entrenched inefficient practices but also gave misleading signals to the market.
- *Unwillingness to allow firms to fail.* It is often argued that governments are faced with a difficult trade-off between the need to achieve economic efficiency and the demands for economic and political stability. Most Asian countries have tended to favour the support of inefficient firms rather than risking the trauma that would result from their failure. This, it is argued, simply stores up trouble for the future, as inefficient firms become a greater and greater burden on the rest of the economy.

These attempts to place responsibility for the Asian crisis squarely on the policy failures of the governments involved have been countered by a number of authors who have instead pointed to failures in the international system. Most influential among these is Joseph Stiglitz, a former Chief Economist at the World Bank and Chair of President Clinton's Council of Economic Advisors. In a recent book (Stiglitz 2002), he has given detailed evidence on US economic policies in Korea, arguing that these were central to the onset of the crisis. As early as 1993, there were discussions within the US government about ways of opening up the lucrative Korean market to a variety of US companies. In particular, Wall Street was keen to see the liberalization of the Korean capital market to allow greater foreign penetration. A number of critics urged caution, arguing that this action was premature and needed to wait until the necessary legal and regulatory frameworks had been developed in Korea otherwise there was danger of serious instability. However, local US interests prevailed and Korea was pressured to undertake rapid deregulation. The result was a very rapid inflow of capital for a time, but when the panic of 1997 set in there was an equally dramatic reversal. The fragile financial system could not cope, and this premature liberalization of the capital account is regarded by Stiglitz as the single most important cause of the crisis. This theme of the paramount importance of outside pressures has also been taken up by Chalmers Johnson (2000) who, in addition, has raised the question of US pressure on Asian governments to purchases large quantities of US armaments.

Whatever the truth of these allegations, they are certainly believed by large segments of the population in many Asian countries. Many Korean businessmen, for example, have privately expressed their anger at the pressures on them to sell their companies, which they worked hard to establish, to American companies for what they regard as ridiculously low prices immediately after the crisis. The consequence has been the development of what Higgott (2000) has called 'the politics of resentment', widespread anti-American feeling in the region. One result has been a concerted attempt by Asian governments to build stronger financial defences around the region, to work more closely together, and to develop a strong regional financial body to reduce any possible future dependence on the IMF. This is the logic of a number of recent initiatives, such as the agreement in Chiang Mai to establish a regional monetary agreement, moves to strengthen Asian co-operation through the 'ASEAN plus three' system, and discussions about the establishment of an Asian Monetary Fund. Asian countries have also been very much to the fore in discussions about reform of the architecture of the international financial system, to provide greater protection to nations from the impact of speculation and unchecked money flows of the kind that destabilized Asia in 1997 (Eichengreen 1999).

Recently, a new and rather longer-term explanation of crisis in various Asian countries has emerged around the theme of regime theory, which was introduced earlier in this chapter. Crisis, it is argued, can be interpreted as the instability that results during a transitional period from one regime to the next. In Japan, for example, the old development system based on the guarantee of lifetime employment, government assistance to the private sector and a range of other mechanisms already discussed could no longer be maintained and the economy lost competitiveness in many areas. But transition to a new regime has proved difficult, resulting in several years of stagnation (Gao 2001). McKay (2003) has applied a similar analysis to Korea, arguing that the old model of the developmental state became outmoded, but the piecemeal introduction of market reforms was not viable either. What was need was a true regime shift, and the onset of the crisis underlined this point and facilitated the emergence of a new regime This has some of the features of the old regime, plus some new elements, but brought together in a uniquely Korean way that is consistent with Korea's history, culture and institutional configuration.

Crisis in Latin America

The situation in Latin America is in some ways a combination of the deep-seated and extended structural crisis described for Africa and the shorter but very dramatic shock that affected Asia. The problem for Latin America is that, while its structural problems are not as severe as those in Africa, they are still very serious, and the financial crises that have afflicted the region have been both regular and very deep.

We have already seen in Chapter 2 that a number of scholars from Latin America have been very influential in the initiation of new ideas in development thinking, especially in exploring the ways in which the region has been adversely affected by outside exploitation. One of the most influential of these thinkers in recent years has been Fernando Henrique Cardoso, who, in a widely-quoted book (Cardoso and Faletto 1979), argued that the association of national and international capital could never lead Brazil to the goal of independent industrial development: rather it would deepen existing inequalities and result in a loss of control over national development. There was some excitement in the development profession, then, when Cardoso was elected President of Brazil in 1994. The result has, however, been a disaster for the Brazilian people (Rocha 2002). Instead of following his own warnings about the dangers of unequal alliances with foreign capital, Cardoso argued that the last decade of the 20th century had seen the unprecedented growth of capital and its availability, something not foreseen by earlier theorists. Countries such as Brazil could gain great benefit from being one of the major destinations of these capital flows. Thus, he embarked on a reform programme very much along the lines of those advocated by the IMF. The capital account was liberalized, earlier protectionist barriers were removed and state enterprises were privatized. In order to attract more foreign capital, interest rates were increased to the highest levels in the world. After some good early results, the long-term impact was just as Cardoso had predicted in his earlier book. Locally owned industries collapsed under the pressures of high interest rates and increased foreign competition, and as the economic indicators started to deteriorate, still higher interest levels had to be imposed. But in the end this did not prevent a serious flight of foreign capital. Unemployment levels increased and income inequality became worse than ever. It was not surprising, then, that in the Presidential election following the end of Cardoso's term in 2002, the left-wing opposition candidate Luiz Inacio 'Lula' da Silva should gain such a clear victory. One of his first steps in office was to delay the purchase of new fighter jets for the air force, diverting the funds instead to anti-hunger projects. With the likely establishment of the Free Trade Area of the

Americas, many commentators in Latin America are expressing serious concern about the power and influence of the United States on Latin America, often repeating Cardoso's earlier warnings.

But all of this is not to deny that there have been some serious internal problems in Latin America as well. As we saw in Chapter 2, a number of studies have compared the growth experience of Asia and Latin America, and attempted to explain why Asia has been so much more successful. The most commonly cited explanation is the difference in the behaviour of the governments and the elites in the two regions. Peter Evans (1995), for example, has argued that it was the nature and motivation of the state that was important. Developmental states in Asia were both *autonomous* – able to act in the national interest rather than on behalf of particular class interests – and *embedded* – closely enough integrated into societies to allow them to be effective managers and co-ordinators. Asia has had its problems of corruption and cronyism, but it has also had some very effective and clear-sighted governments, something that has been very rare in Latin America. Thus, as in the case of Africa, we come back to the question of *state capacity* as a key variable in successful development strategies.

Despite these problems, there have been times when Latin America has been held up as an example of successful development and effective reform. Both Mexico and Chile have at various times been cited as having implemented genuine reform, but it is the examples of Brazil and Argentina that have attracted the most interest (Buxton and Phillips 1999, Frieden *et al.* 2000, Haber 2000). At various times they have been held up as shining examples of how reform should be designed and managed. As we noted earlier, the first years of the Cardoso presidency saw rapid deregulation and privatization in line with IMF recommendations. Similarly, in 1997, as Asia was mired in crisis, Argentina was held up as a favoured country for investors wary of the instability and risk. Following the economic chaos of the 1980s, the orthodox policies of President Menem were credited with a period of growth and low inflation. However, the spillover from the Brazilian crisis in 1998 and other problems heralded a spiral into first recession and then deep crisis, culminating in the bank closures and related riots of December 2001.

Not surprisingly, the Brazilian and Argentinian examples have elicited a wide range of opinions as to the causes of the rapid reversal, and, in particular, the role of the IMF. Some commentators have argued that the IMF policies were not implemented with sufficient vigour, and the IMF was partly responsible for not ensuring that the government did not go further to ensure greater fiscal responsibility (Mussa 2002). In the case of Brazil, Williamson (2002) has suggested than many of the fundamentals of the economy are sound, and one of the roles of the IMF should be to break the cycle of panic by helping to restructure Brazil's debt in an orderly and sustainable fashion. Once again, Latin America has been urged to follow the good example of Asia, which has responded positively to its crisis and has (with the notable exception of Indonesia) recovered very quickly. Others have been much more critical of the IMF policies, arguing that, in fact, Argentina had followed the orthodox policy advice. Certainly, the electorate of Brazil now seems to be convinced that the old IMF orthodoxy is not capable of delivering the freedom from crisis that they need so desperately.

Conclusion

Given this range and complexity of experience it is difficult to generalize about the causes and consequences of economic crisis, much less suggest some effective and generally applicable policy responses. We have seen that economic crises of various kinds have frequently caused great hardship, loss of employment and destruction of assets. We have also reviewed some evidence suggesting that the contemporary global system may be more vulnerable than ever to disruptions of this kind. There is no consensus about the causes of economic crisis, and in particular the balance between internal and external (structural) factors. What is clear, however, is that periodic crises allow us to see much more clearly the structure of the international system, and assist us in identifying some of its weaknesses. It is also clear that these traumatic events are periods of great change and adjustment as one form of economic organization gives way to something else. As recent events in Latin America and Indonesia have also demonstrated, economic crises can often result in dramatic political realignments. For all of these reasons, economic crises represent an important focus within development theory and practice.

Chapter 7

Political Development

DAMIEN KINGSBURY

Development has traditionally been regarded as exemplified by economic growth, which, in turn, has implied technical solutions to development's problems. Development has been seen, in this sense, as value free, with economics claiming to be an objective science rather than a debate about the allocation of resources. However, the allocation of resources, which determines how people live, is perhaps the singularly most intense political subject. The idea that economics was value-free therefore implied the monopoly of a particular ideological framework, rather than the employment of an ideologically free science. Moreover, even where a competing economic paradigm was available, e.g., socialism, it was still encouraged to be applied with equal commitment to ideological singularity. Indeed, it was this contest between economic paradigms that came to define the political competition between the West and what was referred to as the Soviet bloc. Within that, wide-ranging political abuses were committed in the name of one ideology or the other, more often than not with attendant low levels of material development. It therefore became obvious that politics was a key subject of the development process.

In this sense, development is arguably best understood as 'emancipation' or, as Sen (2000) puts it, 'freedom', and while this should have a material aspect, emancipation is primarily understood as a political quality. This has been emphasized by the failure or near failure of a number of states due to low levels of political development, and the role of political development in governance and hence in safeguarding economic processes.

The most successful illustration of political development in the post-war era has been the process of decolonization and the establishment of new, independent states that have enjoyed most of the formal qualities of sovereignty. The political claim in almost every case was to emancipation from colonialism and subsequent self-determination. The political models this established ran the full gamut from monarchy (e.g. Morocco, Brunei) to constitutional monarchy (Thailand, Malaysia) to plural republicanism (India, South Africa), and various forms of authoritarianism (various Latin American states) and totalitarianism (post-unification Vietnam, Cambodia 1975–1979, post-1962 Burma, and numerous sub-Saharan African states at various times). In most cases, the shape of post-colonial states has reflected the style of colonial government and, more importantly, the process of decolonization. In most cases, where decolonization followed a military struggle, the military asserted authority in the post-colonial state, usually with authoritarian or totalitarian implications. Indeed, while there have been worthy exceptions, the political history of post-colonial states has largely been one of various forms of authoritarian or totalitarian government of both left and right ideological persuasions. In terms of analysis, it has taken the failure of many states to develop economically, and for there to be a considerable shift in the global political climate, for the focus to traverse the field from the narrow modernist political paradigm of replicating developed countries, to comparative or relativised ('post-modern') politics. It is suggested here that the next phase of theoretical political development has moved again towards a more grounded, but still reflexive, political position.

Origins of the debate

The idea of political development derives from the key political contests in the history of Europe and the US, in which the nature of the relationship and balance of power between the individual and the state were periodically rewritten. The first real contest of this type was in 6th century BC Athens, whereby all free adult males directly participated in a simple majority vote, from which is derived the idea of democracy. However, there was at this time also an established history of oligarchy and tyranny that would have later echoes. The first of the 'modern' revolutions to sow the seeds of political development was that of England of 1688 (though sometimes dated from 1646, when Parliament first operated without a king), while the American Revolution (1775–1783) created the first modern democratic republic. The republican model (or the parliamentary alternative) became the common form for new states during the 20th century. The main debates have thus been about the ideological form of government, the spectrum running along two intersecting lines, from right (reactionary) to left (socialist) and from liberal to totalitarian (see Figure 7.1). Some analysts actually suggest that the distinctions between 'left' and 'right' in politics is less important than the differences between liberalism and authoritarianism, because a truly liberal society embodies many of the egalitarian hallmarks associated with socialism, while authoritarianism or totalitarianism of both left and right reflects little difference in its application.

During the period of the Cold War, political development occurred primarily within the context of one of the two competing models, the right

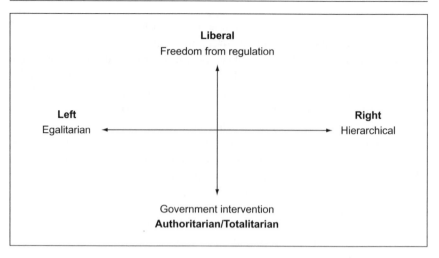

Figure 7.1   *Spectrum of politics*

dominated by capitalism and the left dominated by state socialism, or struggling to find a space in between (such as the Non-Aligned Movement). As a consequence of economic, military and political support from the two major power blocs, the governments of many developing states were often unable to be held accountable by their citizens and tended to form authoritarian and sometimes despotic political systems of both ideological extremes (see Bates 2001: Chs 4–6). So far as 'development' was concerned, the intention was to make states economically self-sufficient, without compromizing their political loyalty to one or the other of the two primary ideological causes.

What was to pass for a nuanced understanding of political development at this time was located in the 'comparative' school of politics (e.g. Pye 1985, and Harrison and Huntington 2000), although the relativization of politics this tended to encourage – that politics could be understood as a product of culture of history – could also be seen as excusing the perceived necessities of the Cold War. It has only been with the end of the Cold War and external support for such states, that developing country governments have had to increasingly fend for themselves and consequently, in many cases, become more accountable. This movement towards accountability has given renewed impetus to ideas about political development. It has been suggested by some commentators that as a consequences of the terrorist attacks in the United States on 11 September 2001 there has been a concerted US effort to establish the 'new world order' first enunciated after the US-led war to oust Iraq from Kuwait in 1991. Some have further commented that the support for, and in some cases imposition of, pro-Western governments has altered the development politics framework, and that this marks a new era in development akin to that of the Cold War era. It is correct to say that the United States has, since '9–11', taken a more assertive stand on what constitutes acceptable and unacceptable polities, and that this has steered US development aid. However, it is far from clear that, in the uni-polar global environment that has existed since the end of the Cold War, this has had any meaningful impact on the development process as such, or political development in particular. The primary change has been in the division of thought over Huntington's *Clash of Civilizations* thesis (1993, 1996) which views the world as divided along 'cultural' lines. Interestingly, proponents of this view, in both the West and Islamic countries, tend to be more authoritarian, while opponents of this view tend to be more liberal.

What is 'political'?

It could be argued that any decision concerning more than one person involves interest and is hence 'political'. This is especially so when the group is a more broadly constituted community, as a 'nation', or within the framework of a state. It is also increasingly argued that apart from the symbiotic relationship between politics and economics there are a range of other considerations that people regard as important and which are directly affected by political processes. Examples of these include the freedoms to express, associate, and worship, to build one's social group or explore one's culture, to have some sense of control over one's own destiny, and to enjoy some personal, social and cultural integrity in the process of making those decisions.

Ideas about what constitutes development broadly defined have therefore shifted more or less in line with challenges to the economic development paradigm (for example, see Sen 1999), critiques of classical economics, related questions about global and local economic distribution and the relationship between the two, and over issues such as the tension between social and political corporatism (aggregate interest, sometimes referred to as communal interest) and individual development (individual interest). Linked to questions about the political means by which global and local economic distribution is gained and sustained – the processes of government and governance – has been an increased concern with human rights issues and related assessments of the development process. This human rights orientation has, in turn, countered the focus on relativized politics, or the politics of comparative development in which the level of political development is predicated upon economic and cultural contexts. This, then, raises issues about how political processes form and transform, and about how political goals are broadly conceived and manifested, and about what political values can and should be considered across contexts.

To distinguish between two closely related but logically distinct fields of inquiry, the politics of development can be understood as a systematic analysis of the types of political processes that have occurred in developing countries. While this can engage issues of political development, in (too) many cases the politics of developing countries do not reflect political development as such. Further, political development is not exclusive to developing countries and refers to the process of political 'progress' as such, which may also advance and retract in what are otherwise developed countries. Political development does have particular relevance to development politics, however, in that most developing countries aspire to political development, at least in rhetoric, and almost all have undergone significant political change over the past 50 or so years.

Some definitions

In any discussion about political processes, there will always be debate and disagreement. However, much debate is semantic. To this end, the following definitions are proposed, which, in turn, help constitute what is intended by the term 'political development'.

At one level, politics is the process or organizational principles of government, or the gaining, exercise and maintenance of authority or power. At another level, however, politics can be anything that posits the interests of one person or group in opposition, competition or variance with another, including the way such opposition, competition or variance is manifested. While politics can exist at a very local level – the politics of family relations, office politics and so on – within the context of political development it usually applies at a more broad social level, involving communities, nations and states.

In this, political development is intrinsically linked to other aspects of development; broadly understood, development is constrained if good governance is not in place, and such governance is a key category of political development. There is also the idea that political development, including ideas such as self-determination and emancipation, is, or should be, a goal in its own right.

The state

As the key political institution in the international arena and the organizational model for national aspirations, the state continues to be the point upon which political development turns. While the idea of the state has been challenged by globalization, it continues to be the prime actor in international relations, as the manifestation of collective political will, and as the arbiter of the conditions of the lives of its citizens. Yet, in the most simple, anthropological, sense, a definition of the state could simply be a shared agreement between a group of people about the rules under which they jointly live. It may, indeed, imply a form of government without a state in the physical sense of the term (Krader 1970: Ch2, see also Gamble 1986, Crone 1986) However, this view of the state does not include more 'explicit, complex and formal' agencies of government, which are the usual markers of state existence (Krader 1970: 13)

Another, more common, marker of the state is its internal integration. In this, social cohesion and the sense of social 'investment' in the state, which is in turn reliant on 'social capital', are key factors in the success of the state. In less successful states, or in states where integration is less, claims to state control are far more rhetorical than actual. This is particularly notable in a number of sub-Saharan African states.

In a physical and institutional sense, the state refers to a specific and delineated area in which a government exercises (or claims to exercise) political and judicial control and claims a monopoly on the legitimate use of force (Morris 1998: 45–6, Laski 1934: 21–4) In terms of the delineated area of the state, its spatial quality 'is integral to its functions and agencies' (Smith 1986: 235). That is, the area of the state defines the functional reach of its agencies. In a contemporary sense, this implies a reach up to the limits of its borders and sovereignty within them, although in more 'traditional' (pre-Westphalian, see pp. 170) societies this border area was far more ambiguous or pliable. This conception of the 'state' is distinct from that of the 'nation', which refers to a group of people who regard themselves as possessing a common political identity, most often based on language and other fundamental cultural signifiers.

The state functions as a marker of political development in that the state is, in the contemporary world, the primary agent of political development. If a state 'fails' – if it loses functional control over all or part of its territory or its institutions cease to function – the process of political development also fails. Within a given territory, the state can be identified by the activities of its agencies. Such agencies include the administrative bureaucracy, the armed forces, educational institutions, state industries, the judiciary, police and the penal system. State agencies and institutions are the functional manifestation of the state, and, to the extent that they fulfil the needs of citizens, can be said to represent the level of political development. It should be noted that the role of the state has come under challenge, from ideological influences, from world bodies such as the International Monetary Fund and from globalized economics (see Chapter 4, also Weber and Bierstaker 1996: 282, Hinsley 1978: 285–286, Camilleri 1994: 130–131, Camilleri and Falk 1992). However, while there are serious challenges to the state at both local and global levels, in many senses these are little greater than in the past, and the state retains its role as the central organizing principle in political affairs. Further, the 'modern' aspects of the state, including its administrative and bureaucratic functions, while slightly reduced, remain central to the capacity of the state to function, in principle, on behalf of its citizens. The functioning modern state, therefore, remains the model to which developing states aspire, and it is within the context of the modern state that aspirations towards political development remain most commonly met.

This, then, raises the issue of the relationship between the government and the state. In principle, the modern state has an existence independent of the government and, with its institutions, continues while governments come and go. However, the distinction between the state and the government was historically less clear. Prior to the colonial period the strength or ability of a government or ruler created, maintained or expanded the state. With the loss of that government or ruler, the state was often prey to other states or dissolved due to a lack of internal cohesion. This can still be seen in failed states.

As noted above, the state is defined by a number of characteristics, and to the extent that a state does not address these criteria it can be said to fail as a state. As outlined by Morris (1998), the state and its institutions must have an enduring quality, in particular being able to survive changes of government or political leadership. These agents must be differentiated from non-state agents and must, if the state is to function, be co-ordinated with each other. For example, the police and the judiciary must be co-ordinated in their support and application of the rule of law, while the executive and the military must act together to protect the sovereignty of the state.

Within that territory, the agents of the state should have full (i.e., not shared) and equally distributed authority. The territory of the state must be sovereign (or claim to be sovereign), in that the state can legitimately claim a monopoly on the use of force within its territory. Jurisdiction must extend to the full extent of the territory of the state. The legitimacy of the state and its right to claim a monopoly on the use of force (or compulsion) should preferably be by consent and must be adhered to by members of the state, and, in that the state is recognized as the ultimate authority (Morris 1998: 45–6, Laski 1934: 21–4) This adherence should be in the form of allegiance to the state, superseding all other allegiances, although to ensure this allegiance, the state would usually have to function to protect and promote the interests of its members. This, then, implies voluntary, rather than compelled, allegiance to the state, which, in turn, implies an aspect of political development.

The idea of the state as it is understood in this contemporary sense is relatively new, formulated in Europe from the time of the Treaty of

Westphalia in 1648 and only in the nation-state sense from the early 19th century. As an idea, it is still disputed in areas where the authority of the state is challenged by assertions of the nation. The most obvious examples of this are the former USSR, the former Yugoslavia, the former Czechoslovakia and, to a lesser extent, in Belgium, Italy and Canada. Across Asia, India, Indonesia, Burma, the Philippines, Thailand and Laos all have localized 'nationalist' rebellions against the spatial–functionalist claims of the state, while much of Africa has been rife with rebellions based on ethnic distinction. In spite of these protests against incorporation into established states, these rebellions are not opposed to the idea of the state as such and, indeed, are aimed at reforming or creating new states.

One broad critical understanding of the state derives from a broadly Marxist or 'political-economy' perspective, summarized as 'analysis of the development of capitalist relations of production and the development of a class of capital accumulators' (Robison 1985:298). In this, the state is crucial because of its strategic role in the process of capital accumulation and, consequently, class (aggregate) formation and conflict. This role of the state in capital accumulation has indeed been critical in many developing countries and classes, in the conventional industrial sense, have in some instances emerged. However, their emergence in developing countries has, in many cases, been fitful and weak and class conflict has often been less important than communal relations. In the case of capital accumulation, in some cases this has occurred not through conventional capitalist practices, but through economic systems that rely on patronage, cronyism and corruption, which imply a lack of political development.

The other main analytical grouping in the political economy field employs a 'dependency approach', which supports the idea that economic classes are often too weakly developed to constitute a political basis. Instead, it proposed that networks of patrons and clients provided a more substantial basis for political organization (Robison, paraphrasing Mortimer, 1985: 298) The relationship between the governments of developing countries and foreign capital, has been more complex than just an outflow of surplus, as indicated by the 'dependency' school theorists. A considerable surplus also accumulated to indigenous (*comprador* and 'nationalist') elites, and there have also been some cases of considerable economic strengthening of the state and its infrastructure. Further, broad living standards have improved as well as declined in developing countries, depending on a range of conditions and circumstances. This means that the generalizations of the dependency approach were a useful critical tool but not fully adequate (Tornquist 1999: 42–3, 70–3). To that end, a more nuanced 'neo-dependency' critique has arisen as critical method for examining world global systems such as 'free trade'.

A further characteristic of the state, and one that directly reflects levels of political development, is the degree to which it is established and, similarly, the degree to which it can operate independently of external agencies. This idea of the 'embededness' of the state refers to the degree to which the state is able to implement its programmes and policies within its given territory. Similarly, the extent to which the state and its institutions are functionally autonomous from non-state interests is also a critical marker of political development within the state. Evans (1995) applied these criteria of embededness and autonomy to a number of examples in sub-Saharan Africa, and often found them wanting. Just before complete state failure, Evans identified what he called the 'predatory state', in which the state (or its agents) survived by 'feeding' off the citizens of the state. Hutchcroft (1998) also applied Evans' criteria of state failure to the Philippines, and in principle much of this could have further been applied to a number of Latin American states, while the predatory qualities could continue to apply to states such as Burma. (e.g., as discussed by Evans 1995:12, 43–7)

As noted above, most, though not all, states are marked by a type of 'social contract', in which the ruler and the ruled agree to conditions of participation in the state (as discussed by Hobbes, Locke and Rousseau, amongst others, although rejected by Mill, 1961: 552). This implies a type of *modus vivendi* connected with a sense of mutual consent (Plamenatz 1968: Ch 1) or mutual advantage (Rawls 1991: 4), but might in fact be a non-jural consideration; that is, being born into a particular state and with few or no realistic options for change or flight, participation in and effective acceptance of state rules might be just the way things are.

Morris has noted, in particular, that strong (authoritarian) states have a greater tendency to engage in harmful behaviour towards their own citizens or others, and that democratic states have not yet gone to war with each other (Morris 1998: 14–19). The implication of this is that where the power of the state is not in balance with a duty to its citizens it can act contrary to their interests. Such a balance is most recognizably achieved through the agencies of the state being accountable to the government and the government, in turn, being accountable to the citizens. Accountability is, therefore, perhaps the most important criterion of political development.

Failed states

A 'failed state' is one that has so grievously damaged itself or has been damaged that it no longer effectively functions (see Jackson-Preece 2000, Bilgin and Morton 2002, and Spanger 2000, for further discussion).

Because states are comprised of both external recognition and internal function, even states that no longer function internally may still receive external recognition and may be able to reconstitute themselves. An example of this is Cambodia from 1975 until late 1978.

In one sense, Afghanistan has also been a failed state, having not functioned as a state in any meaningful sense for decades, with the political collapse of the 1990s a continuation of that situation. Like Cambodia, Afghanistan can be said to have been a victim of external rivalries being played out in the domestic field. But such rivalries found fertile soil in what, at its most cohesive, has only ever passed for an internally riven pre-modern kingdom.

Some completely or partially failed states included Cambodia, especially from 1975 until 1992, Afghanistan, Solomon Islands, and, in Africa, Somalia, Sudan, Rwanda and Congo. The failure of a state in regard to territorial control could imply the development of a competing centre of power and an alternative form of political development (i.e., rebellion or revolution). This applies, in particular, to secessionist movements, which usually claim to better represent the aspirations of a constituent 'nation'. In other cases, the introduction of the idea of the state, and its institutions, is incomplete, testing the relationship between governmental institutions that are only shallowly embedded and a society that has previously had little or no functional contact with state institutions. Examples of this, and where the idea of the state is only slowly being implanted, could include Papua New Guinea, West Papua (Indonesia) and parts of sub-Saharan Africa.

A relatively recent phenomenon has been external intervention in failed states, notably through multilateral military forces and, later, various official and NGO aid agencies. UN intervention in Cambodia effectively rebuilt the political structure of the country in 1992, although the subsequent elections and the 'coup' of 1997 saw the re-entrenchment of the pre-existing dominant political party, the Cambodian People's Party. Despite this, there have been some important moves towards political development in Cambodia since 1992 (see Downie and Kingsbury 2001), and the state is considerably more cohesive than prior to 1992. In Afghanistan, the establishment in 2002 of a new government, with nominal writ over the sovereign territory, has been sorely tested by feuding regional warlords and clan rivalries. This has threatened to plunge the state back into failed status, requiring the long-term commitment of foreign forces (in this case NATO).

Other states that have been able to claim less international attention, such as Somalia, Sudan, Rwanda and Congo, amongst others in Africa, have not had the 'benefit' of an external stabilizing force. Foreign intervention, in these cases, appears to be a short-term palliative to deep, structural problems, including historically rooted and culturally embedded ethnic fragmentation, profound elite corruption, and sharply differing development visions. This intervention has sometimes undermined the efficacy and long-term commitment that external intervention seems to require.

Interest

The failure or near-failure of states, or the violent overthrow of governments, reflects a fundamental competition of political interest. This may reflect an ideological division or separation on the basis of ethnicity, religion or other group association. In this, a common interest is the defining characteristic of political identity. Interest, as such, can be manifested as 'self-interest' (sometimes understood in economic terms as 'incentive'), which is primarily aimed at securing the fortunes of oneself and one's immediate family or group; 'aggregate interest', which sees one's fortune as concurrent with the wider group; 'enlightened self-interest', which identifies the securing of the fortune of oneself through helping secure the fortunes of others; and 'altruism', which is primarily to benefit others. Of these types of interest, self-interest and aggregate interest tend to dominate most societies, although aspects of the latter two types of interest are also notable and are often held up as the public ideal, especially in mythology (hagiography of national heroes being a prime example).

Shared or aggregate interest is the basis of joint claims and, as such, is the foundation of political groupings (groups acting out of shared interest) and equally has the capacity to define political groups not just in their own terms but in opposition to each other (competing interest). Such aggregate interest can be the (non-communal) basis of political parties, and is a key marker of political development.

Types of interest fall into further sets of categories, being defined as vertical interest and horizontal interest. Vertical interest is where localized interest is expressed as a distinct political identity in competition with the state, and horizontal interest is expressed as localized interest vis-à-vis other local groups. Modernist political conceptions locate aggregate interest as the most common in industrially developed, literate and contiguous political communities, identifying interest across communities similarly located within an economic framework (e.g. factory workers, 'middle class', etc.) but who are unlikely to personally know each other. This in turn corresponds to Anderson's 'imagined communities', which developed a sense of common bond despite unfamiliarity through the use of a common language and the availability of print (Anderson 1991). Such communities, which express their aggregate interest as policy preference, are the basis of modern political parties, are identified with more 'advanced' or modernist conceptions of political development, and are usually regarded as necessary for the functioning of a modern national polity.

When there are few social stresses, such as competition for resources, political societies based on communalism can function in a relatively cohesive manner. However, most societies experience competing interest within them, which manifests as social tension. In times of such tension, communally based political societies tend to retreat to ethnic or communal loyalty despite what might otherwise be an underlying material commonality of interest between groups, or division of interest within a particular group. Communal violence between ethnic Hutus and Tutsis in Rwanda was a particularly bloody illustration of this. Such 'horizontal' distinctions between communal groups tend to be made on grounds of social or cultural identification and, indeed, their primary focus may well not be political in an explicit sense, hence they are sometimes are not well equipped to address complex policy issues. Political parties can, and often do, retain aspects of communalism, and, indeed, in many less politically developed societies political parties may be based on communal (ethnic, religious) identity. In theory, however, they at least aim to address issues that extend beyond the immediate communal group and may distinguish within such a group fundamental differences of interest.

Vertical or proto-nationalist interest, expressed as separatism from the state, tends to have colonial or pre-colonial foundations, some of which were enhanced by colonial and post-colonial processes. These could include the development of regional economic disparity, the encouragement of regional identity for the purposes of divide and rule, the use of soldiers from one area against the peoples of another, and through the displacement of indigenous populations who develop a 'national' identity in response to loss of homeland. With the advent of increased levels of communication, political communities can and do exist across quite wide and dispersed geographic areas, although, if voluntary, such communities must enjoy a fairly high level of political cohesion and mutuality, and hence political development, in relation to one another. This form of voluntary political community is, therefore, based upon the political status of the constituent members, its citizens.

As the subject of the state, a 'citizens' is entitled to such political and civil rights that exist within the state, and owes an obligation of duty as defined by the state. Within the context of political development, the balance between a citizen's rights and obligations in regard to the state can vary. Citizenship also implies being a constituent member of a state, being subject to its laws, the rights under which might vary considerably, and being internationally recognized as such.

Prior to the formation of modern states, the idea of a 'citizen' did not effectively apply. In pre-modern, pre-colonial and colonial states, the population were subjects of the ruler (if sometimes via a proxy representative). Prior to the colonial period, the state often granted little political status to those other than the ruling elites and their functionaries. It is only with the establishment of the modern state, in particular with delineated borders, constitutions and (at least theoretically) full and equal legal authority up to those borders, that citizenship became available and applied to the people of developing countries. Under this application, citizenship has usually been regarded as universal for all legitimate inhabitants of a state, although how this has been defined has varied considerably. Being a product of a normatively voluntary political association, citizenship manifests itself as a legitimacy of political existence, which may seek to correspond with like-minded groups or individuals outside of the formal structure of government. This is what is known as civil society.

Civil society

In political development, the idea of political parties and civil society are closely related. Without civil society, political parties tend to function exclusively as a means of social mobilization for elite interests. In one sense, political parties are the ultimate expression of civil society, in that they are the primary form of political organization aimed at shaping policy, which an active civil society would see as its long-range goal. In this sense, civil society can be seen to include interest and lobby groups and minor political parties. But more importantly, as an expression of the political health and development of a community, civil society is also the multi-faceted availability of different types of political expression, including non-government organizations, the media, trade unions, students groups, artists, intellectuals, public protesters and others who make it their business to contribute to public debate.

Like human rights, the strength of civil society is an important indicator of political development. It offers a broad contribution of ideas to public debate and helps to ensure as complete as possible a range of policy options. It ensures that the government is held to be accountable for its decision making and that there is general public awareness of the values of government decisions. It represents, in a sense, a society in discussion with itself and with its government. In most cases where civil society is active, government tends to be more responsive.

Where civil society is unable or not allowed to be in discussion with itself or its government, there is usually a high level of political repression and a retreat from or blockage of political development. This has been a common characteristic of many developing countries that have suffered from political repression (as well as some industrialized countries that have evolved an extreme form of state corporatism, such as fascism or communism). In this sense, civil society acts not only as a contributor to the political health of a society, but also as an indicator of that health. Although prone to criticism for its many real and imagined failings (see, for example, Chomsky 1994, Chomsky and Herman 1988), the news media have come to represent perhaps the forefront of civil society in political development. This is because the news media is (at least when it is allowed) a conduit for public expression. Of course, many would correctly argue that the news media tends to reflect different sets of interests, not all of which can be said to represent general public good. But the news media is in the interesting position of having to appeal to the public to survive, so as well as helping shape public discourse it is also shaped by it, or else loses its audience. There are, of course, further issues of interplay and hegemony (see Lukes 1974, Gramsci 1971), although this presupposes potential, if not actual, high levels of internal social friction, which not entirely coincidentally is less prevalent where the media is freest.

Social capital

An important idea that extends from civil society is that of 'social capital', drawing in part on the work of the social theorist Robert Putnam (1995, 2000, Putnam, Leonardi and Nanetti 1993; see also Coleman 1990: Chs 5, 8, 12, as a foundation for Putnam's work). In Putnam's terms, social capital is that store of values, information and common identity that may accrue to an individual or, through them, to a society. Where social capital is high, society will tend to work more cohesively towards commonly agreed goals. Where society has a lower level of social capital, such as where values, information and common identity have not built up or have depleted, then society will tend to be more fractious, unco-ordinated and unable or unwilling to act in a mutually beneficial manner. In the former case, a high level of social capital could be seen as a key indicator of a healthy civil society and much more likely to be associated with a higher level of political development. In the latter case, a lower level of social capital would most likely mean that civil society was weak and divided and was more likely to be associated with a lower level of political development.

In determining social capital, education seems to be a key indicator (see WBPNL 2001). However, there have been examples of low levels of civil society activity and accumulated social capital that have still resulted in outcomes that rank fairly highly on the political development index. These could be said to include popular participation in the 1993 elections in Cambodia, the 1998 elections in Indonesia and the 1999 ballot on self-determination in East Timor. In the cases of Cambodia and East Timor, there was a high level of informal political education as a consequence of living in a highly politicized environment. Interestingly, in both instances the United Nations played a key role in supervising the electoral process, imposing some formal structures (and temporarily removing some impediments) with the effect of constructing conditions ordinarily associated with a higher level of political development.

Ideology

As a political society develops, it coheres around a particular policy framework, it can be said to have adopted a particular ideological position (e.g., liberal capitalism, socialism, theocracy, etc) as a basic or first principle set of ideas through which an intellectual order is made of social and political experience. Ideology is not necessarily dogmatic and all views of how the world is, or how it should be, are ideologically grounded. For an ideology to function as such, it must have a relatively high degree of internal coherence. Internal incoherence constitutes a lesser form of political development, so the development of ideology constitutes a higher form of political development (although, because of often artificially structural rules, ideological dogmatism does not).

All political systems and levels of political development represent ideological assumptions, even where such assumptions are not explicit. That is to say, political leaders might claim to be pragmatic, to assert the good of the state or the nation above ideology, or to represent not contemporary ideologies but traditional patterns of political behaviour. But in each case, they are usually representing ideas that derive from classical or neo-classical economic theory, from Leninist interpretations of Marxism, from nationalist ideologies or from resurrected feudal or pre-feudal traditions. Such has often been the case where political rhetoric, say on land redistribution (El Salvador, the Philippines), free markets (the United States, Singapore), socialism (Vietnam, China), the role of the armed forces (Burma, Indonesia) or human rights, is not matched by corresponding political practice.

Some better known examples of ideologies include absolutism, variations on Marxism (see Marx 1967, 1973 for his own idealistic thoughts on political development), anarchism, fascism and liberalism, although religious beliefs such as Christianity or Islam, or ideas about the nation ('nationalism') or the state ('uniterianism', 'federalism'), can also function as ideologies. Even 'consensus' can be an ideology.

As a means of containing dissent within a competitive political framework, the idea of consensus has been employed by a number of developing countries to reduce the greatest objections to arrive at a workable compromise. The origins of the consensus model is generally held to be the village, in which face to face contact is regular and in which harmonious social relations is important. To this end, when a matter affecting the broader community was to be decided, it was by reducing the objections of the minority to make the outcome more broadly acceptable. As a political system in developing countries, however, consensus is often decided by elites, who favour consensus for its ability to ensure continuing elite control of political processes. A consensus candidate for the presidency, for example, would ultimately not be beholden to any group, but rather amorphously to 'the nation'. This then opens the possibility of the abuse of power, and of corruption. Consensus may therefore be a means of avoiding conflict and building superficial social cohesion, but it represents only a small step towards political development.

As noted, it can also be claimed that 'nationalism' is an ideology. The detailed form of this ideology varies from place to place, for example from the organicist (proto-fascist) idea of the Indonesian state to the Leninist model of the Vietnamese state. What they feature in common, however, is not just a desire for independent unity and, consequently, self-determination, but the creation of an idea of a common bonded identity (see Anderson 1991, Smith 1986: 231–235). Means of creating such a common identity are various in developing countries (and previously in what are now developed countries), but usually revolve around a (sometimes manufactured) common history, a (sometimes imposed) common language, shared (or imposed) cultural values and, importantly within the post-colonial context, the bond born of fighting against a common colonial enemy. In this last sense, the common aspiration and struggle for 'liberation' has been a strong component in forging a common identity in many developing states. This common bonded identity, then, has been regarded as the basis for an assertion of legitimate control over the 'nation's' territory (see SarDesai 1997: Chs18, 24).

The modern adoption (or imposition) of fixed borders has clashed with the ebb and flow of traditional polities, not to mention the drift of migrants from one region to another. In the contemporary political world, the free flow of people is regarded as challenging state control of its borders, may upset patterns of established land use and ownership and may threaten loyalty to the state. Historically, however, such migration was often encouraged, as a means of strengthening the state in both economic and military terms. This had implications for pre-colonial state formation and how that has influenced contemporary states. Ideas that derive from the pre-colonial period also inform, sometimes consciously and sometimes sub-consciously, the way political leaders look at their own country and those around them. The establishment of European colonies delineated authority at less than, to or beyond the limits of the state as they found it. This, in turn, has implications for setting the boundaries of post-colonial states, particularly where the boundaries reflected geo-spatial rather than 'nationalist' considerations, in turn deeply affecting the viability of numerous post-colonial states.

As a consequence of the role of the military in some instances of the liberation, and hence state-creation, process, military thinking has also come to exhibit characteristics of an ideology (see Huntington 1957). This is especially relevant in terms of the relationship between the state and its institutions and individual citizens, and in terms of more broad conceptions of power, hierarchy and authority. The lessening of military involvement in political affairs has usually been regarded as a sign of the political maturity of the state; the state is capable of assuming responsibility for its affairs (Dodd 1972: 50–54).

Authority and legitimacy

One view of political development is that it should be appropriate for 'local' circumstances, a political relativism that may imply a variety of non-democratic options. The major problem with this claim is that in non-participatory and non-representative political systems, there is no verifiable means of knowing whether or not there is genuine acceptance of alternative political models. This then raises the issue of the legitimacy of political processes, or the right of the exercise of political power that, within an organizational context, is translated as authority (the other manifestation of power being force). Without the legitimacy of a government (and even a state), a state cannot be stable and will therefore be prone to problems with economic and social development (Smith 1996: 357).

Of the various formulations of legitimacy, Weber's model of three, usually interactive, sets of criteria continues to illustrate the primary political styles, both in developed and developing countries, and corresponds to levels of political development. In discussing legitimacy, Weber noted that the perceived legitimacy of authority reflected in acquiescence might be a product of inflexible or repressive circumstances. Therefore, what passes as political legitimacy in some circumstances might only be so through a lack of free choice on the part of the 'citizen'. Otherwise, legitimacy can be understood to mean the rightful or appropriate rule or exercise of power based on a principle, such as consent, which is accepted by both the ruler and the ruled. Such a relationship might imply force within particular, usually prescribed, circumstances, such as the enforcement of the above-noted codes of acceptable behaviour (laws) (Weber 1964: 326).

Weber's three 'idealized' types of legitimate authority were 'rational-legal', 'traditional' and 'charismatic' authority. 'Rational-legal' authority corresponds to a higher form of political development, and was based on the acceptance of 'the legality of patterns of normative rules and the right of those in authority under such rules to issue commands (legal authority)'. Rational-legal authority could be said to apply to most democracies (accurately defined). Both the 'rational' and 'legal' aspects of this type of authority not only provide a sound and consistent basis upon which most citizens can base their lives, but also, by so doing, they enhance the opportunities for them to be economically productive, hence accelerating material aspects of development. This material development, in turn, establishes an environment in which 'rational-legal' authority is less likely to be challenged. Most developing states have compromised 'ration-legal' authority, which, in part, stems from a retreat to 'tradition' or communalism, and, in part, from corruption. It has been suggested, not entirely persuasively, that a lower level of rational-legal authority can stem from a lower level of economic development. However, it is certain that a lower level of rational-legal authority will contribute to lower levels of economic development.

As a lower level of political development, 'traditional' authority can be seen in authoritarian states that call on culture in order to legitimize government style. Political loyalty is based on allegiance to a 'personal chief' (Weber 1964: 341), 'especially a military force under control of the chief, traditional authority tends to develop into patrimonialism.' The primary means of support for such patrimonial authority is armies or paramilitary police (Weber 1964: 347), while growth is usually hampered by the 'chief's' personal ambitions and ability to influence economic direction (see Weber 1964: 355). These are common conditions in failing states.

Weber's third type of authority, that is 'charismatic' authority, might be said to apply to a revolutionary leader (Weber 1964: 328). This type of authority figure was especially prevalent in developing countries in the immediate pre- and post-decolonization period, often as the leader of an independence movement. Such figures were frequently necessary to weld together disparate groups in pursuit of a united goal. But their post-revolutionary organizational capacity, especially in the face of complex and often difficult economic circumstances, was frequently lacking, sometimes complicated by ego and personal ambition.

Governance

Within the idea of 'rational' decision making is that of 'governance', or more usually 'good governance'. Good governance corresponds to the idea of rational decision making in that political decisions pursue a particular interest, that they do so as competently as possible, and that they are transparent. The issue of transparency is critical within this context, as without transparency there is no guarantee that the actions of governments are as they claim. In this, good governance also implies the consistent, equal and impartial application of the rule of law, and of freedom of inquiry and expression, thus linking ideas of governance into the 'legal' aspect of political development, and into critical aspects of human rights.

In so far as a degree of certainty about rules and responses is a requirement for legitimacy, consistency in the application of the rule of law is a key criterion for legitimacy (Morris 1998: 24, 105–111, Rawls 1991: 7). In each case, the political systems and processes adopted by states reflect not just a range of styles and types, but indicate that even within the respective categories there remains considerable scope for interpretation and reformulation to suit the needs and interests of prevailing political groups or organizations. In this respect, the failure of the separation of powers between the executive and the judiciary does not just allow laws to be interpreted inconsistently, but allows for the development of tyranny (see Morris 1998: 287). In such cases, where major problems with legitimacy of the state have arisen, it has often reflected the state taking on a life of its own, separate from or above those citizens it represents.

Parallel to the idea that the state cannot logically have an interest separate from that of its citizens, the state as the state cannot claim to have a legitimate interest in the preservation of particular laws. Laws that do exist owe their legitimacy to popular support, so it would be analogous that those laws are or should not be immune from popular rejection or change (Schauer 1982: 190). Implicit in the notion that law is not beyond popular change is the idea that government legitimately represents the interests of its people and that amongst those interests is free expression in favour of such representation. Notions of justice, on the other hand, are not predicated on the legitimacy (or otherwise) of governments and the rule of law, but find their home in conceptions of natural rights. To that end, the question of political development resides less with what label a political system is given but whether or not it is a representative and, hence, responsive state, or whether it is an authoritarian and, hence, coercive state. This, then, turns to the issue of civil and political rights, usually referred to as human rights.

Human rights is central to a definition of political development, being

a general moral claim. It is the assertion of a just entitlement pertaining anywhere, anytime, ... to the enjoyment of certain goods or the satisfaction of particular interests deemed fundamental in some way. (Pettman 1979: 76)

As a general moral claim, the rights pertaining to being human are not contingent upon their cultural or political location. Pettman argues that there is a universal basis to human rights, not only based on common humanity but, in UNESCO, 'globally shared norms' agreed to by 'transcultural consensus'. Such consensus includes social solidarity, the sense of self, the value of life and the duty to protect the lost, sick or weak, the idea of the legitimacy of power and a duty to rebel when power's legitimacy is lost, the limitations to be placed upon the arbitrary exercise of power, the idea of juridical impartiality, the civil freedom to travel and to work elsewhere, the freedom to think and publicly criticize, tolerance of social rights (to strike, work and so on), securing freedom by securing material well being, the right to knowledge and learning, the right of a people to their identity and the universality of human enterprise or endeavour (Pettman 1979: 80). This assessment is supported by key evidence presented in the diverse survey of Inglehart *et al.* (1998).

It has also been widely claimed across developing countries, at various times by various people, that the whole idea of 'human rights' is culturally specific, being based on dominant European values and not reflecting local values and traditions. Notions of human rights, particularly civil and political rights, *do* derive from European tradition generally and the Enlightenment in particular. However, Hindu and Buddhist texts also focus on the human condition, while notions of human virtue and compassion characterize early Confucianism. Islam also has a strong emphasis on justice. Many local traditions include sanctions on the exercise of power, the reciprocal nature of political relations, and often high degrees of local autonomy. And of course, culture is not static, and what is represented as 'official culture' is very often a reification or indeed invention of values to suit the interests of particular elites. Related to this issue is the source of such socially shared values that may impose themselves as a consequence of an unequal power structure, that notions of rights and consequent ideas about political development reflect particular interests. Such values may or may not be accepted or internalized, but it cannot be claimed that they are 'natural' or immutable. A further issue is that by taking the structure of the nation-state, the developing states have adopted a form of political organization derived from the West in which there are certain organizational and structural arrangements. One of these is the identification of citizenship, which implies certain basic rights.

Apart from culturally relativised reasons for rejecting the universality of notions of human rights, the Marxist–Leninist approach to the role of the individual in the state, based on that of Hegel, and its co-option by quasi-Marxist states such as Vietnam and Laos, is that notions of human rights are a liberal subterfuge. The general Marxist critique is that human rights are ineffective because a capitalist world order requires human rights abuses as a method of enforcing hegemony. Such rights are held, in such an argument, to be only genuinely possible within complete economic, political, social and cultural emancipation (Campbell 1983: 7). This argument represented a utopian condition for the enjoyment of more prosaic human rights and, as such, failed in a less than utopian world.

A theoretically different critique of human rights derives from the 'organicist' or 'proto-fascist' model of the state, in which the citizen is regarded as an integral part of the state and without an independent political existence. This was the model first conceived of in the foundation of Indonesia, and in a practical sense informs states such as Burma, some African and Latin American states and, to some extent, countries that base their political system on the Leninist model of the state (see Liebman 1975: 444–448). This is close to fascism, based on the similarly Hegelian principle of top-down rule with the state being the supreme manifestation of the 'will of the people' (see Hegel 1967). It is this common top-down state focus of both political models, with the attendant suppression of the constituent members of the state, that has widely discredited them.

The question of human rights, including social and political rights, economic rights (see UNHCHR 1999) and so on, is therefore a site of significant political contest. There may be no absolute answer to this debate, but it is very much at the core of social contentment or, more often, discontent and how that manifests itself in power relations within states. This, in turn, is a key indicator of levels of political development.

A similar point to limiting political development to allow or enhance economic development has been raised in arguing that limits to political development have also been a necessary precondition for 'nation' building; that when there are competing interests within a new and often fragile state, state leaders have to restrict political activity in order to secure the state and construct the nation. This position relies on two, related ideas, the first being that nations can be successfully constructed, as opposed to forming through mutual interest, and that if they can be formed they should be; and the second that the state has a concrete existence and interest in its existence beyond that of its citizens. On one hand, it could be argued that a cohesive 'nation' allows a secure state, and that this is a necessary precondition for the establishment of efficient state institutions. These, in turn, assist and are a part of the process of 'development', broadly defined (e.g., the capacity of the state to raise taxes impacts directly on its capacity to provide conditions of development, such as education, health care, infrastructure, etc). On the other hand, the artificiality of 'nation' construction and the almost inevitable human cost involved in such a process can beg the question of the value of the exercise. The methods of 'nation' creation also often recall political methods that have been widely villified, such as notions of 'organicism' and fascism, while it has been argued that the state and its institutions are intended not to have a life of their own but to exist solely for the collective good of the citizens. The outcomes of the process of political development have sometimes lost the original rationale for such a process along the way, and have manifested action that would seem to subvert those original, usually emancipatory, intentions.

Nettl summed up the original and often lasting dilemma of politics for many developing countries:

> ... too many armies, too much bureaucratic parasitism, too much unequal distribution and not enough production, too much concentration on display projects and neglect of infra-structure, too much articulation of conflicts between communities, in short too much politics for the elites, not enough authentic participation for the masses. (Nettl 1969:19, see also Feith 1962)

Democracy

If people are to be emancipated, in any real sense of the term, they must be able to make political decisions, which returns to the idea of 'rule by the people', or democracy. However, because of its rhetorical power, the term 'democracy' has been grossly overused and abused. Collier and Levitsky identify more than 550 sub-categories of 'democracy' along a conceptual scale (in Haynes 2000: 5). 'People's Democracies' are very often nothing of the sort. Alternatively, those states that can claim to have some sort of functioning democracy do not possess a monopoly on its definition, their versions are not necessarily applicable elsewhere, and, in some cases, the models in use are not sustainable (see Haynes 2000: Ch 2).

The ending of Cold War tensions saw a reconsideration of support for a number of authoritarian or totalitarian regimes that, during the Cold War, were supported to shore up strategic alignments. Without external support, a number of such regimes collapsed (e.g., Indonesia's New Order, and a number of Latin American governments). However, the process of transition from one political form to a normatively more desirable alternative has not proven easy, not least because of internal and external economic pressures, and a number of states have consequently moved backwards and forwards between more and less open or democratic forms of government, or have allowed a 'hollowing out' of 'democracy' (see Diamond 1999). To illustrate, while Thailand now appears to be an open, stable democracy, in its recent history its democratic process have been overthrown by military intervention (in 1971, 1976, and 1991), with various subversions of the government in between (1986, 1988). More positively, however, there are more developing countries that are defined as 'democratic' (or 'free') now than at any previous time since the early 1970s (Freedom House 2002).

Democracy, as a normative component of political development, is understood to mean a political society that allows (or encourages) the direct or representative participation of its citizens in the political process, through representation that is either direct or indirect. That is, the governance of the people is either directly or indirectly through an inclusive, rather than exclusive, process. Such a system might elect a president as the head of state or as the chief executive of state, or it might elect members of a party who in a majority or a coalition choose a parliamentary leader. A state can have a monarch or monarchical representative and an elected legislature and still be a democracy (constitutional monarchy) if the monarch's role is symbolic rather than functional and is accepted by the majority of people of the state. A democracy should also have an open and competitive political system under the rule of law by which all parties to it are willingly bound.

This, somewhat idealized, version of democracy is tested in practice, however, by a series of qualifications. One such qualification is that not all voices in a political society may be heard, or heard equally, as a consequence of unequal access to means of communication. This could, in turn, reflect access to wealth, which could be said to subvert the best democratic intentions. Related to this, political ideas that challenge deeply vested interests often find themselves strongly challenged or undermined by those interests although, no doubt, such interests would claim that they are themselves simply defending their own 'rights' through the political process. Similarly, access to education might differentiate political understanding based on intellectual sophistication although, as noted, the cases of Cambodia and East Timor have proven that political awareness does not necessarily have to equate to formal education.

Political structures, too, can limit political access or participation, especially where one or two parties have a stranglehold over the political process. Some communist or religious states are seen to be dictatorial, although they might in fact have a number of parties that operate within an agreed system. While it is generally correct that there are very real political constraints in such societies, more 'open' political societies could also be challenged on the grounds that the options are also narrow – for example, two versions of relatively conservative, pro-capitalist parties in the United States. This limited choice asks questions of democracy, especially when voter participation is close to or less than half.

It is probably worth noting that there has been a fair amount of criticism for the more comprehensive versions of democracy by some political leaders, such as Singapore's Lee Kuan Yew and Malaysia's Mahatir Mohamad, saying that it is undisciplined and has led to high levels of crime, social delinquency, and so on. More sophisticated versions of such arguments have been put by theorists such as Chan (2002), although they continue to rely on the assumption that because development has been possible in non-democratic states, democracy may therefore be a hindrance to development. However, the two may be also unconnected, and Chan's argument does not account for economic development in more or less democratic societies. But, most importantly, Chan's position continues to define 'development' in narrowly economic terms, and in any case because economic development has been achieved in some states without democracy it does not logically imply that democracy would hinder such development. Indeed, the issue of governance, in which accountability is critical, would seem to indicate that economic development can be greater in democratic societies.

Apart from the criticisms of political leaders such as Lee and Mahatir being gross generalizations and exaggerations, they are usually a blind for criticism of their own authoritarian forms of government, which masquerade thinly as democracies. It is also worth repeating the claim that, perhaps due to the accountability of its politicians, no democracy has ever suffered a famine, and nor have any two democracies gone to war with each other. Such accountability is the strength of this political form. To quote the late English politician, Sir Winston Churchill: 'No one pretends that democracy is perfect or all-wise. Indeed, it has been said that democracy is the worst form of Government ... except all those other forms' (1947).

Political development

Based on the above discussion, it is clear that what does or does not constitute political development remains open to a high level of debate. This is especially so if political development is taken to mean a state following a predetermined course, such as 'Westernization' or 'communism', or simply 'modernization'. Tornquist acknowledges the tension between universalist ideas of political development, which tend to correspond to models, and particularistic definitions, which define development within the cultural context of the political community

(Tornquist 1999:13, 28, 54–61). Pye (1985), for example, argues that political development is precisely a reflection of national culture, and that political styles are embedded in and inextricably linked to cultural styles. This, of course, begs questions about the plurality of cultures within a particular political context, the particular assertion of power interests and the depth and stasis of culture as a determinant on basic human behaviour. It is quite correct to argue that culture does define bonded social groups, and that aspects of culture do (sometimes deeply) inform political styles. But culture is not static, nor is it inflexible, and it is equally correct to note that core issues such as the use, maintenance and legitimacy of power arise in all political contexts and that these core issues are fundamentally more important than cultural influences. If this were not the case, there would be no way of understanding, for instance, the shift between authoritarian and liberal regimes that have occurred in many developing countries, notably in Latin America (Chile, Peru, Argentina) and Asia (South Korea, Taiwan, Thailand, Philippines, Indonesia) and also, although to a lesser extent, in Africa. It is, therefore, proposed here that there are some important, definitive criteria for measuring political development, and that these are less based on the variables of culture or on the subjective interests of individuals (or institutions) than they are on what begin to become broadly accepted, in some cases functionally universal, values (see Inglehart *et al.* 1998 for an assessment of the consistency of key values in 43 countries).

Based on the above discussion, one broad version of a definition of political development could include a range of criteria that reflect the political sophistication of a society. These include the increased complexity and specialization of political roles and institutions within a particular society, increased levels of education and political literacy, the enlargement of an educated political elite, and the emergence of broad (rather than parochial) political issues. Linked to these criteria could be related issues such as urbanization, economic growth and social formation, and the inter-relationship between these and political processes. If there is one flaw with this outline, it is that it assumes that population growth or aggregation is a necessary precondition for political development, which precludes a range of other, perhaps smaller or disaggregated political unities that might also reflect high levels of political sophistication or maturity, such as collectives, trade unions and so on.

In a less contested part of the field, higher levels of social organization, including the widely accepted making and recognition of codes of behaviour, and the distribution of material goods sufficient to avert social dislocation could be held to represent a higher level of political development than, say, a low level of social organization with no agreed codes of behaviour and with material distribution unbalanced to the point of disrupting social cohesion. This represents a basic type of 'social contract' – this term being used somewhat more loosely than by Rousseau (1987) – where the terms and conditions of that 'contract' might vary quite considerably according to a range of internal and external criteria. Assuming that some forms of social organization are more or less likely to promulgate acceptable or desirable codes of behaviour or allow distribution of economic goods (or, indeed, 'good' more abstractly defined) those that promote more acceptable or desirable codes of behaviour and have a wider (and sustainable) distribution of economic goods within a particular social context could be said to be more developed. The converse also applies. There is also a linkage between codes of behaviour (laws) and the distribution of economic goods (economics) and systems of political organization. Some systems are more or less accountable to the constituent members of that political community, and higher levels of accountability tend to produce more widely acceptable outcomes.

Conclusion

Political development has been argued here to comprise social decision making and the exercise of power in that process. The criteria for measuring security and well being have been argued, in some other cases, to be relative to the culture or conditions prevailing at the time. However, it has been argued here that the basic criteria for security and well being are not contextually dependent and that, given an equality of circumstance, they reflect primary values common to all people. That is, relativized notions of political development are rejected as logically redundant.

It has been posited that there have been different forms of politics, and that each has been based on a variety of circumstances, many of which find their origins in material and related forms of interest. The development aspect of this process is present when the decision-making process most equitably represents the interests of the widest number while at the same time ensuring the security and well-being of all. Political processes that militate against such outcomes are, therefore, less developed, and political processes that enhance such outcomes can be said to be more developed. Finally, in the debate between form and function, or what is and what is said to be, as argued elsewhere (Kingsbury 2001: 418), in the final analysis it is important not so much what is said to honour the agreed values of political development, but what is done, that counts.

Chapter 8

Poverty and Development: The Struggle to Empower the Poor

JOE REMENYI

The assertion of this chapter is that there can be no development without poverty reduction. At base, the study of poverty and development must always comes back to the fundamentals of 'what it means to be poor', not in theory but in reality. Most agree that poverty means having insufficient money when money is needed, it means vulnerability arising from the inability to plan for the future with any degree of certainty, and it means standards of consumption that are below those that the community at large judges to be acceptable or adequate to sustain a full and meaningful life. The study of the relationship between poverty and development is the study of the causes of these observable characteristics of 'being poor'.

This chapter begins by looking at the broad macro and global context of poverty and development, before concluding with a household-level view of poverty reduction planning and micro-level poverty policy analysis. The philosophical foundation of what is presented is the belief that so long as poverty is treated as a welfare problem, chronic poverty will persist. Improvements in individual welfare and capacity for self-reliant escape from poverty is as much about ensuring that the poor have a voice that is heard in the corridors of power, as it is about increasing the success with which poor people graduate to better jobs, achieve higher levels of consumption, and participate in the process by which wealth creation and accumulation is realized.

A poverty of poverty theory

In the literature of free market economics there is no 'theory' of poverty. Economists have not felt a need for a theory of poverty, because it has always been possible to address issues of poverty from perspectives that arise out of theories that explain demand management, production economics, fiscal policy, the gains for trade and exchange, or the causes of the wealth of nations. In essence, poverty has been dealt with in a manner that, by implication, depicts it as the outcome of failure; the consequence of circumstances that are deficient in the essential requirements for economic progress. Poverty is, therefore, associated with an absence of growth and an absence of wealth creation.

Throughout almost the whole period since 1950, poverty reduction has taken a back seat to the 'goal' of 'development', and 'economic development' in particular. Development as modernization relegated poverty reduction to a lesser place in development priority setting, well below the need to create and nurture the exemplars of modernity that would encourage traditionalists to embrace the changes needed for modernity to flourish. In South Asia, in particular the India of Nehru and the Ghandi administrations, the creation of technically competent national economies able to 'build-machines-that build-the-machines' was given priority over poverty reduction. Until the economy was modernized, the consumption needs of the poor would have to be sacrificed to the investment needs of modernization. In Latin America, a similar choice was taken, but the argument was different. In this case the proponents of modernization identified technological 'catch-up' as fundamental to the successful establishment and growth of 'infant industries'. Modernization behind the comfort zones offered by high protective tariffs for new industries was favoured as a way of achieving development that would trickle down to the benefit of all. Hindsight shows that nothing of the sort happened. Protective tariffs merely encouraged non-sustainable development strategies that needed ever-larger transfers of wealth, public expenditures and private savings to keep the new industries afloat. The success with which the elite cadres in developing countries, especially the wealthy in South America, followed soon after by the powerful in Africa and most recently by the cronies of corrupt governments in South-East Asia, have convinced governments to choose priorities supportive of these dubious investments, is also a measure of the failure to give poverty a high priority in development.

Despite the readily justified rhetoric that links poverty reduction closely to the success with which modernizing economic growth can be sustained, it is only very recently, since the early 1990s at best, that mainstream thinking has stressed the importance of 'pro-poor' growth over economic growth as such. Pro-poor growth is growth that is the result of poverty-reducing economic activities. Hindsight unequivocally shows that, while sustained economic growth has been a constant priority in the development plans of developing countries, poverty reduction driven by policies for pro-poor economic growth have not been the 'main game' in contemporary development until the closing decade of the 20th century.

Whether one examines the development record through the activities of the World Bank, the IMF, the UN, most donor supported bilateral development programmes; or through the development plans of almost all developing countries, it is impossible to conclude that poverty reduction was the one clear goal of development until after, (i) the appearance of the first issue of UNDP's Human Development Report in 1990, or (ii) production began on the first Poverty Reduction Strategy Paper (PRSP) by the World Bank and the IMF for their African 'clients' some years thereafter. PRSPs are a relatively new strategy for the World Bank and the IMF. It was only at the September 1999 Annual Meetings of the World Bank Group and IMF, that Ministers endorsed the proposal that country-owned poverty reduction strategies provide the basis of all World Bank and IMF concessional lending, and should guide the use of resources freed by debt relief under the enhanced HIPC Initiative. This strategy provides a context for the preparation of a PRSP by country authorities, with broad participation of civil society and technical assistance from donors and multilateral agencies. The PRSP, in effect, translates the Bank's Comprehensive Development Framework (CDF) principles into practical plans for action that are indicative of national development priorities relevant to realization of sustainable poverty reduction.

Internationally agreed poverty reduction targets

A positive step in global poverty reduction was taken at the end of the 20th century when the UN and donor nations agreed to a set of international development goals to reduce poverty by 2015. These goals, which are listed in Table 8.1, have established not only clear benchmarks against which progress can be measured, but also an unequivocal link between development and poverty reduction. For the first time, the international community has taken a stand and made it clear that development without poverty reduction is an unacceptable oxymoron.

Some critics claim that the targets agreed to in the international development goals (IDGs) are too ambitious with little prospect of achievement. This may be so, and if the first few years of the new millennium are anything to go by there can be no doubt that the realization of these targets will be difficult. The diversion of global attention from development to the war on terrorism and the jingoism of securing borders against refugees has not served the interests of the poor in the world. Nonetheless, the targets set by the world community are worthy targets. In 'normal' circumstances, they are achievable targets. In abnormal circumstances these IDGs are only achievable if there is the political will among developing and donor counties to want to see them realized. With

Table 8.1 *International development goals to reduce poverty by 2015*

Poverty reduction target	50% reduction of people in extreme poverty
Social development targets	Universal primary education for all Eliminate gender disparities in primary and secondary education Reduction in infant mortality by two-thirds Reduction in maternal mortality by three-quarters Access to reproductive health services for all

Source: Compiled from IMF *et al.*, 2002, 'Global Poverty Report', and 'A Better World for All', G8 Okinawa Summit, July; Full texts and discussions of progress in achieving the IDGs is available at www.paris21.org/betterworld.

adequate resolve the global development targets for a less poor, a fairer, and a more just world, with a higher quality of life for all, is not a pipe dream.

It should be noted that people in extreme poverty are taken to be those who continue to live on an income of less than US$1 per person per day. When this standard for a global poverty line was first proposed by the World Bank and the UN in the late 1980s, it was a far more generous standard than it is some 15 years later. In most developing countries a more realistic poverty line during the first decade of the 21st century is US$2 per person per day. Even this standard is 'mean'. There is reason to believe that the poverty line ought to be drawn at a standard that is equally applicable in rich economies, such as the USA, Australia or Europe, as it is in developing economies, whether the poor or the poorest. A poverty line of this sort might, for example, define income poverty as consistent with an income below one-half of the GDP per person per annum. At this standard, the proportion of people in developing countries who are in poverty more than doubles to between 40 and 50 per cent of the people. This is so whether one uses raw GDP per person data, or statistics that are adjusted for differences in local currency purchasing power between donor and developing country economies. Clearly, the task ahead in development is to make ever-more-bold in-roads into the incidence of poverty. It is high time that the global community should have declared itself committed to poverty reduction as the first goal of international development.

Trends in the incidence of poverty in developing countries

There are many competing methods by which the incidence of poverty can be measured. Some of these methods will be examined in closer detail later in this chapter. Tables 8.2 and 8.3 provide a summary of the current situation, together with some data on long term trends in numbers of people in poverty in developing countries.

There is now clear evidence that the incidence of poverty in developing countries is falling, both in relative and absolute terms. However, the greatest gains have been made in East Asia, especially China. Is China an anomaly? After all, if China is one of the more regulated and least democratic countries in the world, should it not also be the country with the greatest chronic poverty problem? The answer to this question is both yes and no. On one hand, the period of most rapid decline in the incidence of rural poverty in China is also the period characterized by the most rapid spread of democratic reforms at the local level. On the other hand, since 1995 at least, poverty reduction trends in China have stagnated or reversed, which is a period associated with a slackening of the move to democratic reforms in China.

Table 8.2   *Poverty trends in developing countries*

	< US$1 per day		< US$2 per day	Per cent of population	
	1990	2000	2000	1990	2000
		Number of poor (millions)			
East Asia	452	289	> 500	28	15
South Asia	495	522	> 950	44	40
Sub-Saharan Africa	242	290	> 500	48	46
Latin America	74	78	> 150	17	16
Eastern Europe & Central Asia	7	> 25	2	5	
All developing countries	1276	1200	2800	29	24
Population (millions)					
All developing countries	4468	5412			
DAC countries	816	948			

Sources: Compiled from Global Poverty Report, G8 Okinawa Summit, July 2000; WDR; World Bank, various years; HDR; UNDP, various years; OECD.

Table 8.3 *Selected poverty indicators in developing countries*

Poverty indicator	1960	1970	1980	1990	2000
Children out of school					110
Infant mortality per 1000 live births		107			59
Primary school enrolment rate (%)			78		84
Adult literacy rate (%)	< 40	53			74
Increase in illiterate adults since 1970 (millions)					41
Percentage of developing country population in urban areas			30		50
Incidence of HIV/AIDS					30
Income of richest 20 economies as multiple of poorest 20	15				30
Life expectancy in developing countries (years)	45	55			65
Life expectancy in DAC countries (years)	69	78			

Sources: Compiled from Global Poverty Report, G8 Okinawa Summit, July 2000; WDR; World Bank, various years; HDR; UNDP, various years; OECD.

In all other areas trends have improved in relative terms only, with the result that the total number of poor people in Africa, Latin America, and Eastern and Central Europe has increased through the 1990s and through most of the preceding decades too. Moreover, if we move the poverty line to an income level of US$2 per day instead of a miserly US$1 per day, the absolute number of poor in the developing world increases quite dramatically, typically more than proportionately.

Income per person is an important, but not the only, relevant indicator of poverty. The quality of life is made up of many more elements than income earned and received. In Table 8.3 we consider some of the poverty indicators that are especially important as determinants of trends in personal quality of life.

History shows there is no investment more important as a determinant of personal access to an improving quality of life than education and the accumulation of human capital. When asked what assistance they want, poor people invariably point to education for their children (see, for example, UNESCO 2001, World Bank 1999). Yet, the diversion of resources to education is difficult for the poor, with the result that the absolute number of illiterate poor has not fallen in many developing countries. Progress in eradicating illiteracy must await a revision of domestic public-sector expenditure priorities to increase the proportion of government expenditure devoted to education. In the face of improving enrolment rates in primary education, falling infant mortality rates and rising life expectancy, education must play an ever more important role in pro-poor development priority setting.

It has sometimes been lamented that in many developing countries development has exacerbated the gap between the rich and poor. It is clearly possible for inequality to be the outcome of exploitation and economic activities that are unacceptable in most democratic societies. But, it is also true that pro-poor economic growth strategies will give rise to economic opportunities that benefit the non-poor more in absolute terms than it benefits those below the poverty line. A 10 per cent growth rate equally distributed will always benefit the person on a high income more in absolute terms than the person on a low income. As such, the increase in inequality that results is not bad, to be avoided at all costs; if economic history has anything to teach it is that poverty reduction goes hand in hand with growth that benefits the rich more than the poor. Consider the growth rate data in Table 8.4.

Growth rates have not been uniform across developing countries. In the earliest development decades, South Asia and Africa under-performed compared to all other developing countries and the world at large. During the 1980s and the 1990s, on the other hand, economic growth in Asia, especially East Asia, which is centred on China, dominated the global economy. It would have dominated even more had the Asian economic crisis of 1997–1999 been avoided. In contrast, the situation in Africa and the European nations formerly tied to the Soviet economic bloc deteriorated as economic growth moved into negative territory. In Africa and much of the old Eastern Europe, inequality increased with negative

Table 8.4 *Comparative growth rates*

Real GDP per capita growth rate	1965–1980	1980–1989	1990–1999
DAC countries	2.8	2.5	1.6
All developing countries	3.4	2.5	1.7
East Asia	4.8	6.7	6.1
South Asia	1.2	3.2	3.8
Latin America	3.4	−0.6	1.7
Sub-Saharan Africa	2.0	−2.2	−0.2
Eastern Europe and Central Asia	4.5	0.8	−2.9

Sources: Compiled from Global Poverty Report, G8 Okinawa Summit, July 2000; WDR; World Bank, various years; HDR; UNDP, various years; OECD.

economic growth as dominant elites moved to ensure that the burden of economic decline was not shouldered by them. Where inequality improved, it typically did so because economic decline impoverished the middle class and brought even the wealthy down to a lower common denominator.

Institutionalizing poverty creation

Development and poverty alleviation ought to go hand in hand, but they have not. In the late 1940s and 1950s the study of 'development' in former colonial territories and newly emerging states came into its own as specialist sub-disciplines in the mainstream social sciences, especially economics, sociology, geography and political science. The focus of these early studies were coloured by the recent memory of the 1930s depression, the 'beggar-thy-neighbour' trade wars of the 1920s and 1930s, and the impact of government-led economic planning during the years when war made the efficient functioning of the military–industrial alliance essential to ultimate allied victory in 1945.

The war had spurred the rate of technical progress in vehicle manufacture, and all forms of heavy industry, electronics, aeronautics, chemistry, shipping and macroeconomic management. The spectre of fierce competition from cheap labour economies in the tropics combined with potential oversupply from demobilized, technologically advanced manufacturing enterprises in North America, Britain and Europe was deeply felt. The prevailing view was that the integration of newly emerging countries into the global economy should and can be 'managed' to avoid the worst effects of competitive devaluations, structural change under duress, and unfair competition. But the locus of poverty that this strategy served was not poverty reduction in poor economies but fear of mass unemployment and poverty in the world's most mature economies. The developing world offered the world economy a new source of investment opportunities and new markets to be served, extant poverty in former colonial territories and other developing countries notwithstanding.

A second factor pushed poverty reduction off the development agenda – the concept of modernization rather than poverty reduction. Indeed, modernization demanded the diversion of national production from consumption to investment, which would further reduce already too low consumption levels. The designers of India's development plans from the 1960s through the 1970s openly admitted that modernization would impose austerity and deprivation 'for at least a decade' (see Mahalanobis 1963: 17f, 29, 48). In other words, development involves, indeed requires, a period during which poverty increases before it falls. This myth again diverted attention from the living standards of the poor to investments intended to lift the technical sophistication of emerging economies. Consequently, the appropriate indicators of development were not trends in consumption per capita or number of people living below the poverty line, but per capita and absolute growth rates linked to indicators of modernization.

A third, and in some ways a far more pernicious, factor was also at work. This factor is the emphasis that development advisers (from bilateral and multilateral agencies especially, but also from domestic pressure groups with a vested interest in access to technology-based imports), gave to the importance of development priorities that would secure on-going capacity to import. The primary strategy that serves this goal is export promotion and export-led growth, but international borrowing and favourable terms offered to direct investment by foreign-owned firms, often multinationals, serves a similar goal. In labour surplus economies, the effort to ensure continuing competitiveness in international export markets left exporters of non-renewable resources and labour-intensive simple manufactures with little or no option but to cut wage costs if foreign sales were to be secured. With wages already low, the unfortunate workers found themselves at the end of a losing strategy that exporters could only win by forcing wages ever lower. Such perverse outcomes may not have persisted had developing countries not developed equally self-defeating commitments to overvalued local currencies, the purposes of which served not the poor, but elite interests committed to easing the burden of debt repayment and ensuring on-going access to foreign exchange to service high-income consumers in the import market.

From 'growth first' to pro-poor growth

Neither classical economics nor contemporary free market theories of economic development, such as Arthur Lewis' surplus labour 'model' or Ruttan and Hyami's 'induced innovation' explanation of 'economic progress', give any attention to the *constraints* that prevent poor people from *escaping* poverty. The notion that we have to come to understand and address the constraints to escape from poverty for pro-poor growth to become sustainable is therefore quite new. The focus on constraints to successful self-help and self-reliant escape from poverty is not conventional to the pro-market, neo-liberal thinking that dominates current economic planning.

During the 1990s, the influence of development practitioners gradually displaced that of the theoreticians, with the result that thinking on poverty and development shifted to increase the emphasis given to development strategies that were pro-poor and founded on information and priority-setting processes that are 'participatory' and responsive to 'what it means to be poor', why people remain poor, and the constraints that have to be overcome if poor households are to pull themselves above the poverty line. The governance strategies associated with, for example, macro-level development planning for poverty reduction, such as is associated with preparation of World Bank-sponsored PRSPs in the world's most indebted poor countries, are meant to be inclusive of the poor and their real-world understanding of poverty. Similarly, at the micro-level, bilateral and multilateral donor agencies are increasingly successful in engaging recipient governments and other beneficiaries of foreign aid in poverty reduction project design and implementation arrangements that are pro-poor growth friendly and involve grass-roots participation in process and governance. The success of PRSPs and the growing adoption of participatory processes in all aspects of development, are indicative of a spreading recognition that effective poverty reduction planning and pro-poor project and programme design, demands programme management and project-level implementation processes that are inclusive of the poor. The essential characteristic of this inclusiveness, however, is the use of management systems grounded in information sources and stakeholder relations that are participatory in all phases of the project cycle, from initial appraisal and project identification through to progress monitoring and final impact assessment (see Hulme and Shepherd 2003: 413, 418).

The importance of capital

Associated with this shift was the need to reconsider the role that capital accumulation can play. There is an abiding idea that economic backwardness and the levels of poverty associated with backward areas is tied to the absence of 'capital', which involves a diverse set of 'deprivations'. The best known of these concerns, the absence of money in the pockets of poor people, is very important to an adequate appreciation of the role that the absence of capital plays in chronic poverty, although this does not negate the equally important need to also understand the six other forms that capital takes in the poverty economy:

(i) Financial capital

Poor people do 'save'. In fact, poor households exhibit surprisingly disciplined, effective and productive savings habits. The problem is that even 20 or 30 per cent of a very small income is an even smaller absolute amount saved. As a result, the capacity of the poor to finance development initiatives from current income is limited. Typically, the poor overcome this financial capital constraint by seeking additional resources from 'outside' their immediate household, either in cash or in kind. Borrowing is a way of bringing 'forward' savings to meet expenditures that are greater than can be paid from cash at hand. Debt is the poor person's constant companion. However, if the uses to which the debt of the poor is put can be made more productive, or the cost of the debt reduced, the benefit is an immediate improvement in their financial circumstances.

(ii) Human capital

Just as it is not true that poor households cannot or do not save, so too poor people do not lack human capital. The problem of the poor is that the sorts of human capital they have are also those that are in greatest supply relative to demand. Human capital, however, is not only about skills. It is also about the quality and the vulnerability of the labour power available in poor households. Suspect environments, inadequate nutrition, substandard sanitation and unreliable access to quality drinking water can seriously undermine the stock of labour power that a poor household can rely upon. In these cases, the dependency ratio is high, and poverty chronic as the earning capacity of the economically active members is limited. When the skill-set available is small, the number of dependents high, and opportunities for rewarding employment scarce, the climb above the poverty line is an almost insurmountable task without external assistance. Nonetheless, in the long term it is the accumulation of human capital that enables sustained poverty reduction to be achieved.

(iii) Institutional capital

Poor communities are often characterized by an absence of institutional depth. The availability of a school will influence the ease and the expense of keeping children in attendance. The presence of a health centre can make the difference between prolonged health problems and speedy recovery. The availability of access to a branch of a financial institution can make the difference between getting a loan and not getting one when it is needed. Institutions, however, are not just about education, health, finance or recreation, and can also cover the institutions of governance and due process to which poor people have access. Participatory approaches are an important new element in the process of giving poor people the authority and the ability to determine and make their own livelihood decisions. In order to enact participatory processes, institutional innovations at the local government level are needed, if only to fill the gaps in priority setting for village development left by a long history of centralized, top-down development and poverty alleviation planning.

(iv) Social capital

The ability of a community to reach out and help its members overcome setbacks that exacerbate the slide into poverty or prevent poor people from escaping poverty is determined, in large measure, by the social capital that can be mobilized in times of need, especially natural disasters. Poor communities are more often than not located in geographic regions that are vulnerable to misadventure and natural calamities. A community with significant social capital will have the wherewithal to help poor people recover from setbacks more quickly, more effectively, and more easily than one with limited social capital.

(v) Natural capital

The resource base of a village or a household defines its natural capital. Weather patterns, the fertility of the soil, the availability of common land with open access rights, and the ease with which markets can be reached, are all part of local natural capital. The effectiveness with which natural capital can be used to stimulate job opportunities, investment by households in enterprise development, or the availability of social safety nets can be significantly strengthened by judicious investment in natural capital management, conservation or transformation.

(vi) Liquid capital

The most liquid form of capital is money. As rural communities have become integrated into the broader cash-economy, the importance of money in household budgeting and financial planning has become more important. The purchase of hybrid seeds, fertilizer, chemical herbicides and pesticides, and non-food production raises the share of output that has to be monetized to pay for cash costs. Similarly, the spread of user-pays policies for services accessed from local government or private-sector providers, including education, health, power, water and transport services, has accelerated the importance of cash flow as a key determinant of whether or not a household is 'poor'.

Pro-poor growth: investing in poverty reduction

The common goal of participatory poverty reduction and pro-poor growth strategies is to enhance the creation and accumulation of these six types of capital. Wealth creation associated with additions to the stock of each of these six types of capital lifts the productivity of poor households to levels that will reduce the need for on-going subsidies or welfare transfers to the chronically poor. Pro-poor growth achieves this by choosing to emphasize capital accumulation options that achieve economic growth through investments in poverty reduction rather than poverty reduction through investments in economic growth.

Contemporary thinking on pro-poor growth for poverty reduction is intimately tied to participatory approaches to poverty planning, poverty project design and poverty reduction implementation practices. Pro-poor growth is seated in governance structures that give priority to the needs of the poor. At heart, the aim is to make growth 'inclusive' of the poor and to take deliberate steps to ensure that the sources of growth in which the community and the public sector invests are those that also reduce poverty.

To be inclusive and relevant to the needs of the poor, pro-poor policies and projects need to be based on information that is accurate and realistic about the assets available to the poor and the constraints poor households must overcome if they are to escape poverty. Pro-poor strategies of poverty reduction also arise out of intensive consultation with poor people to identify the best ways in which the opportunities for employment, income and wealth generation available to poor households can be increased, and how solutions to problems can be facilitated, supported and sustained in ways that build self-reliance and the capacity to manage setbacks.

The goals of pro-poor growth strategies can be summarised as follows – pro-poor growth loosens the constraints that keep poor people poor by:

- reducing unemployment and under-employment
- increasing the capacity of poor households to save
- enabling entrepreneurship and innovation to flourish
- facilitating realization by poor households of their savings-investment plans
- allowing new markets to be explored and served
- enhancing risk management to avoid misadventure, ill health and economic loss
- removing vested interests limiting economic opportunities of the poor
- addressing gender equity issues that contribute to institutionalized poverty
- compensating for the impact of market failures on economic opportunities of the poor
- augmenting access to assets that the poor need for growth in self-reliance and productivity
- attending to environmental issues critical to sustainability of livelihoods above the poverty line, and
- ensuring that procedures are in place to achieve good government and the absence of corruption.

Capital to the people?

It was once thought that economic development is a process, first and foremost, of bringing capital to the economies in which poor people live. The decades immediately following the Second World War were characterized by the belief that if only enough capital could be transferred into poor economies, modernization would happen and the achievement of 'take-off' would be merely a matter of time. If take-off did not happen, then the reason was not to be found in a failure of thinking on development, but in a failure to transfer enough capital.

It would take several decades after the launch of Truman's Point Four programme (see p. 27) before *development in practice* took seriously the long understood view in liberal market economics that the scarcity of capital in poor economies is not just the result of limited absolute capacity to save. The reality is that it took development planners a good deal of time to realize the importance that must be given to the lesson that the market signals were showing: i.e., that the scarcity of capital in poor countries is a reflection of the hostile environment that exists for all forms of capital accumulation. No amount of foreign aid would alter this fact unless it was directed at the system causes of this hostility, in particular the *constraints* that poor households must overcome in order to escape poverty. Capital is also scarce, however, because the relative return to investment in a prosperous and rich economy is less risky than a similar investment in a poor and moribund economy. Throwing foreign aid at the problem of scarcity of capital is no solution to the root causes of low absolute levels of savings, high risks, and low estimated future returns to investment.

Capital inflow, from whatever source, does little to help the poor if it is not targeted at the needs of the poor, which has been the case since the 1950s. If the poor have benefited, it has primarily been because of domestic reforms and domestic development investments that created jobs, generated greater income flows into village households and facilitated savings and investment activity by poor households. International capital flows have done little to help the poor because these flows have rarely been targeted at improving consumption by poor households or the creation of long-term job opportunities for the able-bodied poor seeking paid work.

It has taken the development community more than a generation to appreciate that pro-poor growth demands more than international capital inflow, whether via official development assistance (ODA), direct private investment (DPI) or foreign-trade earnings. It also needs domestic policy and organizational changes that increases investor's expected future returns while also deliberately making poor people and poor communities 'partners' in the development process.

Key ideas in sustained poverty reduction

Seven words – Justice, Compassion, Freedom, Education, Opportunity, Prevention and Peace – summarize the fruits of successful development. Justice is important to the poor because it is fairness of opportunity that the poor want and deserve, not charity. Charity is a relief exercise that all too often creates situations of dependency. Compassion, on the other hand, is essential if the poor are to be allowed to take their rightful place in open, transparent and accountable decision-making circles. We can judge the success of development by examining the manner in which a community treats its most vulnerable members. Freedom is what one feels in circumstances where one is free of duress. Education comes with victory over ignorance and the absence of knowledge. Opportunity, prevention (of risk situations) and peace are self-explanatory.

Understanding Poverty

Understanding poverty can be assisted by considering the outward signs of what it means to be poor. Consider the following list:
Poverty means –

Economic constraints
- absence of access to cash
- low productivity
- few assets
- low absolute savings capacity
- low income
- chronic unemployment

Social constraints
- being dependent
- subject to violence and duress
- vulnerability to misadventure
- feelings of hopelessness
- behavioural passivity
- alienated within one's community.

The poverty that development addresses is the poverty that robs people of their freedom. In a very real sense, the poverty that development ought to eradicate is another form of violence done to vulnerable people because of the duress under which their choices are made. Many of these choices would not be made but for the duress of cash, income, and asset poverty.

Levels of poverty

The many different ways in which poor households experience poverty can be used to construct a hierarchy of deprivations. The levels of poverty shown in Figure 8.1 form a sort of 'poverty pyramid'. Immediately below the poverty line, the primary impact of poverty is to reduce consumption below what society judges to be adequate for a meaningful and fulfilling life. As poverty deepens, consumption declines further, with the use made of services, especially those that are user-pays based also reduced. Cuts to consumption and service usage are short-term, immediate responses to the slide into poverty. As one's place in poverty is entrenched, assets are liquidated to maintain a semblance of normality, expanding the base on which systemic poverty and poverty traps are built. Over time one's level of security and sense of dignity are eroded by poverty, further limiting individual capacities to redress one's circumstances. Finally, poverty leads to alienation with the community, robbing the poor of even what little access they have to the social capital available to the community at large. At this point, the base of the poverty pyramid has expanded considerably, reflecting the low level of productivity associated with chronic poverty.

The picture of poverty we get from characterizations such as that shown in Figure 8.1 is useful to explore the nature of poverty traps, which consist of mechanisms, typically systemic, that keep poor people poor, the willingness of the poor to work hard and honestly notwithstanding. The fact that the poor have fewer assets limits the opportunities they have to

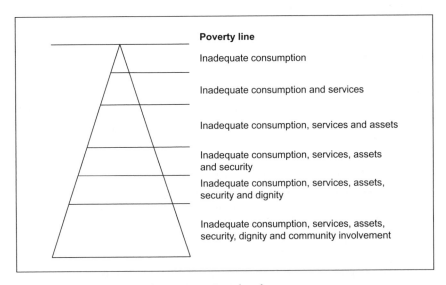

Figure 8.1 *Levels of poverty*

generate more income or wealth. If additional saving is required, it can only be at the expense of already low levels of consumption, which may put at threat the health and well-being of household members.

There are few things more destructive of a poor household's attempt to climb out of poverty than the sudden onset of health expenses. The normal health status of the poor is not robust, and they have limited community networks to assist when necessary. Access to social capital falls the further is the slide into destitution. If alcohol abuse, drug dependence, or HIV/ AIDS are added complications in the poverty trap, permanent deprivation, long-term unemployment, lingering ill health, chronic malnutrition, disability and family violence are also likely to be present.

When people fall on hard times, their response to poverty is often precisely what is needed to ensure that the slide into poverty is deep and permanent. An immediate and natural response to the onset of poverty by a household that has been used to being self-reliant is to cut back on its expenditures and its consumption. Food intake and the quality of the diet slip, followed by decisions not to spend to maintain household assets. In the absence of piecework, the economically active members of the household will undertake food-for-work as the next best opportunity available. Once this option no longer presents, foraging, borrowing from the extended family or friends, and the sale of household assets follows. Children are removed from school and welfare entitlements are explored, before begging and recourse to criminal activities are the only options left. The downward spiral of the poverty trap does, therefore, pass through stages of vulnerability that gradually remove the poor from the very social support systems that they need to reverse their fortunes.

Beyond welfare

There is a strong tendency in many countries for poverty to be considered a 'welfare' issue, with temporary relief tending to be offered. There will always be certain categories of poor people who can only be regarded as welfare clients, especially the aged, the infirmed, the disabled, the vulnerable, such as small children and pregnant women. These groups of poor are ubiquitous among the chronically poor, in part because it is a fundamental characteristic of their condition that they cannot be expected to achieve self reliance no matter how determined they are to look after themselves. A community-based welfare response to their condition is an appropriate response. This is not so in the case of the able-bodied poor. The aim of sustainable poverty reduction is to give every able-bodied poor person the best opportunity to achieve a level of self-reliance above the poverty line.

A livelihood and gender-sensitive poverty pyramid

As useful as Figure 8.1 is in understanding poverty and the relationship that poverty has to development, the deprivation approach to characterizing poverty is a negative and welfare-orientated vision. The focus in the figure is on the consequences of poverty rather than the causes of poverty. The deprivation approach is inadequate to ensure that poverty-reduction policies and projects deal appropriately with the causes of poverty, and discriminate between these causes according to those that are most relevant to particular groups or types of poor households.

One of the greatest challenges to a development professional operating in the field is to know how best to organize in a meaningful way the flood of information on poverty at household level that is available from householders. It is, therefore, essential to come to understand in considerable detail the sources of livelihood on which poor households rely for their sustenance and expenditure planning. The poverty pyramid presented in Figure 8.2 is a device that can be used for this purpose.

The poverty pyramid is simple framework for characterizing a household's poverty 'place' and the structure of poverty in a poor village or community. The livelihoods that poor people rely upon for access to cash flow, production activities, and sources of saving for the future are the springboards from which escape from poverty must be built. Consequently, the core of the poverty pyramid is a combination of the prime income-generation sources of poor households, the relative importance of these functional characteristics of households to income flows, and the number of individuals or households that rely on each prime category of livelihood.

In Figure 8.2 the percentage contribution to household income from different sorts of livelihood types is measured on the vertical axis. The poorest livelihoods are at the bottom of the scale, and the least-poor livelihoods are shown at the top, with households that are vulnerable to slipping back below the poverty line shown as the *near poor* just above the poverty line. On the horizontal axis we show the number of males and females in each livelihood category. Instead of measuring the number of males and females in each category of livelihood source on the hotizontal axis, it is also possible to substitute the number of male-headed and female-headed households instead of individuals.

The bottom stratum is occupied by the Vulnerable Poor. This group consists of the children, the infirm, the aged, the disabled, and pregnant mothers. In most poor communities the Vulnerable Poor is a substantial group of people, often accounting for between one-third and two-fifths of the population. Their 'functionality' (i.e., their contribution to household livelihood), is not zero, but nor is it very significant.

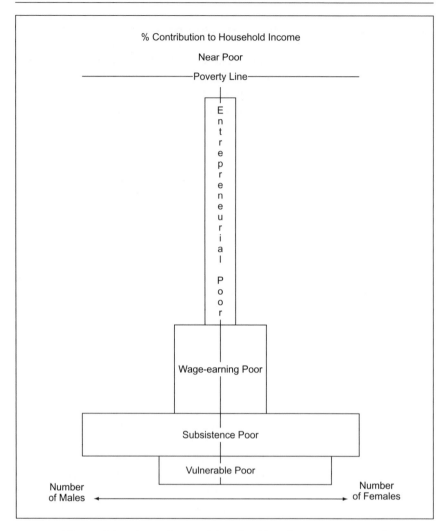

Figure 8.2 *A gender-sensitive, livelihood poverty pyramid*

There tend to be more females than males in this group, largely because men do not get pregnant and women tend to outlive men. There may also be reason to believe that the females in this group are more productive as contributors to household survival and asset creation, but, for the purposes of illustration, Figure 8.2 shows both vulnerable males and vulnerable females contributing similarly to household production and annual cash receipts.

In many developing countries the group immediately above the Vulnerable Poor consists of those villagers whose major source of livelihood is from subsistence agriculture. In Figure 8.2 this group is called the Subsistence Poor, in keeping with their primary functionality or contribution to household production. The essence of subsistence living is consumption by the household of what is produced by the household, with little or no portion sold to generate a cash income. In the contemporary environment, however, there are very few purely subsistence communities. The great bulk of the households that are members of the Subsistence Poor rely on farming, transhumance 'nomadic' pastoral activities, or fishing for the greater part of their households consumption and annual cash and non-cash income.

The Subsistence Poor category is shown as consisting of both male and female members, but the number of males is greater than the number of females. The opposite is likely to be the case in many African countries where subsistence farming by females, often in female-headed households, is still the backbone of rural livelihoods. Nonetheless, note that the higher productivity of subsistence farming over the economic activities of the Vulnerable Poor is shown on the vertical axis. The greater the productivity of subsistence farming, the higher the vertical distance occupied by the Subsistence Poor on the vertical axis of the pyramid. Any intervention that increases the productivity of subsistence farming would be reflected in Figure 8.2 as an increase in the proportion of household income generated from this source.

The third tier in the pyramid is given to typically landless poor households whose survival is dependent upon the success with which the able-bodied members of the household can sell their labour to an employer. In the figure this group is termed the Wage-earning Poor. The wage earned for a day's work is often well in excess of the international poverty line of US$1 per day, but the number of days of paid work found per year is so low that the average daily wage falls well below this level. Nonetheless, the average wage earned tends to be higher than that realized by subsistence households, and is well in excess of the average value of the daily contribution that the Vulnerable Poor make to household income. Subsistence farmers can be conceived as paying themselves an 'own wage', equal to the value of the output that they produce or consume. Where we observe subsistence farmers abandoning their farms to take on day labouring in agriculture, construction, or other employments, we can conclude that the wage they are paid exceeds the own wage earned in subsistence production. If the own wage is the farmer's 'opportunity cost', outside employment opportunities will always be taken up when the wage offered exceeds the own wage.

In Figure 8.2 this is shown by the vertical height associated with each level of the pyramid. It is indicative of the fact that the Vulnerable Poor are typically less 'productive' than the Subsistence Poor, who are, in turn, less productive than the Wage-earning Poor. Nonetheless, in some communities the Wage-earning (landless) Poor are less well-off than the subsistence poor, indicative of the impact on productivity associated with asset ownership and in such cases, the pyramid would look different from the one included here.

The fourth level of the pyramid is often occupied by the Entrepreneurial Poor. These are people who work for themselves and make their living by selling what they produce. Some even employ other people in their 'businesses', but relatively few and rarely on a full-time or even an on-going part-time basis. We could include in this group those rural households that process and sell a portion of their output, thereby benefiting from the value adding that is associated with such activity. In the main, however, the self-employed Entrepreneurial Poor are micro-enterprise operators whose example can be an important source of new sources of income, employment and wealth generation opportunities for households in lower tiers of the poverty pyramid. A key strategy of escape from poverty by the Subsistence Poor is to increase the level of their marketed surplus and the opportunity they have to engage in value-adding through processing of what is produced before it is sold.

A household is allocated to a particular stratum of the Livelihood Poverty Pyramid according to it primary source of livelihood. Hence, while a subsistence household will engage in some cash-sales of produce, and is also likely to avail itself of waged employment when the opportunity arises, the household remains in the Subsistence Poor category so long as the proportion of household livelihood drawn from subsistence production is at least 50 per cent of household annual cash and non-cash income. Once the share of household livelihood derived from the sale of output produced exceeds 50 per cent, that household graduates to join the other micro-enterprise-dependent households in the Entrepreneurial Poor strata. Alternatively, if waged employment rises so that annual household income derived from off-farm employment exceeds all other sources of livelihood, then the household is reallocated to the Wage-earning Poor category. Only if total household cash and non-cash income rises above the poverty line does the household graduate from the Poverty Pyramid.

There is an important fifth group that needs to be acknowledged as integral to the Livelihood Poverty Pyramid. This group is called the *Near Poor*, characterized by households that have managed to climb above the poverty line, but remain vulnerable to falling back into the pyramid should misadventure strike. The Near Poor may have achieved levels of productivity well in excess of that associated with lower strata in the pyramid, but experience has shown that sustained poverty reduction demands explicit attention to the economic requirements that will make it possible for the Near Poor to remain above the poverty line, economic setbacks notwithstanding.

The Livelihood Poverty Pyramid is useful in identifying key pressure points for poverty reduction, the importance of productivity improvements if households are to graduate above the poverty line, and the contrasting contributions of cash and non-cash sources of livelihood. It is also useful framework for field-based poverty analysis. In part, this is because poor villagers find it easy to say which households in their community are where in the hierarchy. As the incidence of poverty changes, the number of households in each stratum will also change. It takes a bit more skill to be able to identify levels of productivity associated with each stratum, or to document the relative impact of changes in the policy, institutional or economic environment. Nonetheless, by drawing our attention to the great diversity of poverty experiences between different strata of the poverty pyramid, the framework facilitates a strategic and tailored approach to understanding the causes of chronic poverty within each stratum. It is also clear that poverty reduction policies that are intended to raise the productivity of the Vulnerable Poor are unlikely to also overcome the key barriers that prevent the Subsistence Poor or the Entrepreneurial Poor from climbing above the poverty line. Effective poverty planning deliberately and decisively discriminates between poor households at different levels of the Pyramid because the constraints each faces in their efforts to be more productive are different. In this sense the Livelihood Poverty Pyramid is a 'heuristic' device for coming to a better understanding of the task of poverty targeting, poverty reduction planning, and monitoring of the impact on poverty of publicly funded development interventions.

Poverty indicators

Measuring and monitoring poverty are important for poverty targeting, for learning from experience, and for pro-poor development planning. However, the statistics on income per person, doctors per 1000 population, average daily calorie intake, school enrolment rates, and the incidence of unemployment often fail to identify the real plight of the poor, especially the hard core poor. The divorce that exists between the statistical indicators of poverty and the human experience of poverty has made it difficult for the best intentions of development professionals to result in a true understanding of the poor and the constraints that must be addressed for genuine and sustainable poverty reduction.

It is common for poverty analysts to select a range of what received wisdom regards as indicative of the incidence of poverty by type, importance and impact. The most commonly used indicator is income per person, normally expressed at the macroeconomic level as GDP per capita. As already observed, it is not necessarily the case that growth in GDP per capita also means a similar level of improvement in the income of the poor households. During the 1990s, for example, GDP per capita in China grew at twice the rate of household income for the poorest 20 per cent of households. In other words, growth in GDP per capita was not benefiting the rural poor at anywhere near the rate at which GDP per capita was growing for the country as a whole. Income poverty is an important 'type' of poverty, but it does not necessarily accord with how the poor experience their poverty, and the importance they would attach to the many characteristics of being poor. The impact of poverty on the capabilities of poor households for self reliance, the entitlements the poor need to become more self reliant, and the opportunities that would be meaningful to poor households as escape routes from poverty are issues on which there are few better 'experts' than the poor themselves.

The Human Poverty Index (HPI) published annually by the UNDP is a popular indicator of poverty. It is a composite index consisting of data on:

- GDP per person
- the percentage of the population expected to die before the age of 40 years
- the percentage of adults (15–65 years) who are illiterate
- the quality of life as reflected in the incidence of malnutrition among children 1–14 years, and
- the percentage of the population with 'easy' access to health services and potable water.

The UNDP and others have made great capital out of the HPI, and have used it to highlight the lack of progress made in poverty reduction throughout almost the whole of Africa, as well as the rapid gains in poverty reduction in North Asia, especially China. The HPI for several ASEAN economies does show that the incidence of poverty has increased in South-East Asia since the Asian economic crisis of 1996–1998. However, the most recent statistics, supported by anecdotal evidence, show that the increase in poverty has been greatest in urban areas and among public sector employees whose real incomes have collapsed, especially in Indonesia, Thailand, Laos, and the Philippines. In contrast, many rural communities that relied on export of their agricultural produce, often horticultural products such as flowers, fruits, fresh vegetables, handicrafts and fish, have experienced a mini-boom as heavily depreciated local currencies boosted the return on exports when expressed in local currency terms. As a consequence, there has been some reversal of the rural–urban drift in ASEAN economies as employment opportunities in rural export sectors responded to the jump in profitability that has flowed because of currency devaluations.

While governments and development planners feel that it is useful to know what is happening to trends in the HPI and other indicators of poverty (such as the *Head Count Index*, which is the percentage of the population below the poverty line, the *Poverty Gap* as measured by the difference between the average income of the poor and the official poverty line, and the *Severity of Poverty* arising from the unequal incidence of income poverty among the poor), the judgement of poor households on which indicators are the best statistical proxies for how they experience poverty plays no part in the construction and interpretation of the HPI, the Head Count Index, the Severity of Poverty Indicators, or indicators intended to measure the capacity of poor households to participate in local community life. Pro-poor policies may not, therefore, be adequately served by the HPI or similar indicators, especially if these are the principal indicators used to track the incidence of poverty and monitor changes. Is there a solution to this dilemma?

Table 8.5 sets out three types of poverty and eight associated poverty indicators consistently selected by poor households in several of China's poorest provinces as critical to describing the poverty experience of rural communities. The indicators identified as appropriate to measuring the incidence of poverty and progress in reducing poverty are less obvious. For example, income is not among the eight poverty indicators. In place of income poor villagers identified access to cash-flow (i.e., liquid capital), and kilograms of grain produced as critical to their experience of poverty. This substitution does not reject the importance of income as a measure of poverty, but stresses that poverty is associated by the poor with an absence of access to money and the presence of food insecurity.

When it came to the gender base of poverty, villagers did not look at the division of labour between the sexes, nor the relative productivity of men and women. Instead, they identified the number of days lost in a year to health problems of women as the key variable. The choice of this indicator by the poor serves to highlight the crucial role that women play in the fortunes of poor households. It also emphasizes the very high importance that poverty-reduction priority setters and policy makers ought to give to ensuring that women's health issues are not neglected.

The importance of labour as a resource for income and wealth creation by the poor is reflected in the choice by the poor of three indicators immediately relevant to the availability of labour power in the household, the consequences for labour productivity of isolation, and cost to the household of time needed to access potable water at a distance. Relief in any or all of these three areas is perceived by the rural poor as important for sustainable poverty reduction.

It comes as no surprise that poor villagers look to the future through their children. Initially, the research team had expected that villagers

Table 8.5 *Poverty indicators consistently selected by poor villagers in China*

Type of poverty	Characteristic	Proxy	Poverty Indicator
Human resource	Gender	Household health status	Days lost to health problems by women
	Dependency	Labour constraint	Hours per day devoted to accessing potable water
	Social capital	Social safety nets	% of eligible children not attending school regularly
Livelihood	Cash flow	Finance constraint	Yuan per person per year
	Nutrition	Food security	Kg of grain produced per person per year
	Shelter	Quality of housing	% of houses in the village constructed from brick
Infrastructure	Isolation	Geographic access	% of natural villages with access via all weather road
	Community development	Infrastructure maintenance	% of households with access to reliable electricity

would distinguish between school attendance by boys and girls as crucial to future stocks of social capital and human capital accumulation. In fact, this was not the case. Villagers consistently pointed to the capacity of households to ensure that all eligible children attend school regularly as the relevant indicator, sex of the child notwithstanding. Quality of life was also not neglected by villagers in their choice of poverty indicators. Two features proved most important to respondents, being the quality of housing available, and access to reliable electricity.

Lessons from international experience

Poverty planning does not have an auspicious history in the modern period of economic development. Development studies has always acknowledged that there are winners and losers as a result of the socioeconomic, legal, institutional, or environmental changes that development involves. Time has merely served to confirm the universally accepted dictum that *successful* development leads to economic growth that will be good for the poor as well as the rich. Experience and hindsight notwithstanding, the idea that economic growth is a legitimate proxy for successful challenges to the incidence of poverty in poor economies still retains currency.

Through most of the 1950s and the 1960s, poverty planning in developing countries took a back seat to sectoral modernization and development investments associated with technology transfers. Poverty-reduction planning was married to the establishment of complex manufacturing industries, described by the head of India's Planning Commission, P. C. Mahalanobis, as involving public-sector support for producer goods industries to ensure that local economies developed the capacity to 'make the machines that make the machines'. A modified form of Soviet-style forced-pace development represented the model that India and other technologically backward economies believed would propel them into modernity. It went without saying that the achievement of modernity was also supposed to herald gains in poverty reduction that mirrored the full-employment conditions that appeared to characterize modern donor economies in North America, Europe and Australasia from the mid 1950s through to the early 1980s.

The development community was not long into the 1970s before concerns began to be expressed about the apparent absence of *progress* in developing countries. Throughout the 1960s, famines persisted and the widespread incidence of deaths from starvation highlighted the fact that for many developing country citizens development planning was not delivering an improved quality of life or freedom from food insecurity. However, the belief that economic growth is good for the poor remained as unassailable a proposition as ever. The inability of development planning to deliver reductions in the incidence of poverty and deaths from starvation in developing countries was, however, not attributed to deficient thinking about the role of economic growth in poverty reduction planning. Instead, development professionals found deficiencies in the technology transfer process, best understood as the catapult from which the 'Green Revolution' was launched. There is some truth here, but it took the world community with a stake in development of poor areas an excessively long time to realize that technology transfer is not a simple matter of choosing solutions from a shelf of past discoveries and existing knowledge. The success of the technology transfer associated with Green Revolution technologies has been the vast amount of applied and fundamental research that has adapted biological materials and rural production methods to the unique geographic and environmental situation of farmers in developing countries.

There is considerable debate over the long-term benefits of the Green Revolution and its impact on poverty. But lower food prices and increased availability of basic staples meant that rice bowls once empty were near half-full by the time the 1970s drew to a close. Nonetheless, the number of poor in the developing world was not falling, while the gap between the rich and poor was increasing. Development planners were again drawn to rethink why more progress was not being made, three decades of economic growth notwithstanding. Economists were aware that new thinking on distribution issues had to be a part of the solution, but the time was not yet right for development planners to make the intellectual leap needed to realize the importance of disaggregating the concept of economic growth beyond the traditional approach of economics to the problem of distribution.

Throughout the 1980s, therefore, development planners were at a loss to know what more to do to ensure that concern for the poor is more than good sounding rhetoric. A lifeline was discovered in the view that development had to be 'humanized', with the policy recommendation that more attention had to be given to policies that would ensure that the poor are given access to the basic needs that are essential for a person to be an active economic actor. The basic needs thesis forced development thinkers to re-examine why poor people do not have access to such basic needs. This re-examination highlighted the systemic basis of chronic poverty. It was then a much shorter intellectual step to ask how economic growth could be made more *pro-poor*. Nonetheless, it was not until the mid to late 1990s that the concept of pro-poor growth was to attain widespread legitimacy.

An important step toward the elevation of pro-poor strategies onto the centre stage of development planning and poverty reduction planning in particular, was the coming to a head of the debt crisis in developing countries. The IMF-led Washington consensus imposed structural adjustment programmes on some of the world's poorest and most heavily indebted countries in ways that reflected a very naive view of the link between economic growth and poverty (see Shah 2002). The manner in which the IMF and other agencies subsequently interpreted it and pursued its goals corrupted the consensus to emphasise recovery of the ability of poor countries to resume or maintain their debt service payments over the reduction of poverty. There were 10 areas of policy reform that made up the Washington consensus:

(i)   Fiscal discipline, to reign-in bloated government deficits that fed chronic balance-of-payments crises and high inflation.
(ii)   Pro-poor public expenditure priorities which would switch public expenditures towards basic health and education.
(iii)   Tax reform to broaden the tax base.
(iv)   Removal of interest rate controls.
(v)   Freely floating exchange rates.
(vi)   Movement to freer international trade.
(vii)   Liberalised inward foreign direct investment.
(viii) Smaller government through privatization.
(ix)   Promotion of greater competition in the operation of domestic markets.
(x)   Regularization of informal sector activities to provide operators with the security of legal property rights.

A global lobby of NGOs and developing country governments brought pressure onto the IMF and the WB to re-examine the impact of structural adjustment programmes on poverty in highly indebted poor countries. The results showed that without deliberate attention to the needs of the poor, the costs of policy reform would be shifted onto those groups in the community with the least political power, typically the poor.

This is, briefly, how thinking in the development community arrived at a current consensus on development planning and strategies for poverty reduction. Economic growth remains at the centre of contemporary thinking, but the link between economic growth and poverty reduction has been seriously re-assessed. Pro-poor economic growth reflects a belief that poverty reduction will not follow economic growth unaided. The pro-poor consensus recognizes that powerful structural, institutional, social and cultural constraints form systemic barriers that favour the non-poor in competition for resources, employment opportunities, government assistance and access to markets. It also acknowledges that economic growth will benefit the poor minimally, if at all, unless deliberate steps are taken to ensure that economic growth and the economic development that follows is pro-poor. Poverty targeting has, therefore, come to take centre stage in poverty reduction planning.

International experience with pro-poor poverty reduction planning, which includes the welter of evidence now available in the many country specific *poverty reduction strategy papers* produced in association with the IMF, IDA and the WB, has resulted in a new agreement that constitutes a framework for achieving pro-poor economic growth. (PRSPs for the world's poorest and most indebted countries can be accessed via the websites of the World Bank or the IMF.) This framework consists of twelve 'guidelines' drawn from the lessons of international experience, for the planning, design and implementation of pro-poor sources of economic growth which are listed in order of priority in Figure 8.3.

---

1. Poverty planning should be informed by participatory analysis and incorporate in the solutions proposed, where practicable, participatory methods in the design, implementation, monitoring and final-impact assessment procedures recommended.
2. Poverty planning must be explicit and deliberate in its targeting of the poor, including those just above the poverty line but at risk of falling back into poverty proper.
3. Poverty planning must address the systemic and resource constraints that prevent poor people from escaping poverty through their own efforts.
4. The outcomes of poverty planning must enhance the capacity of the poor and the near-poor to become more self-reliant if they are to climb above the poverty line and stay above it.
5. Poverty planning must pay special attention to increasing the flow of cash receipts into poor and near-poor households.
6. Poverty planning must address the need to raise the productivity of the functional poor at all levels of the poverty pyramid if sustainable poverty reduction is to be achieved.
7. Poverty planning must address each of the major types of poverty that poor people from all levels of the poverty pyramid identify as critical to their experience of poverty.
8. Poverty planning must nurture an environment in which poor and near-poor households are able to participate in wealth creation activities through improved resource management, access to additional resources, and/or increased opportunities for investment in self-improvement.
9. Poverty planning must be gender sensitive and make explicit provision for the active involvement of women, the mobile aged and children.
10. Poverty planning must be inclusive and not ignore the needs of the vulnerable and powerless, including children, the near-poor and pregnant/lactating women.
11. Poverty planning must embrace pricing strategies that are consistent with the opportunity costs faced by the relevant target population.
12. Poverty planning must give explicit attention to the role of health issues as a cause of on-going poverty.

Figure 8.3   *Pro-poor poverty reduction planning guidelines*
(in order of priority)

From the twelve guidelines outlined in Figure 8.3 it is possible to construct a *framework* for assessing the poverty reduction potential of competing poverty reduction proposals. In brief, this framework can be summarized as follows:

A framework for assessing poverty reduction potential

A. Which levels of functional poverty does the proposal target?

B. Will the proposal increase the productivity of the poor by:
- facilitating activities that increase cash flow into poor households
  - better marketing of products sold
  - lower costs of living
  - lower and less regressive taxes
- enabling the value of output from poor households to increase through
  - increased output
  - more profitable mix of production
  - better prices
  - higher total revenue from sales
- reductions in underemployment
  - enabling better use of household skills
  - offering cash paid employment
  - accessing new markets
  - facilitating access to complementary resources
- lower cost of wage-goods
  - food, clothing, housing, energy
  - transport, education, health
  - communications, leisure
- improved asset base
  - wealth creation assistance
  - security of tenure
  - access to key productive resources
    - financial capital
    - intellectual capital
    - natural capital
    - social capital
  - good government
- removing constraints to self reliance
  - facilitate profitable enterprise development
  - remove obstacles to technology transfer
  - remove subsidies
  - insist on sustainability planning
  - protect the vulnerable
  - address market failures?

C. Does the proposal liberate/empower the poor by:
- ensuring good government
- being inclusive of the poor
- listening to the poor
- addressing systemic constraints to self-reliant escape from poverty?

The framework presented above represents a checklist of things that one ought to consider in assessing the most propitious ways in which donor agencies and governments can assist the poor to escape from their poverty. The principles on which the framework rests are not mysterious, but they do rely on determined commitment to ensure that poverty reduction is the one over-riding consideration in development expenditure priority setting.

Chapter 9

Community Development

DAMIEN KINGSBURY

Development is meant to be about improving the lives of people so it is logical that development should start with people. Community development is the basis of community participation, and lack of it reflects a failure of the capacity or the will of governments to meet the development needs of people in localized, usually rural or minor urban areas. It also reflects the notion that development, broadly conceived, is about the enhancement of the potential of people to emancipate themselves. That is, it is intended to give them greater control over their own lives. This is usually referred to as 'empowerment'. This 'empowerment' approach to development 'places the emphasis on autonomy in the decision making of territorially organized communities, local self-reliance, direct (participatory) democracy, and experiential social learning' (Friedman 1992: vii). However, like many other good ideas that have been encapsulated in a single word or phrase, 'empowerment' has been used so widely and by so many people and organizations for so many different purposes that it has started to lose meaning: 'in some countries, governments talk glibly of empowerment of the poor in their development plans, having stripped the term of any real meaning' (Gardner and Lewis 1996: 118).

Like all ideas about development, what community development, or empowerment, means is contested, reflecting the range of interests that come to play when theory meets practice. There are two primary foci for community development, the first being encapsulated in the idea that it is about development of and for the 'community', and the second is about development via community decision-making processes. The 'community', in this instance, is usually defined as the local group or otherwise as small groups of people, usually living in relative isolation, which are characterised by face-to-face relationships. In this, the 'community' size is determined by the needs of co-operation and consensus. To this end, the size of a viable community can vary from place to place, and is not able to be determined on a universal basis (Hodge 1970: 68). As a consequence, community development programmes must involve a capacity for modification according to local circumstances and, indeed, to suit local needs. What should be noted is that both 'external' and 'internal'

approaches to community development reflect a fundamental re-orientation of development towards a grass-roots or local-level process and
outcomes, usually implying some sort of participation in the process. This
is in contrast to macro-level or infrastructure development projects that
only indirectly affect people at the local level, and in which local
communities have very little say if any, and usually little or no
participation.

Bottom-up versus top-down

A focus on community development has been shown, in a number of cases,
to produce real, tangible and appropriate benefits for local people, as well
as providing a greater sense of self worth and empowerment. It also works
within and helps to preserve aspects of local culture that give meaning to
community life and which assist in maintaining and enhancing the social
cohesion that is necessary when engaging in a process of change.

The failure of 'top-down' or macro aid projects and decision making to
deliver tangible benefits to many people, including the most marginalized,
is addressed by adopting a 'bottom-up' or 'flat' local structure for decision
making about local needs. Despite longer-term recognition of this, many
larger scale projects fail to meet the needs and desires of ordinary people at
the local level, are often not based on local experience and are frequently
unsustainable once the aid provider had left. In all, such aid often benefits
the aid provider, in that they are given a job and a social purpose, but has
little, and sometimes negative, longer-term impact on the aid recipients.

According to the World Bank:

> ... economic growth is necessary but by no means sufficient to achieve
> widespread poverty reduction in the world. The [World Development]
> Report [on Poverty] lists three essential pillars – opportunity, security,
> and empowerment – to achieve a significant rate of sustained poverty
> reduction amongst the poorest population groups. By the same token,
> the recently released book on The Quality of Growth, published by the
> World Bank Institute, also clearly demonstrates the shift from a
> predominantly 'economic growth' development model to an approach in
> which the development of human and socio-cultural capital is deemed a
> sine qua non for achievement of balanced and sustainable development.
> For instance, the book demonstrates, using quantifiable indicators, that
> in countries with a relatively low level of inequality and a medium level
> of economic growth, the chances for large-scale poverty reduction are
> considerably greater than in countries with high economic growth and
> high levels of income inequality. (World Bank 2001a; see also World
> Bank 2000b)

However, not all decisions taken at a local level are appropriate. Some decisions are based in a sense of desperation and are, hence, very short term in nature. Other are based on a limited understanding of opportunities, or of the consequence of their decisions. In yet other circumstances, decisions can be taken or limited by traditional elites who retain power or influence in local settings, often in their own interest, or again, with a limited understanding of options or outcomes. Within many traditional societies, hierarchical power structures often removed from ordinary people not just the power to make larger decisions about their collective lives but constructed a social psychology of deference towards power holders. The issue of social power is a complex one, and can be inconsistent across cultural contexts, despite what might otherwise be seen as commonalities of interest at particular strata of society, and very often the common material conditions applying to particular circumstances. As Weitz, amongst others, notes: 'when involving entire communities in development, the social planner must be capable of using existing social relations advantageously'. That is, a failure to recognize and sensitively employ traditional leaders and others can lead to failure (Weitz 1986: 167, see also Warren 1993).

External involvement

A further problem with local decision making can be that, in a context that needs assistance, advice, or information, outside aid providers can (sometimes unwittingly) shape local agendas or inappropriately insert themselves into local decision-making processes, which may not be sustainable and which may destabilize local social relations. Perhaps the most difficult issue in community development, especially when it is focused on empowerment, concerns the role of the development worker. In simple terms, while a situation might require the intervention of an external agent to create circumstances that allow change, that external intervention by definition must, at some stage, precede empowerment, and often displace it. Based on the assumption that if communities could change themselves they would have done so, it is a rare and extraordinarily sensitive community development project that is able to allow local people to lead.

In all discussion about community development, it must be noted that external factors, from the environment to government to broad economic conditions, will have a constraining influence on what is or is not achievable within a local context. According to Friedman: 'local action is severely constrained by global economic forces, structures of unequal wealth, and hostile class alliances' (1992: iix). If development is to look to communities as the source of change, they must also seek to transform social power into political power and engage in national and international issues (Friedman 1992: iix).

Yet, in helping to create an environment in which people can make decisions for themselves, decisions are often made for them. The first decision is whether or not they wish for such intervention in their lives. Further interventions tend to flow from that, including decisions about what aspects of community development are or should be available, what the priorities for community development are, the nature of local social and hierarchical relations and decision making, and so on. This is especially the case if there is an explicit assumption on the part of development planners that there should be co-ordination between local and wider development goals (Weitz 1986: 79). This is despite acknowledging the necessity of recognizing the 'needs, beliefs and abilities of traditional peoples' (Weitz 1986: 78). However, as Friere (1985) noted:

> Attempting to liberate the oppressed without their reflective participation in the act of liberation is to treat them as objects which must be saved from a burning building, it is to lead them into the populist pitfall and transform them into masses which can be manipulated.

Korten also notes that it is not really possible for one person to 'empower' another. People can only empower themselves (1989: 118–19).

Oliver recognized the potential conflict between the ideas of development planners and local people when he noted that it should be 'the first task of a voluntary organization ... to encourage the people to speak up when aid projects go wrong' (Oliver 1983: 137). Weitz similarly noted that there needed to be an active 'feedback relationship' to allow constant revision of local development projects to conform with field realities (Weitz 1986: 174). In this, Weitz and Oliver were primarily referring to covering up aid programmes that were failing or that had failed, in order to save official embarrassment, but which allows for such failure to be repeated. Similarly, Jain, Krishnamurty and Tripathi suggest that, 'the basic reason for the failure of rural development and poverty alleviation programmes is the exclusion of the people from participation in the development process and the abandonment of the institutions of democratic decentralization and the related electoral process' (Jain, Krishnamurty and Tripathi 1985: 15). Democratic decentralization, in this context, means 'recognizing multiple centres of power' (sometimes referred to as 'Public Interest Partnerships'), which assist in ensuring accountability, transparency, participation, equity, predictability and efficiency. In this sense, what is broadly referred to as governance becomes essential, reflecting the authenticity of local electoral democracy. In simple terms, 'good governance is good for development' (Gonzales, Lauder and Melles 2000: 165).

However, the principle of appropriate development programmes and the necessity for vocal local input remains valid. Weitz (1986: 174) similarly noted that there needed to be a bottom-up 'feedback relationship' to allow constant revision so that programmes could conform to local realities.

Background to community development

Ideas about community development were first commonly propagated in the early 1970s, following what was widely seen as the failure of the 'decade of development' of the 1960s, in which decolonization did not automatically result in development and in which explicitly modernist or industrial policies were mistakenly regarded as the universal path to 'take-off'. What occurred instead, in many developing countries, was a mixture of semi-development, development experiencing losses and then gains in succession, or just simple under-development, in which a number of countries increasingly went backwards. The overall result, at a time when the West remained optimistic, was an overall decline in developing countries, and especially amongst the majority poor of developing countries. As Mortimer noted, this was in large part due to the blind faith held by Western planners in the value of modernization and, consequently, in the lack of value accorded to 'peasants' (Mortimer 1984: Ch 3).

There can be real debate about the sources of inspiration for a change in policy in the west generally and in the United States in particular. But it is worth noting that one of the key strategists in the Vietnam conflict during the 1960s, John Paul Vann, advocated local development projects as a means of winning the support of South Vietnam's peasantry to the cause of the South Vietnamese government. However, while Vann advocated local development projects, he did not envisage local people taking control of such decisions. During this time of revolutionary upheaval in South Vietnam, such a move would have potentially handed local political processes over to the National Liberation Front (see Sheehan 1988). As the main protagonist in favour of prosecuting America's involvement in the war in Vietnam at this time, Secretary of State Robert McNamara was introduced to Vann's ideas.

In response to continuing and increasing poverty in developing countries, the later as president of the World Bank, McNamara outlined the Basic Needs or 'redistribution with growth' approach to development, which focused development on local initiatives. McNamara's then ground-breaking view was that poverty alleviation for the world's poorest 40 per cent was of primary importance, although this should not be undertaken in ways that would damage prospects for economic growth (UNICEF 1996: Ch 3). In this, McNamara was influenced by the 'peripheral' work of NGOs, and thinking such as that expounded by British economist E. F. Schumacher in his seminal work *Small is Beautiful*, which turned away from large-scale industrialization and macroeconomics towards more appropriate medium levels of technology and local economics.

Yet, while this shift in focus was important, the origins of community development can be traced to some of the first thinking about development as a part of the process of decolonization, pre-dating the optimistic and sometimes grandiose ideas of the 1960s. The original United Nations position on community development, for instance, was that it 'is a technique for improving the levels of living, particularly in underdeveloped areas, community development being interpreted as a process creating conditions of economic and social progress for the whole community with its active participation and the fullest possible reliance upon the community's initiative'. (UN 1958: 21) In this sense, the community may be relatively passive in the development process, or the decision-making processes that are intended to lead towards development. In so far as there was a view that the community itself should be brought into the decision-making process, it was via what has been described as via a methodology combining social work and public administration models (Ponsioen 1962). More recently there has also been an increasing emphasis on local decision making contributing to local employment, and in the development of particular expertise.

Education as development

Even though the use of education was an early approach to community development, its history dates back even further, being first conceived of by the British Colonial Office in the 1920s, although it was not applied, in Africa, until the 1940s. Ghana launched its first mass literacy and education campaign in 1951, which was soon after adopted by the nearby French colonies (Manghezi 1976: 41). In this, community development was seen as 'a vehicle for progressive evolution of the peoples to self-government in the context of social and economic change' (Manghezi 1976: 39–40). The idea of community development was not well developed initially, although even at this stage it was recognized that education was a critical component, which found translation as the opening of 'development area schools' and similar projects (Manghezi 1976: 41). The idea of education generally and literacy in particular was later seized upon as a critical factor in community development, both for broader utilitarian purposes and to directly enhance the knowledge base (and hence capacity for decision making) of individuals.

In the sense that education allows participation and opens opportunities, community development is seen to be about enhancing local decision-making processes, via the 'empowerment' of people who are the targets of development projects, and to give them more practical political power over the goals and outcomes of the development process. The idea of empowerment, in this context, is reflected in the ideas of Paulo Friere (1985, 1976), based on the need to develop people's abilities to understand, question and resist structural conditions for their poverty, and to have the capacity to change those conditions. In this, education generally, and literacy in particular, are seen as critical criteria for individual and group development. Friere's critique was essentially derived from a 'bottom-up' perspective of social and economic relations, and was predicated upon the idea of reflection (via education) leading to action (praxis) (Friere 1985: Ch 3). Perhaps the biggest difference between Friere's revolutionary pedagogy and that role of education in a more contemporary community development is that the latter is based upon a more localized and, hence, contained basis, and that it seeks to allow its recipients to participate in wider economic and political spheres, rather than to overthrow them.

Literacy, as the most fundamental aspect of education, has thus remained a key issue in empowerment and participation of local communities, and remains both an obvious means to individual and local development as well as feeding in directly to the capacity of the state, via its constituents, to pro-actively pursue its own wider development goals. Literacy can also be argued to be an end in itself, in terms of enhancing the scope of individuals to participate in a literate world, as noted by the author on a field research trip to Managua and the Nicaragua–Honduras border in November and December 1983. To illustrate this point, after the Sandinistas literacy campaign had taken hold across the state, and at a time when the country was weathering attack by the US-sponsored Contras, one individual in Managua remarked: 'the Somosistas may return, but we can now read and write, and they can never take that away from us'. For many in Nicaragua at this time, despite other hardships, literacy was regarded an important form of liberation in its own right, and the most direct means of empowerment of a previously repressed society.

In a not dissimilar fashion, literacy has been cited as being useful to individuals as well as for 'development' in Bangladesh (although this nominally assumes the odd distinction between the welfare of individuals and 'development'). A literacy programme was developed by the Friends in Village Development Bangladesh for landless men and women, which was based on small groups, and was combined with organizational support, savings and credit schemes, technical assistance for income generation and the rebuilding of a sense of self-worth. 'Literacy is therefore linked to generating local group structures and capacity-building,' not least of which is the capacity to participate in the development process (Gardner and Lewis 1996: 117). It is worth noting here that those developing countries that have performed best, such as the 'newly industrialised countries' of East Asia, invested heavily in education as a precondition for their growth. In particular, the centrality of education to Confucian thinking resulted in massive investment in education in Singapore, Taiwan and South Korea, in each case with dramatic results.

While literacy has been identified by most governments of developing countries as a, and probably *the*, critical development issue, it has not been free of problems, both internally and externally. One of the internal problems with education campaigns is that they do not necessarily address the educational imbalance that can occur between people with and without power. That is, a person with power who is probably already literate may have their literacy enhanced, while an illiterate person may achieve only a basic level of literacy and, in terms of complex written information, still be at a significant disadvantage (especially if their literacy is tested via, for example, a contract or other complex device). Literacy is also most useful when combined with other technical support or enhancement. Literacy alone has the capacity to breed resentment through a greater awareness of structural imbalances or other 'unfairness' that cannot be changed in the short term. Indeed, this has been a major problem in places where literacy and structural unemployment are both relatively high, such as post-ballot East Timor. General estimates of unemployment in East Timor in 2002 were in the order of 75–80 per cent. However, this did not take account of the subsistence nature of much rural employment, although it was a fair reflection of the extent of the non-cash economy. And beyond this, mass education, by definition, assumes that all people's educational needs are the same, or should be the same, whereas in a number of cases this is incorrect. Milburn noted early on that 'the concept of mass education, while it served a particular phase, was essentially a contradiction in terms. Community development with its emphasis on communal co-operation, initiative and self-help has tended so far to overlook the problem of the maladjusted individual' (Milburn 1954–5: 24).

From an external perspective, education campaigns have often been amongst the first to be affected by externally imposed 'structural adjustment' programmes, in which government spending is cut to reduce public expenditure and debt. While this can be seen as a 'soft' option for governments seeking to reduce expenditure in the face of an unsustainable burden of debt, it is very often recommended by external 'consultants' whose concerns are less for the welfare of ordinary people or, indeed, for enhancing the productive capacity of workers than they are for short-term macro-economic outcomes. This disregard for the personal and social value of education very often reflects an unstated ideological bias against mass participation that is potentially occasioned by mass education.

Social distinction

Within any given social context of a local community in a developing country, there is likely to be a marked distinction between elites and others. That is, people with political or economic power (or other forms of social capital) will, in most cases, tend to be somewhat set apart from the vast majority who do not enjoy political or economic power, even though they will necessarily interact and may display elements of a type of social contract. In particular, what once might have been a more simple dichotomy has become complicated by shifting patterns of patronage, land ownership and employment. As well as traditional elites, who might operate as a hereditary or quasi-elected village or district head and enjoy certain privileges as a consequence of that, there has become a new category of political or administrative elites who owe their appointment to political associations or patronage that may be more connected to larger urban centres and modernist or quasi-modernist political formations such as parties. It is almost needless to say that power holders will invariably attempt, often vigorously, to retain or enhance their social, political and economic power (see Burkey 1988: 165).

Associated with such localized political clients or *apparatchiks* are lesser functionaries who may also obtain some personal benefit by way of political association, perhaps through their or their family members' appointment to jobs, business concessions, protections or favourable treatment. Shopholders and other small business owners might also be seen as falling into this category. In a critique on the value of encouraging small enterprise, Fromm and Maccobey noted that '... entrepreneurs do not solve the village's economic problems... They become middlemen, money lenders, and store keepers... the result is to increase dependency and powerlessness of the landless' (Fromm and Maccoby 1970: 205). In more traditional societies, such a localized sub-elite might occupy regularized positions within the community hierarchy, such as legal or religious advisor (often the same), or local constabulary or peace-keeper.

In contrast to localized elites and related sub-elites are 'urban masses' (town-dwellers), migrant workers, and rural peasantry. Urban masses, or more commonly in a local context, town dwellers, are largely those people who function at the lower end of the cash economy, as employees, small stall holders, as the under-employed (e.g., hawking minor trinkets, matches, newspapers, voluntary traffic or parking attendants, and so on), or as the unemployed. Town-dwelling unemployed may include victims of economic downturns or other loss of gainful employment, peasants who have lost their land, single parents (usually mothers), street children (functional orphans), the mentally and physically disabled, and others who, for various reasons, have slipped through the rather threadbare social networks that help sustain people in difficult times.

Migrant workers often constitute a separate group of town-dwellers, not necessarily being fixed to social networks, living in fringe communities (in both figurative and literal senses), living outside local social structures and not being a part of local decision-making processes. They may be structurally precluded from relative equality of access to material well-being, such as through lesser pay, access to potable water or electricity, education for their children, and so on. Migrant workers may also be employed on a seasonal basis, and either be transitory or unemployed during 'off' seasons. As a consequence, migrant workers are excluded from decision-making processes at a number of levels, and there is often resistance to their incorporation into local decision-making processes.

Interactions between the various strata of society, and the subsequent capacity for or interest in power sharing, do find broad commonalities across the development context. But there are also regional differences, usually borne out of local experience over a long period. Illustrations of these differing contexts come from as far apart as Mexico and Indonesia. Within the rural Mexican context, the taking and giving of orders may be unpopular with peasants who are productive and who tend to hoard. Authority or 'leadership' suggests exploitative bosses and this has strong negative connotations, and is therefore not popular. There is, in this, a lack of interest in forcing compliance on the part of others (Fromm and Maccoby 1970: 209). In such a respect, local organization requiring leadership can be difficult to obtain. In a different cultural context, there is a widespread view that village office should neither be coveted nor too highly rewarded. One consequence of this, though, is that villagers might content themselves with mediocre leadership for long periods without concerted attempts at replacement' (Warren 1993: 123).

Notions of authority and hierarchy vary from context to context, and the role of authority in local decision making and how that is employed is not consistent. In some cases authority is a capacity not to be trusted, or to be used with caution. Warren noted that in Bali, members of the traditional aristocracy, civil servants, and agents of political parties who were seen to have status, office, or wealth (that is, traditional patrons) had difficulty in presenting their views publicly in what was seen to be the disinterested manner that is otherwise regarded as a cultural ideal. Hence, orators without such *manjar* significance, but who have influence based on personal qualities, including knowledge of local *adat* (customary law) and skills in public speaking, are often in as strong or a stronger position to persuade local people of the value of an idea.

As a consequence of this public distinction between formal and informal authority figures, a dual leadership pattern can emerge. However, within this, while corporate ideals were supposed to predominate, formal or traditional decision makers still exercise informal influence on orators. 'Although close association with patrons would compromise an orator's credibility, covert alliances develop and orators are able to use their skills to frame factional interests of powerful patrons in terms of principles acceptable in the public forum.' This presentation of a shadow leadership pattern, allied to formal and informal political arenas and codes of expression, shares certain features with Bloch's proposition (1975: 6, 12) that formalized rules and speech forms are essentially vehicles of traditional authority and established power relations. That is to say, even though this social environment might portray itself as formally egalitarian and moral, it actually remains hierarchic and instrumental (Warren 1993: 73). In such cases, deeply ingrained notions of structural hierarchy mean that it may be difficult to achieve local development projects without the consent or participation of local authority figures, or that their involvement will more likely guarantee the success of a project.

In other cases, it can be difficult to achieve successful local projects without the support of local leaders. Warren has noted that the Indonesian family planning project, which has been generally regarded as successful, achieved its greatest success on the island of Bali. This has been identified as being a direct consequence of what was called the *Sistem Banjar* (Neighborhood Association System), in which the village community was a conduit for family planning. By way of illustration of its success, in 1985 Bali had the highest rate for use of contraceptives (74.5 per cent) in Indonesia, compared with the national 52.2 per cent average (Warren 1993: 217). In order to achieve this level of contraception usage, heads of *banjar* (neighbourhood or hamlet associations) were sent to training seminars and liaised with district family planning field workers to provide information and contraceptives. *Banjar* heads were also responsible for registering eligible couples, compiling statistics on contraceptive use and motivating acceptance in communities (Warren 1993: 218). According to Warren, the *klian* (head) of Banjar Tegah said the contraceptive campaign 'would not ever have succeeded if it hadn't gone through the *banjar*. Before everyone was embarrassed to talk about such matters. Now it is normal. At each assembly meeting we discussed family planning until everyone understood sufficiently'. (Warren 1993: 218). This conformed to Weitz's view that, 'when involving entire communities in development, the social planner must be capable of using existing social relations advantageously'

(Weitz 1986: 167). However, this also reflected the broad interests, and reinforced the status of, the local elite.

Apart from local elite input, Warren said there was no difference in contraceptive use based on social or economic status, although there was variance between *banjar* (between 30 and 60 per cent acceptance), which correlated to the distance between *banjar* and the local family planning clinic (Warren 1993: 219), and between support or otherwise of *klian* for the programme (Warren 1993: 220). Proximity to both the source of the programme and the motivator for the programme was critical to the success of a local programme. Warren noted that while local leadership was important, and was influenced by proximity, discussion of leadership or local institutions also need to take account of Balinese conceptions of the 'popular', which were unquestionably influenced by modern ideas about democracy as well as traditional practices and status orientation (Warren 1993: 123).

Social organization

Even local projects, in which autonomy is meant to be paramount, there can continue to be a heavy reliance upon external agencies for assistance, in which the local community provides only part of the total requirement to undertake a local project. One such illustration of this, from Indonesia, is where local funding and communal labour (*gotong royong* – mutual help) supplemented a quarter of the cost of a local project, which was established by the Public Works Department. Notably, two weeks labour was provided by a local military unit under the *Angkatan Masuk Desa* (Army Enters Village) programme for local public works. This programme was developed in the mid-1980s as a means of bringing the army closer to the people, to enhance 'development' more generally, and to cement the military's role in the development process.

Yet, even though this was a government-sponsored scheme, and that the military component was supposed to be paid for out of the military's own budget, the *klian banjar* was still required to make a 'donation' of a monetary 'gift' to the military commander as repayment for the assistance provided (Warren 1993:225). In such instances, most of the 'gift' of cash would be kept by the local military commander, although a portion of it would be paid to his own superiors (or those above him in his patron–client network) and a portion would be spent on or distributed to the soldiers who actually undertook the work (as improvements in their living conditions or as supplementary wages). In this way, the autonomy of village projects was still compromised by broader state projects, patron–client relations, and notions of hierarchy and authority, the unofficial but socially constructed reciprocal elements of which most villagers found impossible to escape.

In relation to Indonesia's primary education campaign begun in 1973, central-government funding via sub-provincial districts allowed villages to subcontract or manage construction of new schools themselves. This was regarded as

> one of the most beneficial and least controversial development programmes, expanding rural employment while broadening educational opportunities. The effect of Inpres SD (the presidential decree that launched the programme) was to raise primary enrolment across Indonesia to a claimed 85 per cent by 1980 (the World Bank said enrolment was 78 per cent in 1984, indicating a tendency for the government to over-inflate its claims).

Because of the benefit to both local education and local employment, under this programme, 'villages devoted considerable energy to this task'. A *klian* of one of the *banjar* in Desa (Village) Siang said: 'besides giving work here, the buildings are better. Why? Because they are ours. If they call in someone from outside, I wouldn't trust them' (Warren 1993: 215).

Even in what was widely considered to be a successful community development programme, there was still some disquiet with the reliance of the programme on outside sources. In this case it was due to corruption at the next level of government up from the village: 'leaders in Tarian and other *desa* expressed frustration at the substantial loss in real value of materials received for projects when delivery was managed through the *kabupaten*'. In this, some building materials were stolen, while others that had to be purchased through the sub-provincial district administration were overpriced (Warren 1993: 230). The role of the *klian banjar* also retained some capacity for capriciousness in development projects. In another village studied by Warren, which was built over the water of a bay, the village head dominated the use of the fresh water tank and left the other two unused tanks outside his home. Fresh water was supplied, at a high cost, by an enterprising Bugis merchant (Warren 1993: 229). However, despite such problems, and reflecting the balance in favour of meeting development objectives, *banjar* continued to be used to balance local decision making and central needs and objectives.

Because of the 'balancing of central needs and objectives', while Indonesia's primary education and fertility reduction programmes both recorded a relatively high degree of success, there were also concerns about how genuinely independent much decision making was. For example, while local communities and community leaders were co-opted into supporting government programmes, there was little community discretion about what programmes it might pursue. That is, if the most pressing need in a particular village was, say, water supply or sanitation, if this did not correspond to a greater external plan it would almost certainly not receive any external support. Further, the linkage between local implementation and higher-level involvement was frequently used as a means of exercising political surveillance and control over local communities. As a result, 'many critics of development ... view participation as a degraded term, which has only served to 'soften' top-downism and has been successfully stripped of its previously radical connotations' (Gardner and Lewis 1996: 111).

Co-operatives

The world's single biggest traded crop is coffee (following oil as the world largest traded commodity), and it is the dominant export of non-oil producing developing countries. Yet, apart from plantations, most coffee is grown and harvested by small landholders, who are entirely at the economic mercy of local buyers who, in turn, sell to the world's trading houses. The price of coffee is set not at the point of sale of the original product, but in the world's stock exchanges. However, given the vast gulf in the price between coffee as a globally traded commodity and the price paid at the farm gate, it is perhaps the ideal product for a co-operative venture. Collective bargaining power that can increase the growers' price for coffee can make a major difference to the income of coffee farmers, yet barely register a blip on the global pricing radar.

As a long-standing but much debated area of economic community development, co-operatives were originally designed to pool the resources of a number of local people, including labour and machinery, into a common enterprise. Co-operatives continue to demonstrate their usefulness, especially in the areas of better buying and selling power, and removing middlemen from such arrangements. Co-operatives can also allow a division of labour and specialization of labour, which, in principle, should allow for greater efficiencies of production (Fromm and Maccoby 1970: 210–211). Weitz also recognized the benefits of co-operative arrangements, noting that they could make available technology and equipment too costly for individuals, transform small-scale farmers into significant economic blocs, that they made production more efficient, and that they could expand opportunities to acquire new markets and suppliers (Weitz 1986: 163). However, Weitz also noted that expectations of what co-operatives could achieve were sometimes overstated, and that expectations exceeded their capacity to deliver, especially in the shorter term. This, he said, needed to be clarified to co-operative participants to ensure that their expectations corresponded to an achievable reality, and to preclude disappointments that could undermine the co-operative enterprise (Weitz 1986: 164).

Even with such clarification of the capacity of co-operatives to produce results, some members of co-operatives have also felt that their respective labour is not always adequately rewarded, especially for those who feel they contribute more but receive back a share based on the number of contributors but not the effort committed. This perceived or real reduction in incentive has led, in some instances, to a reduction in productivity, especially where co-operative members are rewarded at the same rate regardless of how hard or otherwise they work. Constructed as 'collectivization', this form of co-operative was shown to be a failure in China and Vietnam, with overall losses in farm productivity due to the loss of small-holder incentive. In other cases, however, such as Israel's *kibbutz*, co-operative/communal ventures have been far more successful. And the traditional 'mutual assistance' of many villages communities has worked as one model for co-operation, bringing with it a powerful cultural recognition of the need for village units to work cohesively at important times of the year. But especially as an imposed model of local economic organization, co-operatives have had a very mixed record of success. Where co-operatives or co-operative endeavour has a higher degree of voluntarism it also has a much higher degree of relative success.

Translating the idea of voluntary co-operation into year-round co-operation, or shared wealth, is sometimes less straightforward, and in a number of cases production has failed due to a perceived or real lack of incentive, rather than increased through greater efficiencies. Even in the case of public-works projects, which tend to have a better record of co-operation, anti-co-operative attitudes rooted in a hoarding character may still prevail. Balanced against this, the social stigma attached to not contributing a small amount to public works raises problems of anti-social orientation (Fromm and Maccoby 1970: 208). Further issues can also arise from assuming a leadership role in social projects. In some cases, such as a voluntary contribution to a local social project, villagers work more successfully together in public-works projects rather than co-operative enterprises as such, by contributing money or, if too poor, labour (Fromm and Maccoby 1970: 206). In this there can be an expectation that the rich will spend more on public events or, alternatively, public works, by way of displaying their status and, at least as importantly, helping to retain economic balance and social harmony in a type of 'social contract'.

In comparing co-operatives in Maharasthra and Bihar in India, and in Bangladesh, Blair noted that the success or failure of co-operative enterprises resulted from a combination of factors. The success of a co-operative included having adequate infrastructure and hence access to loans, and the co-operative's financial structure (including having a built-in repayment system for loans to avoid defaults). Issues of land tenure, the size of landholdings as an incentive or otherwise towards co-operative behaviour, social cohesion, political culture and, of course, competence, all contributed to success or failure (Blair 1997). Jain, Krishnamurty and Tripathi also noted the issue of landholding size as a factor in co-operative success, indicating that small farmers were more likely to want to be involved in co-operatives. They also noted that, regarding co-operative finance, there was 'no evidence to suggest default is more frequent among small farmers than among large farmers' (Jain, Krsihnamurthy and Tripathi 1985: 57).

In principle, co-operatives can and often do give greater productive capacity and greater independence to local farmers or other groups of small-scale workers. And in forming what amounts to small companies, they do return the benefits of their joint labour to the 'share-holders' – the co-operative members themselves. But questions of adequate or appropriate management, equity, and so on, all need to be addressed in a co-operative enterprise. Perhaps the most successful co-operatives are those that pool resources, and in some cases labour, for certain aspects of a co-operative project, but which retain independence of co-operative stakeholders in terms of clearly delineating inputs and, hence, proportionate outcomes. This 'reward for effort' is perhaps the key formal distinction between a co-operative enterprise and a communal enterprise. The point, however, is that community development is most enhanced when local people voluntarily come together around a local project which is to the benefit of all. In making a decision to work co-operatively towards a shared goal and then by undertaking the work, people in the local context combine practical resources and skills, potentially increase their efficiency through specializing tasks, and achieve economies of scale not available to individuals. However, at least as important, by doing so local people also take their material circumstances into their own hands and, by forming what amounts to a political collective, empower themselves in terms of what they can achieve, but also through increasing their economic and political autonomy for their own benefit.

Expecting the unexpected

Anthropologists have noted that one of the most critical factors that affect development programmes, especially those that are located within and run by the local community, is the impact of development on local patterns of behaviour and economic, social and political relations. That is, development programmes that alter a local environment are not free from flow-on effects, nor are they free of importing external values (such as consumer materialism), despite the implied belief that all societies can potentially adopt with relatively little disruption to the development paradigm. In seeking the advantages of development and in focusing on its potential for positive contribution, there is frequently too little concern for potential negative consequences, meaning that 'unexpected' problems can and do arise, sometimes to the extent of derailing the development process. That is '... social change often entails costs that are neither expected nor planned for' (Appel 1990: 271).

In recognizing that there are impacts from the local development process that are often not planned for, Appel noted seven principles of social change within the development context. They are:

1. Every act of development or modernization necessarily involves an act of destruction.
2. The introduction of a new activity always displaces an indigenous activity.
3. The adaptive potential of a population is limited, and every act of change temporarily reduces this potential until such time as that change has been completely dealt with.
4. Given such reduction, each act of change has the potential to cause physiological, psychological, and/or behavioural impairment in the subject population (such as stress or 'social bereavement')
5. Modernization erodes support and maintenance mechanisms for managing social stress.
6. Change always produces psychological loss, as well as compensation for such loss.
7. Change threatens the nutritional status of a population, and there is often disruption to traditional nutrition patterns. (Appel 1990: 272)

In identifying these factors, Appel also notes that they are all exacerbated by the speed of change. That is, the speed of change might not just have a quantified impact – that twice the rate of change will produce twice the potential problems, but that the quality of the impact can increase disproportionately to the rate of change (twice the rate of change could lead to a greater multiplier of related problems) (1990: 273). The encouragement given to a shift to cash cropping, for instance, can damage local ecology and lead to a loss of subsistence crops. The loss of access to locally sourced food can and often does have a direct impact on the nutritional status of local communities (Appel 1990: 273–4). Not only is the variety of nutritional sources not always available in a purely cash context within a local community at the lower end of the development scale, but cash crops may be subject to total failure (mixed crops tend to be subject to partial failure), hence depriving the grower of access to any return. Further, the trajectory of prices for cash crops has, on the whole, declined in real terms since the late 1970s, with regular dips in pricing depending on the extent of oversupply and relative competition on global markets. This, by definition, reduces the potential income to a subsistence crop grower and, hence, their capacity to secure adequate supplies of food. This then returns to the observations made by Weitz, Warren, Friedman and Oliver; that in any community development process, there needs to be primary recognition given to the knowledge, values, needs, and desires of the local people, which is what, at base, community development is supposed to be about.

Community development at work – the East Timor experience

In assessing the practical potential for community development, the most recent significant programme (at the time of writing), East Timor's Community Empowerment and Local Governance Project (CEP), stands as a useful illustration. The CEP in East Timor showed what was available through community development, but it also pointed up some of the problems that continue to dog local development projects. The CEP was a World Bank-funded project intended to encourage community level development projects and to encourage democratization at a local level in a society that prior to its commencement, apart from one violent and externally organized election, had never previously experienced the democratic process.

The formative stages of the CEP came into being soon after the UN returned to East Timor in late September 1999, following the Indonesian army's 'scorched earth' policy in response to the UN-supervized ballot in which East Timorese voted to separate from Indonesia. Already the equal poorest province in Indonesia, East Timor had about 80 per cent of its buildings and infrastructure destroyed by the retreating Indonesian army and its militia proxies. Prior to the vote, East Timor had been under Indonesian occupation since late 1975, during which time there were limited attempts to introduce literacy and centrally planned development programmes, the latter mostly contributing to larger Indonesian-owned enterprises. Development at the local level was decided upon by Indonesian government appointees (sometimes through a nominal electoral process) and, if at a lower level of implementation, followed a standardized Indonesian model, with even less functional democracy than existed in most of the rest of Indonesia under that country's decidedly authoritarian New Order government. Prior to the Indonesian occupation, East Timor had a few scant weeks of independence, though no meaningful democracy, following a history of Portuguese colonial neglect punctuated by occasional bouts of intense, mostly regionalized violence.

After the first year of the incipient CEP, in November 2000, the US$21.5 million programme largely shifted from the control of foreign employees to an indigenous management team. From this time, the small management team in Dili supported 60 sub-district facilitators, more than 800 village facilitators, and one district project accountant and a district monitor in every district, all of whom were East Timorese.

Recognising East Timor's history of not having experienced democracy (assuming the deeply flawed Indonesian electoral process between 1975–1999 is not included), the key CEP objective was to introduce and establish transparent, democratic, and accountable local structures in rural areas to make decentralized decisions about development projects. While providing the opportunity for local communities to rehabilitate basic infrastructure and revive local economies, the local councils established under CEP were intended to be a vehicle for the local expression of development needs and desires, and for implementing projects. This was, at the time, regarded as a good example of 'bottom-up' development planning and as representing a new policy direction by the World Bank, which funded the project. The former UN Transitional Authority in East Timor head of District Administration, Jarat Chopra, described the CEP as 'an introduction to local democracy, as well as a functioning form of self-determination in the reconstruction process' (La'o Hamutuk 2000).

After its first 12 months, the CEP had funded over 600 sub-projects and supported the formation of 57 sub-district councils. More than 400 village development councils were founded in all districts, between them accounting for a total of 6270 representative council members. One notable aspect of this programme was that the council positions were equally divided between men and women. (World Bank 2000a, TFET 2000) This was in contrast to East Timor's deeply entrenched culture of male domination. However, while this division of representation by sex was broadly regarded as appropriate (not least by many East Timorese women), it was a very clear example of the imposition of external values on a sometimes reluctant indigenous society. This external imposition was not unwelcome, but it did lead to a number of problems:

In many ways, the CEP councils are creations of the 'international community' – albeit with the expressed support of the CNRT [Timorese National Resistance Council]. In this regard, they are not as legitimate and vibrant as socio-political structures that have emerged out of local, long-term processes. As the 'Joint Donor' report noted, '[A]t present the talent and energy at village level is more likely to be found around the chief and the old clandestine structures than within the council'. It is such structures that the report contends 'must be built upon if the country's urgent rural development problems are to be solved.' What the report calls their 'control mentality and gender bias,' however, run counter to international notions of democracy, as well as to the official positions of the CNRT. How the CEP will reconcile its praiseworthy principles with the need to respect indigenous beliefs, practices, and structures is an ongoing challenge. In this regard, working more closely with local and national organizations – such as East Timorese women's groups, for example – might go a long way toward realizing many of the CEP's goals. (La'o Hamutuk 2000)

As a result of the post-ballot destruction, local communities largely chose to invest CEP funds in rebuilding or repairing community and personal infrastructure. Some 43 per cent of funding was allocated for the construction of community meeting halls, a quarter for small roads linking up to larger ones and for the repair of agricultural infrastructure, 15 per cent for the restoration of household assets (such as pots, pans, plates, cups, and/or spoons shared by villagers) and productive equipment (such as simple, communally owned farm equipment, lathes, or saws), 10 per cent for repair of water supply infrastructure (wells and pipes), and 7 per cent for schools or clinics. 'Vulnerable groups' and others, such as orphans and widows, were targeted for CEP support, as were local NGOs and the development of community radio (La'o Hamutuk 2000, Estefa 2001). (It has been common experience in developing countries since the advent of transistorization that radios are the cheapest and most accessible form of mass communication.)

While the CEP was seen as relatively successful in introducing democratization to East Timor, and in improving the social, economic and political position of women, it also had some failures. The introduction of localized democratization necessarily led to tension with traditional power structures, and in cases where traditional leaders prevailed it served to strengthen their political position, as well as offering them the chance to exploit economic opportunities offered by the projects. Similarly, although the CEP served to strengthen and democratize local decision-making, there was an initial lack of co-ordination between villages, and between villages and the district level administrations. This was, in large part, resolved through the establishment of District Advisory Boards providing such linkages. The position of women in such CEPs was also not a universal success, with a continuing 'culture of silence' on the part of many women (and expected by many men), and otherwise a lack of active participation on the part of many women. Further, not all CEP elections were as democratic as intended, with some 30 per cent of elections undertaken by 'acclamation' of candidates who had been chosen by local leaders. Village were also frequently inactive, in part due to a lack of training, in part due to lack of reward and in part due to concern over introducing opportunism to impoverished environments. According to a senior CEP official, Chris Dureau, the CEP's project of dispersing money to districts had in fact undermined democratic principles, mostly because the processes intended to ensure participation were in many cases short-circuited to ensure the efficient dispersal of funds (Dureau 2003).

On balance, however, the CEP was widely regarded as having achieved a number of its goals, not least of which was the locally directed repair of the physical fabric of East Timorese society. Between the CEP and externally supervised elections for the legislature and the presidency (and following the vote for independence), notions of participatory and representative democracy were overwhelmingly enthusiastically received, and were becoming ingrained into the thinking of many, perhaps most, local people as a desirable and legitimate means of decision making The biggest threat to this process related not to the success or otherwise of the CEP, but to the broader economic conditions of the fledgling state, and the social dislocation caused by unmet economic expectations, externally sourced provocation, and the social trauma of a quarter century of brutalization that, pro rata, was on a scale equivalent to that of Cambodia under the Khmer Rouge. Set against this backdrop, the CEP functioned to restore or establish some order of normality and, broadly conceived, 'progress.' However, as a programme with a finite tenure for external funding, there was real concern about its viability after its external sources of funding ended. When that time came, the real test of the success of the programme could be measured.

Local versus global

Regardless of the value attached to it, there is little doubt that the world is in many ways becoming a smaller, more-connected and integrated place. Interestingly, however, while the world grows smaller local cultures are increasingly asserting themselves in ways that were initially unnecessary and then, for a while, difficult if not impossible. That is, as remote corners of the globe are increasingly exposed to the glare of international exposure, the people within them are seeing themselves as a separately identifiable component of a diverse and overwhelmingly culturally heterogeneous global population. This is nowhere more pronounced than in relation to states, many of which as developing countries have only made the transition to statehood in a qualified manner, perhaps reflecting the specific historical and material origins of the world's first (and to date more successful) states. The failure of many states to meet, or be able to meet, the needs of many of their citizens, and the broad sweep of globalization, has meant that many communities have turned back to themselves for development, if in fact many of them ever ceased to do so.

For many in developing countries, what is called 'development' but which in other contexts might just be a simple, perhaps minor improvement in a standard of living, is the product of local conditions, effort, imagination, and capacity. Governments can and do develop major infrastructure projects, and sometimes these have a direct positive benefit on local people. But very often they do not, and in too many cases the effects are deleterious, or are simply not sustained and, hence, become a larger economic burden. Yet, there is no quality of government that exceeds its desire to involve itself down to the most local level of its population, in part certainly to be able to claim some equality of care of its citizens but, almost as surely, to regulate and control them as well. It is at this point that exists the juncture between state and local aspirations for development.

There is no doubt that some local development projects have to fit into a wider development scheme. For example, and short of particular political claims to the local, it would be rather pointless developing a local educational facility of the language being taught was not consistent with a wider literacy programme. So too a road project, in which roads to a proposed bridge faced each other at points that did not correspond. Equally, however, the one-size-fits-all model of development can also fail to address specific local needs, impose inappropriate development, and silence the voice of the local community. Even with the best of intentions, external authorities can only rarely presume to know how people think without actually asking them. Added to this, of course, are all the usual inefficiencies of a larger hierarchical or bureaucratic structure, the continuation of patron–client relations, modified forms of economic status and deference, and the consequent potential for corruption and a reduction of service at the final point of the process.

It is not accurate to say that all the problems of development decision-making can be resolved by devolving responsibility for such decisions to the local level. Even amongst local communities, there are specific interests, conflicts and tensions that can and do derail local decision making processes, or which default to traditional, often non-representative and usually exclusive power structures. There are also problems with awareness and education, and technical competence. These are real issues that need to be addressed. Yet, in acknowledging such issues, the legitimacy of direct representation in local decision making remains valid, the sensitivity and awareness to local needs, concerns, and values is most acute at the local level, and the capacity for inclusiveness in and, hence, ownership of the development process is greatest at the local level. Development is not just about the accumulation of material resources, but about the allocation of such resources. The decision-making process that determines such allocation is a key development issue.

Chapter 10

Gender and Development

JANET HUNT

Whatever the prevailing trend in development, one thing remains constant – gender implications of development processes are neglected. In the years immediately following the Second World War, when the concept of 'development' evolved, issues of gender equity were not even considered relevant to the economic development of Third World countries. Today, after much debate about approaches to development, after significant advances made during the United Nations Decade for Women (1975–1985), and following a period of crisis, debt and adjustment in the 1980s and 1990s, the challenge of making development gender-equitable remains a significant one.

Gender inequality remains a feature of every region in the world, though it is most pronounced in South Asia, sub-Saharan Africa and the Middle East. Women are said to be 70 per cent of the world's poor; have only about 10 per cent of all parliamentary seats in most countries; and in developing countries, on average, they earn only 73 per cent of male earnings. There is not a single developing country in which women and men enjoy equal rights under the law. In particular, women are discriminated against in areas such as their right to land and property, and their right to conduct business independently (World Bank 2001b, UNDP 1995, UNIFEM 2000). The result is that women are more vulnerable to poverty than men, especially as a result of widowhood, separation or divorce, and the consequent loss of access to productive assets.

The future will remain unequal in many parts of the world. Girls represent 60 per cent of all primary school age children not enrolled in school worldwide. In sub-Saharan Africa, the gender gap in school enrolment has remained much the same for the 20-year period 1970–1990. Only 14 per cent of girls are enrolled in secondary school (World Bank 2001b). Denied education, poor girls will grow up to become poor women and the cycle will continue.

Sex and gender: what are we talking about?

In raising the issues of gender inequality, early writers focused on *women* in development. The more recent emphasis on *gender* signals a change in perspective and approach. While women and men differ biologically – that is their *sex* is different – the behaviour and socially learned characteristics associated with their maleness or femaleness, is their *gender*. The learned behaviours and roles associated with being male and female may vary from culture to culture. For example, in one culture males take care of money. In another, it is the women who control the purse strings. Thus, roles associated with each gender may vary from place to place, as well as over time. They are not totally fixed. In the economic sphere, men and women often undertake different activities. Women may plant certain crops; men may plant others. Harvest work may be gender-specific. Men may take care of large animals, women the small ones. Men may hunt; women may gather berries, fruits and wild foods. But, in each setting, we have to be clear what the roles are and how they inter-relate.

A recent study of rural households in Vietnam (Kabeer and Anh 2000), for example, notes that Vietnamese women have always been active traders, making up half the trading labour force in the 1960s unlike their counterparts in South Asia and the Middle East, who comprised only about 10 per cent of traders at that time. By the late 1990s in Vietnam some 90 per cent of men and women were involved in income-earning economic activities, but women were more likely than men to be found in 'catering, food and beverage manufacturing, wholesale and retail trade, and garment and leather industries. Men predominated (80 per cent) in storage and transport services, mining and fishing' (Kabeer and Anh 2000: 11). In terms of agricultural labour, Kabeer and Anh cite research from the Red River Delta that indicates that women alone were 'largely responsible for sowing, transplanting and weeding; both men and women were active in soil preparation and in harvesting'. Animal husbandry was women's responsibility in about 50 per cent of households and a joint activity in 33 per cent. Homestead gardening was done solely by women in 30 per cent of households and jointly in 43 per cent (Kabeer and Anh 2000: 12). Such detailed and localized analysis is required to identify gender roles and responsibilities, and thus to identify appropriate development strategies.

Early development workers, however, made false assumptions, largely based on their own experience of male and female roles in Europe and North America in the early 1900s. It was assumed that women's roles were largely as mothers and 'housewives' in the European sense. Their extremely significant *economic* roles in the household or as farmers were entirely overlooked. As early as 1929, Nigerian women were resisting their loss of land and their reduced status as farmers, as a result of colonists' efforts to 'modernize' agriculture (Boserup 1970, Mies 1986).

Thus, early development projects ignored women, and neglected to understand the diverse roles they were playing in social and economic life. As a result, some early development projects made life worse for women, depriving them of land, which was taken over for the development project's crops, denying them access to technical assistance, providing resources, training and education to men, and often, unknowingly adding to women's work burden (Rogers 1980). Any income from the 'development' activities went straight to the men, creating wider inequalities than already existed.

One early example of a failed project resulting from such assumptions is documented by Dey (1982). The project attempted to promote irrigated rice growing in the Gambia by offering incentives such as credit and cheap inputs as well as marketing assistance to men. Worse, the land proposed for irrigated rice farming was actually common land over which women had use-rights. Women's traditional subsistence rice-growing was forced onto marginal lands, and women showed little enthusiasm for a new role as labourers in the irrigated ricelands. The result was a very disappointing one for the project, and disruption to women's previous rice production for home consumption and exchange.

Where there were development activities for women, they were generally either mother–child health projects (generally with more focus on the child than the mother) or family planning projects to encourage women to adopt family planning methods to reduce population growth (Rogers 1980). Women were seen only as mothers, often of too many children! Such projects did nothing to enhance women's status or promote their equality, although they may have been of some practical support to women, especially those with children.

Integrating women into development

Ester Boserup's seminal work, *Women's Role in Economic Development* (1970), challenged all this. The book documented different household and farming systems in Asia and Africa, pointing out that there were vast differences between the social and economic arrangements in the various household types, and in what she termed male and female farming systems. She observed that women played a very active role in agriculture in Africa, particularly in areas of extensive farming and shifting cultivation. In Asia, on the other hand, in intensive, settled agriculture where the plough was used, women took a far lesser role, and their labour was replaced by male landless labourers. She drew attention to the significance of land tenure arrangements and stimulated a plethora of empirical research to explore these issues in many different contexts. Boserup also drew attention to the economic significance of polygamous households, where extra wives provided a source of free agricultural labour to the household. The European nuclear family model was shown to be a context-specific arrangement, not a universal model. Furthermore, she argued that women could play a much more active role in industrial development and the modern sector, and that economic growth would be enhanced if this were encouraged. Her view was that, contrary to popular belief, women would not take jobs from men, but would expand the available labour force and hence the opportunities for economic growth (Boserup 1970).

Boserup's work stimulated the emergence of the Women In Development movement (Moser 1993), a movement that was gaining in strength at the same time as the movement for the New International Economic Order, in the mid-1970s. While the latter movement argued for a redistribution of the world's resources in favour of developing countries, women argued for a redistribution to balance gender inequalities.

The Women in Development (WID) movement embraced modernization, and argued that women should be 'integrated' into development. If there was to be economic growth, women were to contribute to it and get their fair share of its benefits: women's subsistence farming should be given access to credit and extension services equally with men; women should have equal access to educational opportunities to give them the opportunity to participate in the modern sector. The language of 'efficiency' was adopted by the WID advocates, to convince development planners to involve women in development. It was a language the latter understood, although it was clear they had little idea of how to implement the approach (Moser 1993, Rogers 1980).

Early efforts to respond to WID advocates resulted in the establishment of Women's Projects and Women's Desks in development agencies. They tended to be peripheral to the main development effort going on, which simply remained unchanged. Thus, projects for women were supported in areas such as 'home economics', and traditional crafts, as well as credit for income-generation. The theory was that women's poverty resulted from their underdevelopment, and all that was required for development to occur was to increase their productivity through provision of credit (Moser 1991). Many of the credit programmes were poorly conceived and managed, and they often turned into welfare-type projects that avoided any resource competition with men (Buvinic 1986).

The mainstream of development was barely touched. Even as late as 1995, a study by Jahan of four major donors and two Southern aid-recipient countries found that the donor agencies had taken the easy path, and had avoided hard choices 'creating underfunded mandates, adding a few projects to their existing portfolios, and supporting research, training and the development of operational tools and techniques' (Jahan 1995: 126). WID had become a technical fix, not an issue of empowering women and genuinely transforming development. WID training, WID guidelines, and WID checklists were all embraced with differing degrees of comprehension and commitment (Jahan 1995). But the fundamental development theories on which the whole development 'project' rested were not up for question.

Women AND development: a new critique

While modernization was being critiqued by the school of dependency theorists, feminists were developing their own Marxist-based critique of modernization. Marxist feminists saw that the accumulation of capital resulted not simply from the exploitation of 'peripheral' countries, but from the free subsidy of women's unpaid reproductive and subsistence labour. Maria Mies argued that capitalism could not spread without the subjugation and exploitation of women (Mies 1986) . Her research found that, contrary to the former belief that men were the preferred labour force, women were being employed in some key areas at lower wages and in poor conditions. She found that poorly paid 'compliant' women were the labour force of choice in many multinational companies, particularly in the electronics, textile and garment industries in free-trade zones, and in large commercial agricultural companies. Their work was seen as 'supplementary' to the male 'breadwinner' so they were paid less, and their employment was often on a casual basis, making them vulnerable. Women had indeed been integrated into development, but in such a way as to perpetuate inequality and their own subordination (Mies 1986: 114).

Anything between 60 per cent and 90 per cent of Asia's one million workers in free-trade zones in 1986 were women, typically earning only 50–75 per cent of male wages, working long hours – 12–14 hour days are common – and in poor health conditions. The garment factories are often damp, crowded, noisy and poorly lit, and women are at risk of allergic reactions from chemical dyes. In the electronics industry women are vulnerable to a range of hazards, such as acids, solvents, and carcinogenic chemicals (Mies 1986, Pearson 2001, Pyle and Dawson 1990). Mies' case that low-paid women are being exploited for capitalist development seems borne out by the evidence of the free-trade zone experience – a significant part of such countries' export-orientated national development policies (Pyle and Dawson 1990).

Mies' work was published a year after the Nairobi Women's Conference to mark the end of the UN Decade for Women. At Nairobi, a new 'southern' women's network, DAWN (Development Alternatives for Women in a New Era), also made a strong critique of current development approaches, with the publication of Gita Sen and Caren Grown's book, *Development Crisis and Alternative Visions: Third World Women's Perspectives* (Sen and Grown 1987).

In the introduction to their book, Sen and Grown explain that implicit in many of the activities and discussions about women and development it is assumed that:

> ... women's main problem in the Third World has been insufficient participation in an otherwise benevolent process of growth and development. Increasing women's participation and improving their shares in resources, land, employment and income relative to men were seen as necessary and sufficient to effect dramatic changes in their economic and social position. Our experiences now lead us to challenge this belief.... A development process that shrinks and poisons the pie available to poor people and then leaves women scrambling for a relatively larger share, is not in women's interest..... Equality for women is impossible within the existing economic, political and cultural processes that reserve resources, power and control for small sections of people. But neither is development possible without greater equity for and participation by women. (Sen and Grown 1987: 11, 15)

Thus the DAWN women were also challenging the Women in Development (WID) approach, and its assumption that modernization just needed to incorporate women.

DAWN, and many women working in non-government development organizations around the world, recognized that to challenge this development orthodoxy, women needed to be mobilized and empowered to realise a different development vision.

Gender and development

The focus on women's empowerment became one thread in the next phase of work to promote gender equity in development. But the main thrust was to shift attention from women themselves to the *relations between men and women*, and particularly to analyze the unequal power relations between them at every level, from the household to the national economy. Gender workers recognized that all social, political and economic structures needed to be examined in this light, with the intention of transforming development to become a more gender-equitable process (United Nations 1999).

Development organizations replaced their Women in Development policies with Gender and Development Policies, guidelines and procedures. These were supported by Gender Analysis Training, Gender Planning approaches, and an attempt to achieve 'gender mainstreaming' across the institutions (Moser 1993, Ostergaard 1992, Rathgeber 1990).

An important contribution to the analytical work was made by Caroline Moser (Moser 1993). She distinguished between women's 'practical' and 'strategic' needs, and highlighted the interrelationships between women's different roles – reproductive, productive, and community managing. Women's 'practical needs' were those that resulted from their current subordinated position, and might include assistance in areas such as education, improved health care, agricultural advice, etc. But their strategic needs are those that might help to transform their situation. These might include legal reform to remove gender discrimination; an end to violence against women; and more politically aware, active, and better-organized women. Such changes would contribute to an end to women's subordination. Moser challenged development programmes to address women's strategic gender needs, not just their practical ones. Her call for better understanding of women's triple roles would also help shape development programmes to avoid increasing women's workload, and focus on improving their lives.

At the same time, feminist economists were trying to deal with economic models of the household which were still far from accurate. In general, development economists treat the household as a single unit, and much data collected at the household level is not gender-disaggregated. Bina Agarwal (1997a) has developed a gendered 'bargaining model' of the household, which explores how men and women interact within households to meet their subsistence needs, have access to resources necessary for subsistence, and frame the 'social norms' within which such bargaining takes place. In addition, she outlines the external factors in the market, at the community level and at the level of the state, which shape the bargaining power available to different household members. Thus, a woman's ability to bargain favourably to have equal access to resources for subsistence, such as land, may be affected by laws relating to inheritance, her access to government officials who deal with land registration matters, her educational level and legal literacy, the community's view about the legitimacy of her claim (whatever its legal merits), and her ability to support herself independent of counter-claimants (such as brothers, or uncles) (Agarwal 1997a: 14).

Such detailed analysis of gender at the household level and its interaction with wider factors has been important to continue to challenge development planners to check their assumptions, carry out their prior research, and pay greater attention to the gendered effects of different policies and programmes.

But most institutions have found gender mainstreaming difficult to achieve. In the late 1990s, the Commonwealth Secretariat published a range of guides to 'gender mainstreaming' in different aspects of development planning, including finance, public service management, trade and industry, and agriculture and rural development. Gender, it said,

> is mainstreamed when the development process and frameworks are transformed in ways which ensure the participation and empowerment of women as well as men in all aspects of life and especially in decision-making structures. (Taylor 1999: 7)

Few nations or development agencies have implemented this approach. High staff turnover, poor resourcing, inadequate staffing levels, and lack of corporate commitment have dogged efforts to gain better gender policies and programmes in many development agencies (CIDA 1995, Reality of Aid 1998).

Gender and adjustment

While efforts were underway to make development policies and programmes more gender-sensitive, many countries were facing enormous problems of indebtedness. From the early 1980s, the Philippines, Mexico and many African countries were undergoing the rigours of structural adjustment. Governments had to reduce spending, currencies were devalued and there was a strong push to trade more and open the economies to foreign investment (Beneria 1999).

As the DAWN women explained in Nairobi, women became the 'shock absorbers' in this process. In the name of 'economic efficiency', the policies shifted a considerable burden on to women to make up for the austerity measures that were imposed. At the household level, women's workloads increased as they struggled to make ends meet and provide for their families.

The effects on women of structural adjustment programmes have been well documented (see, for example, Beneria 1999, Elson 1991, Sparr 1994, De Pauli 2000, Commonwealth Expert Group 1989, Floro and Schaeffer 2001). As formal sector employment shrank for both men and women, women increased their activity in the informal sector, working long hours in petty trading, selling sweets and drinks, cooked food, handcrafts, and the like, as well as making clothes and other small items such as purses, bags and baskets. The informal sector workforce in Zambia almost doubled in the period from 1986 to 1996, during Zambia's adjustment process, with women comprising over two-thirds of the 3.4 million informal sector workers in 1996 (Floro and Schaeffer 2001).

The cutbacks in public expenditure on food subsidies, health care and education hit women too. As income fell, food prices rose for many staples, such as maize in Africa, rice in Asia, and oil and cooking fuel.

Women were faced with trying to provide for their families on less. They extended their food growing to try to overcome the impact of reduced household income. But even those who grew food were not immune from the crisis. Zambia, for example, deregulated the price of maize, which tripled in cost. However, the increase in income for women maize farmers was insufficient to offset a seven-fold increase in the price of fertilizers. Many small maize farmers (mostly women) went out of business, and maize output fell by 46 per cent (Floro and Schaeffer 2001).

The reduced health services meant that mothers with sick children had to walk much further than before for any medical help, the cost of drugs increased, and health generally suffered, particularly as women often ate less and anaemia increased. The introduction of user-pays fees in education often meant that the girls of the family dropped out of school, leaving boys to continue (Sparr 1994).

Not all women were affected negatively. The employment effects of export-promotion varied from place to place, with some women gaining employment and increased status. In the Philippines there was a growth in urban industrial employment, especially for young women, but this was mainly focused in the garment and electronics industries in the free-trade zones. While in the rural areas, the shift from maize for home consumption to sugar for export, displaced women agricultural workers as men were hired to cut the sugar cane (Floro and Schaeffer 2001).

Overall, though, it became widely recognized that the gender impacts of structural adjustment policies had been overlooked, and women were bearing the brunt of them. This only served to reinforce feminists' views that current development approaches were negative for women. It also highlighted the need for women to focus on macro-economic policies rather than just development programmes, since the gender impacts of these policies could be significant and widespread.

Gender and the environment

By the early 1990s, global attention shifted to the environment. Women became actively involved in lobbying around the 1992 Earth Summit, held in Rio de Janiero, as it offered another opportunity, seven years after the end of the Decade for Women, for women to mobilize globally to have an impact on policies and programmes in an area of deep concern.

Women have been intimately concerned with environmental problems in many parts of the world, often being the ones who felt the effects of environmental destruction most keenly. In Kenya, the Green Belt Movement, a national women's movement, has had a massive impact through its collection of indigenous seeds, development of tree nurseries, and tree planting programmes across the country (Rodda 1991). In North India, the 'Chipko' movement of women made world news by hugging trees to stop them being felled (Shiva 1989). In Papua New Guinea (PNG) women have actively opposed logging operations that have affected their environment and their livelihoods. I described the multiple negative impacts of one forestry operation on women in PNG thus:

> The forestry operation is controlled by a foreign company, employing foreign workers, as well as some locals. The landowners receive some royalty payments through a landowner company controlled by a handful of powerful men. These men are bribed by trips to Port Moresby, and the promise of immediate cash into allowing all the land to be logged. Water in the river is now very muddy and oily. Yet it is the only water for drinking, washing, and cooking. Fish and seafood are becoming scarce – women have to travel longer distances to get crabs. The river banks have been eroded and the gardens are flooded more often, so women are discouraged from gardening. The river is drier too at other times of the year, and it is now impossible for men to easily float sago logs down the river – so women now go deep into the bush to cut and drag back sago. Cash brought into the area has caused increases in gambling, alcoholism, prostitution and violence against women. (Hunt 1996)

It is hardly surprising that women, faced with these sorts of problems, have been at the forefront of environmental campaigning.

Women mobilized extremely effectively around the Rio Earth Summit to gain valuable commitments to recognize women's role as environmental managers and to enable women to participate more in environmental decision-making. However, the central assumption of the final statement, that more economic growth is needed to provide the resources to solve the world's environment problems, is seen as an inherent contradiction by many feminists (Braidotti *et al.* 1997). Indeed, writers and activists such as Vandana Shiva see this approach as nothing less than destructive maldevelopment.

Shiva's ecofeminist views derive from her experience working with Indian peasant women farmers coupled with her intellectual critique of Western science. Shiva says that Western patriarchal science is reductionist – that is, it reduces everything to its parts. It achieved dominance as a mode of thinking by:

> excluding other knowers and ways of knowing ... in contrast to the organic metaphors, in which concepts of order and power were based on interconnectedness and reciprocity, the metaphor of nature as a machine was based on the assumption of separability and manipulability. (Shiva 1989: 22)

Thus, the narrow mode of thinking that Western scientific thought represents is seen as the major contributor to destructive, violent approaches to development. This, says Shiva, is because this mode of thinking was deliberately designed to support a particular mode of production, emerging in the industrial revolution, in which each firm or industrial sector was aiming to maximize its own profits. Thus, the focus is on profit-making within a limited framework, without consideration of the ecological and social costs: 'the ultimate reductionism is achieved when nature is linked with a view of economic activity in which money is the only gauge of value and wealth' (Shiva 1989: 25).

Shiva contrasts this mode of thinking with the Indian cosmology which is holistic, creative, dynamic and integrated. The relational aspects of all parts of life and nature are understood, and this includes the relationship between the 'natural' and the 'supernatural':

> Contemporary Western views of nature are fraught with the dichotomy between man and woman, and person and nature. In Indian cosmology, by contrast, person and nature (Purusha-Prakriti) are a duality in unity. They are inseparable complements of one another in nature, in women, in man. (Shiva 1989: 40)

Shiva's book contrasts the way women have traditionally managed food, water and forest resources in a sustainable manner, and how new approaches (e.g., the 'Green Revolution') have damaged the ecology and undermined women's traditional methods of nurturing their environment.

One example she cites is the introduction of high-yielding, short-stalked strains of irrigated sorghum in South Asia. These were grown alongside local drought-resistant sorghum varieties traditionally interspersed with other crops such as pulses and green leafy vegetables, including the highly nutritious *bathua* and a drought-resistant crop called *save*. The new high-yield varieties of sorghum needed large quantities of water and pesticides. The latter then destroyed the predators to a pest, the *midge*, which attacked the local sorghum, eventually wiping it out. This led to a severe reduction in sorghum straw, an important fodder crop for the livestock, leading to a reduction in the number of animals a family could keep. This, in turn, reduced the natural fertilizer available. Thus, in Shiva's view, the scientists and agricultural 'experts' who focused on increasing the output of one crop, sorghum, neglected to recognize that the traditional farming system was a complex and ecologically balanced one, with multiple produce that withstood drought conditions and provided good nutrition for growers' families. There was no miracle of high yields in the new system, when the total production of the old one was taken into account. In fact, the new varieties left people far more vulnerable to crop failure in drought conditions (Shiva 1989: 122–131).

More recently, Shiva has challenged a great deal about the way seeds have been controlled, and the way trade laws emanating from the World Trade Organization have affected local producers' ability to continue to manage their natural resources in traditional ways. She is particularly angry about 'biopiracy' – the way in which intellectual property of indigenous peoples (their plants) is being co-opted by large multinational corporations and patented as private property. In particular, farmers are unable to survive since they now have to purchase hybrid seed varieties, that cannot be saved and replanted, and that require large quantities of expensive pesticide and fertiliser to produce a crop. The loss of water resources, due to heavy use of water sources for agribusiness and other industrial and mining uses, only exacerbates this situation, impoverishing many Indian farmers (Shiva 2000).

Shiva has been criticized for romanticizing the traditional farming system and for 'essentialism' – or conflating all women with poor rural Indian women, and suggesting that only these women have the solutions to the environmental crisis. In fact, Agarwal argues that Shiva only draws on Hindu women's cosmology, not that of other Indian religions. It is also suggested that by linking women so closely with nature Shiva's approach encourages the continued subordination of both. Agarwal adds that Shiva's emphasis on the negative impacts of Western colonialism neglects local dynamics of power and inequality. This latter argument seems not to be well supported by a close reading of Shiva, since she certainly recognizes that local men can become caught up in commercial forestry against the wishes of the women, even though she attributes this to colonialism of their minds (Agarwal 1997b).

Perhaps a more sophisticated approach, similar in perspective to Shiva's, but recognizing that women are enjoying differentiated losses and benefits from global economic development is typified by Wee and Heyzer's work (Wee and Heyzer 1995). They recognize that some women have benefited from prevailing patterns of growth, but their concern, like Shiva's, is the depletion of the natural resource base on which rural women in particular, but in the end all of us, depend. Thus their main concern is extreme global inequality and the fact that a small percentage of people and corporations can control so much of the natural resource base – they can deplete it to enrich themselves, but in the process they impoverish others. It is the relationship between the creation and appropriation of wealth and the creation of poverty, that is the significant concern that they address.

They provide numerous examples, but the issue of shrimp-farming in the Philippines, Thailand, Bangladesh, India and Malaysia illustrates their point very clearly. These countries have provided favoured sites for aquaculture farms which produce tiger prawns and other marine produce for export, particularly to the USA, Europe and Japan. These are huge commercial ventures, quite different from traditional aquaculture, which has been practised sustainably for generations. The new systems destroy wetlands and mangroves, and displace traditional fisherfolk; they create huge amounts of waste and draw not only on sea water, but on large quantities of ground water as well, depleting the water sources for local people. In India, scientists found that the new systems caused many 'serious social and ecological effects, including the spread of salt water over farms (causing a loss of agricultural lands and drinking water): loss of mangrove ecosystems; loss of landing grounds for traditional fishermen; increased health ailments of people living nearby due to pollution; increased unemployment due to displacement of livelihood in surrounding communities'. The benefits, of course, go to the companies, but the considerable costs are borne by local people and local authorities (Wee and Heyzer 1995: 114–15).

Wee and Heyzer argue that what is required is that the many realities experienced by different people need to be reflected in development decision-making. The current development paradigm, based as it is on a single worldview which makes others' views invisible, has to be challenged by alternative realities. The empowerment of poor women so that their reality can count as much as anyone else's, is critical to this transformation of development. They suggest that the efforts to make visible (and to place a value on) women's unpaid work, and the hidden free subsidies that the natural environment provides to development, is an important part of the process of making alternative realities visible.

Marilyn Waring (1988) has developed a pithy critique of the United Nations System of National Accounts (UNSNA), the system used by all countries to establish their economic results. As she so clearly demonstrates, women's unpaid work and the 'free' contribution of nature is never valued, and hence not recognized in the national accounts of nations. This results from a series of gender-blind bureaucratic decisions about definitions of what is measured. A huge amount of women's reproductive work is excluded. If such services were provided commercially – water and fuel purchased from utility companies, food bought in the market, meals purchased in a restaurant and child care provided in a child-care centre, all this would be included in the national accounts. But when a woman provides it herself, she is a housewife, economically inactive! Lewenhak (1992) has provided detailed proposals about how women's work could be valued and counted for national statistics, but as yet, no country has adopted such an approach, although some are developing 'satellite accounts' to value women's unpaid work, as recommended in the Beijing Platform for Action (United Nations 1995).

Post-modernism and difference

The post-modernist school of thought, which questions the 'grand theories' of the past and the idea that rational thinking and technological solutions will bring 'progress' to the world, reinforces Wee and Heyzer's view that what is needed to transform development is to open it up to different voices, different meaning systems, and different realities.

Post-modernists draw attention to how the category 'woman' or 'man' is constructed, and how particular categories of women (poor women, Third World women, Asian women) are constructed, and by whom. Mohanty has been particularly critical of Western feminists who have presented the 'Third World woman' as implicitly, if not explicitly, 'ignorant, poor, uneducated, tradition-bound, domestic, family-oriented, victimised, etc' in contrast to Western women 'as educated, as modern, as having control over their own bodies and sexualities, and the freedom to make their own decisions' (Mohanty 1997: 80). Such categorization has colonialist overtones, and is firmly (and correctly) rejected by feminist writers from the developing world. The 'women in development' literature has, unfortunately, been the most prevalent source of such representation of women in the developing world.

Parpart's 'feminist post-modern critique' of much development dis- course highlights the significance of 'difference' in gender debates. As she explains, the practical implications of this critique are to get planners to take seriously the realities of women's lives, especially to explore different women's views about what changes they want from development: 'this approach to development recognizes the connection between knowledge, language and power, and seeks to understand local knowledge(s), both as sites of resistance and power' (Parpart 1995: 264).

It is this perspective that demonstrates the importance of women being organized, documenting their own lives from their own perspectives as subjects, not objects, of research (validating their own knowledge), and having a key role in development decision-making. This is particularly important for minority women, indigenous women, women who are old, or who have disabilities, or who may be particularly marginalized in development planning. Yet, such women may not readily want to form groups, except perhaps in crises (Khan 2000).

The focus on gender, combined with the whole focus on how categories and meanings are constructed, has finally also led to some focus on men and 'masculinity' in development. The Men's Group for Gender Equality at UNDP argue that an important issue to explore is how men contribute to reproducing inequalities in gender relations, and how they can help transform the situation (Greig *et al.* 2000). There are complex issues involved, as men all benefit from their gender privilege in relation to women, but recent work is suggesting that as some men's traditional roles disappear or change following economic restructuring, they are left with very low self-esteem, which manifests itself through their descent into alcoholism, and increased violence and abuse towards women (Narayan *et al.* 2000, Silberschmidt 2001, Snyder and Tadesse 1997). Their definitions of 'masculinity' appear to be challenged by their new circumstances.

Narayan *et al.* identify a phenomenon they call 'gender anxiety' in poor households as men and women adjust their roles in the face of economic crisis. The crisis has created stresses and strains on both men and women, who respond, according to Narayan *et al.*, in 'gender specific ways'. Men may desert their families through shame that they cannot provide for them, while women struggle on.

Community development approaches

If the latest approach to development is to be more participative and inclusive, then we have to ask what happens in gender terms when participative methodologies are used? It is not at all clear that gender equity will result from more community participation, particularly unless special measures are put in place to give voice to the views and wishes of women, especially women who may be more marginal in the community (Gujit and Shah 1998).

Community participation approaches, such as Participatory Rural Appraisal, can easily lead to a false consensus being derived from the views of those with power and influence in a community. Thus, the views of the most significant problems and appropriate strategies to address them, can overlook issues that are difficult for women to raise, particularly while men are present. An obvious example would be domestic violence, which is unlikely to be raised using the methodologies of mapping, village transects, and other visual tools, nor while the perpetrators are present (Gujit and Shah 1998, Cornwall 2001). Separate opportunities for women to participate are necessary, but in some parts of the world not always easy to arrange, since women are secluded or accompanied by male relatives wherever they go.

The complexities of communities have often been overlooked, and as Cornwall explains, one cannot assume that women's interests will always compete with men's, or that all women will have an investment in changing the status quo. Women in positions of privilege may well resist change designed to benefit poorer women. Facilitators of community participation approaches need to be sensitive to gender and power dynamics within a community and have strategies to address them.

Too often, culture and tradition have been used to prevent women overcoming discrimination and enjoying basic human rights. It is easy for men to suggest that feminist ideas from the West are being brought in to a developing country in a colonial manner. However, things are rarely that simple. In all countries there are local women who are struggling for women's rights – whether this be to prevent violence against women, female genital mutilation, and so-called 'honour killings', or to achieve equality under the law, access to education or adequate health care, protection of their environments and adequate income. In a globalized world they are likely to have information from women elsewhere that may help or inspire them, but their efforts are grounded in their own experience and reality. Women are struggling for their own empowerment in many different ways.

The concept of women's empowerment is itself an interesting one. Jo Rowlands (Rowlands 1995) has identified different approaches to power: power *over* (a relationship of domination and subordination); power *to* (having decision-making or problem-solving power); power *with* (people organizing together to achieve their goals) and power *within* (self confidence to act). As she points out, the women's movement has stressed the last two forms of empowerment, noting that empowerment is not simply about offering opportunities for participation in decision-making, but encouraging people to have confidence and a sense of entitlement to participate.

However, in the development world, the concept of empowerment has been interpreted largely to mean economic empowerment of individual women through credit programmes (Oxaal and Baden 1997). While these may have been valuable, the social aspects of empowerment may have been more important to women than the economic benefits alone. In a recent paper, Kilby (Kilby 2001) explores what Indian women themselves define as their own empowerment. He interviewed 80 self-help women's groups which had been formed by NGOs to provide savings and credit programmes, each of around 20 women. He asked them a simple question 'What is the most important change in your lives over the past few years? Women identified four major areas:

- mobility – the capacity to go beyond the house independently
- increased respect and dignity – within the family
- assertiveness – women becoming bolder within the family and in dealing with officials
- solidarity and support – mutual support they receive from the self-help groups.

As he commented, 'the first thing that struck me from these testimonies was that there was very little mention of economics or income.... The responses in terms of change were about their own personal 'agency' (Kilby 2001). Indeed, the changes that seemed most significant to them related to power *within* themselves and power *with* the other group members.

The approach to empowerment articulated by groups such as DAWN (Sen and Grown 1987) gives strong emphasis to women organizing themselves to achieve significant structural changes, such as legal reform to end gender discrimination, campaigns for reproductive rights and to prevent violence against women, and mobilization of women for political participation. The need for such an approach is very evident. To achieve gender equitable development one needs many factors in place:

- A legal and institutional environment that promotes gender equity, rather than reinforcing gender discrimination
- Women organised and vigilant at national, regional and local levels to ensure that laws, policies and programmes are consistent with gender equity, and to promote proactive approaches to improving the situation of women
- Individual women with self-esteem and confidence to actively participate and negotiate on their own behalf at the level of the household, community, and nation
- Men willing to recognize that gender oppression affects them too, and able to subject 'masculinity' to critical scrutiny in terms of how it affects them, as well as openness to change the way they benefit from their gendered privilege from the household to the international level.

Clearly, if the community development and women's empowerment approach is the development approach for the future, development planners and workers need a better understanding of gender dynamics within community development processes, and they need a more sophisticated understanding of women's empowerment, at different levels and in different spheres, whether political, economic, social, or personal. For example, having a gender equality clause in a constitution will have little if any practical effect on the ground if it is not developed into specific laws in areas such as discrimination in employment, land inheritance, access to services, and prevention of violence against women. Furthermore, such laws will be of little practical use if women are unaware of them, or if it is difficult, or impossible, to get them enforced. Thus, top-down strategies must be complemented (if not preceeded) by community-level strategies that might have practical benefits for women. For example, the use of community shaming strategies may be of more practical use to prevent men being violent to women than distant laws in a country where the legal system is weak and obtaining justice is expensive.

Cambodia is one country with a relatively recent constitution, which has a gender equity clause. However, the situation in Cambodia remains extremely tough for women. Narayan *et al.* (2000) report that many young women have gone into sex work for survival. Poor women they interviewed offered three reasons for the dramatic increase in young women taking up this work:

> First, most families face acute shortages of money and everyone will have to work hard. Second, farm work is less and less available and so girls seek non-farm employment. Third, as instances of domestic violence increase, divorce rates have surged in Cambodia. After separation she has no means of subsistence, and she has no right to the family land. (Narayan *et al. 2000: 193*)

Gender inequities in relation to land, the prevalence of domestic violence, and the few alternative employment opportunities are forcing young women into a trade which endangers their health (through transmission of HIV/AIDS and other sexually transmitted diseases) and leaves them socially vulnerable. The reality falls far short of the aspirations in the constitution.

Gender and globalization: the way ahead

Whilst a shift to a more participatory and community-orientated approach to development is welcome, it is clear that it may not automatically improve gender equity. Furthermore, the major economic trends of globalization may have far wider gender effects, which must not be ignored.

To date, the research on the gender effects of trade liberalization is limited, and there are conflicting findings, mainly because the gender impacts vary according to a range of factors, particularly women's role in the export sectors of specific national economies.

UNIFEM's website suggests a number of possible effects of the current trade liberalization regime through the World Trade Organization, among them (www.unifem.undp.org/trade):

- Women competing with each other internationally to provide cheap labour for export industries, thereby undercutting each other (for example, women who make traditional Kenyan sisal bags are losing market share to cheap Asian copies)
- Promotion of export-orientated agriculture at the cost of women's subsistence agriculture

- Displacement of small women's service businesses by large multi-national companies entitled to operate in the country under 'national treatment' rules (i.e., on the same terms as local businesses).
- The loss of women's ability to control local genetic resources and biodiversity as companies take out patents over seed varieties under WTO rules
- A possible rise in employment in the textile and garment industries as quota controls on textile imports to the US and Europe are phased out over the next 10 years.

Most trade agreements make no reference to gender equality, and are implemented with no consideration of the gender implications (Espino 2000). Cardero (2000), studied the gender effects of structural adjustment and trade liberalization in Mexico over the period 1980–1997. NAFTA entered into force in 1994, but the whole period was one of economic restructuring and change. Women's employment in Mexico increased more rapidly than men's, but over 70 per cent of the jobs are in services, the retail sector and informal sector. NAFTA appeared to stimulate a huge rise in jobs for women, but most were in food processing (tortilla making). However, pay has dropped significantly (22 per cent in 1995 alone). Women have also been increasing their employment in agriculture, but their piece-work hours in the agricultural export sector have lengthened and they still undertake all the household work. Two-thirds of women working in agriculture earn no wages (Fontana *et al.* 1998).

In the textile and apparel industries the picture is complex, but it seems that the absolute number of jobs has increased significantly, but, relative to men, women's proportion of those jobs has reduced. Women are also overwhelmingly represented in the low-skilled, low-paid positions, with men three times more likely to be in technical or managerial positions. Many of the new jobs for women are in small enterprises where conditions are poor, and wage rates have fallen significantly (in the garment industry, wages almost halved between 1980 and 1996). Substantial growth has taken place in the 'in-bond' maquiladoras, but a geographical differentiation has also occurred, with more women employed in maquiladoras in some of the central provinces away from the US border, and men's employment growing in the more high-tech plants close to the border. The wages are lower in the fast-growing in-bond areas than other manufacturing sectors, and women's wages are lower than men's (Cardero 2000).

Another major study (Fontana *et al.* 1998) examined the gendered employment effects of trade liberalization on six countries: Ghana, Uganda, Sri Lanka, Pakistan, Bangladesh and Jamaica. Fontana *et al.* found that trade liberalization had different impacts for men and women in different contexts, and these were related to factors such as: gendered patterns of rights in resources, female labour force participation rates, education levels and gaps by gender and patterns of labour market discrimination and segregation, as well as socio-cultural environments (Fontana *et al*. 1998: 2).

They note the growth of female employment in the export-orientated manufacturing industries, especially in Asia, as well as in Latin America and the Caribbean, and suggest that this has had beneficial effects for younger women. They recognize, however, that there are issues to do with employment conditions and longer-term benefits.

Their findings indicate that women benefit most:

- 'where wages for women relative to men are highest
- where new trade-related employment represents the greatest increase in income earning opportunities compared to alternatives
- where new opportunities entail the greatest change in social practices of seclusion and subordination of women.' (Fontana *et al*. 1998: 48)

But the picture in sub-Saharan Africa is rather different. There, women have not generally benefited from increased agricultural export production, as they have limited land rights and their unpaid labour is used without them gaining control of the income. Worse, their labour may be diverted from subsistence crop production and the nutritional status of the household may suffer, or girls may be kept out of school to take up that work. Fontana *et al*. comment: 'there is a danger that the intensification of female labour in export production, often unpaid, may undermine other developmental gains, particularly in the education and health status of women and girls' (Fontana *et al*. 1998: 48).

These general findings lead them to suggest two major areas of policy action:

- 'In countries where female participation in wage labour in export industries is high, emphasis on reducing labour market discrimination
- In countries where agriculture is the main focus of export activity, emphasis on strengthening and enforcing women's property rights in land.' (Fontana *et al*. 1998: 48)

They highlight the need for action to reduce gender discrimination against women in employment conditions, and promote women workers' rights, and the particular need to address the situation of women outworkers and those working in the informal sector. Again, the need to support the organization and advocacy efforts of women workers is emphasized.

Another area with little understood gender effects is greater deregulation of capital accounts. Zammit (2000) has undertaken a study of the gender implications of rapid movements of capital, and to the extent that such movements plunge economies (such as Indonesia's in 1997) into crisis, the effects are likely to be differentiated by gender, with women suffering more, particularly if the downturn is long and deep. Liberalization of such accounts is also on the agenda of those driving this economic orthodoxy, but its gender implications are unlikely to be high on their minds.

What is emerging is a dual-track system of global rule-making. On the one hand, is the system of rules for trade and financial services, which is increasingly brought under the oversight of the World Trade Organization, with its sanctions and penalties for countries which breach the rules. This system operates without any serious consideration of gender equity concerns. In contrast, the alternative global rules system, is the system of human rights instruments, and the 'soft law' agreements negotiated through the series of United Nations Conferences throughout the nineteen eighties and nineties. The Convention for the Elimination of All Forms of Discrimination Against Women (CEDAW) and the Beijing Platform for Action are the key documents within the latter system. Sadly, there is no connection between these two rules-systems, and the one that takes precedence and has far more impact due to its tough penalty regime, is the World Trade Organization rules system. This suggests a need for reform of global governance structures to bring these systems into alignment, and ensure that trade and financial liberalization takes place within a framework with the goals of achievement of human rights and gender equity, as well as environmental sustainability.

Gender and governance

The language of 'governance' offers one way forward at a global level, yet to date, the interest in 'governance' has been largely focused at a national level and has been largely gender blind. Governance in development jargon generally refers to economic management, public-sector reform, legal reform and civil-society programmes. The example above suggests that gender considerations rate very low in economic governance priorities at a global level. At the national level, the picture is equally biased. The economic governance agenda is clearly about the promotion at national level of the global economic orthodoxy already discussed (Taylor 2000).

One valuable economic governance initiative is the concept of gender budgeting. As Budlender remarks, the budget 'is in many respects the single most important policy or law passed by any government, determining the resources to be allocated to its policies and programmes' (Budlender 2001: 323). In South Africa, for example, a Women's Budget Initiative has had a remarkable impact. Unlike the original Australian exercise, in which the analysis was undertaken within the bureaucracy, this initiative was a collaboration of women's NGOs, women researchers, and women parliamentarians. Its success in generating a debate about budget impact on women, boosting funding allocations in some key areas for women, and inspiring other African countries to undertake a similar exercise has been important. Budlender feels, however, that the greatest effect is opening up budget discussion, formerly the preserve of white, male, businessmen, to women of all races across South Africa. She recognizes that the technical economic language is an obstacle to wider understanding of economic decision-making, but nevertheless argues that the Women's Budget Initiative has been very significant in bringing gender issues, including the unpaid work of women, into economic debates in South Africa.

The second area of governance is the public sector reform agenda that has been associated with the economic restructuring taking place in many countries. Public sectors have been 'downsized', and privatized with little consideration for the gender effects, both in terms of women's employ-ment, and the provision of essential social and other services. Legal reform, the third area, may include incorporation of the CEDAW provisions into national law and reform of laws to eliminate gender discrimination through the statutes, but Das Pradhan (2000) points out that there are many difficulties associated with attaining gender inclusion in legal development programmes and projects. However, this aspect of the 'governance' agenda is potentially a very useful one. Fourthly, civil society programmes may include support for women's organizations, an essential factor if gender equity is to be achieved. However, studies of civil society programmes to date have rarely focused on their gender aspects, so it is unclear how much these may have contributed to gender equity. Support to strengthen women's groups, especially those involved in promoting women's human rights and empowerment, could undoubtedly be enhanced.

However, the general principles of governance agenda – especially transparency, accountability, efficiency, equity and participation *in theory* should provide a useful set of principles on which gender advocates can base their case. But to do so, they will clearly need to challenge orthodox assumptions about these concepts. At what level and for whom, is efficiency to be judged, for example? What might real accountability to women mean and how might it be strengthened? How can governments that signed on to the Beijing Platform for Action be held to account to implement the many policies embedded within that document, particularly in the face of the alternative rules emanating from the WTO? The advocacy of women's groups has to date been the main source of pressure on governments to put their words into action so greater support for their efforts is vital.

The way ahead

There are now three major areas for attention. The first involves ensuring genuine institutional commitment, resources and strategies for gender mainstreaming in all development institutions, whether these are national development planning bodies, donor agencies, or non-government agencies. Few development institutions make gender equity a goal or objective of their work, yet this should be explicit, and clear strategies and plans should flow from it, with regular monitoring and evaluation of progress towards it. Mainstreaming brings with it the risk of complacency, 'policy evaporation' and oblivion. To avoid this, there has to be a deepening of commitment, knowledge, skills and approaches. One strategy is for institutions to undertake serious gender audits of their work and act upon them. However, few have done this to date (Hunt 2000).

A second, related area, is to bring gender considerations into macro-economic institutions, policies and programmes. This needs to be highlighted because of its importance and neglect. Feminist economists are making an important contribution at an academic level, but their impact at policy level has mainly been restricted to greater visibility of women's work in national accounts and promoting more gender-sensitive alternatives to orthodox adjustment policies for indebted countries (Beneria 1995). Serious efforts are now underway to develop a dialogue about how to 'engender macro-economic and international trade models' (Grown, Elson and Cagatay 2000) and to undertake training that brings gender experts and macroeconomists together (Pearson 1995). However, most mainstream economists would not recognize or accept that gender equity should be a deliberate goal of economic policy. They may argue that it will result from greater economic growth (World Bank 2001b), and achieving that is their primary objective, however, how many would have considered the agreements made at Beijing, or the implications of CEDAW for their work? Yet unless economic policies at all levels explicitly try to support gender equity, they may well undermine it.

Thirdly, while the alternative United Nations rules framework deserves strong support, it nevertheless fails to challenge the fundamental development model, which feminists like Wee and Heyzer, Shiva, and the DAWN network roundly condemn as unsustainable and unjust. This is the critical question. How significant will it be to have gender equality on a development path which is utterly unsustainable? How can women and men concerned about the nature of the development that we are pursuing, work in a gender equitable way to turn it around and make it sustainable for generations? If we seriously assess development to date, this is the fundamental challenge ahead – and it is a truly global challenge, for the developed nations as much as for developing ones, and for market actors as much as state and community sector ones.

Chapter 11

Environment and Development

DAMIEN KINGSBURY

It is a truism to say that without the environment there can be no development. Any capacity to develop, no matter how it is defined, must occur within its physical context; the land we grow food on, the water we drink, and the air we breathe. Our rush to achieve material development has been predicated on the capacity of the physical environment to support it. In some cases the environment has been despoiled, and in others it is simply running out of resources. Nurturing of the environment, and its use in a sustainable and affordable manner, are critical issues in the development process.

The rise in interest in the environment in developing countries reflects a growing awareness of such issues in developed countries and, hence, among many bilateral and multilateral aid agencies and aid organizations. This has, in turn, been communicated to developing countries, although in many developing countries awareness of environmental issues has come from direct experience with environmental problems. The growth of industrialization, often quickly and with few if any environmental safeguards, and swelling populations, have had a real and substantial impact on many developing countries.

The environmental record of development has, to date, been poor, and environmental degradation has continued at a pace that has already had a major impact on the capacity of some societies to continue to function. South Korea, for example, became so heavily polluted during its drive towards industrialization in the 1960s and 1970s that many of its rivers had become 'dead' and air pollution had become a health hazard. By the late 1980s the government had imposed strict environmental regulations and had begun to spend what was to become billions of dollars on major clean-up programmes. By 1996, Korea was spending more than six billion dollars per annum on pollution control measures (Cho 1999). Similarly, the best export prospects to Taiwan had become pollution control equipment, a trade that was worth almost one billion dollars a year. While most developing countries had not yet reached the level of industrial development of South Korea or Taiwan, the industrialization process in the vast majority also showed serious signs of failing to implement environmental safeguards, the rationale being that as developing countries they could not 'afford' such safeguards. This did not to begin to include over-logging, land degradation, run-off from herbicides, insecticides, and human waste pollution.

Within the environmental debate there are questions about how long current development processes can continue before local ecological systems collapse as, in some cases, they have already done. There is also concern about the effects on global ecological systems. Environmental damage may occur in one country and be a consequence of that country's policies, but environmental degradation does not respect arbitrary state divisions. Damage in one country can easily impact upon another country, or many countries, and widespread environmental collapse is no longer a matter of if, but when and where, should there not be a fundamental shift in development thinking, planning and implementation.

One of the critical and most controversial issues in environmental development revolves around the capacity of the earth to sustain people. There are those who believe that the earth has greater capacity than currently exists, and those who believe that the earth is already being taxed beyond its capacity. There is no doubt that there are some parts of the world with a much greater carrying capacity than others, especially if people who live there are prepared to adopt a more simple, less consumption-orientated life. Even where the earth has shown that it has a high carrying capacity, this is usually enhanced by the use of fertilizers, pesticides, and high-energy transport, all of which adds a cost that is not often factored in to economic assessments (see Milbrath 1996: Ch 10). The use of agricultural pesticides can and often does enhance productivity but it also has implications for water quality, for example (UNCSD 2002b). In this respect, the full cost of economic growth is usually greater than the simple single bottom line formula used by most accountants, in that it also uses 'public good' (clean air, water, habitat, other amenity) that is not properly, or often at all, costed. In particular, there is conflict over the notion of 'public' or shared resources, especially where this 'free' resource (e.g., water, air) is used excessively or unwisely, and impacts on 'non-market' activities (Portney 1982: 4). In this sense, private markets may allocate resources inefficiently, and the 'externalities' generated by private development may impact on a wider 'public good'. (Portney 1982:6) In one sense, the over-exploitation of some resources by some parts of the earth's population, or 'resource capture', produces a structural imbalance in access to resources (Homer-Dixon 1999: 15–19) and potential for conflict.

There are significant parts of the world that have a very limited carrying capacity and are vulnerable to degradation due to over-exploitation. These marginal areas, such as Africa's Sahel, are growing in size, and their capacity to support life is reducing. And apart from the consumption of non-renewable resources, it would appear that at some point there must, logically, be a limit to the carrying capacity of the earth, regardless of how sensitively and wisely it is used.

Neo-Malthusianism

There have been, as Homer-Dixon has noted (1999:53) distinct physical trends in global change, and while these have occurred over varying time-scales and in different locations, their effects have become increasingly global and inter-related. Homer-Dixon noted an interconnectivity between, for example, human population growth, rising energy consumption, global warming, ozone depletion, rising cropland scarcity, tropical deforestation, rising scarcity of free water, declining fish stocks and a more general loss of biodiversity.

In particular, the sheer increase in the global population, the consumption of natural resources implied by such growth, and the human and industrial pollution that has been produced is perhaps the single most important issue. Of the world's 6.257 billion people at the end of 2002 (USCB 2002), 5 billion live in developing countries, and about 3 billion live in rural areas and depend largely on agriculture for their income or subsistence. Korten notes that while the world's poor only add marginally to environmental degradation, if they were to achieve higher levels of development the already unsustainable consumption of natural resources would quickly move into the critical zone. Yet, the alternative is to condemn these poor to underdevelopment in perpetuity (Korten 1989: 166). And there is also a view that suggests poverty actually increases environmental degradation, through more desperate use of resources. The only way to raise global standards of living to a higher, more equitable level is to reduce global consumption, mostly readily through reducing the global population.

Assuming no change in human behaviour – that is, no move away from a global tendency to increasingly consume natural resources – or the adoption of less resource-reliant technologies, it would appear there needs to be a considerable, perhaps drastic, reduction in the world's population in order to accommodate limited natural productive capacity and to find alternative and more sustainable finite natural resources. However, the only signs of absolute population reduction, apart from natural or human calamities, has been amongst the most developed societies (although many countries have reduced the rate at which they are increasing their population). This implies that global society will have to develop significantly further before there is any in-built tendency towards population reduction and, frankly, all indicators are that there is not time before environmental catastrophe for this 'natural' process to take place.

The argument that suggests there are limits to the earth's capacity to sustain an increasing population is sometimes referred to as Malthusianism, or neo-Malthusianism. This follows the precepts of the late 18th/early 19th century British economist and demographer Thomas Robert Malthus, who argued that efforts to raise the poor beyond subsistence level would lead to an unsustainable increase in pressure upon resources that would, in turn, restore an economic imbalance, thus creating more poor people. Malthus' answer was to reduce population pressure, through 'moral restraint'. A later version of 'neo-Malthusianism' posited that as resources are finite, and larger families in any case contributed to poverty, birth control and subsequent population reduction were necessary conditions for sustainable development.

The world's total population was about 1.65 billion in 1900; by the end of the 20th century it had grown to more than 6 billion, nearly a fourfold increase. The annual growth rate, while slowing since the late 1960s, was still in the order of 80 million a year (Homer-Dixon 1999: 13). Added to this has been a massive shift in consumption patterns over the 100 years, currently doubling each 30 years, notably in industrialized countries but also in developing countries. The massive increase in hydrocarbon (oil and gas) consumption, which is expected to peak between 2007 and 2019 (McKenzie 2000), and its consequences for the environment (e.g., greenhouse effect, enhancing desertification), is one illustration of the shift in consumption, as is the world's increasing demand for timber and timber products, including paper, which is leading to increased deforestation.

The main criticism of neo-Malthusianism derives from governments and policy makers who claim that large populations sustain markets that are necessary to increased growth, and are also capable of caring for increasingly larger older populations, which are especially noticeable as a consequence of fertility 'booms' such as those following the Second World War and the Green Revolution. Some governments also continue to argue that a large population is necessary for defence purposes, although the linkage between the two rather more reflects a pre-modern view of strategic advantage. And apart from cultural traditions, in which larger families are regarded as a safeguard against abandonment in old age, some religions (such as Roman Catholicism) actively encourage propagation to increase the numbers of their followers. The rationalization of this position is that the earth is intended for the consumption of humanity, and that it has the capacity to sustain a much greater overall consumption. Many policy makers (including the Catholic Church) also argue that the earth's problems less reflect overall consumption and more reflect the unequal distribution of consumption (see Homer-Dixon 1999: 35–7).

Having noted that, by the 1960s the governments of some of the more heavily populated countries decided that their population 'bomb' was already ticking, and took steps to limit population growth (see Ehrlick 1968, for one of the first, most critical, though somewhat alarmist discussions on the subject). The 1960s were critical in this respect, as not only had a number of countries recognized that there was about to be a major problem with excessive population, but at the same time fertility rates were growing, to peak at 2.1 per cent a year between 1965 and 1970 (Homer-Dixon 1999: 13). Nowhere was population growing more quickly than in Asia, with Korten noting that population growth in developing countries was at an average of 2.5 per cent (Korten 1990: 11).

As a consequence, in Asia, by 1966, 12 of 22 states had taken measures to curb fertility (Ness and Ando 1984: 18). The world's first, second and fourth most populous countries, China, India and Indonesia, are three prominent examples of countries that have active population control policies, and while the heavy-handedness of these policies in India and particularly in China have given ammunition to the 'pro-fertility' lobby, they have served as recognition that population growth has costs as well as benefits. However, the success or otherwise of these programmes was less the issue than a recognition of the basic problem. And not all countries with large populations, high population densities, or limited environmental capacities support the idea of limiting their populations. Ness and Ando noted that contrasting with the Asian experience, only four of 26 Latin American countries, three of 40 African states and three of 18 Mediterranean states had adopted fertility control measures (1984:19). This reflected the Asian lead in the fertility control field that was itself predicated a public recognition that median and mean populations densities were generally higher in Asian countries, and tended to be higher in other countries that also adopted fertility control programmes (Ness and Ando 1984: 22–3). The success of those programmes further reflected the actual strength of implementation of the programme (Ness and Ando 1984: 132–9). Not surprisingly, the timing of the move towards controlling fertility rates corresponded with more localized policy planning as a result of independence, rapidly increasing populations as a consequence of the 'Green Revolution', and access to new and more widely available methods of contraception.

Unlike developing countries, industrialized countries have not employed active fertility control programmes where it could be argued that their existing populations exceed the environmental capacity to support them, with the United States and Western Europe (and their heavy reliance on imported oil) perhaps being the prime examples. However, policy planners in most industrialized countries argue that their populations have either slowed in their rate of natural expansion or that they are, in fact, in decline. This reduced fertility rate has a direct correlation to greater urbanization, education, and income capacity, and can also be seen occurring amongst more educated, urbanized workers in developing countries. As noted above, this has created a new concern that, apart from having a reduced domestic market for locally produced goods and services, older generations will not be able to be supported by younger ones and will, thus, become an unsustainable burden on a reduced economic base.

Deforestation

The impact of population spread and consumption is perhaps most visible in terms of loss of forests and associated desertification, and is equally the world's most significant environmental problem. Such deforestation has a number of implications, including soil erosion, land degradation (in particular degradation of arable farmland) and desertification, loss of habitat for various animal species and reduction in other biodiversity, the absorption of carbon dioxide (with a resulting increase in global warming) and a reduction in the production of oxygen, upon which all animal (and human) life depends (FAO 2001). Estimates vary, but at the current rate of deforestation, some of the world's major forests, such as in Indonesia/ Borneo, Papua New Guinea and the Amazon Basin, will be completely deforested within 30 years, and possibly sooner. Chile, with approximately one-third of the world's temperate rainforest, at current rates of logging, could be completely deforested by 2022.

Brazil contains the world's single largest forest, in the Amazon Basin, but existing logging, which has been driven by the timber industry and new settlements and farmland, has depleted the forest at an unsustainable rate. Between 1978 and 1996, some 52 million hectares, or 12.5 per cent of the total forest, was cleared, representing a loss of around 2.9 million hectares a year. Logging, continuing at the rate of 13,000 hectares a day, or 4.75 million hectares a year, received renewed impetus at the beginning of the 21st century as Brazil struggled to meet external loan repayments. The president of the Amazon Working Group (representing some 350 regional NGOs), Claudionor Barbosa da Silva, said that 90 per cent of funding to Amazon conservation programmes had been cut to meet IMF loan schedules, along with two-thirds of rainforest protection capacity and demarcation of lands belonging to indigenous peoples. Austerity measures resulting from the IMF programme were also expected to force people to illegally log the forest (Knight and Aslam 2000). Other countries looking to address critical economic problems through increased excessive logging of old-growth forests included Russia and Indonesia, which, along with Brazil, were home to just under half of the world's old growth rain forests.

While environmental policies in Indonesia were always very poor, the decentralization of government following the end of the New Order in 1998 further impacted on the environment, in particular exacerbating the loss of Indonesia's tropical rainforests. Already very poor, local environmental protection has slid further, due to less central control over logging, short-term local government economic priorities, and the decentralization of corruption. The annual deforestation rate between 1985 and 1997 was estimated to be 1.7 million hectares (Resosudarno 2002). Since 1998, that level is believed to have increased significantly. In one district in Central Kamlimantan, for instance, logging permits that were already running at an unsustainably high level, had tripled in the six months to December 2000 (Resosudarno 2002: 4).

In other areas in Kalimantan, in the face of a larger economic collapse, illegal logging has increased dramatically, although local governments have turned less than a blind eye towards it, by taxing the logs that are illegally taken to continue to raise revenue: 'in the months of April, May and June 2000 alone, the district [of Kotawaringin] raised 24 billion rupiah by taxing illegal timber coming out of [East] Kotawaringin.... This initiative is effectively "legalizing" illegal timber' (Resosudarno 2002: 8). And as Resosudarno notes, much illegal logging has taken place in protected and conservation areas (2002: 9–10). This type of experience is common in many developing countries, where forests are seen as a resource with almost unlimited exploitable potential (see, for example, Vitug 1993)

In some areas, it can be simple government policy that leads to excessive logging. In Burma, between 40 and 50 per cent of the state remained under forest cover by 1995. However, Burma's military government has been desperate for hard currency to finance its military following the collapse of its economy. The international community has condemned its opium/heroin trade so it has increasingly turned to logging. At the same time, anti-government guerrilla groups have also engaged in logging to support their campaigns, while allowing corrupt Thai generals and businessmen to also illegally log across the border. Where once forests covered around 55 per cent of Thailand, they now cover around five per cent, with half of the remnants being held in reserves. Thailand, once a wood exporter, now imports timber and paper (similarly to Nigeria). In this, Thailand has been effectively logged out and further logging is now banned there (Gallasch 2001: 8–9, 11, see also Bryant in Hirsch and Warren 1998).

Interestingly, while developed countries have called on developing countries to preserve their forests, in particular rainforests, some leaders of developing countries have pointed out that such calls are somewhat hypocritical given that most developed countries almost completely depleted their own stands of forests in the process of industrialization.

Desertification

Drought and desertification, resulting from global climate change and direct human activity, threatened the livelihoods of more the 1.2 billion people across 110 countries (Juara 2000). Drought is a generally natural variation towards lower rainfall in what are already lower rainfall areas. However, rainfall patterns can also be affected by changed global weather patterns (such as the 'El Nino' effect), and global warming due to the emission of 'greenhouse' gases.

Desertification, or the degradation of drylands, involves the loss of biological or economic productivity and complexity in croplands, pastures, and woodlands. Desertification occurs mainly as a consequence of climate variability and unsustainable human activities, with the most commonly cited forms of unsustainable land use being over-cultivation, over-grazing, deforestation, and poor irrigation practices. Seventy per cent of the world's drylands (excluding hyper-arid deserts), or some 3600 million hectares, are degraded. Excessive use of lands generally and drylands in particular is allowed by unregulated access, but is usually driven by economic necessity. In many cases, even where people know their practices are not sustainable, they are looking to survive to next week, rather than next year. The future of the environment can, in such circumstances, start to look like a luxury many people cannot afford. There are also cases of ignorance of dryland farming, where new settlers farm drylands in rainy times, only to have the drylands revert to normal soon after, exposing often inappropriate farming methods (UNCCD 2002a).

Once land is degraded, while it can recover, its capacity to do so is reduced, which has longer-term physical and socio-economic consequences. Physically, degraded topsoil can be blown away by wind or washed away by rainstorms, and it becomes prone to erosion, waterlogging and salination. Excessive grazing of hooved animals can also damage soil and kill off existing vegetation, which, in turn, reduces the capacity to maintain topsoil and further reduces vegetation, or allows the growth of inappropriate vegetation. Other consequences of land degradation include the loss of topsoil during rains that silt waterways, killing fish stocks and making such water unpotable. More than 1.2 billion people around the world do not have adequate access to potable water (Homer-Dixon 1999: 13), almost entirely due to the degradation of waterways, most often due to silting. Examples of the degradation of marginal lands include during the 1930s in the US, in the 1950s in the former USSR, in Australia, and notably in the Sahel region along the southern edges of the Sahara Desert, in places such as Mauritania, northern Burkina Faso, north-western Niger, central Chad, much of Sudan, parts of Eritrea, and across areas of northern China and Mongolia.

Apart from environmental degradation, desertification reduces the capacity for food production, that in already marginal areas can result in famine. Whitehead notes that while acute famine crises usually coincide with catastrophic events, they tend to occur in areas that are already affected by scarcity and thus escalate a problematic situation into one of 'complete disaster' (in Friday and Laskey 1989:82). Such complete disasters tend to displace people which, in some cases, leads to conflict. There has been little formal study of the economic consequences of desertification, by a UN report quotes an unpublished World Bank study as noting, in Africa, that the depletion of natural resources in one Sahelian country was equivalent to 20 per cent of its annual GDP. The UNCCD estimates that the lost annual income due to desertification is approximately US$42 billion each year (UNCCD 2002b).

Desertification is widespread, occurring in Africa, across Asia, Latin America and parts of the Caribbean, the northern Mediterranean, central and eastern Europe, and Australia. However, of all these places, desertification has its greatest impact in Africa, much of which has been affected by frequent and severe droughts, which has been further complicated by the debt crisis and frequent civil conflict. Two-thirds of Africa is desert or drylands, amongst which are extensive agricultural areas, almost three-quarters of which are already degraded to some extent. Many African countries are landlocked, have widespread poverty, and depend on subsistence agriculture. Despite its natural problems, in 1970, Africa was self-sufficient in food production. But by 1984, due to frequent and severe drought, population increase, drought, soil erosion, desertification, government policy failure and political turmoil, a quarter of Africa's population was being kept alive by imported grain (Manley and Brandt 1985: 157, see also UNCCD 2002c). This has been the prime contributing factors to Africa having the most marginal dietary energy supply, lowest per capita GDP, and highest infant mortality rate of any continent (Whitehead, in Friday and Laskey 1989: 84).

Because programmes designed to deal with desertification in Africa must be sustainable, they have increasingly been focused on local communities:

> local communities have valuable experience and a special understanding of their own environment. When the responsibility for natural resource management is taken away from them, their use of land and other natural resources can become highly inefficient. The result is often land degradation. Participatory development recognizes the rights of local communities over their resources. (UNCCD 2002d)

The UNCCD notes, however, that the participatory process is time-consuming and labour-intensive, that many affected member states continue to need stronger civil society and public security to participate, and that governments needed to construct a conducive environment for community participation: 'the community has to go through a long learning and confidence-building process in order to take full advantage of the new resources it now receives and manages directly. Due attention is also paid to gender issues and the involvement of the more marginalized social groups' (UNCCD 2002d).

Water

Related to the issues of deforestation and desertification, the use and pollution of the world's waterways for human and industrial purposes has reduced the amount of available potable water and has negatively impacted on plant and animal life, in particular fisheries, in streams as well as in oceans in areas near outlets. This has again impacted severely on marginal populations who rely on the supply of protein and potable water for everyday needs. As Harrington and Fisher have noted: 'of all the threats to biological resources, habitat modification in its various forms is by far the most serious' (Harrington and Fisher, in Portney 1982: 122). What was once considered to be an inexhaustible abundance of fish has begun to diminish in ways that have meant that some species of fish have become extinct and other are threatened with a reduction in numbers that might preclude their continued viability as a species.

Habitat degradation and pollution are critical factors in sustaining fish stocks. The critical factors in the depletion of fish stocks include the drainage of coastal wetlands and swamps, along with the conversion of land for houses, farms, and roads also destroying breeding grounds for fish through increased run-off of silt, industrial chemicals and human waste into spawning areas. Industrial spills in the South-East Asian archipelago have led to vast quantities of fish simply being killed, much less losing their breeding grounds.

However, probably the biggest impact on fish stocks is overfishing, which has taken place, both through need and commercial opportunity and has subsequently become a common problem in many parts of the world. One area of international co-operation has been over the large, slow breeding Southern Bluefin Tuna (SBT), the numbers of which have been in decline since the 1960s when annual catches reached 80,000 tonnes. By the mid-1980s it became apparent that catches would have to be limited to preserve the remaining stocks, and while there has been considerable international debate and disagreement, and some illegal fishing, there is now agreement between the primary SBT fishing states to control fishing of the species (CCSBT 2002). A similar programme of conservation has also been enacted for the Atlantic Bluefin Tuna. Even stocks of that most feared fish, shark, have become depleted in a number of specific locations due to overfishing. Improper or wasteful fishing methods have also depleted other, often localized, fish stocks at an unsustainable rate. The use of explosives and dragnets kill many species in addition to those that are actually sought after. Even Lake Victoria, which is bordered by Kenya, Uganda and Tanzania, and feeds millions of people, was facing a depletion of its fish stocks due to overfishing, illegal fishing, and improper fishing methods (PNA 2001).

According to Proyect, advances in fishing technology mean that the world's fishing fleets have the capacity to exceed global fish stocks. The introduction of sonar and fishing boats that could carry much greater hauls meant that between 1970 and 1992, the average tonnage taken by each fishing boat increased by almost double to 26,000 tonnes. Of this, about a third of the total catch, or some 27 million tonnes, is discarded as waste. (Proyect 1998)

One means of controlling fishing and of securing adequate supplies of fish stocks has been the age-old practice of aquaculture. Aquaculture, which is the planned breeding of fish, on the face of it appears to be a rational response to declining fish stocks in a world that continues to require fish protein. At a local level, aquaculture has been able to use local ponds for breeding fish. Communities in the protein-poor north-east Thailand have been experimenting with diversified, self-sufficient food programmes since the mid-1980s, and notably since the economic crisis of 1997, including breeding fish in local ponds and cages, to supplement the traditional net fishing in the region's limited waterways. This has provided a steady source of protein to local families and villages, and helped to reduce the fluctuations in food supply that occur as a result of seasonal variation, drought-induced crop failure and changes in demand and price for the basic cash crop of rice. Similarly, in lowland Vietnam, local villagers have responded creatively to the permanent scarring of much of their countryside by using the thousands of remaining bomb craters as fish-breeding ponds. In addition, both Thailand and Vietnam have been turning rice paddies into fish breeding ponds, as a way of meeting both local and export demand.

However, while localized aquaculture is a practical response to securing protein, larger scale or globalized aquaculture has had some negative consequences, especially through the introduction of 'exotic' species into unfamiliar environments, which has resulted in the depletion of original indigenous fish stocks. For example, the introduction of a particular type of prawn (shrimp), *Panaeus Japonicus*, from Japan to Europe has resulted in the species' colonization of vast marine areas (TWR 1998) and the loss of local species.

Drinking water

The loss of fish stocks and the depletion of coastal and ocean habitat is a major threat to both ecological balance and to the sustainability of a key source of protein for human consumption. But even more importantly, lack of access to potable (drinkable) water is perhaps the world's most immediate environmental issue. Access to potable water is critical for the obvious reason that people must have potable water in order to survive. But what is less appreciated is that the quality of available water is at a level where it continues to be the single biggest contributing factor to general illness, a situation reflected in infant mortality rates (Fordham 2002). That is, lack of access to potable water not only directly impacts upon the health of people who have no choice but to drink unsuitable water (notably through nutritional and fluid loss, primarily through diarrhoea), but this, in turn, limits their capacity to work and consequently has a direct economic impact on their capacity for development (see Whittington and Swarna 1994, also Latham 2000, and Strauss, esp p. 168, in Pinstrup-Andersen 1993 for discussion on nutrition and development).

The combination of industrialization, the increased use of herbicides, insecticides, growth promoters, deforestation, and human population growth have all impacted negatively of the world's supply of potable water. As Baur and Rudolph (2001) have noted, the simple question of whether there is enough fresh water for each person is already a critical issue. Around 3800 km3 of fresh water is withdrawn annually from the world's lakes, rivers and aquifers, which is about twice the amount extracted 50 years ago. Agriculture uses around two-thirds of available water, industry uses slightly less than one–fifth, and municipal and domestic use accounts for slightly less than 10 per cent. The world's population, as noted, is over six billion people, and is expected to reach between seven and ten billion before it stabilises or falls. Each person requires up to 50 litres of water a day for drinking, food preparation, sanitation, and bathing (with around 20 litres considered a practical minimum). Yet at the turn of the century, more than a billion people did not have access to potable water (Kothari 2002), or had access to less than the required amount (Baur and Rudolph 2001). Not surprisingly, access to water is not evenly distributed, with a number of countries occupying what are considered 'water stressed' (semi-arid and arid) zones. One-third of these countries are expected to face severe water shortages this century. By 2025, there will be approximately 3.5 billion people living in water-stressed countries. In simple terms, there are more people than there is available water, especially in less supportive environments. And where the environment has a greater capacity to support higher populations, those populations are placing such stresses on water supplies that its supportive capacity is diminishing.

In Jakarta, although no-one would ever consider drinking it, the 'water' running in the city's canals is so heavily polluted that simply falling in to it can result in critical skin infections, burns, and even death. Problems with water pollution, primarily of rivers but also of paddies, affects much of Indonesia (see Lucas in Hirsch and Warren 1998). And in many rural areas where there remains no access to running water, water drawn from wells or ground pumps is increasingly affected by chemical and human pollution seeping into the water table.

Loss of potable water, due to inadequate or failing waterways is a significant factor in the development profile of a number of cities in developing countries. In Pakistan, a large majority of the country's 135 million people do not have access to drinkable water, primarily due to industrial waste and agricultural run-off. (Yes.Pakistan 2002) Infrastructure projects, often funded by multilateral lending agencies such as the Asian Development Bank, are being undertaken in places like Karachi and Manila, to reduce this unnecessary loss of drinking water. However, the extent of the problem, the rate at which it continues to grow worse, and the cost involved in fixing it, as well as ensuring the reliable supply of potable water to urban systems, means that the larger problem is expanding faster than it can be addressed.

While many developing countries do have restrictions on polluting waterways (and other controls on pollution), these restrictions are very commonly observed in the breech. And in any case, governments of developing countries are more inclined to go softly on such industry, as they cite economic inability to provide alternative means of waste disposal while pointing out the contribution of industrial development and enhanced food production to self-sufficiency, employment, and economic development.

One suggested answer to declining water stocks is the privatization of water. That is, water should cease to be (in principle) a generally freely available resource and should become a commodity like any other. While most countries do charge for water access, they do so through governments that regard the provision of water as a broad social responsibility. The World Bank has estimated that the world water market was worth almost one trillion dollars at the beginning of the 21st century, although that only accounted for the approximately 5 per cent of the world's water consumers who obtained water through corporations. Two of the world's major private water suppliers, Suez Lyonnaise des Eaux (SLE) and Vivendi SA own or control water companies in 120 countries, with each distributing water to more than 110 million people (Ondeo 2002, Vivendi 2002). However, the privatization of water assumes two points. The first point assumed is a capacity to pay, although it is fair enough to say that when there is no choice people will, if they can, pay for water as a primary necessity. However, many of the world's most poor would be unlikely to be able to pay for privatized water, while there are questions about the benefit to those who can do so. The second point assumed is that everything can be commodified, and that what has for most people traditionally been an assumed public right, somewhat like breathing air, can or should be regarded as the preserve of private interest. Regardless of private business's poor record on environmental issues, there are deep philosophical questions attached to the idea that what was once a common public good is available for private ownership. However, in principle, such questions go to the core of the nexus between humankind and the environment, and how we organize our affairs in ways that are equitable or otherwise, and which are sustainable or otherwise.

Political economy of the environment

Although it is sometimes posited in these terms, environmental degradation is not just a consequence of unthinking people mindlessly destroying the world they live in. For many people, notably the most poor in developing countries, drawing down on environmental resources is a matter of survival, of being able to secure their livelihood from one day to the next. Logging to clear land for farming can occur because of population pressure or displacement, the need to a earn cash income or the provision of fuel wood for cooking. Washing clothing and bathing in streams is a common practice in developing countries, but adds detergents and soap to waterways that not only support fish stocks and other species, but which are also used for supplying drinking water. Yet, on the face of it, there appears to be few alternatives. Similarly, even where people construct toilet facilities away from waterways (and they often do not), seepage through ground water can and does lead to a high level of bacteria in streams and wells, with negative consequences for the health of people who use such sources. In some cases, environmental degradation is a consequence of a lower level of awareness or lack of education. But in most cases, poor people engage in the practices they do not through choice, but through sheer necessity. For other communities, unsustainable resource exploitation is a consequence of living in marginal environments, or environments that are unable to comfortably sustain growing populations, as was noted in the observations about desertification and localized logging. However, many people who had previously come from subsistence societies have increasingly been encouraged to participate in mono-culture cash cropping. With world commodity prices tending to fall since the 1970s (non-energy commodity prices falling by about half between 1980 and 2000 (GCM 2000)) and increasing tariff barriers to value-added food products, cash-cropping requires more exploitation of a given area to produce the same income (or what is most often in reality less real income).

Yet for others, environmental degradation is a consequence of a desire to accumulate wealth, usually at the expense of others. It is, of course, correct to say that it is possible to produce wealth which is not at the expense of others. That is, it is possible to be a net contributor to the overall wealth of a community. However, rates of wealth creation are usually well below those achieved by specific individuals, which implies that in order for some to increase their wealth others must, to some extent, lose. And this overall increase in wealth creation, even where it is not at the expense of others, almost always continues to draw down on some aspect of the environment. Unfortunately, in most developing countries, the quickest and most lucrative wealth is to be made by selling off resources, usually without value-adding (e.g., raw minerals, saw-logs, wood-chips), or by cutting costs such as those expended on environmental safeguards (e.g., dumping pollutants into waterways).

While local exploiters often operate for personal profit at the expense of their fellows and the environment, the wider relationship between the local and the global comes in to play, in determining what resources are in demand, how much is to be paid for them, what alternatives a local economy might have for income generation and, arguably, the direction in which local economies can operate. The price of commodities alone can determine environmental impact, not through steering providers away from lower-priced commodities but through increasing production to make up for shortfalls in prices. That is, if a product, say sawlogs, is reduced in price by half, at least twice as many logs (due to higher marginal costs) will need to be produced to return equivalent levels of income. The reduction in the price of sawlogs can be a consequence of simple reduced demand, but at least as likely it will be a consequence of major buyers pitting primary commodity producers against each other to bargain down prices. Where prices for particular commodities fall to levels that become socially or environmentally unsustainable, the option is to seek alternative sources of income. However, most developing countries are locked into deriving the large proportion of their income from relatively few commodities, and immediate demands for income generation preclude time-consuming and sometimes costly diversification into other economic areas. This tendency can be exacerbated by demands for developing economies to repay loans to multilateral agencies (such as the IMF), which, in turn, impose conditions on the shape of economic development to produce the greatest short-term results.

External actors are not always, or indeed often, able to achieve the types of arrangements in individual countries or localities that they would like to. In such cases, they allow local agents to undertake the domestic arrangements for production of commodities, and to deal directly with them. In either case, however, the interests of such local agents are primarily in self-enrichment and in assisting the enrichment of external actors. The economic interests of these so-called 'comprador elites' rarely coincide with those of local people, and, consequently, their concern for the material circumstances of local people are minimal (see Frank *et al.* 1996, Cardoso and Falletto 1979). That is to say, if the priorities of such comprador elites are primarily for self-enrichment, often at the impoverishment of their fellow citizens, there is little likelihood they will have much concern for their material environment. In this respect, comprador elites act to facilitate the interests of outsiders, who are similarly concerned with the extraction of profit with little or no sense of social contract, much less an 'investment' in the future of the locality being exploited. As a consequence, care for the environment is very low down on the list of priorities, if existing at all.

Beyond the rapaciousness of international carpetbaggers and their proxies, there is some awareness of (if not respect for) the problems caused by the iniquity of global allocation of resources. In a world that continues to be dominated by a version of *realpolitik* (in which there is understood to be no higher law making body than the state, and in which the state achieves advantage through capacity to impose its will), state leaders are only answerable to their constituents, amongst whom are international businesses. They are not answerable to the citizens of other countries, nor is there any agreed global regulatory system that apportions wealth on the basis of effort or need (see Morganthau 1978). As a consequence, if the benefits to their own citizens are at the expense of another's citizens then, in simple terms, it is the citizens of the other state that are disadvantaged. The primary consequence of this is that states that have less advantage in international relations tend to be exploited, or at best not have their interests considered, in the arranging of international trade, with the consequence that if they are not further impoverished in absolute terms then they are least allowed access to fewer opportunities to relative development. This, then, relates to the earlier mentioned desperation that many people in developing countries find themselves facing, meaning they are often forced into environmentally unsustainable practices to survive, or that pressures to retain 'comparative advantage' comes to include a disregard for the environment or environmental regulations.

One response to this state of affairs, primarily from more developed countries, is that developing countries must implement a range of practices to ensure that they escape from the trap of economic underdevelopment and desperation. However, the policies that are recommended to implement are, at best, often environmentally damaging, and, at worst, only replicate the cycle of poverty that led to them in the first place (see GE 2002). In reality, those countries that control large proportions of the world's economy have the capacity to direct global pricing, by driving up or down world prices for key commodities, and resource management, through demand. And where, in rare circumstances, a country does manage to escape from this structural imbalance in capacity to determine prices and hence opportunity for development, it can find itself on the receiving end of anti-competitive tariffs, an economic embargo or blockade, or direct intervention. As a consequence, in a bid to engage in the global economy and seek the benefits that can have to offer, many impoverished countries continue to be structurally obliged to engage in environmentally unsustainable economic practices.

Alternatives

Recognition of environmental problems stemming from and hindering development has become, by the beginning of the 21st century, a fundamentally uncontested issue. There continues to be debate about the extent of environmental degradation, the capacity of natural resources, and technological 'fixes'. But there is little argument that the global climate is changing, that forests – and their capacity to produce oxygen – are disappearing at a rate that is unsustainable, that deserts are growing rather than shrinking, and that, despite exceptions, air, water and land pollution continues to constitute a major problem. There is only slightly more debate about the contribution of absolute population size to environmental degradation, the imbalance in resource distribution, the symbiotic relationship between scarcity and conflict, and the necessity of moving towards environmental sustainability.

Environmentally related conflict is identified by Dabelko (1996) as falling into two broad resource categories; renewable and non-renewable. Dabelko regards conflict over non-renewable resources as being more conventional conflict, focused on economic benefit. Examples of such conflict include Iraq's invasion of Kuwait and the subsequent US-led attack on Iraq (oil), Morocco's conflict with the Polisario Front (phosphate), South Africa's occupation of Namibia and conflict in Angola (diamonds), the Khmer Rouge's occupation of western Cambodia (gems, as well as timber), Burma's conflict with separatists (gems, as well as timber and opium), Nigeria and Biafra (oil), Russia and Chechnya (oil), Indonesia and Aceh/West Papua (oil, liquid natural gas/copper, gold), and many others.

Conflicts related to renewable resources, and more from particular resource scarcity, tend to operate from a less naked desire for economic control. Conflicts may arise is relation to losses of renewable resources in one area and availability in another, or through over-population relative to available resources. But one less clear source of renewable resource conflict is relative to population growth, in which there is chronic poverty, or in which there is a pointed lack of consensus about the legitimacy of common political organization via the distribution of resources within it (especially if that is understood as related to ethnic identity). In such cases, resultant institutional weakness can lead to a breakdown in authority, and civil conflict. This relates to Homer-Dixon's proposition that environmental 'stress' has 'social effects, that lead to conflict both within and between states' (Homer-Dixon 1991: 76–77).

Where internal 'stress' can and too often does manifest is in abuses of the human rights of people protesting about the degradation of their land in various ways. And importantly, where human rights defenders often try to support such protesters, or to protect them from attack, they themselves are victim of attack and human rights abuses, including arbitrary arrest and detention, torture, and extra-judicial killing. In this there is a clear link between environmental and human rights issues – over the capacity of ordinary people to be able to speak freely when things directly, negatively affect their own lives.

Appropriate development

As a consequence of the high costs of development, in environmental as well as other terms, there has increasingly been discussion about 'appropriate development' and 'sustainable development', two ideas that often overlap. What is commonly referred to as 'appropriate development' is where the level of technology is suitable for the needs and conditions of the area undergoing the process of development and does not require environmentally destructive or economically unsustainable industry. Sustainable development similarly means the idea that development can be sustained primarily in ecological terms, but also economically, politically, and socially.

Although there is no universal agreement as to what constitutes 'appropriate development', and even less about 'sustainable development', some key ideas include its capacity to be locally operated and sustained without requiring either external expertise or capital. In this respect, sophisticated technology is regarded as far less important than technology that works, can be maintained at little or no expense, and has few environmental side effects. An example of inappropriate development, for example, is the use of diesel powered electric generators in poor, oil importing countries. Appropriate development might rely on solar, wind,

284 Environment and Development

geothermal or water (stream, dam, wave or tidal generated) power (Dunkerley at al 1981), while there has been development of alcohol and oilseed (such as rapeseed) as a replacement for petrol and diesel as transport fuels. Solar power is also advancing very quickly, and while it might remain a relatively capital expensive form of energy, its cost is reducing while practicability is increasing through the use of photo-voltaic cells that can provide power on a cloudy day, or by moonlight. They are relatively capital expensive, but a lot cheaper than similar cells were a few years ago, and have effectively no running or environmental costs. However, in the shorter term, there might simply have to be, in some cases, an acceptance that such sources of power are not available, economically affordable, or suitable to a particular environment. By way of illustration, in the 1980s, an acquaintance volunteer aid worker returned from Solomon Islands with the story about how, when a village generator broke down it was flown to the capital, Honiara, to be repaired. While it was away, the villagers lived as before the arrival of electricity. When the generator was eventually returned, as it was being unloaded from a seaplane to a canoe, it fell into a lagoon, and after being retrieved had to be returned to Honiara for further repairs. Between the cost of fixing the generator and its clear lack of necessity, the villagers decided they were better off without it, and voluntarily returned to living without electricity.

The issue of access to energy, in particular electricity, is the source of considerable tension in environmental debates. Up to two billion people in developing countries do not have access to electricity. Even in countries that currently employ fossil fuels as their primary energy source, current prices are unlikely to be sustained and they will become prohibitively expensive, a situation that is expected to develop well before fossil fuels run out. As a consequence, there will be an increasing economic necessity to consider alternative forms of energy producing technology. That is, while there has been some move towards exploring alternative forms of energy, the major research and development will only occur when fossil fuels become prohibitively expensive, which they are expected to do by the end of the first quarter of the 21st century. However, while this applies to developed countries, and countries that produce, subsidise or have low taxes on oil products, there are many countries that already struggle to meet their fuel import bill. And the environmental issues related to fossil fuel use are increasingly critical, not least of which is air pollution in many of the world's major developing cities. In particular, with an increasingly urbanized population, Asia has some of the world's most polluted cities, including Beijing, Tianjin, Shanghai, Jakarta, Bangkok, Manila, Mumbai, Calcutta and Delhi (Haq *et al.* 2002: Chs 1–7), although urban sprawls such as Mexico City have also recorded dangerously high air pollution levels.

Renewable energy

Renewable energy has been noted as one means of retaining existing energy consumption levels while maintaining relatively high levels of environmental sustainability. There is, not surprisingly, some debate about the ecological credentials of all renewable fuels, especially hydroelectricity, which was the most widespread form of renewable energy in use at the time of writing. About one-fifth of the world's agricultural land is irrigated, and irrigated agriculture accounts for about 40 per cent of the world's agricultural production. Half the world's large dams were built exclusively or primarily for irrigation, and an estimated 30 to 40 per cent of the 271 million hectares of irrigated land worldwide (around 15 per cent of the total) rely on dams. Dams producing hydroelectricity also produces close to 20 per cent of the world's total electric supply, with 24 countries depending on hydroelectricity for 90 per cent of their power supply. Dams also inhibit flooding, which between 1972 and 1996 affected of around 65 million people, which is more than war, drought or famine combined (Baur and Rudolph 2001).

Less positively, however, large dams have proven to be only marginally cost effective. The main problems with large dams has been cost over run, a tendency to fall short of projected power targets, and a return of less revenue than anticipated. Dams also impact upon fish stocks, flood plain agriculture, and reduce habitat through flooding. It is worth noting that less than half of the dams commissioned during the 1990s had environmental impact assessments (WCD 2000, Baur and Rudolph 2001). Dams have also been shown to have a high social cost, especially in terms of displacing local peoples. Baur and Rudoplh (2001) suggest that between 40 and 80 million people have been displaced by dam construction, with more than half of those coming from India and China (see Fuggle and Smith 2000). The Narmada River dam project in India, which includes some 30 large dams and 3000 small dams, has been highly controversial and the site of resistance by local people opposed to being removed from their homes. There has also been extensive criticism of the project over inaccurate costing, benefits and returns (see Rangachari *et al.* 2000). (On large dams in Indonesia, see Aditjondro in Hirsch and Warren 1998.)

While some developed countries such as Norway have fully developed hydroelectric schemes, others, such as Australia, discovered that the headlong rush towards hydroelectricity had become self-perpetuating, regardless of energy needs, while itself having a significant environmental impact. In 1981, the Australian government overrode the Tasmanian state government in its bid to dam the Franklin and Gordon Rivers on the grounds that hydroelectric power supply already exceeded industrial demand, which was declining, and because both rivers had high ecological value. They were both later listed as a World Heritage Area. There has also been moves to increase the flow of water to rivers draining from the watershed now contained by the Snowy Mountains Hydroelectric Scheme, which is Australia's biggest ever infrastructure project.

In land-locked Laos, which has least-developed (LLDC) status, a major hydroelectric project on the Theun River (Nam Theun) was intended to produce sustainable energy for both consumption in Laos and selling-on to Thailand (which, at least in the short to medium term, had reduced its electricity demand due to the Asian economic crisis of the late 1990s). The project was heavily criticized for saddling Laos with international debt, and for flooding a significant forest area. However, the Lao government agreed that the area to be flooded be logged first, and has restricted legal logging in much of the rest of its forests. With around half the country under forest cover, Laos arguably remains among the most densely forested countries in the world. (There is debate about this – the government claims its is 55 per cent forested, while the World Rainforest Movement says that it is now less than 40 per cent forested, down from 70 per cent in 1940 (WRM 2000).) While the Nam Theun II dam project has been subjected to international scrutiny, due to local deforestation, social displacement, and questions about the demand for the power it will generate, such controversy has at least ensured that the project has been closely monitored, with an eye to ensuring it proceeds according to agreed criteria (Iverach, in Stensholt 1997: 69–70, 76). Large dams required to generate hydroelectricity have also been highly controversial in many other cases, in Latin American, across Asia and throughout Africa. Up to 10 million people are said to have been displaced by large dam development since 1948, with most not returning to their former standard of living, while many older dams are now beginning to silt up, reducing their capacity and future potential (IRN 2001). By the end of the 20th century, there were over 45,000 large dams in over 150 countries, with an average age of 35 years, which meant they were mostly coming to the end of the useful water storage life (Baur and Rudolph 2001).

Support for large dam projects, which has cost some 125 billion dollars in multilateral and bilateral aid since 1950 (although as little as 15 per cent of total costs), has been challenged on the grounds of cost-efficiency. Especially with the advent of micro-turbines, there is greater consideration being given to smaller, cheaper and more environmentally friendly forms of hydroelectricity.

Beyond those forms noted above, there is also what its supporters are fond of calling 'the fifth fuel' – energy conservation. Consumption drives resource exploitation, and is in turn driven by two criteria. The first is that the world's population continues to grow, in simple terms providing a multiplier effect for existing consumption. The second criterion is that technological development has led many and perhaps most of the world's population to, if not expect, then at least to want more, of almost everything, as the developed world has and continues to do. For example, chlorofluorocarbons (CFC) are internationally recognized as depleting the earth's ozone layer, and manufacturers of refrigerators that use CFCs have been banned by most countries. However, CFC refrigerators are cheaper to produce than non-CFC refrigerators, so when China embarked on a programme to ensure that each family has a refrigerator it turned to the cheaper CFC refrigerators. The international community expressed its dismay at the prospect of tens of million of CFC-producing refrigerators that would be added to the world's total, but the Chinese government replied that its people could not afford non-CFC refrigerators, and yet it was not prepared to deny them the right to preserve food. Similarly, when the international community condemned the Malaysian government for unsustainable logging of old-growth tropical forests in northern Borneo, it replied that it would not be denied the right to also achieve developed status, to which such logging would contribute. And, it pointed out, that the West in particular had developed in part through deforesting its own lands, and that it was hypocritical for it to now tell other states they could not do the same.

What this implied was that industrialized states were beginning to be forced to reconsider their own patterns of consumption, and to look at ways of modifying and ultimately reducing them. The Kyoto Agreement, for example, was intended to reduce greenhouse gas emissions by 8 per cent of 1990 levels by 2012. Greenhouse gasses are identified as carbon dioxide, methane, nitrous oxide, perfluorocarbons, hydrofluorocarbons, and sulfur hexafluoride. While 73 countries had signed the agreement by mid-2002, including all European Union states and Japan, countries that had not ratified the agreement still accounted for 64 per cent of greenhouse gas emissions, including the US, which alone accounted for 36 per cent of emissions, and Australia, which remains the world's greatest greenhouse polluter on a per capita basis (primarily due to the production of electricity through burning brown coal, and the high level of automobile use).

One means of encouraging more environmentally friendly practices has been the policy of 'greenhouse trading'. Greenhouse trading is essentially a credit system by which industries that emit greenhouse gasses are encouraged to reduce emissions by being able to claim reductions against taxation or other methods of payment, e.g., one tonne of greenhouse gas could be worth, for instance, US$2. The savings (or payments) would then be invested in seeking non-polluting means of industrial capacity. However, while greenhouse trading was emerging as one means to resolve greenhouse gas emissions problems, its emergence was fitful and uncoordinated (Pew Centre 2002). The problem of greenhouse trading for developing countries is, of course, that governments have to be prepared to subsidise the credit system, or be prepared to impose penalties on polluting industries. However, given limited financial liquidity and often influential or otherwise impervious industries, this policy option has not been seriously considered in developing countries, and would require considerable multilateral backing for it to be at all successful. In this, the political economy of development continues to run counter to the needs of the environment, and privileges economic development in the hierarchy of development outcomes.

By contrast, appropriate development usually (although not always) posits that social and ecological outcomes have precedence over economic outcomes, and that development should, and indeed must, occur at the local level, relying on renewable, local inputs with little or no negative impact on the environment, where it has a direct and tangible benefit, rather than at the macro level. In this respect, increased self-sufficiency may have little or no benefit to the GDP, but does have the capacity to markedly improve quality of life (see, for example, Trainer 1995, Dunkerley *et al.* 1981: 203–11).

In terms of local sustainability, mixed agriculture can also be more economically and environmentally sustainable than mono-culture cash-cropping in what is broadly a declining market in real prices. Sustainability is also enhanced both in terms of varying usages of land to allow it to regenerate and in supplying a wider variety of foodstuffs for local consumption as well as for sale. This is especially so if the mixed cropping is based on indigenous plants, which do not require fertilizers, pesticides or herbicides to ensure their growth. In this respect, notions of sustainable development include those that allow people to live in economic or material terms, but ensuring an adequate supply of nutrition, which are not captive to fluctuating market forces, which are affordable to develop and do not require expensive external inputs, and which do not damage or otherwise unbalance the local ecology.

Like many important ideas, 'sustainability' has been quickly recognized but then co-opted by a range of parties to support their respective causes and to essentially dilute or detract from the meaning of the term. Some uses of the term 'sustainability' have referred to the capacity of political organizations to retain themselves in power, or for businesses to continue to be profitable. The World Bank employs a 'multi-dimensional' meaning, as noted earlier in this chapter. To illustrate this point, when the United Nations Johannesburg Summit noted two critical features of sustainability, it failed to do so in meaningfully applicable terms. Its first point was the observation that since the 'Earth Summit' of 1992, poverty and environmental degradation had worsened rather than improved (UNDESA

2002a). The second point was that the 'key outcomes' of the summit aimed at halving poverty and the number of people who were slum dwellers, without access to safe water and sanitation, to promote renewable energy, to be more socially responsible in chemical use, to encourage appropriate use of fisheries, and so on (UNDESA 2002b). The key issue in this, however, was that amongst all the laudable aims, there were very few concrete steps to be taken, no form of enforcement, and little likelihood that the various timelines proposed for 'halving' various measures could or would be met. Indeed, the idea of 'sustainability' was no where formally spelled out, as though it was either too ambiguous or too contentious an idea to put precise meaning to.

'Sustainability' was intended in its original contemporary usage to primarily mean *environmental* sustainability. That is, there is no future without a natural environment within which to live, and use of the natural environment must be in a way that can be sustained; that is, to ensure the future of the species, people can use resources only in ways that are renewable or which do not permanently deplete the earth's resources. Sustainability may allow growth, but does not imply it. Indeed, in most cases it would be difficult to talk about further growth in simple per capita GDP terms while also aiming for sustainability. However, sustainability does not preclude greater equity of distribution, nor does it preclude growth in non-consumption areas, such as the growth of knowledge (education) or culture. Indeed, sustainability encourages a return to a somewhat simpler and less technologically dependent society. This does not imply a wholesale retreat from technology, but a recognition that not all technological development is necessary, or 'appropriate', and that some types of simpler, and therefore less commercially profitable, technology may in fact be equally or more suitable for many requirements. As Korten noted:

> Current development practice supports increases in economic output that depend on the unsustainable depletion of the earth's natural resources and the life-support capabilities of its econ-system. Such temporary gains do not represent development so much as theft by one generation of the birthright of future generations. (1990: 4)

Triple bottom line

In the process of development, understood as industrialization, there has been a fixed competition between economic development and environmental considerations, 'with one side trying to force through new rules and standards, and the other trying to roll them back' (Elkington 1999: 108).

However, taking a line from economists Porter and van der Linda, soon 'resource productivity will be directly linked both to environmental protection and competitiveness. Environmental constraints drive innovation and, as a result, eco-efficiency.... The conclusion ... is that top executives should spend less time resisting new environmental legislation, and more rethinking the nature and future of their businesses to ensure they are well adapted for the sustainability transition' (1999: 109). Elkington argues for what he calls a 'triple bottom line' for business management, which focuses on economic prosperity, environmental quality and social justice. This idea could be as readily applied to the development paradigm, especially when it is noted that Elkington draws strongly on the notion of globalization that 'embraces not just economic dimensions but also social and environmental dimensions' (1999: 385).

A similar, 'multi-dimensional' paradigm has been defined by the World Bank as 'sustainable development', which focuses on various types of capital. It should be noted here that this is a relatively 'soft' version of the various interpretations that have been applied to the idea of 'sustainability', but does employ economic criteria in its definition. Indeed, the language of sustainability is defined in economic terms, with sustainability applying to various types of 'capital'. The first type of capital is financial, implying sound macroeconomic planning and prudent fiscal management. Physical capital refers to infrastructure, while human capital applies to health and education, and social capital applies to skills and abilities, and institutions, relationships and norms about the quantity and quality of social interactions. Finally, natural capital refers to both commercial and non-commercial natural resources, and 'ecological services' including potable water, energy, fibres, waste assimilation, climate stabilization and other aspects of the natural environment that relate to maintaining life (World Bank 2001c).

One aspect that impinges on Elkington's model, though, is that of the role of government in establishing parameters for social and environmental as well as economic outcomes. To this end, notions of governance come into play, in which governments are not only accountable and responsible, but also have the capacity to retain an institutional distance from sources of pressure (such as short-term focused businesses). In this sense, 'governance' becomes a critical issue in ensuring that broader communities act together for a common benefit, rather than individuals or individual organizations acting separately for their own, limited benefit.

The environmentalists' slogan, 'Think global, act local', necessarily reduces a complex range of issues to a simplistic argument. But in doing this, it retains the seemingly true premise that where we live is local, and how we act where we live has a local impact. Additionally, it implies that our local actions, cumulatively, have the capacity to impact on a much wider scale. The impact of one person on the environment is negligible, no matter if they try to do their worst. The impact of hundreds of millions, or billions, though is quite another matter. Therefore, conversely, one individual who behaves responsibly can similarly have no meaningful impact on the greater environment, but may inspire many others, and large numbers of individuals can. In this respect we are all members of the global community, and all share in global responsibility. The advantages of one are often at the cost of another, while the sacrifices of one, for example *not* cutting down trees, must be shared by the greater community that benefits. There is little doubt that we are, as a global community, beginning to bump into the edges of the earth's capacity to indefinitely sustain what has been to date an ever-expanding human population. And while the consequences of these limits will affect some more than others, especially in the short to medium term, in the longer term they will affect all. As a consequence of these totalizing aspect of globalization, and the finite extent of the globe, Elkington's argument in favour of environmental and social responsibility as well as economic prosperity, are functionally non-negotiable: 'to refuse the challenge implied by the triple bottom line,' he says, 'is to risk extinction'. (1999: 2) More positively, there seems to be a growing awareness of this probable outcome, which reduces its chances of occurring.

Bibliography

Adade, C. (1991) 'Cut: drastic reductions likely in Soviet support', *New Internationalist*, 216.

Addison, T. (2000) 'Aid and Conflict', in F. Tarp (ed.) *Foreign Aid and Development*, pp. 392–408.

Adelman, I. and Taft Morris, C. (1973) *Economic Growth and Social Equity in Developing Countries* (Stanford, Ca., Stanford University Press).

Agarwal, B. (1997a) '"Bargaining" and gender relations: within and beyond the household', *Feminist Economics*, 3 (1): 8–9.

Agarwal, B. (1997b) 'The Gender and Environment Debate: Lessons from India', in N. Visvanathan, L. Duggan, L. Nisonoff and N. Wiegersma (eds), *The Women, Gender and Development Reader* (London, Zed Books), pp. 68–74.

Agarwala, A. N. and S. P. Singh (eds) (1958) *The Economics of Underdevelopment* (Oxford, Oxford University Press).

Agenor, P.-R., Miller, M., Vines, D. and Weber, A. (eds) (1999) *The Asian Financial Crisis: Causes, Contagion and Consequences* (Cambridge, Cambridge University Press).

Ahlburg, D. *et al.* (1994) *Independent Enquiry Report into Population and Development* (Canberra, AGPS/ADAB).

Amacher, R. D., Haberler, G. and Willett, T. D. (eds) (1979) *Challenges to a Liberal International Economic Order* (Washington, DC, American Enterprise Institute).

Amin, S. (1976) *Unequal Development* (London, Monthly Review).

Amin, S. (1977) *Imperialism and Unequal Development* (Hassocks, Harvester).

Amin, S. (1978) *Some Thoughts on Self-Reliant Development, Collective Self-Reliance and the NIEO* (Stockholm, Institute for International Economic Studies).

Amsden, A. (1989) *Asia's Next Giant: South Korea and Late Industrialization* (New York, Oxford University Press).

Anderson, B. (1991) *Imagined Communities* (revised, 2nd edition), (London, Verso).

Anderson, J. (1985) *Research and Agricultural Progress* (Armidale, University of New England).

Anderson, J., Herdt, R. and Scobie, G. (1986) *Science and Food: The CGIAR and its Partners*, Vols 1–4 (Washington, DC, CGIAR).

Anderson, M. (1999) *Do No Harm: How aid can support peace – or war* (Boulder, Lynne Rienner Publishers).

Appel, G. (1990) 'Costing Social Change', in M. Dove (ed.), *The Real and Imagined Role of Culture in Development: Case Studies From Indonesia* (Honolulu, University of Hawaii Press).

Ariff, M. (ed.) (1998) *APEC and Development Cooperation* (Singapore, Institute of South East Asian Studies).

Arrighi, G. (2002) The African Crisis: World Systemic and Regional Aspects, *New Left Review*, 15: 5–38.

AusAID Aid (2001) Budget Summary 2001–02, from www.ausaid.gov.au/budget/summary (accessed 22 May 2001).

Ayres, R. (1983) *Banking on the Poor: The World Bank and World Poverty* (Cambridge, Mass, MIT Press).

Bass, T. A. (1990) *Camping With the Prince and Other Tales of Science in Africa* (New York, Penguin).

Bates, R. (2001) *Prosperity and Violence* (New York and London, Norton).

Bain, I. (1996) 'The China Country Program', in Kilby, P. (ed.), *Australia's Aid Program: Mixed Messages and Conflicting Agendas* (Melbourne, Monash Asia Institute and Community Aid Abroad).

Balassa, B. (1971) *The Structure of Protection in Developing Countries* (Baltimore, Md, Johns Hopkins University Press).

Battaile, W. (2001) *ARDE 2001: Making Choices* (World Bank Annual Review of Development Effectiveness).

Bauer, J. and Bell, D. (1999) *The East Asian Challenge for Human Rights* (Cambridge, Cambridge University Press).

Bauer, P. (1971) *Dissent on Development* (London, Weidenfeld & Nicholson).

Baur, J. and Rudolph, J. (2001) 'Water Facts and Findings on Large Dams as Pulled from the Report of the World Commission on Dams', *Development and Cooperation*, No 2.

Bebczuk, R. and Gasparini, L. (2000) 'Globalization and Inequality: The Case of Argentine', paper to *Poverty and Income Inequality in Developing Countries: A Policy Dialogue on the Effects of Globalization*, Paris, OECD, 30 November–1 December 2000.

Beck, U. (2000) *What is Globalization?* (Cambridge, Polity Press).

Ben-David, D., Nordstrom, H., and Winters., L. (1999) *Trade, Income Disparity and Poverty Special Studies 5* (Washington, World Trade Organization).

Bell, D. (2000) *East Meets West: Human Rights and Democracy in East Asia* (Princeton, NJ, Princeton University Press).

Belshaw, H. (1947) 'Observations on industrialization for higher incomes', *Economic Journal*, September, 379–87.

Beneria, L. (1995) 'Toward a Greater Integration of Gender in Economics', *World Development*, 23 (11): 1839–50.

Beneria, L. (1999) 'The enduring debate over unpaid labour', in *International Labour Review*, 138 (3): 287–309.

Beneria, L. (2001) 'Structural Adjustment Policies', in L. Beneria and S. Bisnath (eds), *Gender and Development: Theoretical, Empirical and Practical Approaches* (London, Elgar Publishing), pp. 419–27.

Beneria, L. and Bisnath, S. (2001) *Gender and Development: Theoretical, Empirical and Practical Approaches*, Vol. I and Vol. II (London, Elgar Publishing).

Berger, M. and Borer, D. (eds) (1997) *The Rise of East Asia: Critical Visions of the Pacific Century* (London, Routledge).

Bhagwati, J. and Desai, P. (1970) *India – Planning for Industrialization* (London, Oxford University Press).

Bilgin, P. and Morton, A. (2002) 'Historicizing Representations of 'Failed States': Beyond the Cold War Annexation of the Social Sciences?', *Third World Quarterly* 23 (1).

Black, M. (1992) *A Cause for Our Times: Oxfam the first 50 years* (Oxford, Oxfam).

Blair, H. (1997) *Success and Failure in Rural Development: A Comparison of Maharasthra, Bihar and Bangladesh*, Paper presented to Peasant Symposium, Bucknell University, 10 May 1997.

Bloch, M. (ed.) (1975) *Marxist Analyses and Social Anthropology* (New York, Wiley).

Boff, L. and Clodovis (1984) *A Concise History of Liberation Theology* (New York, Orbis Books).

Booth, D. (1999) *Are the International Development Targets Reachable? Reassessing the Prospects in Asia and Africa*, Notes from an ODI Seminar. Presentations by Lucia Hanmer and Felix Naschold, ODI, Stephen Ackroyd (Oxford Policy Management, Susan Joekes, IDS and Rosemary McGee, Christian Aid, from www.odi.org.uk (accessed 1 October 2002).

Boserup, E. (1970) *Women's Role in Economic Development* (New York, St. Martin's Press).

Bourdieu, P. (1977) *Outline of a Theory of Practice*. Trans. Richard Nice. (Cambridge, Cambridge University Press).

Boyce, J. (2002) 'Unpacking Aid', *Development and Change*, 33 (2): 329–246.

Boyer, R. and Hollingsworth, J. (1997) 'The variety of institutional arrangements and their complementarity in modern economies', in J.R. Hollingsworth and R. Boyer (eds), *Contemporary Capitalism: The Embededness of Institutions* (Cambridge, Cambridge University Press), pp. 49–54.

Braidotti, R. Charkeiwicz, E. Hausler, S. and Wieringa, S. (1997) 'Women, the Environment and Sustainable Development' in N. Visvanathan, L. Duggan, L. Nisonoff and N. Wiegersma (eds), *The Women, Gender and Development Reader* (London, Zed Books), pp, 54–61.

Budlender, D. (2001) 'The South African Women's Budget Initiative: What does it Tell Us About Poverty Alleviation?' Chapter 15, in F. Wilson, K. Nazneen and E. Braathen (eds), *Poverty Reduction: What Role for the State in Today's Globalised Economy?* (Cape Town, CROP International Studies on Poverty, NAEP).

Burkey, S. (1988) *People First: A Guide* (London and New Jersey, Zed Books).

Burnside, C. and Dollar, D. (1997) *Aid, Policies and Growth*, Policy Research Working Papers 1777 (Washington, DC, World Bank).

Bush, G.W. (2002) The National Security Strategy of the United States of America, http://www.whitehouse.gov/nsc/nss/html (accessed 23 October 2002).

Buvinic, M. (1986) Article in *World Development*, 14 (5): 653–664

Buxton, J. and Phillips, N. (eds) (1999) *Developments in Latin American Political Economy* (Manchester, Manchester University Press).

Cairncross, A. (1962) *Factors in Economic Development* (London, Allen & Unwin).

Camilleri, J. (1994) 'Reflections on the State in Transition', *Arena*, Melbourne.

Camilleri, J. and Falk, J. (1992) *The End of Sovereignty? The Politics of a Shrinking and Fragmented World* (London, Edward Elgar).

Campbell, T. (1983) *The Left and Rights* (London, Routledge & Kegan Paul).

Cardero, M. (2000) 'The impact of NAFTA on Female Employment in Mexico', in De Pauli (ed.), *Women's Empowerment and Economic Justice: Reflecting on Experience in Latin America and the Caribbean* (New York: UNIFEM).

Cardoso, F. (1982) 'Dependency and Development in Latin America', in H. Alavi and T. Shanin (eds), *Introduction to the Sociology of Developing Countries* (New York: Monthly Review Press), pp. 112–127.

Cardoso, F. and Faletto, R. (1979) *Dependency and Development* (Berkeley, University of California Press).

Cassen, R. & Associates (1994) *Does Aid Work?*, Report to an Intergovernmental Task Force (Oxford, Clarendon Press).

Cernea, M. (ed.) (1985) *Putting People First*, 1st edition (New York, Oxford University Press/World Bank).

Cernea, M. (ed.) (1991) *Putting People First*, 2nd edition (New York, Oxford University Press/World Bank).

CGIAR (1978) *Farming Systems Research at the International Agricultural Research Centers* (Rome, FAO).

CGIAR (1985) *Summary of International Agricultural Research Centers: A Study of Achievements and Potential* (Washington, DC, CGIAR Secretariat).

Chambers, R. (1980) *Rural Poverty Unperceived: Problems and Remedies* (Washington, DC, World Bank).

Chambers, R. (1983) *Rural Development: Putting the Last First* (Harlow, Longman).

Chan, S. (2002) *Liberalism, Democracy and Development* (Cambridge, Cambridge University Press).

Chenery, H. (1955) 'The Role of Industrialization in Development Programmes, *American Economic Review*.

Chenery, H. (ed.) (1971) *Studies in Development Planning* (Cambridge, Mass, Harvard University Press).

Chenery, H. (1979) *Structural Change and Development Policy* (London, Oxford University Press).

Chenery, H. *et al.* (1974) *Redistribution with Growth* (London, Oxford University Press).

Chenery, H. and Syrquin, M. (1975) *Patterns of Development 1950–70* (London, Oxford University Press).

Chirzin, H. (2002) *Globalization, Development and Liberation in the Third Millennium: An Islamic Perspective* http://202.64.82.162/daga/ds/dsp00/dl3m-h.htm (accessed 24 December 2002).

Cho, K. (1999) *Pollution Statistics in Korea in Relation to 1993 SNA* (Seoul, Bank of Korea Research Department).

Chomsky, N. (1994) *Media Control: The Spectacular Achievements of Propaganda* (New York, Open Media/Seven Stories Press).

Chomsky, N. and Herman, E. (1988) *Manufacturing Consent: The Political Economy of the Mass Media* (New York, Pantheon Books).

Churchill, W. (1947) Speech to House of Commons, London, 11 November 1947.

CIDA Review, Ottawa 1995.

Clague, C. (ed.) (1997) *Institutions and Economic Development: Growth and Governance in Less-Developed and Post-Socialist Countries* (Baltimore, Md, Johns Hopkins University Press).

Clark, C. (1940) *The Conditions of Economic Progress* (London, Macmillan).

Clark, J. (1991) *Democratizing Development* (London, Earthscan).

Club of Rome (1972) *Limits to Growth* (Rome).

Club of Rome (1974) *Mankind at the Turning Point* (Rome).

Colclough, C. and Manor, J. (eds) (1991) *States or Markets? Neo-Liberalism and the Development Policy Debate* (Oxford: Oxford University Press).

Coleman, J. (1990) *Foundations of Social Theory* (Cambridge, Mass, Harvard University Press).

Commission for the Conservation of Southern Bluefin Tuna (CCSBT) (2002) 'Origins of the Convention' (Canberra, Commission for the Conservation of Southern Bluefin Tuna).

Commonwealth Expert Group (1989), *Engendering Adjustment for the 1990s: Report of a Commonwealth Expert Group on Women and Structural Adjustment* (London, Commonwealth Secretariat).

Conway, G. R., McCracken, J. A. and Pretty, J. N. (1987) *Training Notes for Agroecosystem Analysis and Rapid Rural Appraisal*, 2nd edition (London, IIED).

Coote, B. (1992) *The Trade Trap: Poverty and the Global Commodity Markets* (Oxford, Oxfam).

Cornia, G., Jolly, R. and Stewart, F. (eds) (1987) *Adjustment with a Human Face*, Vols I and II (Oxford, Clarendon Press).

Cornwall, A. (2001) 'Making a Difference? Gender and Participatory Development', *IDS Discussion Paper*, No 378 (Brighton: Institute of Development Studies).

Cowen, M. and Shenton, R. (1996) *Doctrines of Development* (London, Routledge).

Cox, R. (1996) 'A Perspective on Globalization', in Mittelman, J. (ed.), *Globalization: Critical Reflections* (Boulder, Lynne Rienner Publishers).

Crone, P. (1986) 'The Tribe and the State', in J. Hall (ed.), *States in History* (Oxford, Basil Blackwell).

Dabelko, G. (1996) *The Environment and Conflict in the Third World: Examining Linkage, Context and Policy*, Occasional paper No. 12, Harrison Program on the Future Global Agenda, January 1996.

Danielsen, A. (1982) *The Evolution of OPEC* (New York, Harcourt, Brace, Jovanovich).

Darling, M. L. (1925) *The Punjab Peasant.*

Das Pradhan (2000) 'Engendering Good Governance in Practice', *Development Bulletin*, 51: 6–9.

de Bary, W. (1998) *Asian Values and Human Rights: a Confucian Communitarian Perspective* (Cambridge, Mass, Harvard University Press).

De Pauli, L. (ed.) (2000) *Women's Empowerment and Economic Justice: Reflecting on Experience in Latin America and the Caribbean* (New York: UNIFEM).

de Silva, D. *et al.* (1989) *Against All Odds: Breaking the Poverty Trap* (London, Panos Pubs).

de Soto, H. 1989, *The Other Path* (trans. J. Abbott) (New York, Harper & Row).

de Soto, H. (2000) *The Mystery of Capital: Why Capitalism Triumphs in the West But Fails Everywhere Else* (London, Bantam Press).

de Waal, A. (1989) *Famine That Kills* (Oxford, Clarendon).

de Waal, A. (1997, 1998) *Famine Crimes: Politics and the Disaster Relief Industry in Africa* (Indiana, Indiana University Press).

Dey, J. (1982) 'Development Planning in the Gambia: The Gap between Planners and Farmers' Perceptions, Expectations and Objectives', *World Development*, 10 (5).

DFID (1997) *Eliminating World Poverty: A Challenge for the Twenty-First Century*, White Paper, London, Department for International Development.

DFID (2000) *Making Globalisation Work for the World's Poor: An Introduction to the UK Government's White Paper on International Development*, DFID, London, December.

Diamond, J. (1999) *Guns, Germs and Steel: The Fates of Human Societies* (New York, W.W. Norton & Co).

Diamond, L. 1999. *Developing Democracy Toward Consolidation* (Baltimore, Md, Johns Hopkins University Press).

DiMarco, L. (ed.) (1972) *International Economics and Development: Essays in Honour of Raul Prebisch* (London, Academic Press).

Dodd, C. (1972) *Political Development* (London, Macmillan).

Dollar, D. and Kraay, A. (2002) Spreading the Wealth, *Foreign Affairs*, 81 (1): 120–33.

Downie, S. and Kingsbury, D. (2001) 'Political Development and the Re-emergence of Civil Society in Cambodia', *Contemporary Southeast Asia*, 23.

Duncan, R. (2000) *Globalization and Income Inequality: An International Perspective*, Conference on International Trade Education and Research: Managing Globalization for Prosperity, Victorian Department of State and Regional Development, Melbourne, 26–27 October 2000.

Dunkerley, J., Ramsay, W., Gordon, L. and Cecelski, E. (1981) *Energy Strategies for Developing Nations* (Baltimore, Md, and London, Johns Hopkins University Press).

Dureau, C. (2003) Address to 'Working Together for East Timor' conference, Darebin City Council, Melbourne. 4–5 April.

Dutt, A. (ed.) (2002) *The Political Economy of Development*, Vols 1–3 (Cheltenham, Edward Elgar).

Easterly, W. (2001) *The Elusive Quest for Growth* (Cambridge, Mass, MIT Press).

Ehrlich, P. (1969) *The Population Bomb* (New York, Ballantyne Books).

Eichengreen, B. (1999) *Toward a New International Financial Architecture: a Practical Post-Asia Agenda* (Washington, DC: Institute for International Economics).

Eichengreen, B. and Fishlow, A. (1998) 'Contending with Capital Flows: What is Different about the 1990s?' in M. Kahler (ed.) *Capital Flows and Financial Crises* (Manchester: Manchester University Press), pp. 23–68.

Eicher, C. K. and Staatz, J. M. (eds) (1990) *Agricultural Development in the Third World*, 2nd edn (Baltimore, Md, Johns Hopkins).

Elkington, J. (1999) *Cannibals With Forks: The Triple Bottom Line of 21st Century Business* (Oxford, Capstone).

Elliott, C. (1987) *Comfortable Compassion* (London, Hodder & Stoughton).

Elliot, L. and Denny, C. (2002) 'Top 1% Earn As Much As the Poorest 57%', *Guardian*, 18 January.

Ellis, H. S. (ed.) (1961) *Economic Development for Latin America* (London, Macmillan).

Elson, D. (1991) 'Structural Adjustment: Its Effect on Women', in T. Wallace and C. March (eds), *Changing Perceptions: Writings on Gender and Development*, (Oxford, Oxfam), pp. 39–59.

Ely, R. T. (1903) *Studies in the Evolution of Industrial Society*.

Emmanuel, A. (1972) *Unequal Exchange* (London, Monthly Review).

Escobar, A. (1995) *Encountering Development: The Making and Unmaking of the Third World* (Princeton, NJ, Princeton University Press).

Espino, M. (2000) 'Women and Mercosur: the Gendered Dimension of Economic Integration', in L. De Pauli (ed.), *Women's Empowerment and Economic Justice* (New York, UNIFEM).

Estefa (2001) *Evaluating the World Bank's Community Empowerment Project*, 7 (2).

Evans, P. (1995) *Embedded Autonomy: States and Industrial Transformation* (Princeton, NJ, Princeton University Press).

Faber, M. and Seers, D. (eds) (1972) *The Crisis in Planning* (London, Chatto & Windus).

Feith, H. (1962) *The Decline of Constitutional Democracy in Indonesia* (Ithaca, Cornell University Press).

Firth, R. (1927) 'The Study of Primitive Economics', *Economica*, December: 312–35.

Fishlow, A. (1985) 'Lessons from the Past: Capital Markets in the 19th Century and the Interwar Period' in M. Kahler (ed.), *The Politics of International Debt* (Ithaca, Cornell University Press), pp. 37–94.

Florini, A. (2000) 'Who does what? Collective action and the changing nature of authority', in R. Higgott, R. Underhill and A. Bieler, *Non-State Actors and Authority in the Global System* (London, Routledge).

Floro, M. and Schaeffer, K. (2001) 'Restructuring of Labour Markets in the Philippines and Zambia: the Gender Dimension', in L. Beneria and S. Bisnath (eds), *Gender and Development: Theoretical, Empirical and Practical Approaches*, Vol. II (London, Elgar Publishing), pp. 393–418.

FOE (2002) *Friends of the Earth WTO Scorecard: WTO and Free Trade vs. Environment and Public Health*, http://www.foe.org/camps/intl/greentrade/scorecard.pdf

Fontana, M., Joekes, S. and Masika, R. (1998) *Global Trade Expansion and Liberalisation: Gender Issues and Impacts* (Brighton: BRIDGE, IDS).

Food and Agriculture Organisation (FAO) (2001) *State of the World's Forests 2001* (Rome, Food and Agriculture Organisation of the United Nations).

Fordham (2002) 'Scatter Plot: Infant Mortality versus Access to Safe Water', Stabilization Policy in Developing Countries, Political Economy and Development, Fordham University, New York City.

Forex Capital Management (2002) *An Introduction to Foreign Exchange* (Irvine, Ca, Fordex).

Foster, M. and Leary, J. (2001) *The Choice of Financial Aid Instruments*, Working Paper 158 (London, Overseas Development Institute).

Fox, J. and Brown, D. L. (1998) *The Struggle for Accountability: The World Bank, NGOs and Grassroots Movements* (Cambridge, Mass., MIT Press).

Frank, A. (1966) 'The Development of Underdevelopment', *Monthly Review*, 18: 17–31.

Frank, A. G. (1967) 'Capitalism and Underdevelopment in Latin America', *Monthly Review*.

Frank, A. (1980) *Crisis in the World Economy* (New York: Holmes & Meier.

Frank, A., Chew, S., and Denemark, R. (eds) (1996) *The Underdevelopment of Development: Essays in Honor of Andrew Gunder Frank* (Thousand Oaks and London, Sage Publications).

Frank, A. and Gills, B. (1992) 'The Five Thousand year World System: An Interdisciplinary Introduction', *Humboldt Journal of Social Relations*, 19 (2): 1–80.

Freedom House (2002) *Freedom in the World Country Ratings 1972–3 to 2001–'02* (New York).

Friday, L. and Laskey, R. (1989) *The Fragile Environment: The Darwin College Lectures* (Cambridge, Cambridge University Press).

Frieden, J., Pastor, M. and Tomz, M. (eds) (2000) *Modern Political Economy and Latin America: Theory and Policy* (Boulder, Westview).

Friedman, J. (1992) *Empowerment: The Politics of Alternative Development* (Cambridge, Blackwell).

Friere, P. (1976) *Education: The Practice of Freedom* (London, Writers and Readers Publishing Cooperative).

Friere, P. (1985) (1970) *Pedagogy of the Oppressed* (Harmondsworth, Pelican Books).

Fromm, E. and Maccoby, M. (1970) *Social Character in a Mexican Village: A Sociopsychoanalytic Study* (Englewood Cliffs, NJ, Prentice-Hall).

Fuggle, R. and Smith, W. (2000) *Experience with Dams in Water and Energy Resource Development in the People's Republic of China* (Cape Town, World Commission on Dams).

Fuglesang, A. and Chandler, D. (1986) *Participation as Process: What We Can Learn from Grameen Bank, Bangladesh* (Oslo, NORAD).

Fukuyama, F. (1992) *The End of History and the Last Man* (London, Verso).

Furnival, J. S. (1939) 'Netherlands India: A Study of a Plural Economy'.

Furtado, C. (1964) *Development and Underdevelopment* (Berkeley: University of California Press).

Furtado, C. (1965) *Diagnosis of the Brazilian Crisis* (Berkeley: University of California Press).

Furtado, C. (1970) *Economic Development in Latin America* (Cambridge, Cambridge University Press).

Gagne, G. (2000), 'International Trade Rules and States: Enhanced Authority for the WTO?', in R. Higgott, R. Underhill and A. Bieler (eds), *Non-State Actors and Authority in the Global System* (London, Routledge).

Galbraith, J. K. (1979) *The Nature of Mass Poverty* (Cambridge, Mass, Harvard University Press).

Gallasch, D. (2001) *Taking Shelter Under Trees* (Chiang Mai, Friends Without Borders).

Galtung, J. (1997) 'Grand Designs on a Collision Course', *Development*, 40 (1): 71–75 (reprinted from *International Development Review* 1978: 3–4).

Gamble, C. (1986) 'Hunter-Gathers and the Origins of the State', in J. Hall (ed.), *States in History* (Oxford, Basil Blackwell).

Gao Bai (2001) *Japan's Economic Dilemma: the Institutional Origins of Prosperity and Stagnation* (Cambridge, Cambridge University Press).

Gardner, K. and Lewis, D. (1996) *Anthropology, Development and the Post-Modern Challenge* (London, Pluto Press).

GCM (2000) 'Summary', *Global Commodity Markets* (Washington, DC, World Bank).

GE (2002) *Global Economy: World Bank and IMF* (San Francisco, Global Exchange).

George, S. (1998) *A Fate Worse than Debt* (London, Penguin).

Gereffi, G. and Wyman, D. (eds) (1990) *Manufacturing Miracles: Paths to Industrialization in Latin America and East Asia* (Princeton, NJ, Princeton University Press).

German, T. and Randel, J. (2002) 'Never Richer, Never Poorer', Part IV, World Aid Trends, in *The Reality of Aid: An Independent Review of Poverty Reduction and Development Assistance* (Manila, IBON Books), pp. 145–57.

Ghosh, B. N. (ed.) (2001) *Global Financial Crises and Reforms* (London, Routledge).

Gibb, R., Hughes, T., Mills, G. and Vaahtoranta, T. (eds) (2002) *Charting a New Course: Globalisation, African Recovery and the New Africa Initiative* (Johannesburg, South African Institute of International Affairs).

Giddens, A. (1990) *The Consequences of Modernity* (Stanford, Stanford University Press).

Giddens, A. (1991) *Modernity and Self-Identity* (Cambridge, Polity Press).

Giddens, A. (1995) *Beyond Left and Right* (Cambridge, Polity Press).

Glewwe, P. and van der Gaag, J. (1988) 'Confronting Poverty in Developing Countries: Definitions, Information and Policies', *Living Standards Measurement Study*, Working Paper #48 (Washington, DC, World Bank).

Gonzalez, J., Lauder, K. and Melles, B. (2000) *Opting for Partnership: Governance Innovations in Southeast Asia* (Ottawa and Kuala Lumpur, Institute on Governance).

Gramsci, A. (1971) *Selections from Prison Notebooks*, ed. and trans. Q. Hoare and G. Smith (London, Lawrence & Wishart).

Gray, J. (1998) *False Dawn: The Delusions of Global Capitalism* (London, Granta).

Greenpeace (2001) *Safe Trade in the 21st Century: The Doha Edition*, Greenpeace comprehensive proposals and recommendation for the 4th Ministerial Conference of the World Trade Organisation (Amsterdam, Greenpeace International).

Greig, A., Kimmel, M. and Lang, J. (2000) 'Men, Masculinities and Development: broadening our work towards gender equality', *Gender in Development Monograph Series*, 10 (New York: UNDP).

Griffin, K. and Kahn, A. R. (1978) 'Poverty in the third world: ugly facts and fancy models', *World Development*.

Grown, C., Elson, D. and Cagatay, N. (2000) 'Introduction', *World Development* 28 (7): 1145–1156.

Guillen, M. (2001) 'Is Globalization Civilizing, Destructive, or Feeble? A Critique of Five Key Debates in the Social-Science Literature', *Annual Review of Sociology*, 27.

Gujit, I. and Shah, M. K. (1998) *The Myth of Community: Gender Issues in Participatory Development* (London, Intermediate Technology Publications).

Gurtov, M. (1994) *Global Politics in the Human Interest*, 3rd edition (Boulder, Lynne Rienner).

Gusfield, J. (1967) 'Tradition and Modernity: Misplaced Polarities in the Study of Social Change', *American Journal of Sociology*, 72.

G77 (2002) *Final Communique Adopted by the Thirty-Second Meeting of the Chairmen/Coordinators of the Chapters of the Group of 77*, Geneva, 14–15 February.

Haber, S. (ed.) (2000) *Political Institutions and Economic Growth in Latin America: Essays in Policy, History and Political Economy* (Stanford, Ca, Hoover Institution Press).

Hadjimichael, M. (1996) *Adjustment for Growth: The African Experience* Occasional Paper (Washington, DC, International Monetary Fund).

Hadjimichael, M. T., Ghura, D., Muhleisen, M., Nord, R. and Ucer, E. M. (1995) *Sub-Saharan Africa: Growth, Savings and Investment 1986–93*, Occasional Papers 118 (Washington, DC, International Monetary Fund).

Haggard, S. (2000) *The Political Economy of the Asian Financial Crisis*, (Washington, DC: Institute for International Economics).

Hancock, G. (1989) *Lords of Poverty* (London, Macmillan).

Hansen, A. H. (1941) 'The stagnation thesis', in *Fiscal Policy and Business Cycles*, reprinted in A. Smithies and J. K. Butters (eds) (1955), *AEA Readings in Fiscal Policy* (Homewood, Ill, Richard D Irwin), pp. 540–57.

Hansen, H. and Tarp, F. (2000) 'Aid effectiveness disputed', in F. Tarp, *Foreign Aid and Development: Lessons Learned and Directions for the Future* (London and New York, Routledge), pp. 103–28.

Haq, G., Han, W. and Kim, C. (eds) (2002) *Urban Air Pollution Management and Practice in Major and Mega Cities of Asia* (Seoul, Korea Environment Institute).

Harberler, G. (1948) 'Some economic problems of the European recovery program', *American Economic Review*, September: 495–525.

Harrison, L. and Huntington, S. (eds) (2000) *Culture Matters: How Values Shape Human Progress* (New York, Basic Books).

Haynes, J. (ed.) (2000) *Democracy in the Third World* (London, Routledge).

Healey, D. (1973) 'Development policy: New thinking about an interpretation', *Journal of Economic Literature*, 10: 760ff.

Hegel, G. (1967) *Hegel's Philosophy of Right*, trans. T. M. Knox (Oxford, Oxford University Press).

Held, D., McGrew, A., Goldblatt, D. and Perraton, J. (1999) *Transformations* (Cambridge, Polity Press).

Hellinger, S., Hellinger, D. and O'Regan, F. (1988) *Aid for Just Development*, (London, Lynne Rienner).

Herbst, G. (2000) *States and Power in Africa: Comparative Lessons in Authority and Control* (Princeton, NJ, Princeton University Press).

Herfindahl, O. and Brooks, D. (eds) (1974) *Resource Economics: Selected Works of Orris C. Herfindahl* (Baltimore, Resources for the Future, Inc.).

Herman, E. and McChesney, R. (2000) 'The Global Media' in D. Held and A. McGrew (eds) *The Global Transformations Reader* (London, Polity).

Hettne, B. (1995) *Development Theory and the Three Worlds*, 2nd edition (London, Longman).

Hicks, N. (1980) 'Is There a Trade-off Between Growth and Basic Needs?', *Finance and Development*, 17 (2): 17–20

Hicks, N. and Streeten, P. (1979) 'Indicators of development: The search for a basic needs yardstick', *World Development*, 7: 567–80.

Higgott, R. (2000) 'The International Relations of the Asian Economic Crisis: a Study in the Politics of Resentment', in R. Robison *et al.* (eds), *Politics and Markets in the Wake of the Asian Crisis* (London, Routledge).

Hill, S., Elsom, J., Stewart, J. and Marsh, K. (1981) *Development With a Human Face* (Canberra, AGPS).

Hillar, M. (1993) 'Liberation Theology: Religious Response to Social Problems, A Survey', in M. Hillar and H. R. Leuchtag (eds) (1993), *Humanism and Social Issues: An Anthology of Essays* (Houston, American Humanist Association), pp. 35–52.

Hinsely, F. (1978) *Sovereignty*, 2nd edition (Cambridge, Cambridge University Press).

Hiro, D. (1995) *Between Marx and Muhammad: The Changing Face of Central Asia* (London, HarperCollins).

Hirsch, P. and Warren, C. (eds) (1998) *The Politics of Environment in Southeast Asia: Resources and Resistance* (London, Routledge).

Hirschman, A. (1958) *The Strategy of Economic Development* (Yale, Yale University Press).

Hirst, P. and Thompson, G. (1996) *Globalization in Question* (London, Polity).

Hodge, P. (1970) 'The Future of Community Development', in A. Robson and B. Crick (eds) *The Future of Social Services* (Harmondsworth, Penguin Books).

Hoffman, P. (1997) 'The Challenge of Economic Development', *Development*, 40: 19–24.

Homer-Dixon, T. (1991) 'On the Threshold: Environmental Changes as Causes of Acute Conflict', *International Security*, 16: 76–116.

Homer-Dixon, T. (1999) *Environment, Security, and Violence* (Princeton, NJ, Princeton University Press).

Hopkins, M. (1991) 'Human development revisited: A new UNDP report', *World Development*, 19 (10): 1461–73.

Hopkins, R. F. (2000) 'Political Economy of Foreign Aid', in F. Tarp, *Foreign Aid and Development: Lessons Learned and Directions for the Future* (London and New York: Routledge).

Hopkins, T. and Wallerstein, I. (1982) *World-Systems Analysis: Theory and Methodology* (Beverly Hills, Sage).

Hossain, M. (1988) *Credit for Alleviation of Rural Poverty: The Grameen Bank in Bangladesh*, Research Report # 65 (Washington, DC, International Food Policy Research Institute).

Hulme, D. and Shepherd, A. (2003) 'Conceptualizing Chronic Poverty', in D. Hume and A. Shepherd (eds), *Chronic Poverty and Development Policy*, *World Development*, Special Issue (Oxford, Pergamon), pp. 403–23.

Human Rights Watch (2002) 'Bush Should Urge Democratic Reforms in Pakistan', Press Release, 12 September.

Hunt, J. (1996) 'Women's Vision of a Just World Order', in *Towards Sustainable Livelihoods: Report of 1994–95 SID PIED Workshops on Civil Society and Sustainable Livelihoods, held in Asia, sub-Saharan Africa, Latin America and North America*, (Rome, Society for International Development).

Hunt, J. (2000) *Report by Juliet Hunt Churchill Fellow 2000*, The Winston Churchill Memorial Trust of Australia.

Huntington, S. (1957) *The Soldier and the State: the Theory and Politics of Civil-Military Relations* (Cambridge, Mass, Belknap Press).

Huntington, S. (1987) 'The Goals of Development', in M. Weiner, M. and S. Huntington (eds), *Understanding Political Development* (Boston, Little, Brown & Co.), pp. 4–28.

Huntington, S. (1993) 'The Clash of Civilizations', *Foreign Affairs*, 72 (3): 22–50.

Huntington, S. (1996) *The Clash of Civilizations and the Remaking of the New World Order* (New York, Simon & Schuster).

Hurley, D. (1990) *Income Generation Schemes for the Urban Poor*, Development Guidelines #4 (Oxford, Oxfam).

Hutchcroft, P. (1998) *Booty Capitalism: The Politics of Banking in the Philippines* (Ithaca, NY, Cornell University Press).

ILO (1977) *Employment, Growth and Basic Needs: A One World Problem* (New York, Praeger).

IMF (2002) *Globalization: A Framework for IMF Involvement* (Washington, International Monetary Fund).

Inglehart, R., Basanez, M., Moreno, A. and Mendozo, M. (1998) *Human Values and Beliefs: A Cross-Cultural Sourcebook* (Ann Arbor, University of Michigan Press).

IRN (2001) *Manibeli Declaration* (International Rivers Network).

Isbister, J. (1991) *Promises Not Kept* (West Hartford, Conn, Kumarian Press).

Jackson, B. (1990) *Poverty and the Planet: A Question of Survival* (London, Penguin).

Jackson, K. (ed.) (1999) *Asian Contagion: The Causes & Consequences of a Financial Crisis* (Boulder, Westview).

Jackson-Preece, J. (2000) 'Self-Determination, Minority Rights and Failed States' tions', Paper presented to the Failed States Conference, Florence, 7–10 April.

Jahan, R. (1995) *The Elusive Agenda: Mainstreaming Women in Development* (London, Zed Books).

Jain, L., Krishnamurty, B. and Tripathi, P. (1985) *Grass Without Roots: Rural Development under Government Auspices* (New Delhi, Sage Publications).

Jefferys, A. (2002) 'Giving Voice to Silent Emergencies', *Humanitarian Exchange*, 20: 2–4.

Johnson, C. (1987) 'Political Institutions and Economic Performance: the Government Business Relationship in Japan, South Korea and Taiwan', in F. Deyo (ed.), *The Political Economy of the New Asian Industrialism* (Ithaca, NY, Cornell University Press), pp. 136–65.

Johnson, C. (2000) *Blowback: the Costs and Consequences of American Empire* (New York, Little, Brown & Company).

Jolly, R. (1999) 'New Composite Indices for Development Cooperation', *Development*, 42 (3): 36–42.

Jomo, K. S. (ed.) (1998) *Tigers in Trouble: Financial Governance, Liberalisation and Crises in East Asia* (London, Zed Books).

Jomo, K. and Nagaraj, S. (2001) *Globalisation Versus Development* (Basingstoke, Palgrave).

Juara, R. (2000) 'Experts Seek Ways to Combat Desertification', *Third World Network*.

Kabeer, N. and Anh, T. T. V. (2000) 'Leaving the Ricefields, But not the Countryside: Gender, Livelihood Diversification and Pro-Poor Growth in Rural Viet Nam'. *UNRISD Occasional Paper*, 13 (Geneva, UNRISD).

Kamal-Chaoui, L. (2000) 'Halving poverty', *OECD Observer*, 17 April.

Kanbur, R. (2000) 'Aid, conditionality, and debt in Africa', in F. Tarp (ed.), *Foreign Aid and Development: Lessons Learned and Directions for the Future* (London, Routledge).

Kang, D. (2002) *Crony Capitalism: Corruption and Development in South Korea and the Philippines* (Cambridge, Cambridge University Press).

Kaul, I. (1999) 'In Search of a New Paradigm of International Development Cooperation', *Development*, 42 (3): 22–4.

Kearney, A. (2001) 'Measuring Globalization', *Foreign Policy* Washington, DC, May–June.

Kenworthy, J. (1893) *The Anatomy of Misery* (London, W Reeves).

Keynes, J. (1936) *The General Theory of Employment, Interest and Money* (London, Macmillan).

Khan, N. (2000) 'Gender and Livelihood in an Upland Community Forestry Project in Bangladesh', *Development Bulletin*, 51: 77–81.

Kilby, P. (2001) 'Women's Empowerment in India – the Voices of Women', *Paper presented to Gender and Globalisation in the Asia-Pacific Conference*, Australian National University, Canberra, November.

Killick, A. (1976) 'The Possibilities of Development Planning', *Oxford Economic Papers*, July.

Killick, A. (1989) *A Reaction Too Far: Economic Theory and the Role of the State in Developing Countries* (London, Overseas Development Institute).

Kindleberger, C. (1978) *Manias, Panics, and Crashes* (New York, Basic Books).

Kingsbury, D. (1998) *The Politics of Indonesia* (Melbourne, Oxford University Press).

Kingsbury, D. (2001) *South-East Asia: A Political Profile* (Melbourne, Oxford University Press).

Kirby, A. (2000) 'Alternatives to Oil', BBC News Online, 8 September.

Klare, M. and Anderson, D. (1996) 'US and Soviet Military Aid', *A Scourge of Guns* (Washington, Federation of American Scientists).

Knight, D. and Aslam, A. (2000) 'Brazil's bail-out is a time bomb', *South-North Development Monitor*, 18 March.

Kochan, L. (1963) *The Making of Modern Russia* (Harmondsworth, Pelican Books).

Kohl, R. and O'Rourke, K. (2000) 'What's New About Globalization: Implications for Income Inequality in Developing Countries', paper presented to *Poverty and Income Inequality in Developing Countries: A Policy Dialogue on the Effects of Globalization*, OECD, Paris, 30 November–1 December.

Korten, D. (1989) *Getting to the 21st Century: Voluntary Action and the Global Agenda* (West Hartford, Kumarian Press).

Kothari, M. (2002) *Statement of the Special Rapporteur on adequate housing under the United Nations Commission on Human Rights, Mr. Miloon Kothari, World Food Summit: Five Years Later*. 10–13 June, Rome.

Krader, L. (1976) *Dialectic of Civil Society* (New York, Prometheus Books).

Kragh, M. V., Mortenson, J. B., Schaumberg-Muller, H. and Slente, H. P. (2000) 'Foreign aid and private sector development', in F. Tarp, *Foreign Aid and Development* (London, Routledge), pp. 312–31.

Krugman, P. (1994) The Myth of Asia's Miracle, *Foreign Affairs*, 73 (6): 62–78.

Krugman, P. (1999) *The Return of Depression Economics* (London, Allen Lane).

Kuznets, S. (1930) 'Static and Dynamic Economics', *American Economic Review*, September: 426–41.

Kuznets, S. (1966) *Modern Economic Growth* (New Haven, Conn., Yale University Press).

La'o Hamutuk (2000) 'Evaluating the World Bank's Community Empowerment Project', *La'o Hamutuk Bulletin*, 1 (4).

Lapierre, D. (1985) *The City of Joy* (London, Arrow Books).

Laski, H. (1934) *The State in Theory and Practice* (London, George Allen & Unwin).

Latham, M. E. (2000) *Modernization as Ideology: American Social Science and Nation Building in the Kennedy Era* (Chapel Hill, University of North Carolina Press).

Ledgerwood, J. (1999) *Microfinance Handbook* (Washington, DC, World Bank).

Leipziger, D. (ed.) (2000) *Lessons from East Asia* (Ann Arbor: University of Michigan Press).

Lerner, D. (1958) *The Passing of Traditional Society: Modernizing the Middle East* (New York, Free Press).

Lewenhak, S. (1992) *The Revaluation of Women's Work*, (London: Earthscan).

Lewis, A. (1955) *The Theory of Economic Growth* (Homewood, Ill, Richard Irwin).

Lewis, J. (ed.) (1988) *Strengthening the Poor: What Have We Learned?* (New Brunswick, Transaction Books).

Leys, S. (1997) *The Analects of Confucius* (New York, W.W. Norton).

Liebman, M. (1975) *Leninism Under Lenin*, (Trans. B. Pearce) (London, Jonathan Cape).

Lim, D. (1994) 'Explaining the Growth Performances of Asian Developing Economies', *Economic Development and Cultural Change*, 42 (4): 829.

Lindert, P. and Williamson, J. (2002) 'Does Globalization Make the World More Unequal', in M. Bordo, A. Taylor and J. Williamson (eds), *Globalization in Historical Perspective* (Chicago, University of Chicago Press).

Lindsey, T. and Dick, H. (eds) (2002) *Corruption in Asia: Rethinking the Governance Paradigm* (Sydney, Federation Press).

Lipton, M. and Longhurst, R. (1989) *New Seeds and Poor People* (London, Unwin Hyman).

Lisk, F. (1977) 'Basic-Needs Fulfilment', *International Labour Review*, 115 (2): 175–91.

Little, I. (1982) *Economic Development* (New York, Basic Books).

Lovell, C. H. (1992) *Breaking the Cycle of Poverty: the BRAC Strategy* (Connecticut, Kumarian Press).

Lubbers, R. (1996) 'Globalization: An Exploration', in *Nijenrode Management Review*, 1 November: 26–31.

Lubbers, R. and Koorevaar, J. (1998) *The Dynamic of Globalization*, paper presented to Tilburg University, Netherlands, 26 November.

Lubbers, R. and Koorevaar, J. (1999) *Governance in an Era of Globalization*, Paper for the Club of Rome Annual Meeting, 26–27 November.

Lukes, S. (1974) *Power: A Radical View* (London, Macmillan).

Macdonald, D. (1992) *Adventures in Chaos: American Intervention for Reform in the Third World* (Cambridge, Mass, Harvard University Press).

MacDougall, G. (1945) 'Review of Staley, Eugene, World Economic Development: Effects on Advanced Industrialized Countries', *Economic Journal*, June–September: 284–6.

McCracken, J. A., Pretty, J. N. and Conway, G. (1988) *An Introduction to Rapid Rural Appraisal for Agricultural Development* (London, IIED).

McGillivray, M. (1991) 'The Human Development Index: yet another redundant composite development indicator?', *World Development*, 19 (10): 1461–8.

McKay, J. (2003) 'The Restructuring of the Korean Economy Since 1986 and the Onset of the Financial Crisis: the Industrial-Financial Nexus', in MoonJoong Tcha (ed.), *The Economic Crisis and the Korean Economy at the Crossroads* (London, Routledge).

McKenzie, J. (2000) *Oil as a Finite Resource: When is Global Production Likely to Peak?* (Washington, DC, World Resources Institute).

McNamara, R. (1981) *The McNamara Years at the World Bank* (Baltimore, Johns Hopkins).

Mahalanobis, P. C. (1963) *The Approach of Operational Research to Planning in India* (New Dehli, Indian Statistical Institute).

Mahathir M. (2002) 'Globalization and Developing Countries', *The Globalist*, Washington, DC, 9 October.

Mahbubani, K. (1998) *Can Asians Think?* (Singapore: Times Books International).

Maloney, C. (1986) *Behaviour and Poverty in Bangladesh* (Dhaka, University Press Ltd).

Manghezi, A. (1976) *Class, Elite, and Community in African Development* (Uppsala, The Scandinavian Institute of African Studies).

Manley, M. and Brandt, W. (1985) *Global Challenge* (London and Sydney, Pan Books).

Mann, C. (1997) 'Reseeding the Green Revolution', *Science*, 277: 1038–43.

Maren, M. (1997) *The Road to Hell: The Ravaging effects of Foreign Aid and International Charity* (New York, The Free Press).

Markandaya, K. (1954) *Nectar in a Sieve* (New York, Signet for Harper & Row).

Martin, H. and Schuman, H. (1997) *The Global Trap: Globalization and the Assault on Democracy and Prosperity* (London, Zed Books).

Martinussen, J. (1997) *Society, State and Market: A Guide to Competing Theories of Development* (London, Zed Books).

Marx, K. (1967) *Manifesto of the Communist Party* (Moscow, Progress Publishers).

Marx, K. (1973) *Grundrisse* (Harmondsworth, Penguin Books).

Mehotra, S. (2002) 'International Development Targets and Official Development Assistance', *Development and Change*, 33 (3): 529–538.

Meier, G. (1995) *Leading Issues in Economic Development* (Oxford: Oxford University Press).

Meier, G. and Seers, D. (1984) *Pioneers in Development* (New York, Oxford University Press for the World Bank).

Mies, M. (1986) *Patriarchy and Accumulation on a World Scale: Women in the International Division of Labour* (London, Zed Books).

Milbrath, L. (1996) *Learning To Think Environmentally While There is Still Time* (Albany, State University of New York Press).

Milburn, S. (1954–5) *A Study prepared for the UN* UN Series on Community Organisation and Community Development, No. 21 (New York, United Nations).

Mills, G. (2002) *Poverty to Prosperity: Globalisation, Good Governance and African Recovery* (Johannesburg: Tafelberg Publications and the South African Institute of International Affairs).

Ministerial Review Team (2001) *Report of the Ministerial Review Team: Towards Excellence in Aid Delivery: A Review of New Zealand's Official Development Assistance Programme*, Wellington.

Mohanty, C. (1997) 'Under Western Eyes: Feminist Scholarship and Colonial Discourses', in N. Visvanathan, L. Duggan, L. Nisonoff and N. Wiegersma (eds), *The Women, Gender and Development Reader* (London, Zed Books), pp. 79–85.

Morganthau, H. (1978) *Politics Among Nations: The Struggle for Power and Peace* 5th edition (New York, Alfred A. Knopf).

Morris, C. (1998) *An Essay on the Modern State* (Cambridge, Cambridge University Press).

Morris, M. D. (1979) *Measuring the Condition of the World's Poor: The Physical Quality of Life Index* (New York, Pergamon).

Morris-Suzuki, T. (1989) *A History of Japanese Economic Thought* (London, Routledge).

Morrissey, O. (2000) 'Foreign Aid in the Emerging Global Trade Environment', in F. Tarp (ed.), *Foreign Aid and Development* (London, Routledge).

Mortimer, R. (1984) 'Stubborn Survivors: Dissenting Essays on Peasants and Third World Development', in H. Feith and R. Tiffen (eds), *Monash Papers on Southeast Asia No 10* (Melbourne, Centre for Southeast Asian Studies, Monash University).

Moser, C. (1991) 'Gender Planning in the Third World: Meeting Practical and Strategic Gender Needs' in T. Wallace and C. March (eds), *Changing Perceptions: Writings on Gender and Development* (Oxford, Oxfam), pp. 158–71.

Moser, C. (1993) *Gender Planning and Development: Theory, Practice and Training* (London, Routledge).

Mosley, P. and Eekhout, M. (2000) 'From Project Aid to Programme Assistance', in F. Tarp (ed.), *Foreign Aid and Development* (London, Routledge), pp. 131–53.

Mussa, M. (2002) *Argentina and the Fund: From Triumph to Tragedy* (Washington, DC, Institute for International Economics).

Mydal, G. (1957) *Economic Theory and Underdeveloped Regions* (London, Duckworth).

Narayan, D., Chambers, R., Shah, M. K. and Petesch, P. (1999) 'Global Synthesis: Consultations with the Poor', Paper presented at *Global Synthesis Workshop*, World Bank, Poverty Group, 22–23 September, Washington, DC.

Narayan, D., Chambers, R., Shah, M. K. and Petesch, P. (2000) *Voices of the Poor: Crying Out for Change* (New York, Oxford University Press).

Narayan, D. with Patel, R. Schafft, K., Rademacher, A. and Koch-Schulte, S. (2000) *Voices of the Poor: Can Anyone Hear Us?* (New York, Oxford University Press).

Nayyar, N. (ed.) (1977) *Economic Relations between Socialist Countries and the Third World* (London, Macmillan).

Nehru, J. (1950) *Independence and After* (New York, John Day & Co.).

Ness, G. and Ando, H. (1984) *The Land is Shrinking: Population Planning in Asia* (Baltimore, Johns Hopkins University Press).

Nettl, J. (1969) 'The Study of Political Development', in C. Leys (ed.) *Politics and Change in Developing Countries* (Cambridge, Cambridge University Press).

Nisbet, R. (0000) 'The Metaphor of Growth', in *Social Change and History – Aspects of the Western Theory of Development* (Oxford, Oxford University Press).

Nkrumah, K. (1957) *The Autobiography of Kwame Nkrumah* (London, Thomas Nelson & Sons).

Norman, D. (1974) 'Rationalizing Mixed Cropping under Indigenous Conditions: the Example of Northern Nigeria', *Journal of Development Studies*, 11: 3–21.

Norman, D. (1980) 'Farming Systems Approach: Relevance for the Small Farmer', *Rural Development Paper No. 5* (East Lansing, Michigan State University).

Nurske, R. (1953) *Problems of Capital Formation in Developing Countries* (New York, Oxford University Press).

OECD (1989) *Development Cooperation in the 1990s: Efforts and Policies of the Members of the Development Assistance Committee* (Paris).

Ohmae, K. (1991) *The Borderless World: Power and Strategy in the Interlinked Economy* (London, Fontana).

Ohmae, K. (1995) 'Putting Global Logic First', *Harvard Business Review*, January–February: 119–25.

Ohmae, K. (1996) *The End of the Nation State* (London, HarperCollins).

Oliver, D. (1983) *Trickling Up* (Suva, Lotu Pasifika Production).

Ondeo (2002) *Ondeo in the World: Facts and Figures* (Paris, Suez Lyonnaise des Eaux).

Organization for African Unity (1981) *The Lagos Plan of Action for the Economic Development of Africa 1980–2000* (Geneva, OAU).

Ostergaard, H. (ed.) (1992) *Gender and Development: A Practical Guide* (New York, Routledge).

Oxaal, Z. and Baden, S. (1997) 'Gender and Empowerment: Definitions, Approaches and Implications for Policy', *BRIDGE Report*, No. 40 (Brighton, Institute for Development Studies).

Oxfam (2000) *Millennium Summit: Closing the Credibility Gap?*, Oxfam International Policy Paper 8/00 (London, Oxfam).

Oxfam International (2002) *Rigged Rules and Double Standards: Trade, Globalisation, and the Fight against Poverty* (Oxfam International).

Panafrican News Agency (PNA) (2001) 'Concern as Kenyan Fish Stocks Fall', Panafrican News Agency, 13 February.

Parfitt, T. (2002) *The End of Development: Modernity, Post-Modernity and Development* (London, Zed Books).

Parpart, J. (1995) 'Post-modernism, Gender and Development' in J. Crush (ed.), *Power of Development* (London, Routledge).

Patel, I. G. (1994) 'Limits of the Current Consensus on Development', in *Proceedings of the World Bank Annual Conference on Development Economics* (Washington, DC, World Bank), pp. 9–17.

Pearson, R. (1995) 'Bringing it all Back Home: Integrating Training for Gender Specialists and Economic Planners', *World Development* 23 (11): 1995–9.

Pearson, R. (2001) 'Male Bias and Women's Work in Mexico's Border Industries', in L. Beneria, and S. Bisnath (eds), *Gender and Development: Theoretical, Empirical and Practical Approaches*, Vol II (London, Elgar Publishing), pp. 246–76.

Pempel, T. J. (1998) *Regime Shift: Comparative Dynamics of the Japanese Political Economy* (Ithaca, NY, Cornell University Press).

Pempel, T. J. (ed.) (1999) *The Politics of the Asian Crisis* (Ithaca, NY, Cornell University Press).

Perlman, M. (1981) 'Population and Economic Change in Developing Countries: A Review Article', *Journal of Economic Literature*, 19: 74–82.

Petras, J. and Veltmeyer, H. (2001) *Globalisation Unmasked: Imperialism in the 21st Century* (London, Zed Books).

Pettman, R. (1979) *State and Class: A Sociology of International Affairs* (London, Croom Helm).

Pew Centre (2002) 'Report Shows Emerging Greenhouse Gas Market', (press release) (Arlington, VA, Pew Centre for Global Climate Change), 19 March.

Peyrefitte, A (1992) *The Collision of Two Civilisations* (London, HarperCollins).

Pinstrup-Andersen, P. (ed.) (1993) *The Political Economy of Food and Nutrition Policies* (Baltimore, Johns Hopkins University Press).

Plamenatz, J. (1968) *Consent, Freedom and Political Obligation*, 2nd edition (London, Oxford University Press).

Ponsioen, J. (1962) 'Community Development as a Process', in J. Ponsioen (ed.), *Social Welfare and Policy: Contributions to Theory* (The Hague, Mouton & Co.), p. 52.

Porter, D., Bryant, A. and Thompson, G. (1991) *Development in Practice: Paved With Good Intentions* (London, Routledge).

Portney, R. (ed.) (1982) *Current Issues in Natural Resource Policy* (Washington, DC, Resources for the Future, Inc.).

Prebisch, R. (1950) *The Economic Development of Latin America and its Principal Problems* (Lake Success, NY, United Nations).

Proyect, L. (1998) 'Fish Stocks and Malthus', unpublished paper, 23 May.

Putnam, R. (1995) 'Bowling Alone: America's Declining Social Capital', *Journal of Democracy*, 6 (1): 65–78.

Putnam, R. (2000) *Bowling Alone: The Collapse and Revival of American Community* (New York, Simon & Schuster).

Putnam, R. D., Leonardi, R. and Nanetti, R. (1993) *Making Democracy Work: Civic Traditions in Modern Italy* (Princeton, NJ, Princeton University Press).

Pye, L. (1966) *Aspects of Political Development* (Boston, Little, Brown & Co), pp. 104–5.

Pye, L. (1985) *Asian Power and Politics* (Cambridge, Mass, Belknap Press).

Pyle, J. L and Dawson, L. (1990) 'The Impact of Multinational Technological Transfer on Female Workforces in Asia, Columbia Journal of World Business', in L. Beneria and S. Bisnath (2001), *Gender and Development: Theoretical, Practical and Empirical Approaches*, Vol. II (Nottingham, Edward Elgar).

Pyle, J. and Dawson, L. (2001) 'The Impact of Multinational Technological Transfer on Female Workforces in Asia', *Columbia Journal of World Business*: 237–45.

Rahnema, M. with Bawtree, V. (eds) *The Post-Development Reader* (London, Zed Books).

Ramirez-Faria, C. (1991) *The Origins of Economic Inequality Between Nations* (London, Unwin Hyman).

Rangachari, R., Sengupta, N., Iyer, R., Banerji, P. and Singh, S. (2000) *Large Dams: India's Experience* (Cape Town, World Commission on Dams).

Rathgeber, E. (1990) 'WID, WAD, GAD: Trends in Research and Practice', *The Journal of Developing Areas*, 24 (4): 489–502.

Rawls, J. (1991) *A Theory of Justice* (Oxford, Oxford University Press).

Reality of Aid (1998).

Remenyi, J. V. (1976) Core-Demi-Core Interaction in Economics, PhD dissertation, Duke University, Durham, NC.

Remenyi, J. (1991) *Where Credit is Due: Income Generating Programmes for the Poor in Developing Countries* (London, Intermediate Technology Publications).

Remenyi, J. (1994) A chapter in B. Geddes, J. Hughes and J. Remenyi (eds), *Anthropology and Third World Development* (Geelong, Deakin University Press).

Remenyi J. V and Quinones, B. (eds) (2000) *Microfinance and Poverty Alleviation* (London, Pinter).

Resosudarno, I. (2002) *Shifting Power to the Periphery: Preliminary Impacts of Indonesia's Decentralisation on Forests and Forest People*, paper presented to Indonesia Update conference, Australian National University, 18 September.

Rhyne, E. (2001) *Mainstreaming Microfinance* (Bloomfield, Conn., Kumarian Press).

Rist, G. (1997) *The History of Development: From Western Origins to Global Faith* (London, Zed Books).

Rivero, O. de (2001) *The Myth of Development: the Non-Viable Economies of the 21st Century* (London, Zed Books).

Robins, K. (2000) 'Encountering Globalization', in D. Held and A. McGrew (eds), *The Global Transformations Reader* (London, Polity).

Robison, R. (1985) 'Class, Capital and the State in New Order Indonesia', in R. Higgott and R. Robison, *The Political Economy of Southeast Asia* (Melbourne, Oxford University Press).

Rocha, G. (2002) 'Neo-Dependency in Brazil', *New Left Review*, 16: 5–30.

Roche, C. (1999) *Impact Assessment for Development Agencies: Learning to Value Change* (London, Oxfam).

Rodda (1991) *Women and the Environment* (London, Zed Books).

Rogers, B. (1980) *The Domestication of Women: Discrimination in Developing Societies* (London: Tavistock).

Rosenstein-Rodan, P. N. (1943) 'The Problems of Industrialization of Eastern and South-Eastern Europe', *The Economic Journal*, June–Sept, reprinted in A. N. Agarwala and S. P. Singh (eds) (1963) *The Economics of Underdevelopment* (Oxford, Oxford University Press), pp. 245–55.

Rostow, W. (1960) *Stages of Economic Growth* (Cambridge, Cambridge University Press).

Rostow, W. (1971) *Politics and the Stage of Growth* (Cambridge, Cambridge University Press).

Rostow, W. (1984) 'Development: The Political Economy of the Marshallian Long Period', in G. Meier and D. Seers (eds), *Pioneers in Development* (New York: Oxford University Press), pp. 229–61.

Rostow, W. (1990) *Theorists of Development from David Hume to the Present* (New York, Oxford University Press).

Rostow, W. W. (1990) *Theorists of Economic Growth from David Hume to the Present* (London, Oxford University Press).

Rousseau, J.-J. (1987) *The Social Contract and Other Discourses* (Harmondsworth, Penguin Classics).

Rowen, H. (1998) *Behind East Asian Growth: The Political and Social Foundations of Prosperity* (London, Routledge).

Rowlands, J. (1998) 'A Word of the Times, but What does it Mean? Empowerment in The Discourse and Practice of Development', in H. Afshav (ed.), *Women and Empowerment: Illustrations from the Third World* (Basingstoke, Macmillan), pp. 11–34.

Rumansara, A. (1998) 'The Struggle of the People in Kedung Ombo', in J. Fox and D. L. Brown (eds), *The Struggle for Accountability: The World Bank, NGOs and Grassroots Movements* (MIT Press), pp. 123–149.

Rutherford, S. (2000) *The Poor and Their Money* (London, Oxford University Press for DFID).

Ryrie, W. (1995) *First World, Third World* (Basingstoke, Macmillan).

Sachs, W. (1992) 'The Discovery of Poverty', *New Internationalist*, June: 7–9.

Sachs, W. (1992) *The Development Dictionary: A Guide to Knowledge as Power* (London, Zed Books).

SarDesai, D. (1997) *Southeast Asia: Past and Present* (Boulder, Westview Press).

Schauer (1982) *Free Speech: A Philosophical Inquiry* (Cambridge, Cambridge University Press).

Schultz, T. (1962) 'Reflections on Investment in Man', *Journal of Political Economy*, Supplement, October: 1–8.

Schultz, T. (1964) *Transforming Traditional Agriculture* (New Haven, Conn., Yale University Press).

Schultz, T. (1980) 'The Economics of Being Poor', *Journal of Political Economy*, August.

Schumacher, E. (1973) *Small is Beautiful: A Study of Economics as if People Mattered* (London, Blond & Briggs).

Schuurman, F. (2001) *Globalisation and Development Studies: Challenges for the 21st Century* (London, Sage).

Scully, G. (1988) 'Institutional Framework and Economic Development', *Journal of Political Economy*, 96: 622–62.

Seabrook, J. (1993) *Victims of Development* (London, Verso Press).

Seers, D. (1972) 'The Meaning of Development', in N. Bastor (ed.), *Measuring Development: The Role and Adequacy of Development Indicators* (London, Frank Cass).

Seligson, M. A. and Passe-Smith, J. T. (1998) *Development and Under-Development* (London, Lynne Rienner).

Sen, A. (1981) *Poverty and Famine: An Essay on Entitlement and Deprivation* (Oxford, Clarendon Press).

Sen, A. (1983) 'Development: Which way now?', *Economic Journal*, 93, December: 754–757.

Sen, A. (2000) *Development as Freedom* (London, Oxford University Press).

Sen, G. and Grown, C. (1987) *Development Crisis, and Alternative Visions: Third World Women's Perspectives* (New Delhi: DAWN).

Shah, A. (2002) *Structural Adjustment – a Major Cause of Poverty*, August, http://www.globalissues.org/TradeRelated/SAP.asp.

Shah, M. and Strong, N. (2000) *Food in the 21st Century* (Washington, DC, CGIAR/World Bank).

Sheehan, N. (1988) *A Bright Shining Lie: John Paul Vann and America in Vietnam* (New York, Random House).

Sherman, A. (1992) *Preferential Option* (Grand Rapids, MI, Eerdmans Publishing Co.).

Shiva, V. (1989) *Staying Alive: Women, Ecology and Development* (London, Zed Books).

Shiva, V. (2000) *BBC Reith Lecture*.

Silberschmidt, M. (2001) 'Disempowerment of Men in Rural and Urban East Africa: Implications for Male Identity and Sexual Behaviour', *World Development*, 29 (4): 657–71.

Simons, P. *et al.* (1997) Committee to Review the Australian Overseas Aid Program, *One Clear Objective: Poverty Reduction Through Sustainable Development*, Report of the Committee of Review, AusAID Canberra.

Singer, H. (1950) 'The Distribution of Gains Between Investing and Borrowing Countries', *American Economic Review Papers and Proceedings*, May, pp. 473–485, reprinted in Dutt (2002) *The Political Economy of Development*, vols 1–3 (Cheltenham, Edward Elgar), pp. 19–205.

Singer, H. (1993) *Economic Progress and Prospects in the Third World* (Aldershot, Edward Elgar).

Siwakopi, G. (2002) 'Who's aiding whom? Poverty, conflict and ODA in Nepal', in *Reality of Aid*, pp. 81–97.

Slater, D. and Bell, M. (2002) 'Aid and the geopolitics of the post-colonial: critical reflections on New Labour's Overseas Development Strategy', *Development and Change* 33 (2): 335–60, April.

Smillie, I. (1995) *The Alms Bazaar: Altruism under fire – non-profit organisations and international development* (London, Intermediate Technology Publications).

Smillie, I. (1999) 'Public Support and the Politics of Aid', *Development*, 42 (3) September, pp. 71–6.

Smith, A. (1986) 'State-Making and Nation-Building', in J. Hall (ed.), *States in History* (Oxford, Basil Blackwell).

Smith, B. (1996) *Understanding Third World Politics: Theories of Political Change and Development* (Bloomington and Indianapolis, Indiana University Press).

Snyder, M. and Tadesse, M. (1997) 'The African Context: Women in the Political Economy', in N. Visvanathan, L. Duggan, L. Nisonoff and N. Wiegersma (eds), *The Women, Gender and Development Reader* (London, Zed Books), pp. 75–78.

South Centre, The (SC) (1998) *Statement to the Second WTO Ministerial Conference by the South Centre* (Geneva, The South Centre).

Spanger, H.-J. (2000) 'Failed State or Failed Concept? Objections and Suggestions' Paper presented to the *Failed States Conference*, Florence, 7–10 April.

Sparr, P. (1994) *Mortgaging Women's Lives: Feminist Critiques of Structural Adjustment* (London, Zed Books).

Stensholt, R. (1997) *Developing the Mekong Subregion* (Melbourne, Monash Asia Institute).

Stiglitz, J. (2000) 'The Insider: What I Learned at the World Economic Crisis', *The New Republic* (available on-line at http://www.tnr.com/041700/stiglitz041700.html

Stiglitz, J. (2002, 2003) *Globalization and its Discontents* (New York, Norton).

Stiglitz, J. and Yusuf, S. (2001) *Rethinking the East Asian Miracle* (Oxford, The World Bank and Oxford University Press).

Strange, S. (1986) *Casino Capitalism* (Oxford: Basil Blackwell).

Strange, S. (1998) *Mad Money* (Manchester: Manchester University Press).

Stubbings, L. (1992) *'Look What you Started Henry': A History of the Australian Red Cross 1914–1991* (Australian Red Cross).

Supachai, P. (2002) *Director-General Supachai welcomes agreement streamlining LDC membership* (Press release) (Geneva, World Trade Organisation) 3 December.

Tarp, F. (2000) *Foreign Aid and Development: Lessons Learned and Directions for the Future* (London, Routledge).

Taylor, V. (1999) *A Quick Guide to Mainstreaming in Development Planning* (London: Commonwealth Secretariat).

Taylor, V. (2000) *Marketisation of Governance: Critical Feminist Perspectives from the South* (Cape Town, SADEP).

Tehranian, M. (1999) *Global Communication and World Politics* (Boulder, Lynne Rienner Publishers).

Tendler, J. (1989) 'Whatever Happened to Poverty Alleviation?', *World Development*, 17 (7), July.

TFET (2000) *Update No 3* Trust Fund for East Timor World Bank, Asian Development Bank, AUSAID, USAID) 6 October.

Third World Network (TWR) (1998) 'The negative impacts of aquaculture', Third World Resurgence No 93, May 1998, in *Third World Network*.

Thompson, J. (2000) 'The Globalization of Communication', in D. Held and A. McGrew (eds), *The Global Transformations Reader* (London, Polity).

Tinbergen, J. (1976) *Central Planning* (New Haven, Conn, Yale University Press).

Todaro, M. P. (1994) *Economic Development in the Third World*, 4th edition (New York, Longman).

Todd, H. (1996) *Women at the Center* (Boulder, Col, Westview Press).

Tornquist, O. (1999) *Politics and Development: A Critical Introduction* (London, Sage).

Toye, J. (1987) *Dilemmas of Development: Reflections on the Counter-Revolution in Development Theory and Policy* (Oxford: Basil Blackwell).

Toye, J. (1991) 'Is there a New Political Economy of Development', in C. Colclough and J. Manor (eds), *States or Markets? Neo-Liberalism and the Development Policy Debate* (Oxford, Oxford University Press).

Toye, J. (1993) *The Dilemmas of Development*, 2nd edition (Oxford, Blackwell).

Trainer, F. (1995) *Development: Conventional versus Critical Perspectives*.

UNCTAD (2002a) 'What are the Least developed Countries', in *Least Developed Countries Report 2002*   (New York, UN Conference on Trade and Development).

UNCTAD (2002b) *World Investment Report 2002* (New York, United Nations).

UNDP (various years) *Human Development Report* (New York, Oxford University Press).

UNDP (1995) *Human Development Report* (New York UNDP).

UNFPA (1978–2002) *State of World Population* (New York, UN).

UNHDR (1999) *United Nations Human Development Report: Globalization with a Human Face* (New York, United Nations Development Program).

UNICEF (1996) *The State of the World's Children 1996* (New York, United Nations International Children's Emergency Fund).

UNIFEM (2000) *Progress of the World's Women* (New York UNDP).

United Nations (UN) (1945) *Charter of the United Nations* with subsequent amendments.

United Nations (UN) (1958) Series on Community Development No 26 *Report on the Mission to Survey Community Development in Africa*, January–April 1956 (New York, United Nations).

United Nations (UN) (1985) *United Nations Programme of Action for African Economic Recovery and Development, 1986–1990* (New York, United Nations).

United Nations (UN) (1995) *United Nations Fourth World Conference International Platform for Action* (New York: United Nations).

United Nations (UN) (1999) *World Survey on the Role of Women in Development* (New York: United Nations).

United Nations (UN) (2002) *Growth in UN Membership 1945–2002* (New York, United Nations).

United Nations Commission on Sustainable Development (UNCSD) (2002a) *CSD Theme Indicator Framework* (New York, United Nations).

United Nations Commission on Sustainable Development (UNCSD) (2002b) *Indicators of Sustainable Development: Guidelines and Methodologies* (New York, United Nations).

United Nations Convention to Combat Desertification (UNCCD) (2002a) 'The Causes of Desertification'.

United Nations Convention to Combat Desertification (UNCCD) (2002b) 'The Consequences of Desertification'.

United Nations Convention to Combat Desertification (UNCCD) (2002c) UN Convention to Combat Desertification 'Combating desertification in Africa'.

United Nations Convention to Combat Desertification (UNCCD) (2002d) 'Participatory Development: A bottom-up approach to combating desertification'.

United Nations Department of Economic and Social Affairs (UNDESA) (2002a) *The Johannesburg Summit Test: What Will Change?* (New York: United Nations) 26 August–4 September 2002.

United Nations Department of Economic and Social Affairs (UNDESA) (2002b) *Key Outcomes of the Summit*, September 2002.

United Nations Environment Program (UNEP) (2002) *Global Environment Outlook 3* (New York, United Nations Environment Program).

United Nations Population Division (UNPD) (2001) *World Population Prospects: The 2000 Revision* (New York, United Nations).

Uphoff, N. (ed.) (1982) *Rural Development and Local Organisations in Asia*, 2 Vols (New Delhi, Macmillan).

USAID (2002a) *East Timor* (Washington, DC, United States Agency for International Development).

USAID (2002b) *Participatory Practices: Learning From Experience* (Washington, DC, United States Agency for International Development).

USCB (2002) *World POPClock Projection* (United States Census Bureau) 21 November.

USDS (2002) *Patterns of Global Terrorism* (Washington, DC, United States Department of State).

Vaughan, M. (1987) *The Story of an African Famine* (Cambridge, Cambridge University Press).

Vitug, M. (1993) *Power From the Forest: The Politics of Logging* (Manila, Philippine Center for Investigative Journalism).

Vivendi (2002) *Environment* Vivendi Universal public statement.

Wade, R. (1990) *Governing the Market: Economic Theory and the Role of Government in East Asian Industrialisation* (Princeton, NJ, Princeton University Press).

Wade, R. (1996) 'Globalization and Its Limits: Reports of the Death of the National Economy are Greatly Exaggerated', in S. Berger and R. Dore (eds), *National Diversity and Global Capitalism* (Ithaca, Cornell University Press).

Wallace, T. and March, C. (eds) (1991) *Changing Perceptions: Writings on Gender and Development* (Oxford, Oxfam).

Wallerstein, I. (1974) *The Modern World System* (New York, Monthly Review Press).

Wallerstein, I. (1979) *The Capitalist World Economy* (Cambridge, Cambridge University Press).

Wallerstein, I. (1984) *The Politics of the World Economy* (Cambridge, Cambridge University Press).

Waring, M. (1988) *Counting for Nothing: What Men Value and What Women are Worth* (Wellington: Allen & Unwin).

Warren, B. (1980) *Imperialism: Pioneer of Capitalism* (London, Verso).

Warren, C. (1993) *Adat and Dinas: Balinese Communities in the Indonesian State* (Oxford, Oxford University Press).

Washington State (2002) *Best Export Prospects 2002: Pollution Control Equipment* (Taiwan, Washington State).

WB-GNI (2002) *GNI per capita 2000, Atlas Method and PPP*, World Development Indicators Database (Washington, DC, World Bank).

WBPNL (2001) 'Cultural Capital and Educational Attainment', *Social Capital* World Bank Poverty Net Library (Washington, DC, World Bank).

WCD (2000) 'Executive Summary', *Large Dams Cross Check Survey* (World Commission on Dams).

Weber, C. and Bierstaker, T. (eds) (1996) *State Sovereignty as Social Construction* (Cambridge, Cambridge Studies in International Relations).

Weber, M. (1964) *The Theory of Social and Economic Organization* (New York, Free Press).

Wee, V. and Heyzer, N. (1995) *Gender, Poverty and Sustainable Development: Towards a Holistic Framework of Understanding and Action* (Singapore, ENGENDER).

Weiner, M. (ed.) (1966) *Modernization: The Dynamics of Growth* (New York, Basic Books).

Weiss, L. and Hobson, J. (1995) *States and Economic Development* (Cambridge, Polity Press).

Weissman, S. *et al.* (1975) *The Trojan Horse: a Radical Look at Foreign Aid* (Palo Alto, Ramparts Press).

Weitz, R. (1986) *New Roads to Development* (New York, Greenwood Press).

Whittington, D. and Swarna, V. (1994) *The Economic Benefits of Potable Water Supply Projects to Households in Developing Countries*, paper no. 53 (Manila, Asian Development Bank, Economic and Development Resource Centre).

Wigg, D. (1993) *The Quiet Revolution*, World Bank Development Essay #2 (Washington, DC, The World Bank).

Williams, M. (1997) 'The 1970s: a need for reappraisal', *Development*, 40 (1).

Williamson, J. (2000) 'What Should the World Bank Think about the Washington Consensus?', *The World Bank Research Observer*, 15 (2): 251–264.

Williamson, J. (2002) *Is Brazil Next?* (Washington, DC, Institute for International Economics).

Wittfogel, K. (1957) *Oriental Despotism* (New Haven, Conn., Yale University Press).

WN (2002b) *Globalization, Growth and Poverty: Building an Inclusive World Economy* (Washington, DC, World Bank).

Woo Wing Thye, Sachs, J.D. and Schwab, K. (eds) (2000) *The Asian Financial Crisis: Lessons for a Resilient Asia* (Cambridge, Mass., MIT Press).

Wood, B. (1999) *Development Cooperation Into the 21st Century*, the Inaugural K. William Taylor Memorial Lecture Brisbane, Australia, 1 November.

World Bank (various years) *World Development Report* (New York, Oxford University Press).

World Bank (1981) *Accelerated Development in Sub-Saharan Africa: An Agenda for Action* (Washington, DC, World Bank).

World Bank (1981) *A Collection of Farewell Speeches on the Occasion of the Retirement of Robert S McNamara as President of the World Bank, 1968–81*, World Bank Report 13380 (Washington, DC, World Bank).

World Bank (1984a) *Toward Sustained Development in Sub-Saharan Africa: A Joint Programme of Action* (Washington, DC, World Bank).

World Bank (1984b) *World Development Report: Population Change and Development* (New York, Oxford University Press).

World Bank (1986) *Financing Adjustment with Growth in Sub-Saharan Africa* (Washington, DC, World Bank).

World Bank (1990) *Proceedings of the World Bank Annual Conference on Development Economics* (Washington, DC, World Bank).

World Bank (1991) *World Development Report: From Plan to Market* (New York, Oxford University Press).

World Bank (1994) *Population and Development: Implications for the World Bank* (Washington, DC, World Bank).

World Bank (1995) *Strengthening the Effectiveness of Aid: Lessons for Donors*, www.worldbank.org (accessed on 27 September 2002).

World Bank (1998) *Assessing Aid: What Works, What Doesn't and Why*, a World Bank Policy Research Report (Oxford, Oxford University Press).

World Bank (2000a) *First Trust Fund For East Timor Project To Be Handed Over To East Timorese*, press release (Washington, DC, World Bank Group).

World Bank (2000b) *World Development Report 2000–2001: Attacking Poverty* (Washington, DC, World Bank).

World Bank (2001a) 'Community Empowerment and Social Inclusion', in *Social Policy Design* (Washington, DC, World Bank).

World Bank (2001b) *Engendering Development: through Gender Equality in Rights, Resources and Voice* (Washington, DC: World Bank).

World Bank (2001c) *Sustainable Development in the 21st Century* (Washington, DC, World Bank).

World Bank (2002a) *World Development Report 2000/2001: Attacking Poverty* (Washington, DC, World Bank).

World Bank (2002b) *Engendering Development* (Washington, DC, World Bank (http://www.worldbank.org/gender/prr/).

World Commission on Environment and Development (1987) *Our Common Future* (Brundtland Report) (Oxford, Oxford University Press).

WRM (2000) 'Laos: Vanishing forests and growing corruption', *World Rainforest Movement Bulletin*, 35 (Montevideo, World Rainforest Movement).

WSF (2002) *World Social Forum Charter of Principles* (Sao Paulo, World Social Forum).

WTO (2002a) *The WTO in brief* (Geneva, World Trade Organisation).

WTO (2002b) 'Developing Countries', in *The 'WTO in brief* (Geneva, World Trade Organization).

Wu, Y. (1946) 'International Capital Movements and the Development of Poor Countries', *Economic Journal*, March: 86–101.

WWF (2002) *Living Planet Report* (Gland, World Wildlife Fund).

Yes.Pakistan (2002) http://www.yespakistan.com/people/potable_water.asp (accessed 2 December 2002).

Yusoff, M., Hasan, F. and Jalil, S. (2000) 'Globalization, Economic Policy, and Equity: The Case of Malaysia', paper presented to *Poverty and Income Inequality in Developing Countries: A Policy Dialogue on the Effects of Globalization*, OECD, Paris, 30 November–1 December.

Zammit, A. (2000) 'International Capital Flows: Identifying the Gender Dimension', *World Development*, 28 (7): 1249–68.

Zandstra, H. G., Price, E. C., Litsinger, J. A. and Morris, R. A. (1981) *A Methodology for on-farm Cropping Systems Research* (Los Banos, IIRI).

Zimmerman, R. (1993) *Dollars, Diplomacy and Dependency: Dilemmas of US Economic Aid* (London, Lynne Rienner).

Zwart, P. (2002) *Report from the NZ NGO Representative to the Financing for Development Conference*, Monterrey, Mexico 18–22 March.

Index